Comparative Theology and the Problem of Religious Rivalry

AAR
AMERICAN ACADEMY OF RELIGION

Reflection and Theory in the Study of Religion Series
SERIES EDITOR James Wetzel, Villanova University
A Publication Series of
The American Academy of Religion
and
Oxford University Press

CONVERGING ON CULTURE
Theologians in Dialogue with Cultural Analysis and Criticism
Edited by Delwin Brown, Sheila Greeve Davaney and Kathryn Tanner

LESSING'S PHILOSOPHY OF RELIGION AND THE GERMAN ENLIGHTENMENT
Toshimasa Yasukata

AMERICAN PRAGMATISM
A Religious Genealogy
M. Gail Hamner

OPTING FOR THE MARGINS
Postmodernity and Liberation in Christian Theology
Edited by Joerg Rieger

MAKING MAGIC
Religion, Magic, and Science in the Modern World
Randall Styers

THE METAPHYSICS OF DANTE'S *COMEDY*
Christian Moevs

PILGRIMAGE OF LOVE
Moltmann on the Trinity and Christian Life
Joy Ann McDougall

MORAL CREATIVITY
Paul Ricoeur and the Poetics of Moral Life
John Wall

MELANCHOLIC FREEDOM
Agency and the Spirit of Politics
David Kyuman Kim

FEMINIST THEOLOGY AND THE CHALLENGE OF DIFFERENCE
Margaret D. Kamitsuka

PLATO'S GHOST
Spiritualism in the American Renaissance
Cathy Gutierrez

TOWARD A GENEROUS ORTHODOXY
Prospects for Hans Frei's Postliberal Theology
Jason A. Springs

CAVELL, COMPANIONSHIP, AND CHRISTIAN THEOLOGY
Peter Dula

COMPARATIVE THEOLOGY AND THE PROBLEM OF RELIGIOUS RIVALRY
Hugh Nicholson

Comparative Theology and the Problem of Religious Rivalry

HUGH NICHOLSON

OXFORD
UNIVERSITY PRESS

OXFORD
UNIVERSITY PRESS

Oxford University Press, Inc., publishes works that further
Oxford University's objective of excellence
in research, scholarship, and education.

Oxford New York
Auckland Cape Town Dar es Salaam Hong Kong Karachi
Kuala Lumpur Madrid Melbourne Mexico City Nairobi
New Delhi Shanghai Taipei Toronto

With offices in
Argentina Austria Brazil Chile Czech Republic France Greece
Guatemala Hungary Italy Japan Poland Portugal Singapore
South Korea Switzerland Thailand Turkey Ukraine Vietnam

Published by Oxford University Press, Inc.
198 Madison Avenue, New York, New York 10016

www.oup.com

Library of Congress Cataloging-in-Publication Data

Nicholson, Hugh (Hugh R.).
Comparative theology and the problem of religious rivalry / Hugh
Nicholson.
p. cm.
ISBN 978-0-19-977286-5
1. Religions—Relations. 2. Eckhart, Meister, d. 1327.
3. Sankaracarya. 4. Christianity—Relations—Hinduism.
5. Hinduism—Relations—Christianity. 6. Mysticism. I. Title.
BL41.N53 2011
202—dc22 2010028114

9 8 7 6 5 4 3 2 1

Printed in the United States of America
on acid-free paper

To
Francis X. Clooney, SJ
with gratitude

Foreword

I am grateful to Hugh Nicholson several times over for writing *Comparative Theology and the Problem of Religious Rivalry*. The dedication is of course gratifying. It is wonderful to see one's students prosper and pursue their intellectual commitments in the years after graduate school. It is particularly fine to see a student of the caliber of Hugh speak in his own scholarly voice, pursuing issues crucial to comparative theology in his own distinctive way—a way such as I myself did not choose, perhaps could not have mastered. He is notably successful in detecting fissures deep in the writings of earlier scholars who seriously engaged traditions other than their own; such is a matter of historical interest, to be sure, but it also sheds light on who we are as their descendants.

Hugh's formidable analytic strengths are evident in manifold astute insights into what authors mean by what they write, and his insights are commendably accompanied by due investment in the longer historical perspective. Thus, he does very well in noticing the roots of today's "comparative theology discourse" in nineteenth-century ventures deeply intertwined with political concerns and what today we might call the "theology of religions discourse." One might of course go back still farther, for example, studying the major missionary encounters of the sixteenth century, with due attention to Catholic missionary scholarship that, whatever its limitations, never neatly separated comparative study from theologizing about religions. But Hugh's point is well taken: there is no innocent, apolitical theology, no innocent encounter across religious boundaries, no scholar whose work does not have some political positioning at stake, no comparative theology that definitively leaves behind the mixed motives and messages of the past.

His return to Otto's *Mysticism East and West* is an excellent way to get at why people are inclined to take up comparative study. He brings the venerable comparison of Eckhart and Śaṅkara back to life in a remarkably fresh way, well attuned to this new era of comparative studies. That Otto did not enter very deeply into the study of Śaṅkara is well known, and Hugh's corrections in this regard—grounded in Hugh's own seriousness on matters Indological—show why this matters. While Otto's agenda would not have been saved by better Indology, such knowledge would have usefully upset his agenda and enabled him to make better judgments on Śaṅkara and Eckhart, beyond the scope of his original intentions.

In all this, Hugh charts his own path, attuned to the issues of current urgency, particularly regarding comparative theology as a discipline he agrees is important and even urgent. As far as I can see, his approach does not so much correct mine, as indicate how interesting it is when relatively likeminded scholars take up related issues differently. My own interest in Śaṅkara and the Brahma Sūtras is less analytic and philosophical than Hugh's, and relatively untroubled by my early reading Otto. Mine is an on-again, off-again love affair, with a sense that no matter how deeply I read Vedānta texts, I will never have gone deep enough—and yet am still reading as a Roman Catholic, returning to the reading of my own tradition the better for it. Hugh does something else, engaging Otto in argument, and better yet, he shows why the argument need not be posed in the terms Otto favored; Hugh draws on Śaṅkara to explain his position in a way that makes it resistant to merely unfavorable comparisons with Eckhart.

I cannot say whether my work would be better were I more explicit in disclosing an inevitable political agenda, though I do suspect that my commitment to the closer reading of texts "for their own sake" would necessarily be sorely trimmed were I to spend much time discussing contextual issues; but I can say with some certainty that because Hugh has indeed done his work in uncovering the fact and manner of the political, now comparative theology as a field is definitely much better off. There will always be rivalries among those who belong to religions and find themselves studied, those who study them, and those who ponder whether such study can in some way be fruitful; but Hugh's work shows us better how to insure that the inevitable not be reduced to the unnoticed.

Francis X. Clooney, SJ
Director of the Center for the Study of World Religions
Harvard University

Preface

This book addresses the problem of oppositional identity in theological discourse. To be more specific, it attempts to reconcile the ideal of religious tolerance with an honest acknowledgment of the extent to which religious communities mobilize identity on the basis of interreligious differences. What led me to this particular theological problematic was an increasingly acute sense of the politically ambiguous nature of comparing religious traditions. On the one hand, the impetus for such comparison is often an irenic, "liberal" desire to reconcile the teachings of various religions. Indeed, the basic presupposition of the comparative enterprise—that religions are comparable in some way—challenges the absolutist belief in the uniqueness of any single tradition. At the same time, however, the act of comparison brings the differences among religions strongly to the fore. In a comparative context, religious teachings become strongly marked as Christian, Hindu, Islamic, and so on. Even if we stop short of Wilfred Cantwell Smith's assessment that such marking denatures the pristine unity of a transcendental experience of faith, we must concede that, at the very least, it directs our attention to precisely those aspects of religious commitment—parochialism, chauvinism, intolerance, and polemics—that are distasteful to liberal sensibilities.

Up until fairly recently, various forms of pluralist theology gave the reassuring impression that it was possible to affirm religious difference without conceding these more problematic aspects of religious commitment. We can distinguish two basic types of pluralism. The first regards the various religions with their many mutual differences as only so many expressions or manifestations of a more fundamental metaphysical and/or experiential unity. This universalist form of pluralism, which has historical roots in the humanism of the Enlightenment, avoids the more problematic implications of religious difference by relativizing those differences.[1] The second form of pluralism traces its genealogy back to the critique of Enlightenment universalism in Romanticism and that movement's celebration of cultural distinctiveness. It evades the antagonistic dimension of religion not by relativizing religious differences but by reifying and essentializing them. That is, it understands the various religious traditions as more or less self-contained cultural-religious systems that enter into relation with one another only after their essential—and distinctive—character has been determined.[2] In recent years, both forms of pluralism have suffered badly under the impact of postmodern critique. They have each been exposed, against their sincerely held intentions, as hegemonic forms of discourse. The purportedly universalistic presuppositions of the first are now seen to be little more than ideological projections of a particular understanding of religion amenable to Western modernity. The second form of pluralism is hegemonic in that it invariably suppresses the internal diversity of each tradition in its effort to identify that tradition's allegedly essential character. With its understanding religions as more or less self-contained and unified cultural formations, this second variety of pluralism, moreover, fails to recognize the extent to which religious traditions achieve a sense of identity in relation to—and largely in opposition to—rival traditions and movements. With these two dominant forms of pluralism having been called into question, the problem of how to reconcile the liberal ideal of interreligious respect or tolerance with an honest acknowledgment of the oppositional dimension of religious identity asserts itself with renewed force.

The central thesis of Part I of this book is that the fundamental aim of the liberal theological tradition is what might be called, borrowing terminology from the controversial political theorist Carl Schmitt, the "neutralization and de-politicization" of religious discourse and practice. In other words, a major, if not the dominant, trajectory in modern religious thought can be understood in terms of an effort to isolate a putative core of religious conviction and experience from relations of social antagonism.

This thesis challenges what has become the standard reading of the history of modern theology. It has been customary to treat the history of modern theology, at least in North America and Europe, in terms of the problem of apologetics—the problem, that is, of the extent to which the claims of a theological tradition should be recast in terms that the broader culture will readily understand. Classic liberalism and Neo-orthodoxy—and, more recently, their respective contemporary heirs, revisionism and postliberalism—are often presented as the two fundamental theological options; other possibilities tend either to be interpreted as variants or combinations of these two or else marginalized.[3] The fundamental theological challenge is rendering traditional Christian claims plausible and intelligible in secular, post-Christian societies without sacrificing the distinctiveness of the Christian message in the process. Or, stated negatively, the challenge is to avoid the twin pitfalls of cultural accommodation—the danger of a one-sided liberalism—and cultural irrelevance—the danger of a one-sided (neo)orthodoxy.[4] The rereading I propose places this problematic in a larger historical perspective. The problem of apologetics is only a particular aspect or inflection of the more fundamental problem of reconciling religious commitment with an aversion to social antagonism. The priority of the latter problematic can perhaps be most clearly demonstrated with respect to the Enlightenment project of rational theology, the so-called "Religion of Reason." Seen through the lens of the apologetics problematic, the aim of Enlightenment philosophers and theologians like Locke, Toland, and Tindal was to reconcile Christian teaching with a modern worldview shaped by the discoveries of modern science and the development of modern political institutions. There is much truth in this formulation, of course, but I would argue that it fails to get at the heart of the matter. As evident in Locke's preoccupation with the problem of religious "enthusiasm," the fundamental aim of Enlightenment theology, I suggest, was to isolate a putative essence of Christian faith from the sectarian attitudes and passions that were believed to have led to the so-called "Wars of Religion" of the sixteenth and seventeenth centuries. By establishing Christian faith on the universally valid discourse of reason, Enlightenment theologians and philosophers sought to undercut the sectarian loyalties that had visited so much havoc on European societies. Rationalism, in other words, served as an instrument of de-politicization. In chapter 2 of this book, I show how several key moments in the history of modern theology—from Schleiermacher's intuitively based concept of religion, through the Christian universalism of the late nineteenth century and the experiential pluralism of the twentieth, up to the postliberal theology of George Lindbeck and his followers—can be fruitfully understood in terms of this problematic of dissociating religious commitment from social antagonism, religion from "the political."

The understanding of theological liberalism in terms of depoliticization calls for a rereading of the history not only of modern theology, but of the comparative study of religion as well. Many historians of religion are inclined to understand the historical development of their discipline in terms of a gradual emancipation from theology. They readily acknowledge that many of the founders of the discipline like F. Max Müller, C. P. Tiele, and P. D. Chantepie de la Saussaye continued to work with theological commitments. But they tend to regard these commitments as mere holdovers from an earlier time.[5] Such theological commitments, according to this modernist narrative, have subsequently been recognized and eliminated from the discipline in a process that is, to be sure, ongoing and incomplete. Against this view, I argue in chapter 1 that from its inception in the late nineteenth century up until fairly recently, the discipline of comparative religion—or at least a dominant trajectory thereof—is more accurately understood as a moment in the larger liberal theological project of depoliticizing religion. This hypothesis makes sense of the otherwise puzzling fact that many scholars and theologians of the late nineteenth century assumed that an ostensibly impartial science of religion coincided with a universalist theology of Christian fulfillment. In a project that was fully continuous with the rationalist theology of the Enlightenment, early comparativists sought to depoliticize religion by rendering it scientific, that is, by establishing religious belief on a scientific—which in the late nineteenth century meant comparative—foundation. The depoliticization hypothesis also explains the close alliance, illuminatively described by Tomoko Masuzawa in her book *The Invention of World Religions*, between the contemporary academic study of religion and the pluralist ideology that sustains today's discourse of "world religions."

In this book, I reinterpret the respective histories of modern theology and comparative religion in the context of developing a contemporary model of comparative theology. Such a rereading of the history of modern religious thought in terms of the depoliticization problematic, I would argue, is integral to the constructive project of comparative theology. For, as indicated above, the issue of the political comes strongly to the fore when one compares religious traditions. Another way of bringing the connection between the depoliticization problematic and the comparative theological project clearly into view is to consider the historical provenance of the two interpretations I challenge. One could argue that both of these interpretations—the understanding of modern theology in terms of the problem of apologetics and of comparative religion in terms of an emancipation of the study of religion from theology—can be traced to the so-called "theological renaissance" of the 1920s and '30s.[6] With its bold assertion of the incommensurability between revelation and history, faith and "religion," the Dialectical Theology of Barth, Brunner, and Gogarten rendered the activity of comparison, a feature of the liberal theology against which it profiled itself, theologically irrelevant, if not theologically suspect as well. The thesis of an antithesis between faith and religion—of which the divorce between theology and comparative religion was an inevitable consequence—externalized the relation between (Christian) faith and the issue of social antagonism. Of course, the theologies of figures like Barth and Brunner were, if anything, more political, more confrontational, than their liberal predecessors. And yet, the assertion of a radical discontinuity between the vertical, transcendental dimension of faith, on the one hand, and the horizontal-political dimension of religion, on the other, shifted attention away from the question of an antagonistic dimension constitutive of the act of faith. Rather, the question became that of the stance a transcendental concept of faith should take vis-à-vis a fallen world of antagonistic human relations. This externalization of the relation between faith and "the political" is implicit in the apologetic, "Christ-and-Culture" (H. R. Niebuhr) problematic that has since come to dominate theological discussion. A theological approach that makes comparison an integral part of theological method reverses this development, returning the issue of the inherent ambiguity of religious commitment to the center of theological reflection.

The second interpretation I question, the understanding of the disciplinary history of comparative religion in terms of an emancipation from theology, can also be seen as a consequence of the profound theological changes of the 1920s and '30s. At that time, many historians of religion, effectively conceding as normative Neo-orthodoxy's dogmatic (as opposed to apologetic) conception of theology,[7] sought to dissociate the discipline of comparative religion from theology. No longer was the science of religion believed to coincide with a liberal form of Christian universalism as it had in the previous century. Since then, scholars of religion have continually sought to purge their discipline of any lingering traces of theological commitment in their effort to establish the study of religion as a "legitimate" academic discipline. In recent years, the exposure of previously unacknowledged forms of "theologism" in the classic model of the History of Religions exemplified by scholars such as Wach, Kitagawa, and Eliade (to say nothing of the rather patent theologism of phenomenologists of religion like Söderblom, van der Leeuw, Otto, and Heiler) has prompted something of an identity crisis in the discipline. At the risk of oversimplifying matters, we might say that this crisis has split scholars of religion into two basic camps, which we might label, borrowing terminology from Catherine Bell, "modernist" and "postmodernist."[8] The former responds to this challenge of crypto-theology in the classic models of religious studies by pressing on with what its critics might regard as the quixotic task of purging all traces of normative (read: "theological") commitment from the academic study of religion.[9] The latter believes that the future of the comparative study of religions lies in the open acknowledgment, critique, and defense of the inevitable normative presuppositions of the discipline.[10] Implicit in this second response is a rejection of the emancipation model of the disciplinary history of comparative religion, at least in its cruder forms. In chapter 1, I argue that the new comparative theology epitomizes this second approach to the study of religion and theology.

Simply by uniting—or, rather, *re*-uniting—theology and comparison, then, the new comparative theology challenges the way the relation between theology and comparative religion has been conceived since the aforementioned theological renaissance. Given the revisionary implications of comparative theology with respect to the prevailing conception of the theology/religious studies relation, it is perhaps fitting that part II of this book would feature the work of Rudolf Otto, a thinker whose reputation both as a theologian and as a scholar of comparative religion has suffered rather badly as a result of the estrangement of theology and comparative religion. Toward the end of his career, Otto's reputation as a theologian was eclipsed by the Neo-orthodox movement, whose leaders, not coincidentally, included some of his severest critics, Bultmann, Brunner, and Barth.[11] As if in compensation for being passed over by this dominant trajectory in twentieth-century theology, Otto has been recognized as a significant figure in the disciplinary history of the comparative study of religion. More recently, however, his reputation has suffered there as well, as a later generation of scholars have been put off by the openly theological nature of Otto's comparative works. Indeed, Otto's theologically motivated comparisons substantiate and exemplify the charge, leveled by Tim Fitzgerald, Russell McCutcheon and others, that the classic model of comparative religion based on the category of religion as a sui generis and universal phenomenon is essentially theological in character. My hope is that an acceptance of comparative theology as a legitimate, if not unavoidable, way of doing theology in today's world will lead to a rehabilitation of Otto's reputation, not, to be sure, as a disinterested historian of religion—which, it should be noted, he never claimed to be—but precisely as a comparative theologian. While my treatment of Otto is far from uncritical, my decision to use his classic work *Mysticism East and West* as a point of reference for the comparative theological exercise in part II is motivated in part by my belief that Otto was a precursor, and in important respects an exemplar, of the kind of theologically sensitive and philologically rigorous comparative work currently practiced by contemporary comparative theologians like Francis Clooney, James Fredericks, James Keenan, John Berthrong, John Thatamanil, Reid Locklin, and Michelle Voss Roberts, among others.

Perhaps it would be appropriate at this point to say a word or two about my relationship to the emerging field of comparative theology. On the one hand, I write this book as someone committed to the project of comparative theology and its goal of fostering relations of mutual respect and understanding among the religions. I also share its underlying theological conviction that a knowledge of other traditions enlarges our understanding and awareness of God's presence in the world. As a doctoral student of Francis Clooney and a participant (as research assistant) in Robert C. Neville's Cross-Cultural Religious Ideas Project held at Boston University between 1995 and 1999—two experiences for which I am profoundly grateful—I belong to a generation of scholars who have been specifically trained in the practice of comparative theology. That is to say, my academic background differs from a previous generation of scholars whose primary academic training lay in either one or the other side of the comparative theological project. I am neither an area specialist with a side interest in theology nor a Christian theologian with a side interest in other religions.

On the other hand, I find myself somewhat on the margins of what I take to be the discipline's dominant trajectory. In a quite understandable effort to lend to the new discipline a clear sense of identity, pioneering comparative theologians like Clooney and Fredericks have insisted on its distinction from two discourses for which I must confess a certain affinity. The first of these is the theology of religions, pluralist theologies of religion in particular. The second is the academic study of religion. In distinguishing comparative theology from these two discourses, particularly the latter, these scholars have emphasized comparative theology's confessional character. While profoundly influenced by this confessional trajectory of contemporary comparative theology, I find myself by temperament and upbringing more inclined to stress the continuities between comparative theology and the theology of religions, on the one side, and the academic study of religion, on the other. As indicated above, I have a profound sense of affinity toward pluralist theologians like John Hick, Wilfred Cantwell Smith, and Paul Knitter, this despite my willingness to concede the validity of many of the criticisms recently leveled against them. At the same time, I have always had an avid interest in the comparative study of religion, this despite receiving my primary graduate training in a theology program where there was an undercurrent of hostility toward "religious studies." This autobiographical information might provide some context for the argument, put forward in chapter 1, that the reunification of theology and comparison in the new comparative theology challenges the long-standing tendency, maintained on both sides of the divide, to oppose theology and religious studies.

Another way of describing my location within the broader movement of comparative theology is that I see the academy rather than a particular faith community as my primary, though not exclusive, audience and "constituency."[12] That is to say, I identify more with "academic" rather than confessional forms of theology, realizing, of course, that these labels are only relative.

Inasmuch, then, as the particular conception of comparative theology set forth in these pages reflects my own personal background and predilections, I naturally cannot regard it as the only valid or normative one; even while articulating a conception of the discipline that makes most sense to me, I recognize and affirm the legitimacy, indeed the desirability, of a plurality of approaches to comparative theology.

Finally, it gives me great pleasure to acknowledge those who have helped me, either directly or indirectly, in the research and writing of this book. Of all those teachers and colleagues who have taught and inspired me, to none do I owe a greater debt of gratitude than my former dissertation director, Francis Clooney. While my indebtedness to Clooney's work is no doubt evident—perhaps too evident!—throughout this book, so too are the respects in which my understanding and practice of comparative theology diverges from his, most notably in its more critical, revisionary focus. The different perspective I have on the practice of comparative theology reflects a different religious background as well as a set of questions, concerns, and emphases that are characteristic of my generation.

Special thanks are also due to Ted Vial for his interest in and support of this project as editor of the Reflection and Theory in the Study of Religion Series. Before he was committed to my project, Ted generously provided incisive criticism of early drafts of chapters 1 and 3, which helped me enormously as I struggled to focus my thoughts and give shape to the project. This work also benefited greatly from my productive collaboration with Reid Locklin, who read and commented on several early drafts of the manuscript at the same time that I did the same for his excellent monograph, *Liturgy of Liberation: a Christian Commentary on Śaṅkara's* Upadeśasahasri (forthcoming, 2011). I am grateful as well to the two anonymous readers at Oxford University Press, each of whom gave the manuscript a careful and perceptive reading.

Other colleagues and friends who have read and commented on parts of the manuscript or essays closely connected with it include Chris Seeman, Jeff Hoover, Andrew Nicholson, John Casey, Joyce Janca-Aji, and John McCarthy. James Fredericks provided incisive and salutary criticism of an early version of the first chapter.

Somehow I wish I could hold these individuals responsible for the many oversights and errors that are inevitable in such a wide-ranging project as this, but, alas, that would hardly be an appropriate way to reward their generosity.

I would also like to thank those individuals and institutions who supported this project more indirectly. I first began to work out some of the ideas behind this project during the 2004–5 academic year, which I spent as a Senior Fellow in the Martin Marty Center at the University of Chicago Divinity School. Thanks in large part to the participants in the regular Marty Center seminars, including Wendy Doniger and William Schweiker, this fellowship provided the ideal intellectual environment in which to conceive such a project. I am particularly grateful to my former colleague and Department Head, Jeff Hoover, not only for his support for the leave of absence in 2004–5 which allowed me to go to Chicago, but also, more generally, for his professional support and friendship during the eight years I was employed at Coe College. I am grateful also to Harlene Hansen and her student staff at the Stewart Memorial Library at Coe for help with interlibrary loans, particularly in tracking down obscure German articles and books on Meister Eckhart. In the final preparation of the manuscript I received valuable assistance from my resourceful research assistant, Daniel Dion, Ph.D. candidate in Theology at Loyola University Chicago.

An earlier version of chapter 1 appeared in the *Journal of the American Academy of Religion* 77:3 (September 2009): 609–46; it appears here with the permission of the journal. Unless otherwise indicated, all translations are my own.

For her patience and support, thanks, finally, to Susanne, who will not really believe "the book is done" until she holds it in her hands.

Contents

Abbreviations

AU	Aitareya Upaniṣad
AUBh	Śaṅkara, *Aitareya-Upaniṣad-Bhāṣya*. Cited from Umeśānanda Śāstri and Svarṇalāla Tulī, ed., *Aitareyopaniṣad: saṭippaṇa-saṃskṛta-hindī-ṭīkā-dvaya-saṃvalita-śāṅkarabhāṣya-sametā* (Hṛṣīkeśa, U.P.: Śrī Kailāsa Vidyā Prakāśana, 1999).
Bhāskara	Vindhyesvarī Prasāda Dvivedin, ed., *Brahmasūtrabhāṣyam Śri Bhāskarācāryaviracitam* (Varanasi: Chowkhamba, 1991).
BAU	Bṛhadāraṇyaka Upaniṣad
BAUBh	Śaṅkara, *Bṛhadāraṇyaka Upaniṣad Bhāṣya*. Cited from Kāśinātha Śastrī Āgāśe, ed., *Bṛhadāraṇyakopaniṣat, ānandagiri-kṛta-ṭīkā-saṃvalita-śāṃkara-bhāṣya-sametā* (Puṇyākhyapattane: Ānandāśramasaṃsthā, 1982).
CAU	Chāndogya Upaniṣad
BS	Bādarāyaṇa's *Brahma-Sūtra*
BSBh	Śaṅkara, *Brama-Sūtra-Bhāṣ*ya. The Sanskrit text is cited from J. L. Sastri, ed., *Brahma-Sūtra-Śāṅkarabhāṣyam with the Commentaries: Bhāṣyaratnaprabhā of Govindānanda, Bhāmatī of Vācaspatimiśra, and Nyāyanirnaya of Ānandagiri* (1980; reprint, Delhi: Motilal Banarsidass, 1996).
Gītā	Bhagavad-Gītā

GBh Śaṅkara, *Bhagavad-Gītā-Bhāṣya*. Cited from A. G. Krishna Warrier, ed. and trans., *Śrīmad Bhagavad Gītā Bhāṣya of Śaṃkarācārya* (Madras: Sri Ramakrishna Math, 1983).

LW The Latin works of Meister Eckhart cited from J. Quint and J. Koch, eds., *Meister Eckhart: Die deutschen und lateinischen Werke* (Stuttgart and Berlin: W. Kohlhammer, 1936–). The abbreviation LW will be followed by the volume number in the Kohlhammer series. I have cited the following individual Latin treatises, the abbreviated title followed by the numbered section(s) of the Latin edition (e.g. *Comm. Ex.*, no. 61):

Comm. Ecc. *Sermons and Lectures on Ecclesiasticus*

Comm. Ex. *Commentary on Exodus*

Comm. Jn. *Commentary on John*

Comm. Gen. *Commentary on Genesis*

Par. Gen. *Book of the Parables of Genesis*

MHG Middle High German

NHG New High German

Pf. Eckhart's German sermons collected in Franz Pfeiffer, ed., *Meister Eckhart* (Leipzig, 1857). The roman numerals following (e.g. Pf. LVI) correspond to the numbering of the sermons in Pfeiffer's edition.

STh Thomas Aquinas, *Summa Theologiae*. Quoted from: *Summae Theologiae: Latin Text and English Translation, Introductions, Notes, Appendices, and Glossaries* (Cambridge: Blackfriars, 1964–81).

Introduction

> A St. Paul, an Augustine, a Wesley wrote and thought about theology; not about "Christian theology." This latter phrase would have seemed to them bizarre, and limited; would have seemed to concede too much.
>
> —Wilfred Cantwell Smith

A Utopian Quest for Unmarked Faith

"We pray this in the name of the Father, and of the Son, the Lord Jesus Christ, and of the Holy Spirit. Amen." With these words, the Reverend Franklin Graham, son and heir apparent of the famous evangelist Billy Graham, concluded the opening invocation at George W. Bush's inaugural ceremony on January 20, 2001. Graham's invocation of the name of Jesus—the same Trinitarian prayer, but without the appositional phrase, "the Lord Jesus Christ," had been used by his father on the occasion of the elder Bush's inauguration in 1989—signaled a willful repudiation of the long-standing custom of using more generic and inclusive religious language in American public discourse. This deliberate break from what Robert Bellah has called the tradition of "American civil religion" was, if anything, more dramatic in the ceremony's closing benediction offered by the Rev. Kirbyjon H. Caldwell, the pastor of a suburban Houston "mega-church": "We respectfully submit this humble prayer in the name that's above all names, Jesus the Christ. Let all who agree say amen." Caldwell's request for a confirmatory "amen" added a participatory dimension to the exclusory rhetoric of the prayers to Jesus.[1] It divided the audience into those who could say "amen"—those Americans who happened to be Christian—and those who could not.[2]

The divisive effects of the Christocentric prayers did not stop there, however. The rift between Christians and non-Christians ramified to the former group. Graham's and Caldwell's prayers divided the Christian audience between those Christians—evangelicals and conservative Catholics for the most part—who collectively expressed an enthusiastic "Amen!" to the invocation of Jesus' name and those Christians of a more liberal stripe who reacted to the prayers with feelings of ambivalence, uneasiness, and perhaps even a tinge of embarrassment.[3] Members of this latter group found nothing objectionable in the prayers themselves—after all, the prayers were identical to the ones heard every week in mainline Christian churches—but were uncomfortable with the exclusionary connotations that these Christian prayers took on in the context of a presidential inauguration. As the distinguished scholar of American religious history Martin Marty put it in describing this liberal reaction, "People don't mind the prayers; they mind the assumption of exclusivism and Christian privilege."[4]

The ambivalent reaction on the part of liberal Christians to the Jesus prayers reflects an understanding of the nature of religion and religious commitment that is characteristic of the modern era. As I hope to show in chapter 2, it is an understanding of religion whose genealogy reaches back to the Enlightenment project of dissociating a universal "essence" of religion from the sectarian loyalties and intolerant attitudes that were held responsible the for the so-called Wars of Religion of the sixteenth and seventeenth centuries. Characteristic of this understanding of religion is a sharp distinction between the meaning religious utterances have as expressions of faith, on the one hand, and as markers of religious difference, on the other. Thus for the liberal Christians at Bush's inauguration, the exclusory, "political" intention that the Jesus prayers took on in that context jarred with what they regarded as the prayers' more authentic or proper meaning as expressions of Christian faith. The judgment that the use of such prayers in pluralistic contexts is inappropriate reflects an underlying sense that the exclusionary intention they acquire in those settings is somehow alien to the true spirit of Christianity. An interest in preventing this exclusionary dimension of Christian discourse from coming to the fore would explain why liberal Christians tend to ally themselves with secularists in advocating more inclusive, generic language in public prayers and invocations. Far from being a capitulation to the pressures of secularism or "political correctness," this preference for generic theological language can be seen, paradoxically, as a way of preserving the proper sense of Christian prayer. It reflects, in other words, a properly *theological* concern with recovering the authentic faith dimension of public religious discourse from its political excrescences, even if this recovery comes at the cost of some of that discourse's expressive power.

Nowhere is the "two-dimensional" understanding of religion implicit in this liberal discomfort with expressions of religious faith strongly marked as "Christian" more clearly or eloquently expressed than in the writings of the historian of religions cum Christian theologian Wilfred Cantwell Smith. In numerous books and articles, Smith adumbrates a pluralist theology of religions whose salient feature is the recognition of a unitary concept of faith in the multifarious phenomena in the history of religions. At the heart of Smith's theological vision is an acute sensitivity to the difference between what I would call marked and unmarked expressions of faith—precisely the same sensitivity, I suggest, that we saw expressed in the liberal reaction to the Jesus prayers at the Bush inauguration. Noting that the New Testament never speaks of "Christian faith" but simply faith, and that the great theologians of the Christian tradition like Paul, Augustine, and Wesley wrote about theology and not "Christian theology," Smith argues that the adjective limits and denatures the religious concepts, whether "faith," "theology," or "religion," that it modifies.[5] To be specific, it introduces into religious discourse a sociopolitical intention of marking religious difference that threatens to eclipse its reference to the Transcendent. Adjectivally marked religious expressions pertain to the "horizontal," worldly relations between religious communities, while their unmarked counterparts pertain to the "vertical," transcendental relation between human beings and God. The privileged concept in this bi-dimensional conception of religion is the (unmarked) concept of faith, which names this transcendental relation directly. From the observation that the religious insider's orientation to transcendent reality naturally expresses itself in generic, unmarked terms, Smith concludes that this faith dimension is universal.[6] The terms "Christian faith," "Islamic faith," and so on, do not designate independent forms of faith so much as the particular modes that a unitary faith can take; Smith construes such expressions as shorthand formulations for "faith in its Christian form," "faith in its Islamic form," respectively.[7] Faith in this pluralistic conception is essentially one, though its particular manifestations are many.[8] Like the velocity of light in relativity theory, the concept of faith in Smith's theology is an absolute that transcends any historical frame of reference. It belongs to an entirely different order or dimension than the aspects of religion that lend themselves to historical observation.

Much like the inclusive, generic religious language that liberal Christians prefer in civic discourse, Smith's generic concept of faith gives expression to a utopian desire to transcend political, "us" versus "them" distinctions in the sphere of religion. The utopian character of Smith's concept of faith appears most clearly when it is seen in relation to the phenomenon he terms "reification." Reification is the process by which a way of life oriented to transcendence is reduced to a set of observable practices and propositionally expressible beliefs. In other words, reification occurs when a community of faith, in a kind of Augustinian fall from grace, narcissistically turns its attention in on itself to apprehend itself as a sociological cum theological entity—as a *religion*. What typically occasions this preoccupation with outward religious forms and religious differences is a polemical challenge from without. Smith notes that reification usually occurs in situations of religious rivalry and competition.[9] Many of the reifying terms used to denote specific religious groups begin their careers as terms of denigration hurled at a community from without; in a subsequent moment, they are appropriated by the community so designated, with their polarity reversed, as positive terms of self-identification.[10] We might infer from this historical pattern that the reified concepts of religion enshrine relations of religious antagonism in much the same way that the commodity in Marxist thought embodies the unjust labor relations involved in its production.[11] Smith's historical-critical project of thawing out the reified concepts of religion to liberate their transcendental faith dimension can therefore be interpreted as an effort to assert the transcendence of religious faith over attitudes of religious chauvinism and intolerance.

As numerous critiques of Smith's brand of pluralist theology have shown, however, the relation of "faith" to the exclusory, political dimension of religion is more ambiguous than Smith was willing to acknowledge. Critics of pluralist theology like Mark Heim and Kenneth Surin have called into question the putative universality of Smith's conception of faith and—what amounts to the same claim expressed from another angle[12]—the radical inclusivity of the "world theology" founded upon its recognition. As Heim has argued, few religious communities would accept the radical discontinuity that Smith posits between the subjectivistic, existential attitude he calls faith, on the one hand, and the propositional beliefs and observable practices that together comprise the historically conditioned forms of "religion," on the other.[13] It is difficult to avoid the conclusion that Smith's understanding of human religiosity in terms of a personal experience of faith is strongly conditioned by his own Protestant background.[14] And just as Smith's conception of religion as faith is more particular than he acknowledges, so too, his critics allege, is his "world theology" considerably less inclusive than it purports to be. Smith is aware, of course, that many of his Christian coreligionists, to say nothing of the adherents of other religions, will resist his pluralistic vision of theology. But he minimizes the significance of this resistance by attributing it to prejudice and ignorance, to parochial attitudes held in place by lingering attachments to outmoded exclusivist theological traditions.[15] He is confident that such exclusivistic attitudes will become increasingly untenable as a "new world situation" characterized by the large-scale encounter between persons of diverse faiths begins to dawn.[16] Smith's expectation that those who disagree with him will eventually come around to accept his theological proposal as they become more "enlightened" constitutes a refusal to recognize—and ultimately to respect—an alternative theological viewpoint.[17] As Heim, following Surin, argues, the "we" of Smith's world theology, far from being coextensive with all humanity as Smith intends, is restricted to those who share Smith's liberal presuppositions—"a 'we' of liberal intellectuals," as Heim puts it.[18] The fundamental problem with Smith's pluralist theology is that it refuses to acknowledge its own exclusions, a constitutive blindness that it shares more generally with political liberalism, according to some recent critics of the latter.[19] Put differently, Smith's concept of a world theology is *hegemonic* in that it seeks to extend the influence of this liberal conception of religion beyond the circle of those whose basic outlook it expresses.[20] As both Surin and Kathryn Tanner have argued, pluralist theologies like Smith's, as expressions of "Western cultural hegemonism," are unwittingly complicit in the forms of discourse that reflect and support the unequal "neo-colonialist" relations fostered by late-stage, global capitalism.[21]

This critique of Smith's world theology as a form of discourse that masks its particularity and partiality under a pretense of universality can be approached from yet another angle. As I suggested above, Smith's generic concept of faith reflects the same instinctive preference for unmarked over marked expressions of religious commitment that we saw in the liberal Christian reaction to Franklin Graham's prayer at the Bush inaugural. The hegemonic character of Smith's generic concept of faith is implicit in this preference for unmarked religious language. For, as Roman Jakobson has shown in his studies of language, a hierarchic relation obtains between an unmarked term and its marked correlate.[22] Perhaps the most familiar example of such a hierarchic relation is the use of non-gender-inclusive language. The male and female personal pronouns represent, respectively, the unmarked and the marked terms of a binary opposition. As feminist critics have taught us, the use of the male pronoun as the unmarked or default term reflects a situation of male privilege or patriarchy. In an analogous way, the use of unmarked, generic religious language—language, in other words, that a putative mainstream audience experiences as unproblematic—reflects a relation of hegemony over the groups that identify with the marked, particularistic alternatives.

The critique of Smith's pluralist theology as a form of hegemonic discourse thus reflects back upon what might be regarded as its generative impulse, namely, the liberal reaction to strongly marked expressions of Christian commitment like those heard at the Bush inaugural. It suggests that this reaction against particularistic religious language is less innocent and more ambiguous than it might first appear. As we have seen, this reaction embodies a utopian impulse to transcend relations of social antagonism in the sphere of religion. At the same time, however, it expresses, albeit unwittingly and incipiently, a will to maintain a culturally privileged position over those who do not share its underlying presuppositions. The hegemonic character of the generic religious language preferred by liberal Christians can be inferred from the reactions of those for whom such language is neither unobtrusive nor innocuous. Many non-Christians and non-theists, who would prefer that religious references be eliminated from civil discourse altogether, experience the ceremonial deism used in American civil discourse as the imposition of a covert Christian theism. At the same time, some Christian conservatives experience the very same generic and inclusive religious discourse as an imposition of an ideology of liberal pluralism, of "political correctness." Whatever one might think of the respective merits of these points of view, both of these reactions demonstrate, at the very least, that the ceremonial deism that passes for unmarked religious language in American civil discourse is not politically innocent. That is to say, it represents one option, at once contestable and defensible, among a number of alternatives.

The Inescapability of the Political

The foregoing critique reveals the liberal universalism that Smith exemplifies to be a profoundly ambiguous discourse, one that is both utopian and ideological at the same time.[23] It is utopian in that it envisions a radically inclusive form of religious community that makes a clean break with all forms of oppositional identity. It is ideological in that it masks its own particularity in projecting this universalistic vision. Smith's brand of pluralism would thus seem to embody a contradiction. It declares a radical break with religious exclusivism, but does so only through an act of exclusion that it fails to acknowledge. The same critique applies, mutatis mutandis, to cognate pluralist theologies like that of John Hick, and, a fortiori, to the universalistic fulfillment theologies of the nineteenth century, whose underlying presuppositions, as I shall argue below in chapter 2, pluralist theologies like Smith's unwittingly preserve.

A helpful, if provocative, model for understanding the contradictory and ambiguous nature of liberal universalist theologies, I suggest, is the critique of political liberalism of the controversial legal and political theorist Carl Schmitt. Having invoked the name of the man dubbed the "crown jurist of the Third Reich," I should perhaps reassure the reader here at the outset that I personally find many aspects of Schmitt's political thought, quite frankly, repugnant—his tendency, if only on a rhetorical level, to glorify war and "aestheticize" violence,[24] as well as his advocacy of an authoritarian state, to say nothing of his well-documented anti-Semitism and the intellectual support he provided to the Nazi state.[25] Nevertheless, I feel that few writers have grasped the fundamental ambiguity of classic liberalism[26]—of which liberal universalist theology is one expression—with greater clarity or insight.

The central concept in Schmitt's critique of liberalism is his "concept of the political." Schmitt notoriously defines the political as the grouping of human beings into friend and enemy.[27] For Schmitt the political constitutes a fundamental and ineluctable dimension of human societies. Any attempt to eradicate it from social relations only leads to more insidious forms of domination. Schmitt illustrates this point with the concept of humanity, a concept that exemplifies the ambiguity he sees in liberal thought. Schmitt notes that this concept, which, in excluding the concept of the enemy, gives expression to the liberal goal of eliminating antagonism from social relations, has proven extremely useful in ideologies of imperialist expansion.[28] It is well known, of course, that imperialist powers have justified their domination of foreign populations with the notion that they are somehow "civilizing" or "humanizing" the latter. Schmitt perspicaciously notes that wars waged in the name of humanity are often the most inhumane precisely because they refuse to recognize a legitimate enemy. The effective monopolization of the concept of humanity by one of the warring factions can be used to justify the utter destruction of an adversary who has become defined as an enemy of humanity.[29]

This thesis regarding the inescapability of the political forms the basis of Schmitt's critique of liberalism. For Schmitt, the defining feature of liberal thought is its attempt to neutralize and "depoliticize" social relations. Schmitt reads the history of Western modernity as a series of unsuccessful attempts to realize a conflict-free region of human interaction. At every stage in this history, liberal thought seeks to base social relations on a previously nonantagonistic domain of culture, only to find that the chosen domain becomes "political" the moment it becomes the decisive or controlling domain of culture.[30] The paradigmatic example of the unsuccessful depoliticization of society, according to Schmitt, is the twentieth century's effort to base social relations on rational economic principles, that is, to reduce social and political problems to technically solvable economic ones concerning the production and distribution of goods.[31] The emergence of capitalism and communism as antagonistic political ideologies in the twentieth century testifies to the failure of this particular attempt at depoliticization.[32]

Schmitt's thesis regarding the inescapability of the political brings the problematic at the heart of pluralist theologies clearly into focus. The aforementioned critique of Smith's pluralism suggested that the effort to dissociate religion from exclusionary, "us" versus "them" relations ends up merely transposing the act of exclusion to a meta-level where the excluded "other"—in the form of exclusivist theologies—is not immediately recognized. As Heim argues, pluralism's illusion of impartiality is maintained by a specious distinction between, on the one hand, the primary faith positions (i.e., the "religions," Buddhism, Judaism, Islam, etc.[33]) that it includes and, on the other, the metatheories of religion (exlusivism and inclusivism) that it excludes.[34] The exclusory, political character of pluralist theology comes into view when we recognize it as a substantive religious position in its own right.

My use of Schmitt's "inescapability thesis" to describe the problematic of pluralist theology presupposes a corollary to the concept of the political that Schmitt himself does not make explicit, namely, a recognition of unacknowledged exclusion or hegemony as a modality of the political. In our critique of Smith, we saw that pluralist theologies, in their well-intentioned effort to overcome exclusionary, polemical relations in the realm of religion, often yield a situation in which religious exclusion is merely masked, not eliminated. The difference between the two situations has to do with acknowledgment: the second refuses to acknowledge the act of exclusion that the first acknowledges openly. We can thus regard these two situations—which we might term the polemical and the hegemonic, respectively—as representing two modalities of the political. In the first, polemical modality, an adversarial relation is out in the open; in the second, hegemonic modality, this relation is sublimated and misrecognized. Even when the concept of the political is broadened to include relations of hegemony, however, it still refers to an oppositional, exclusory relation and so thus retains the basic sense Schmitt gave to it.

There is yet another refinement that I would make to Schmitt's concept of the political that initially appears subtle but will prove crucial to the solution I will propose for the problem of the political in theology. In appropriating Schmitt's concept of the political, I distinguish between an "us" versus "them" relation, on the one hand, and Schmitt's friend-enemy grouping, on the other. The inescapability thesis, I suggest, pertains to the former but not, as Schmitt believes, to the latter. I thus define the political in terms of an adversarial relation between an "us" and a "them" that stops short of declaring the "them" an enemy. To anticipate the thesis of the first part of this book, I shall argue that when the political is understood in this way, it is compatible with an acceptance of religious pluralism and a respect for religious others.

This revised definition of the political rests on a different understanding of the *basis* of the inescapability thesis. Schmitt based his claim for the unavoidability of political antagonism on a pessimistic, Augustinian view of human nature. Like some of the earlier political theorists he admired, such as Machiavelli, the nineteenth-century Spanish counterrevolutionary Donoso Cortes, and, especially, Hobbes, Schmitt believed that human beings were essentially warlike by nature.[35] He combined this pessimistic anthropology with a vitalist philosophy of Nietzschean provenance that celebrates the existential boundary situations in which human beings prove their "authenticity" as they confront the real possibility of death.[36] According to this understanding of the political, all political struggle carries an intrinsic reference to the possibility of violent conflict, to "the real possibility of physical killing," as Schmitt puts it with a rather unsettling directness.[37] In the final analysis, political behavior is determined by the ever-present possibility of war that hovers over social relations like the sword of Damocles. One could argue that an understanding of the political as constituted by "the real possibility of physical killing" assumes the inevitability of violence and destruction.

Against this vitalist-existentialist understanding of the political, I follow the political theorist Chantal Mouffe in basing the Schmittian thesis of the ineluctability of the political not on an assumed propensity of human beings for war and violence, but rather on the essentially relational or differential nature of social identity.[38] According to a relational conception of social identity, all forms of collective identity are constituted by difference; a group's sense of identity is constituted by the other against which it defines itself. Social identity therefore has an "us" versus "them" structure; it presupposes, in other words, a political moment of exclusion. In contrast to Schmitt's conception of the political, however, this conception does not imply the inevitability of violent conflict. Indeed, for a conception of the political based on a relational understanding of social identity, the physical destruction of the adversary, far from being the logical consequence of the political mobilization of identity, signifies its negation. Put differently, a relational conception of the political recognizes that a sense of political identity is constituted by its adversarial "other," and not, as in Schmitt's theory, by the possibility of their destruction. This revised conception of the political will allow us to make a critical distinction between, as Mouffe puts it, an adversary to be tolerated, even respected, on the one hand, and an enemy to be destroyed, on the other.[39]

The Political Goes "All the Way Down"

As a basic presupposition of religious identity, the principle of political opposition would seem to be integral to the forms of life conventionally categorized as religious. The entirety of religious discourse and practice, in other words, would appear to be implicated, either directly or indirectly, in relations of religious rivalry. The foregoing critique therefore calls into question the presumption that the differential, political dimension of religious commitment is somehow adventitious to an existential core of faith. In other words, it casts doubt on the two-dimensional conception of religion that I suggested was implicit in the liberal aversion to the Jesus prayers at the Bush inaugural and exemplified in Wilfred Cantwell Smith's theology. Ironically, Smith's proposal, precisely by drawing the two-dimensional conception of religion to its logical conclusion, inadvertently prepares the ground for its own refutation. As we have seen, Smith, in what appears to be an almost-desperate effort to preserve a kind of magic circle of religious experience untouched by profane considerations of religious difference, effectively concedes the entire objective and communal side of religion—communicable beliefs and observable practices—to the mundane realm in which relations of religious rivalry hold sway. Once the nonpolitical "essence" of religion has been whittled down to the exceedingly slender thread that is Smith's personal-existential concept of faith, all it takes is a demonstration of the partiality of this concept to shipwreck the two-dimensional conception of religion.[40] The demonstration that Smith's concept of faith forms a constitutive part of a hegemonic—and thus political—form of discourse suggests that the principle of the political runs all the way through religious discourse and practice.

To appreciate just how radical and far-reaching this critique is, we need to recognize that the two-dimensional conception of religion that it calls into question is by no means restricted to pluralist theology, indeed not even to those that are conventionally characterized as "liberal." The foregoing critique extends, for example, to the conviction expressed in the following passage by the Catholic theologian Peter Phan:

> With regard to the question of Catholic identity, this [indirect] approach [that is, an internal apologetic for the Church's teachings that appeals to the habitus of the individual Catholic] is predicated upon the conviction that personal identity and social identity are shaped and maintained not primarily by the specific differences that an individual or a society possesses over against others, which may be many but superficial, but by what might be called "deep structures," which may be few and common to others.[41]

Here Phan assumes that the differential aspect of social identity is relatively superficial; we might infer from this passage that the interiorized "skill" or habitus upon which Catholic identity is based is developed more or less independently of a consideration of rival teachings. It is noteworthy that in this passage, Phan, who represents a moderate, "inclusivist" position in the theology of religions debate, appeals to essentially the same distinction upon which John Hick bases his pluralist theology, namely, a distinction between "that which is most important in Christianity," on the one hand, and "that which is uniquely Christian," on the other, with the former obviously being the privileged category.[42] That essentially the same distinction forms the presupposition of both Phan's defense of traditional Catholic teaching and Hick's "Copernican Revolution in Theology" shows just how deep-seated and widespread the two-dimensional concept of religion is. In chapter 2, I shall argue that the problematic of isolating a nonpolitical core of religious belief and practice extends well beyond the liberal universalism of Hick and Smith. It even includes what is perhaps liberal universalism's most formidable contemporary adversary, the postliberal theology of George Lindbeck and his followers.[43]

A Shift in Strategy

If the assumption of a nonrelational and nonpolitical core of religious experience is no longer tenable, if, that is, one can no longer assume a dimension of religion entirely innocent of "political" considerations, is one therefore obliged to concede the inevitability of what Friedrich Schleiermacher, in a classic expression of the two-dimensional conception of religion, called "the malicious spirit of sectarianism and proselytizing (*der gehässige Sekten- und Proselyten-Geist*)"?[44] Is one obliged, in other words, to abandon the Enlightenment project of dissociating religious commitment from attitudes of chauvinism and intolerance? Or to pose the question in terms of our opening example, must one concede Franklin Graham's brand of combative, "in-your-face" Christianity as the most honest and authentic form of Christian commitment? To draw such a conclusion, I suggest, would be to overlook another side to the relational understanding of religious identity. To be sure, a relational conception of social identity is forced to acknowledge a political moment of exclusion in the consolidation of identity. But at the same time it recognizes a relation of interdependence between a self-identified group and its excluded other. As mentioned above, this recognition implies a measure of tolerance and respect of the religious "other." It fosters, in other words, an ethos of "agonistic respect" between rival religious communities in which the destructive possibilities of religious conviction are held in check.

A recognition of the inevitability of the political in the realm of religion need not imply, then, an abandonment of the Enlightenment's aim of ridding religious commitment of intolerance, which I define, following Kathryn Tanner, as a refusal to respect religious difference.[45] But it does call into question the Enlightenment's *strategy* for realizing that aim, namely, that of isolating a putative essence of religion from its political excrescences. Applying some of the basic insights of political theorists like William Connolly and Chantal Mouffe who pursue a postmodern critique of classic liberalism in the context of a commitment to a pluralistic and democratic society,[46] I propose a change in strategy that reconciles an acknowledgment of the ineluctability of "us" versus "them" contrasts in the sphere of religion with a commitment to the principles of religious pluralism and interreligious respect. The strategy I propose is based on a distinction between two moments in the formation of religious identity. In the first of these moments, a sense of identity is formed through a political act of exclusion. In the second, the form of identity so constituted disavows its relational nature by grounding itself in a set of ostensibly inherent cultural-religious properties. The underlying presupposition of the proposed change in strategy is that religious intolerance—again, understood as a refusal to respect the religious other qua other—stems more from this second, ideological moment of naturalization than from the first, political moment of exclusion. It is only after a group denies its essential relatedness to its constitutive other that it can construe the latter as somehow deviant and therefore unworthy of respect. Having made this vital distinction between these two moments in the consolidation of identity, the strategy I propose shifts the target of critical intervention from the political creation of identity—the first moment—to the ideological stabilization or naturalization of identity—the second moment. In targeting the second moment of identity formation, this strategy seeks to intercept what Connolly calls "the drive to convert differences into modes of otherness."[47]

If we compare this strategy of *denaturalizing* Christian identity to the former strategy of *depoliticizing* it, we see that while the former strategy is far more modest, it might ultimately prove more effective in advancing the goal of religious tolerance and respect. Because it is willing to recognize its detractors as legitimate adversaries, it is less likely to contribute to the resentment that fuels the movements of religious extremism and intolerance that we see throughout the world today.

Demarginalizing Comparative Theology

The recognition of the ineluctability of the political in religious discourse as a—perhaps the—key problem for modern theology brings interreligious relations to the center of theological reflection. For it is precisely in an interreligious context that the political dimension of religious discourse obtrudes as a problem for theology.[48] We recall that it was in the pluralistic context of the Bush inauguration ceremony that the invocation of Jesus' name became obtrusive and problematic in a way that it is not in an ecclesial context of Christian worship. A theology, then, that recognizes and confronts "the political" as a central problem—a theology, therefore, that embodies the change in strategy described above—will most likely be an interreligious or comparative theology, or at the very least will be one with a pronounced interreligious dimension.

This understanding of theology stands in marked contrast to the current state of theological studies, however. Far from being the central or defining mode of Christian theological reflection, the practice of comparative theology—defined by James Fredericks as "the attempt to understand the meaning of Christian faith by exploring it in the light of the teachings of other religious traditions"[49]—is currently a marginal, and in some quarters scarcely recognized, theological subdiscipline.[50] Even the theology of religions, the branch of theology dedicated to the a priori determination of the stance Christianity should assume toward non-Christian faiths, while well established, remains an ancillary branch of theological study. The current marginality of the interreligious dimension of Christian theology is curious when one considers that an awareness of the claims of meaning and truth of non-Christian religions has been an integral part of the hermeneutical situation of Christian theology in Western cultural contexts—to say nothing of non-Western ones—for quite some time. It is difficult to avoid the suspicion that the marginalization of the interreligious dimension of Christian theological reflection is a consequence of the view that the political dimension of religion is adventitious to an authentic core of faith, the fundamental presupposition of what I have been calling the two-dimensional conception of religion. One suspects that the seemingly obligatory appeals to the unprecedented newness of the contemporary pluralistic situation that one typically finds in the introductory chapters of works of interreligious theology, appeals which suggest that this anomaly is due simply to an inevitable time lag in the theological response to situational change, mask a deeper cause, namely, an unwillingness to confront the issue of the exclusions inherent in theological discourse.

The Argument of This Book

This book is divided into two parts. In the first, I argue that the task of reconciling an acknowledgment of the ineluctability of the political in theology with a commitment to religious pluralism sets the agenda for the new comparative theology. This agenda is more or less implicit in the self-understanding of comparative theology as a fresh alternative to the theology of religions.[51] According to one of the new discipline's most articulate spokespersons, James Fredericks, the debate between pluralists and inclusivists that has defined the theology of religions has reached an impasse as each of these camps has exposed the unacknowledged partiality of the other's universalistic claims.[52] Put differently, each has successfully revealed the other to be a hegemonic form of discourse. To the extent that the new comparative theology promises a way out of the current theology of religions impasse, it implicitly advertises itself as a non-hegemonic form of theological discourse and thus as a solution to the problem of the political in theology.

Chapter 1 complicates this understanding of comparative theology by examining its relationship with the theology of religions in light of their common genealogy in the comparative theology of the late nineteenth century. A familiarity with the latter contains an implicit warning against the facile assumption that the current impasse in the theology of religions is due simply to the inherent limitations of its a priori method. For contemporary comparative theologians to imagine that the problem of unacknowledged exclusion or theological hegemonism can be solved simply by adopting an empirical method is to repeat the self-deception of their nineteenth-century forebears, who naively believed that a "scientific" comparative method could inoculate comparative theology against the exclusionary, political element in religion.[53] The chapter goes on to argue, however, that the reunification of theology and comparison in the new comparative theology negates the oppositional contrast between the comparative study of religion and theology. It is by means of this contrast that the former discipline has often sought to legitimate itself as an impartial, "scientific" discipline. Comparative theology challenges this tendency of scholars of religion to project a theological other, a tendency which, paradoxically, has blinded the discipline of comparative religion to its own normative—and often implicitly theological—presuppositions. In this way, the new comparative theology exemplifies a recent shift in the understanding of the comparative method in the study of religion, namely, from a positive method for uncovering putative universal structures of metaphysical and/or psychic reality to a self-critical method for the testing and revision of the conceptual categories through which scholars interpret their data.[54] It is by clearly recognizing and developing comparison as a method of "critical self-consciousness," I argue, that the new comparative theology can avoid the pitfalls of its late nineteenth-century namesake.

Chapter 2 extends the foregoing analysis of the history of interreligious theology to the modern theological tradition as a whole. Specifically, the chapter proposes a rereading of the history of modern theology since the Enlightenment in light of Schmitt's "depoliticization" thesis. It profiles several figures in that history who exemplify decisive moments in the ongoing—and inconclusive—project of depoliticizing theology. In the course of recounting that narrative, the chapter identifies two basic strategies by which Christian theology in the modern period has sought to dissociate theology from the political. The first of these, liberal universalism, has for the most part dominated the avant-garde of modern Christian thought, from the natural theology of the seventeenth and eighteenth centuries, up through the universalist fulfillment theologies of the nineteenth century, to the experiential pluralism of the twentieth. Each of these expressions of liberal universalism has sought to liberate a universal "essence" of religion from the dogmatism, sectarianism, and chauvinism of traditional theology. The second strategy, which we might call, for want of a better term, theological communitarianism, comes to the fore in the postliberal theology of George Lindbeck and his followers. Rejecting the universalist presuppositions of the liberal theological tradition on both philosophical and sociological grounds, it argues for an understanding of particular religions as self-contained cultural-linguistic systems that are, strictly speaking, incommensurable with one another. Building on Kathryn Tanner's trenchant critique of this aspect of postliberalism in her book, *Theories of Culture*, I argue that postliberalism's substantive concept of Christian identity represents yet another way of evading the ineluctability of the political in religion.

The historical survey in chapter 2 sets the stage for the constructive task, undertaken in chapter 3, of developing a theoretical model of comparative theology that directly confronts the problem of the political. Its point of departure is Tanner's theory of Christian identity as internally constituted by its relations with other cultural forms.[55] In the first part of the chapter, I argue that a political moment of exclusion is implicit in a relational understanding of Christian identity like Tanner's. Like other forms of cultural identity, Christian identity is formed on the basis of differences that come to be recognized in the course of social interaction. A concept of group identity is formed when a group transposes the complex and ambiguous web of relations twining it to its cultural environment into an antithesis between isolated elements metonymically standing for their respective wholes. But a relational concept of Christian identity cannot simply end with the formation of an oppositional contrast between an "us" and a "them." A relational concept of identity not only implies a political moment of exclusion, but also a subsequent moment in which past conceptions of Christian identity are revised and reformulated to meet the exigencies of a new situation. In the second half of the chapter, I argue that cross-cultural comparison, when understood in terms of the metaphorical process, serves as an effective technique for deconstructing the oppositional contrasts formed in the first moment. The metaphorical juxtaposition of parallel features from compared traditions reverses the reductive process whereby a complex set of intercultural relations is transformed into a binary opposition. Thus understood, interreligious comparison can be used effectively to circumvent the formation of essentialized contrasts between religious communities.

Part II of the book applies this model of comparative theology to a specific example: the comparison of Meister Eckhart and Śaṅkara as exemplified in Rudolf Otto's classic study, *Mysticism East and West*. Chapter 4 undertakes a genealogical analysis of the Christian apologetic discourse that Otto's book brings into a convenient focus. Otto's comparison reworked an "East" versus "West" apologetic contrast that was and remains constitutive of modern Christian self-understanding. This is the contrast between, on the one hand, the ethical, world-affirming nature of Christianity and, on the other, the allegedly quietistic, world-negating nature of Eastern spirituality, as epitomized by the Advaita Vedānta doctrine of *māyā*. In *Mysticism East and West*, Otto makes an implicit appeal to this Christian apologetic and orientalist dichotomy in order to redirect the charges of pantheism, acosmism, and quietism for which Eckhart has long been accused onto Śaṅkara. And yet, Otto's specific concern with clearing Eckhart's name of these charges complicates his relationship to the apologetic tradition of East versus West comparison. The parallels Otto draws between the two masters leave open the possibility of extending the arguments by which he vindicates the German master to his Indian counterpart, thereby deconstructing the world-affirmation versus world-denial dichotomy.

The remaining chapters of Part II pursue these possibilities through an independent comparative study of Eckhart and Śaṅkara. Chapter 5 explores the parallel between Eckhart's distinction between God and Godhead, on the one hand, and Śaṅkara's distinction between the personal and impersonal aspects of Brahman, on the other. Reading Śaṅkara's commentary on the *Brahma-sūtra* in light of the understanding of Eckhart's concepts of God and Godhead as constituting what Michael Sells calls a "double paradigm," I argue for a dialectical, rather than hierarchical, understanding of the relation between the personal and impersonal aspects of Brahman. This interpretation challenges the long-standing invidious "orientalist" characterization of Brahman as a pale and lifeless abstraction.

Chapter 6 uses this dialectical understanding of Śaṅkara to challenge the conventional understanding of his doctrine of the world as one of "illusionism." This chapter argues that Śaṅkara's declaration of the unreality of the phenomenal world can be understood as a transformative commentary on an earlier, realist form of Vedānta that subverts, but does not efface, the latter's realist cosmology. Reading Eckhart through the lens of Śaṅkara's commentary on the *Brahma-sūtra* allows us to see the former's apophaticism similarly as a transformative commentary on the orthodox Christian model of creation.

Chapter 7 challenges the contrast Otto draws between the activist ethic affirmed by Eckhart and the quietism and moral indifference allegedly espoused by his Indian counterpart. Specifically, it challenges Otto's assumption that the "works" (*gewerbe*) that give spontaneous expression to the soul's participation in the divine life in Eckhart coincide with the "works" (*karma*) that exclude liberative knowledge in Śaṅkara. The chapter goes on to examine Eckhart's critique of instrumental religious activity and his notion of the annihilation of the created will in light of Śaṅkara's polemical contrast between knowledge and action. This parallel focuses attention on the polemical and ideological dimensions of the Eckhartian themes of spiritual poverty and will-less activity, dimensions obscured by a tendency, stemming from the influence of Romanticism on Eckhart's modern reception, to regard these simply as spontaneous expressions of an unmediated religious experience. The parallel with Śaṅkara encourages us to recognize even the loftiest expressions of Eckhart's religious thought as inextricably bound up with the complex and often-contentious relations between the Church and the new religious movements of the late Middle Ages. This reading of Eckhart, then, exemplifies the thesis that the political impacts all forms of religious discourse, even if only indirectly. At the same time, however, the example of Eckhart demonstrates that an acknowledgment of the political dimension of religious discourse need not exclude a capacity of that discourse to inspire and edify.

PART I

Theology and the Political

I

The Reunification of Theology and Comparison in the New Comparative Theology

You will have observed that I have carefully abstained from entering on the domain of what I call *Theoretic*, as distinguished from *Comparative Theology*. Theoretic theology, or, as it is sometimes called, the philosophy of religion, has, as far as I can judge, its right place at the end, not the beginning of Comparative Theology. I have made no secret of my own conviction that a study of Comparative Theology will produce with regard to Theoretic Theology the same revolution which a study of Comparative Philology has produced in what used to be called the philosophy of language.

—F. Max Müller

The various positions one might then articulate in a theology of religions—all religions are one; all religions are merely different; one religion alone is true, the rest untrue; the rest partially true—become interesting only after reading has taken place, when these positions can be refined in light of actual knowledge of one or more religions, and rearticulated as extensions of the practice of reading. Even if one wishes to place the theology of religions at the beginning of one's treatise about religions, this theology is nevertheless best composed only after comparison has already occurred.

—Francis X. Clooney

Publications on interreligious dialogue and comparative theology invariably begin by emphasizing the unprecedented newness of the contemporary theological situation. We are reminded that men and women of different faiths, particularly in urban centers in North America and Europe, now interact with each other on a personal level. Religious pluralism has become, to use Paul Knitter's apt phrase, "a newly experienced reality" for many in today's world. Theology, accordingly, is only just beginning to respond to this new situation of religious pluralism. Up until recently, contemporary North Atlantic theology "had no internal imperative to think about the other religions as anything other than targets for conversion sought by mission programs."[1] According to this narrative, comparative theology, which can be formally defined as theological reflection on the meaning of one faith in light of the teachings of another, represents a largely unprecedented theological enterprise; it marks, in the words of John Thatamanil, "a new stage in Christian theology's encounter with other religions."[2]

Such claims regarding the unprecedented nature of the new comparative theology are not without an element of truth. And yet they can be taken at face value, I would argue, only if one arbitrarily excludes a consideration of the disciplinary history of comparative religion. The assumption that this history is somehow irrelevant flows from an uncritical acceptance of the current disciplinary separation between theology and religious studies.[3] When one examines the formative period of the comparative study of religion in the late nineteenth century, however, one discovers that this discipline was founded on a set of theological commitments that are cognate to those motivating the new comparative theology. A curious fact that can be taken as a convenient sign for this kinship is that an alternative designation for "comparative religion" in the late nineteenth century was, in fact, "comparative theology." As this coincidence of name suggests, the new comparative theology is not nearly as unprecedented as many of its exponents tend to assume.

In this chapter, I argue that the new comparative theology can be properly understood and evaluated only when it is rooted in the historical trajectory of the comparative study of religion. In particular, I show that the tensions and ambiguities of the new discipline can be illuminated, and its nature and task subsequently clarified, when it is compared to the comparative theology of the late nineteenth century.

The Comparative Theology of the Nineteenth Century

"Comparative theology" was originally among the constellation of terms used to describe the nascent scientific (as opposed to confessional) study of religion.[4]

Perhaps the most well-known work to describe and promote comparative theology is F. Max Müller's *Introduction to the Science of Religion*, the text Eric Sharpe credits with being "the foundation document of comparative religion."[5] As suggested by Müller's title, "theology" formed the *object* of comparison, where comparison was assumed to be a method of scientific discovery.[6] What is striking about the comparative theology of the nineteenth century, however, is that this pretension to scientific impartiality did not prevent theology from being the *subject* of comparison as well.[7] Müller betrays his theological convictions when he argues that of all the religions of the world, it is Christianity alone, as the one religion transcending all loyalties to a particular nation or people, which favors the idea of an impartial comparison of the religions of the world.[8] Müller's theological convictions are rather muted, however, when compared with more typical works of comparative theology.[9] For paradigmatic comparative theological works such as James Freeman Clarke's *Ten Great Religions: An Essay in Comparative Theology* or F. D. Maurice's *Religions of the World and their Relations with Christianity*, an impartial study of the religions leads to the conclusion of Christianity's unambiguous superiority over all others. Clarke, for example, writes:

> For we can make it appear, by a fair survey of the principal religions of the world, that, while they are either ethnic or local, Christianity is catholic or universal; that, while they are defective, possessing some truths and wanting others, Christianity possesses all; and that, while they are stationary, Christianity is progressive. . . .[10]

How such works could reconcile a sincere claim of scientific impartiality with unabashed assertions of Christian superiority presents a challenge for today's interpreter.[11] Tomoko Masuzawa, who deserves credit for calling attention to the all-but-forgotten legacy of comparative theology in her book, *The Invention of World Religions*, describes the perplexity elicited by these works as follows:

> It seems to us today rather remarkable that so many nineteenth-century authors of varying attitudes towards non-Christian religions claimed—or, for the most part, assumed—that their enterprise of comparing religions without bias was not only compatible with but in fact perfectly complementary to their own proudly unshakable conviction in the supremacy of Christianity. Nowadays we generally discredit this claim as naive at best, disingenuous at worst. We behold in disbelief the seriousness with which some of those comparativists with strong dogmatic views pronounced that their

surveys of other religions were—not just in principle, but in actuality—"fair," "sympathetic," and "impartial."[12]

The key to solving this interpretive puzzle, I suggest, is to recognize that nineteenth-century works of comparative theology, whether decidedly Christian ones like Clarke's, or arguably post-Christian ones like Müller's, defined themselves in opposition to a particular, albeit dominant, kind of Christian apologetics. Like many later works of *Religionswissenschaft*, as we shall see, their claims of objectivity and impartiality were artificially maintained by projecting a theological other. But this theological other was not coextensive with Christian theology, only with a confessional and dogmatic form of it. As Arie Molendijk has shown in his study of the 1876 Dutch Universities Act, which institutionalized the science of religion in the Netherlands, the science of religion for founding figures like C. P. Tiele and Chantepie de la Saussaye was originally an expression of liberal, "super-denominational" theology. Molendijk argues that these early proponents of *Religionswissenschaft* did not intend to introduce an independent discipline, much less to abolish theology; rather, they wanted to place theology on a scientific basis.[13] What this "consecration" of theology as a science would do is purge theology of those "unscientific" elements—apologetics, polemics, and dogmatics—that were assumed to be adventitious to the essence of true religion.[14]

Another way of stating this thesis is that the comparative science of religion gave expression to the liberal theological project of "depoliticizing" religion that I described in the preceding chapter. The Schmittian concept of "the political" that I employ in my analysis usefully highlights the two features of traditional confessional theology that the scientific discourse of comparative religion sought to eliminate.[15] The first of these was its inherently divisive, sectarian nature. It was believed that the comparative science of religion, inasmuch as it was grounded on the recognition of a common element in religion underlying differences in creed, would undercut the antagonisms sustained by the competing forms of confessional theology. The second feature of traditional confessional theology that it was hoped the science of religion would neutralize was its dogmatism, its tendency to assert claims without a due regard for empirical evidence.[16] Having recognized the political in its twin aspects of dogmatism and antagonism as the defining characteristic of traditional confessional theology, we are in a position to grasp the essential aim of the comparative theology of the late nineteenth century. The latter sought to rid theology of its sectarianism and its dogmatism by bringing religious commitment in line with the universally valid discourse of empirical science. Thus the liberal theological project of depoliticizing religion took the form of establishing a comparative science of religion.

The coincidence of the projects of the scientific study of religion and liberal theology explains why comparative theologians like Clarke were blind to the discrepancy, so obvious to today's reader, between Christian universalism and the scientific ideal of impartial comparison. This blindness is a consequence of the fact that both projects defined themselves over against the same adversary. They shared, in other words, the same constitutive other, namely, the political as instantiated in traditional confessional theology with its dogmatism and its penchant for controversy. The opposition of these two projects to a common adversary effectively effaced the distinction between them.

This thesis regarding the coincidence of liberal theology and the emergent science of religion qualifies the standard history of the discipline of religious studies as a gradual emancipation from theology. As Sigurd Hjelde puts it, if one can speak of the early development of the discipline in terms of an emancipation, it is an emancipation "not *from* theology as such, but *within* its own limits."[17] The development of the comparative science of religion, in other words, takes place in the context of a dialectic internal to theology in which theology seeks to purge itself of its "unscientific" elements by defining itself over against a dogmatic theological other.[18] One could argue, in fact, that much (though of course not all) of the subsequent history of the discipline in the twentieth century, in particular, the classic understanding of the history of religions as a hermeneutical discipline, can be redescribed in terms of a dialectic internal to theological liberalism and thus standing in continuity with the comparative theology of the late nineteenth century.

Few scholars exemplify this thesis better than the historian of religion Joachim Wach (1898–1955). Wach's effort to demarcate the discipline of *Religionswissenschaft* from theology remains firmly ensconced in a liberal theological framework. He argues that the proper task of the history of religions, the understanding of other religions, is distinct from, though complementary to, that of theology, which he defines rather narrowly as "identifying its own confessional norms, . . . of understanding and confirming its own faith."[19] And yet Wach's conception of the history of religions as a hermeneutical discipline rests on presuppositions that his critics would immediately recognize as theological in nature. To interpret religious phenomena properly is to understand them as expressions of a reality that transcends them.[20] A hermeneutical understanding of the history of religions demands an intuitive sense of religion, a *sensus numinis*, which can be understood as a kind of faith, but an ecumenical faith that does not blind one to the meaning of other religions.[21] Wach's conception of the history of religions, then, remains, despite its pretensions to the contrary, an expression of liberal, nonsectarian theology, as even his contemporaries could recognize.[22] The same basic criticism applies to the efforts of his disciple, Joseph Kitagawa, to draw a sharp distinction between a "humanistic" and a "theological" approach to the history of religions. With his commitment to the idea of "a sacred dimension of life and the world" as a fundamental presupposition of the history of religions,[23] Kitagawa remains within a basically theological framework in spite of his explicit recognition of a specifically liberal theology (of the kind on display at the 1893 World Parliament of Religions) as theology proper, and thus to be excluded, along with theology of a more traditional variety, from the method of the history of religions.[24]

It has been recognized for quite some time now that the exposure of various forms of "crypto-theology" in the classic models of comparative religion has precipitated something of an identity crisis in the academic study of religion. One response to this crisis has been to repudiate the "transcendental" approach epitomized by the much-maligned phenomenology of Mircea Eliade in favor of a naturalistic approach that concerns itself with explaining (and not merely interpreting) religious phenomena.[25] Whether the comparative study of religion has finally liberated itself of theology by rejecting the transcendental approach, or, alternatively, whether comparative religion, even of the naturalistic variety, remains an exercise in what Timothy Fitzgerald terms "liberal ecumenical theology" so long as it presupposes a concept of religion as a valid analytic category, is a complex question that lies outside the scope of the present discussion. What seems clear, however, is that from our present vantage point, many previous attempts to demarcate the science of religion from recognized forms of theological discourse, from the comparative theology of the nineteenth century to the phenomenology of religion and comparative religion of the twentieth, now appear as moments within the larger liberal theological project of liberating the discourse on religion from dogmatism and exclusion, in short, from the political.

The New Comparative Theology as a Fresh Alternative to the Theology of Religions

If a major current in the disciplinary history of the comparative study of religion can be understood in terms of the liberal theological project of depoliticizing religion, as I have suggested, then we would naturally expect to find a parallel pattern of development in the tradition of theology proper. And nowhere in the modern theological tradition is this pattern more clearly visible than in the development leading to the "theology of religions" with its threefold typology of exclusivism, inclusivism, and pluralism. As I shall argue below, these three categories can be understood as successive moments in a dialectical process through which the tradition of liberal theology has sought to overcome the principle of religious exclusion and antagonism—the political—only to see this principle reappear in ever more insidious—because easily misrecognized—forms of exclusion, what I have been calling theological hegemonism.[26] Like the project of "de-theologizing" the comparative study of religion, the development reflected in the three theology of religions categories has led to an impasse. Unlike the former, something called comparative theology stands at the end of that process rather than at the beginning.

The theology of religions attained its present configuration with the emergence of the classic pluralist theologies associated with the triumvirate of John Hick, Wilfred Cantwell Smith, and (the early) Paul Knitter. Pluralism is founded upon a critique of the Christian fulfillment theology that had previously served as the standard bearer of Christian liberalism. At the heart of this pluralist critique is the argument that the sharp distinction that the liberal theologies of Christian fulfillment drew between themselves and the generally exclusivist tradition of Christian apologetics was largely specious. The former retains a presumption of Christian superiority that is, in the words of John Hick, no more than "a hangover from the old religious imperialisms of the past."[27] The claim that Christianity includes and fulfills other faiths harbors a barely concealed intention to convert and dominate the latter. Against the Christian absolutism that it sees in both exclusivism and inclusivism, pluralism rejects the notion that any single tradition, Christianity in particular, has a privileged access to divine truth. As captured in Hick's metaphor of the Copernican Revolution in theology, the pluralist shift from a "Christocentric" to a "theocentric" model of the religions marks a clean break with the tradition of Christian absolutism. With their abandonment of the presumption of Christian superiority, the previous generation of pluralist theologians thought that they had finally eliminated the twin forms of exclusion—namely, the open exclusion of theological polemic and the veiled exclusion of theological hegemonism—from theology.

More recent critiques of pluralist theology have shown that this judgment was premature. The classic pluralist theories of religion have found themselves in the ironic position of having to defend themselves against precisely the same charges that they had leveled against inclusivism. Critics of pluralist theology like Mark Heim and Kenneth Surin have argued that pluralists like Hick and Smith have failed to acknowledge the particularity—and exclusivity—of their own perspectives.[28] Such pluralist theologies are therefore little more than inclusivisms in disguise. Thus Hick's well-known "theocentric" model of the religions, in which the positive religions circle the Real like the planets around the sun, places a Kantian philosophy of religion, a perspective every bit as particular as Christian theology, at the center of the religious universe.[29] In a similar way, the unitary concept of personal faith that forms the basis of Smith's vision of religious pluralism betrays the influence of his own Protestant background.[30] In its unwitting universalization of a distinctly Protestant conception of faith, Smith's proposal for a world theology reveals its kinship with the Christian fulfillment theology of the previous century.

Much as the exposure of crypto-theologism in the classic project of comparative religion has brought the academic study of religion to a state of uncertainty, the critique of pluralism—not coincidentally—has brought the theology of religions to an impasse.[31] Following James Fredericks, we can describe this impasse as follows: while the pluralists have called into question the inlcusivists' claim to have made a radical break with the tradition of Christian exclusivism, their critics have turned around and questioned the pluralists' claim to have made a radical break with inclusivism—and therewith, given the pluralists' own critique of inclusivism, with exclusivism as well. The pluralists and their critics have thus successfully exposed the unacknowledged exclusions of each other. They have each, in other words, exposed the other's position as a hegemonic form of discourse.

Speaking on the behalf of a small but growing contingent of theologians, Fredericks presents "comparative theology" as a way out of this impasse. This new theological subdiscipline, which Fredericks defines formally as "the attempt to understand the meaning of Christian faith by exploring it in the light of the teachings of other religious traditions,"[32] avoids the pitfalls of the theology of religions by renouncing the two features that Fredericks holds responsible for the latter's inadequacy. The first of these problematic features of the theology of religions is its a priori method, its pretension to work out a stance towards other traditions independently of an empirical study of those traditions. The a priori method effectively renders its theological judgments unfalsifiable with respect to the traditions it might subsequently encounter.[33] The second defect of the theology of religions is its assumption of a global, totalizing perspective on the religions. This global meta-perspective implies a presumption to know other religions better than their own adherents, whether as the vain products of human presumption, as in Barth's exclusivism, as various expressions of anonymous Christianity, as in Rahner's inclusivism, or as various forms of "Reality-centeredness," as in Hick's pluralism.[34] This presumption to understand other religions better than their own adherents, Fredericks argues, has the effect of obviating a serious and open engagement with other religious traditions. In the case of inclusivism and pluralism, it allows the Christian theologian to disregard the specific claims of the religious other while at the same time somewhat disingenuously claiming to affirm them. By thus discouraging a recognition of the specific claims of other religions despite—or, perhaps, precisely because of—the claim to include them, inclusivism and pluralism promote interreligious relations that can be aptly described as hegemonic.

The new comparative theology is defined by two features that inversely correspond, respectively, to the apriorism and the summitry of the theology of religions. The first and most obvious of these is its empirical method. If there is one claim that defines the discipline of comparative theology, it is that a serious engagement with one or more other faiths is integral to contemporary interreligious theological reflection. Comparative theology's empirical method implies a willingness to revise theological judgments in light of the particular teachings of other traditions. The second characteristic feature of comparative theology is its reluctance to generalize.[35] As a form of theological praxis or reflective practice, comparative theology eschews the kind of abstract theorizing about religious truth characteristic of the theology of religions. Theological reflection emerges only in the context of a practical engagement with specific examples of comparison.[36]

These two features establish comparative theology as the antithesis of the theology of religions. And it is as the antithesis to the theology of religions that comparative theology is able to move beyond the impasse in which the former finds itself. Now, if that impasse can be understood in terms of the problem of unacknowledged exclusion or hegemonism, as I have suggested, then comparative theology, in claiming that it represents a way out of that impasse, effectively advertises itself as a non-hegemonic form of interreligious theological discourse.

Prima facie, then, the new comparative theology, like the figure of Nietzsche's Zarathustra, represents the antithesis of its older namesake. For the older comparative theology, by fostering the misrecognition of specifically Christian theological claims as universal religious principles ostensibly uncovered by impartial, "scientific" analysis, epitomizes the kind of theological hegemonism that one finds in the theology of religions. Upon closer examination, however, the new comparative theology exhibits parallels with its older namesake that temper any expectation that the problem of theological hegemonism will magically disappear simply by adopting an empirical method and refraining from generalization.

A Comparison of Comparative Theologies

To bring this parallelism into view, we take a closer look at the way in which the older comparative theology distinguished itself from the traditional apologetic theology that served as its constitutive other. Proponents of comparative theology like Clarke and Müller, who prided themselves on their fair and sympathetic attitude towards non-Christian faiths, rejected the standard apologetic categories of revealed religion and natural religion to describe Christianity's relations with other religions.[37] They recognized these theological categories to be inherently tendentious; strictly speaking, these categories excluded a comparison of Christianity, the one revealed religion, with the various forms of invented or natural religion. By discarding these categories, the comparative theologians were able to recognize a positive, providential role of non-Christian religions in an economy of salvation.[38] In general, though with some exceptions, the categories that replaced those of revealed religion and natural religion were those of universal (or world) religions and national (or ethnic) religions.[39] The latter categories were ostensibly based on empirical observation, not on unwarranted dogmatic assertion; whether or not a religion had been able to transcend its original cultural matrix and thereby become a universal religion was a matter of empirical determination. And yet, as even a cursory examination of the works of comparative theology shows, the categories of universal religion and national religion did not prevent unwarranted dogmatic assumptions from stealing into the comparative analysis and determining its final conclusions. Such assumptions are plainly evident when comparative theological works proceed to argue, as they invariably do, that the ostensibly universal religions of Islam and Buddhism are merely national religions in disguise and that Christianity alone merits the title of universal or world religion. It is apparent that comparative theology's appeal to ostensibly empirical analytical categories did little more than to conceal from its authors and much of its contemporary audience the dogmatic nature of its conclusions.

That comparative theology should yield basically the same results as the older apologetic theology should come as no surprise when we recognize, following J. Z. Smith, that the division between universal religions and national religions, like all dualistic classifications in fact, "is ultimately a sublimation of the earliest and most fundamental dichotomous division: 'ours' and 'theirs', or 'true' and 'false.'"[40] As I shall argue in more detail in the next chapter, the distinction between universal religions and national religions can trace its genealogy directly to the Enlightenment project of dissociating an "essence" of religion from the principle of social antagonism. The privileged category of universal religion corresponds to the essence of religion freed from its political excrescences. National religion, by contrast, corresponds to religion adulterated by those political elements. In the final analysis, national religion, qua national—that is to say, qua *political*—is not, strictly speaking, religion at all. The distinction between universal religion and national religion, no less than that of revealed religion and natural religion, thus reduces to the age-old polemical distinction between true religion and false religion. There is, of course, considerable irony in the fact that this dichotomous division between religion as such and political religion, inasmuch as it reduces to the fundamental social division between "us" and "them,"[41] is itself an expression of the latter term.

The irony extends, in fact, to comparative theology's effort to define itself over against the older, exclusivist form of apologetics. For when we recognize that the classification between universal and national religions encodes the dichotomy between religion and the political, we see that the dichotomous classification through which comparative theology establishes the superiority of Christianity over other religions is essentially the same dichotomy by which it sets itself over against a rival form of Christian apologetics.[42] Comparative theology's tendentious characterization of Christianity as the universal religion reflects the more fundamental act of exclusion by which it constitutes itself as a new, liberal form of Christian apologetics. This observation suggests that the understanding of Christianity as the paradigm of universal religion is, in fact, essentially a projection of an intra-Christian polemic.

This analysis of the comparative theology of the nineteenth century reveals an unexpected parallel with its twenty-first-century namesake. We immediately recognize a striking parallel between, on the one hand, this distinction between empirical and dogmatic methods by which the older comparative theology defined itself over against traditional Christian apologetics and, on the other, the distinction between a posteriori and a priori methods by which the new comparative theology defines itself over against the theology of religions.

This parallelism should give contemporary comparative theologians pause. It suggests that the categorical distinction that a comparative theologian like Fredericks posits between comparative theology and the theology of religions might prove to be just as specious as the allegedly radical distinction that the older fulfillment theology drew between itself and exclusivist apologetics, or, again, the distinction pluralist theology later drew between itself and inclusivism.

The foregoing analysis suggests that the history of modern interreligious theology might be fruitfully understood in terms of Schmitt's thesis of the inescapability of the political. As we saw in the previous chapter, Schmitt argued that the liberal tradition has sought to establish social relations on a neutral, nonantagonistic cultural domain only to see that domain henceforth become the site of a political opposition.[43] When the history of modern interreligious theology is regarded from the perspective of Schmitt's inescapability thesis, the new comparative theology appears as merely the latest in a dialectical sequence of binary oppositions by which the tradition of liberal theology has vainly sought to dissociate itself from the principle of the political. Classic fulfillment theology, exemplified by nineteenth-century comparative theology, represents the first of these oppositions. As we have just seen, the old comparative theology defines itself in opposition to an older tradition of exclusivist apologetic theology. When Christian fulfillment theology comes to be recognized as an expression of cultural imperialism, and therefore as vitiated by the political, the liberal wing of Christian theology responds by introducing a hitherto unknown distinction between inclusivism and pluralism.[44] This distinction forms the basis of a new opposition. As we have seen, the resultant pluralist theology defines itself by its refusal to recognize a significant distinction between exclusivism and inclusivism, which together comprise liberal theology's newly reconstituted other. The new comparative theology, which emerges at roughly the same time as the bloom falls off the rose of Hickian-style pluralism, introduces a third moment in this dialectic. As we have seen, James Fredericks justifies the new enterprise of comparative theology on the basis of the critique of pluralist theology as inclusivism in disguise. By positioning itself as an alternative discourse to the theology of religions, the new comparative theology sets itself over against the forms of theology—comprehensively enumerated by the three theology of religions categories, exclusivism, inclusivism, and pluralism—that have been reclaimed, as it were, by liberal theology's political other (see figure 1.1). Seen from this broader historical perspective, then, the new comparative theology might appear as the latest strategy on the part of Christian liberalism to retreat and regroup in the face of the ineluctable advance of the political.

Now, one might object to the thesis that comparative theology forms a binary opposition with the various forms of exclusionary, political theology represented by the three theology of religions categories on the grounds that it overlooks the fact that many comparative theologians ally themselves with an inclusivist theology of religions position.[45] When we view the theology of religions categories as successive moments in a dialectic unfolding in time, however, we see that the inclusivism with which contemporary comparative theologians identify is quite distinct from the classic inclusivism associated with the older theologies of Christian fulfillment. Whereas the latter defined itself over against exclusivism by emphasizing the universal scope of Christian salvation, the former defines itself over against pluralism, specifically, pluralism's pretension to transcend any particular religious perspective. By identifying

Modern Interreligious Theology	Political "Other"
Old Comparative Theology (Christian Fulfillment Theology)	Traditional Christian Apologetics (Exclusivism)
Pluralist Theology	Christian Absolutism (Exclusivism; Inclusivism)
New Comparative Theology	Theology of Religions (Exclusivism; Inclusivism; Pluralism)

FIGURE I.1 Three Moments of Depoliticization in Modern Interreligious Theology

themselves with an inclusivist position, contemporary comparative theologians acknowledge and affirm the particularity of their own—typically Christian—theological perspective.[46] A comparative theology that allies itself with the newer "acceptance-model" (as opposed to "fulfillment-model") inclusivism,[47] then, remains an expression of oppositional thinking, only with this difference, that its criticism is focused more narrowly on a specifically pluralist theology of religions, that is to say, on its immediate predecessor in the aforementioned dialectic.[48]

This reading of the modern history of interreligious theology in terms of a dialectical series of binary oppositions through which the latest proposal declares a radical break with its predecessors sheds an interesting angle of light on the feature of the literature on interreligious theology that I noted at the outset of this chapter, namely, the seemingly obligatory mention of the unprecedented newness of the contemporary theological situation. This theme has been a staple of such literature for nearly one hundred years. Compare, for example, J. N. Farquhar's (1913) declaration that, "All the parts of the world have at last been brought into communication...The unity of the human race has become effective for the first time in human history,"[49] to W. C. Smith's (1959) pronouncement of the "new world situation" in the twentieth century, characterized by a "large-scale face-to-face meeting between persons of diverse faith";[50] and finally, to Paul Knitter's (1985; 2005) description of religious pluralism as "a newly experienced reality."[51] A comparison of such pronouncements suggests that the appeal to the radical newness of the contemporary interreligious situation has a curious capacity to replicate itself in successive generations. To be sure, each of the above statements reflects real and important developments in the world historical situation. The present situation of global capitalism, for example, where mass migration and the dissemination of global culture through electronic media have accelerated, expanded, and intensified the processes of cultural interaction to the point of radically transforming the way individuals and groups understand themselves, *is* different, even radically so, from that of late nineteenth-century colonialism or even the postwar period described by W. C. Smith.[52] And yet, one cannot help noticing a certain functional similarity in all these announcements of a radical break with the past; each serves to reinforce the impression of the radical newness of whatever theological proposal is currently being offered. An inevitable consequence of this effort to drive a wedge between the interreligious theology of the present and that of the past is an amnesia with respect to past comparative endeavors, most notably, the comparative theology of the late nineteenth century.[53]

Comparative Theology as an Expression of Global Hegemonism?

What ambiguities might the dichotomy between the new comparative theology and the theology of religions conceal in the former term? To be more specific, if classic inclusivism and pluralism unintentionally and unwittingly embody the logic of cultural imperialism as their critics contend,[54] might the new comparative theology be similarly implicated in hegemonic, neocolonialist forms of discourse? Our lack of historical distance naturally renders any hegemonic dimension of comparative theology difficult to discern and any attempt to describe it somewhat tentative. Nevertheless, I find that some fairly recent critiques of postmodern discourse open up a perspective from which the continuities between comparative theology and earlier forms of interreligious theology become visible.

One of the most thought-provoking of those critiques, particularly in light of the thesis that dichotomization represents a mechanism of ideological blindness, can be found in Michael Hardt and Antonio Negri's book *Empire*. These authors argue that postmodern and postcolonial critical discourses, in their preoccupation with the specific forms of domination associated with colonialism and the modern nation-state, fail to recognize the structurally different forms of domination recently introduced with the advent of late-stage, multinational capitalism.[55] The older forms of "modern sovereignty" that form postmodernism's object of critique operate through two related mechanisms: on the one hand, the positing of binary oppositions that define Self and Other and, on the other, the subsequent subsumption of those binaries in a conception of social totality.[56] Postmodern thought challenges binary division and totalization by highlighting and affirming the cultural differences that both these aspects of essentialism suppress. And yet, as Hardt and Negri observe, postmodernism, in its celebration of cultural difference and its transgression of cultural boundaries, reveals a disconcerting kinship with the ideology of the world market. Consumerism and contemporary marketing thrive on cultural difference, while the world market, with its global flows of media, labor, and capital, works to deconstruct, in postmodern fashion, national and territorial boundaries.[57] To the extent that postmodern discourses coincide with the functions and practices of late capitalism, Hardt and Negri argue, they are ineffective against the particular forms of domination wrought by the latter.[58] Specifically, postmodern discourses unwittingly support a new social hierarchy being formed by the processes of globalization, namely, between a freely mobile, consumer class of (Western and non-Western) elites, on the one hand, and an emerging global proletariat, on the other.

Comparative theology's implicit critique of the theology of religions as a hegemonic form of discourse mirrors postmodernism's critique of "modern sovereignty" as described by Hardt and Negri. The two dimensions of the postmodern critique, namely, the deconstruction of binary oppositions and the disavowal of the universalizing discourses of totalization, find exact parallels, for example, in the comparative theology of Francis Clooney. Against binary division in the religious sphere, Clooney's comparative method, with its relentless focus on particular texts, resists the generalizations used to construct conceptual formations like "Hinduism" or "Christianity" that have traditionally supported and legitimated tendentious oppositions between "East" and "West." His emphasis on the local and particular, in other words, challenges the "modular" conception of the religions presupposed by the theology of religions discourse.[59] At the same time that he highlights the internal differences suppressed by the process of "reification" described by W. C. Smith, Clooney draws attention to theological parallels that cut across religious boundaries.[60] By thus demonstrating that significant theological differences do not always coincide with established religious boundaries, Clooney's comparative theology thus sets itself against binary division in the realm of religion. As for the second dimension of postmodern criticism, the critique of totalizing discourse, we have already seen that a renunciation of a totalizing perspective on the religions is one of the defining features of the new comparative theology.

How exactly might this conception of comparative theology be susceptible to Hardt and Negri's critique of postmodernism? One could argue that to the extent that comparative theology works to transgress religious boundaries and to deconstruct a modular conception of the religions—a conception of religion, incidentally, that seems to be modeled after the concept of the modern nation-state—it finds itself in line with the forces of globalization that, as we have seen, tend to deconstruct national boundaries.[61] We might legitimately ask whether comparative theology's alignment with these forces renders it blind to the particular forms of domination wrought by the latter. Specifically, we might ask whether comparative theology, as a form of postmodern discourse that celebrates the fluidity and porosity of cultural and religious boundaries, finds itself uncomfortably aligned with the "winners" in the processes of globalization—that is, those who experience mobility across cultural and geographical boundaries as liberating—against the "losers" in this drama, who are forced to regard the mobility and indeterminacy of globalization more ambivalently.[62] As if to underscore this point, Hardt and Negri note that, as a general tendency, those in the latter group are apt to resonate with the various discourses of fundamentalism, which remain, in many significant respects, comparative theology's "other."[63]

The ambiguity that attends comparative theology's deconstruction of religious boundaries extends to the other critical dimension of the comparative theological project, namely, its renunciation of a totalizing perspective. To see this, I turn now to Fredric Jameson's incisive critique of the postmodern "war on totality" as set forth in his book, *Postmodernism, or, the Cultural Logic of Late Capitalism*. Jameson makes a distinction between "totality," which suggests the idea of a privileged perspective of the whole that refuses to acknowledge its particularity, and "totalization," which refers more positively to the political project of locating oneself in relation to the larger social and economic structures that condition one's existence and yet lie outside the range of one's immediate experience.[64] The global, "totalizing" dimension of politics that has disappeared in the localized, small-group style of politics characteristic of the postmodern age, Jameson argues, is nothing other than the dimension of the economic system itself.[65] The anti-utopian hostility to totalization functions ideologically to remove those structures from the range of political critique and action. Jameson identifies the historical conditions for the postmodern resistance to totalization in the very success of the capitalist mode of production, its successful penetration into previously uncommodified regions of human experience. The successful advance of capitalism has eliminated those enclaves of social and economic difference from which one could get some purchase on global capitalism as a total, systemic phenomenon.[66] The disappearance of totalization on the level of thought paradoxically signifies its triumph on the level of reality, specifically, in the emergence of the world system of late capitalism.[67]

The theoretical reticence of comparative theologians like Clooney and Fredericks appears more ambiguous in light of this critique of "postmodern nominalism." Just as the reduction of political action to local struggles places the global economic system outside the range of political challenge, so too, in an analogous way, a comparative theological method that focuses on the localized reading of texts leaves the doctrinal superstructure of the compared traditions, with their typically absolutist and oppositional claims, safely intact.[68] One might argue that a comparative theological method that indefinitely postpones theological conclusions—a "patient deferral of issues of truth," as Clooney eloquently puts it—ends up supporting the theological status quo by default.[69] To be sure, in discouraging any expectation that sensational new teachings will result from the practice of comparative theology, Clooney directs our attention to the more subtle, yet arguably more profound and interesting, ways in which religious outlooks are transformed by interreligious theological encounter. Moreover, his comparative method might be more radical than it appears, quietly effecting behind-the-scenes transformations destined to break into manifestation the moment they pass a critical threshold. Nevertheless, the method of localized reading seems to discourage the kind of bold and imaginative theological revisionings offered by the pluralist theologies at their best.[70] In particular—and here the link between the critique of comparative theology and Jameson's critique of the postmodern nominalism becomes more than simply analogical—one wonders whether comparative theology, in its single-minded focus on the local and the particular, effectively renounces a capacity to envision the global dimension of theological praxis, a sense of the particular religious community's position in the global system. Such a synoptic theological vision grounds the kind of interreligious liberative praxis advocated by Paul Knitter.[71]

The foregoing analysis is only meant to be suggestive. I do not wish to claim that there are inherent defects in the methods and aims of the new comparative theology, much less in its execution.[72] Rather, my aim in pushing this line of critique is simply to call attention to the areas of vulnerability, the potential blind spots, of a new discipline still in the process of formation. My basic point is that comparative theology's criticism of its predecessors neither exempts it from ambiguity nor removes it from a history of interreligious theological encounter that has been deeply implicated in colonialism and neocolonialism. Paradoxically, the new discipline is more likely to perpetuate that history the more it attempts to deny it.

Comparative Theology as the Paradigm for the New Comparativism

We have seen how the new comparative theology, by defining itself in opposition to the theology of religions, risks falling into a pattern of projecting a dogmatic theological other, a move that diverts attention away from its own inherent ambiguities. In this respect, it repeats the founding gesture of its discredited nineteenth-century namesake. The liberal theological project of depoliticizing religion seems to have come full circle, poised to repeat the same mistakes.

This danger is considerably offset, however, by the fact that the new comparative theology, in reuniting the comparative method and theological reflection, annuls another oppositional relation that can trace a more direct line of descent to the comparative theology of the nineteenth century. As mentioned above, the modern academic study of religion has maintained its status as an objective, scientific discipline in large part by defining itself in opposition to theology.[73] Now a discipline that has to rely on a projected other in order to secure its intellectual legitimacy is, of course, suspect. Adapting a statement that Paul Ricoeur makes concerning the analogous relation of social theory to ideology, we could perhaps say that the epistemological weakness of a conception of religious studies is proportional to the force with which it denounces theology, where "theology" is understood in the sense of ideology.[74] Ricoeur notes that only a truly positive science like the mathematical physics of Galileo or Newton is entitled to declare an epistemological break with ideology.[75] When a non-positive science like sociology or religious studies makes such a declaration, it therefore exaggerates its claims of scientific rigor. Thus, when works of comparative religion define themselves over against theology, they artificially enhance their claims of scientific objectivity and impartiality. Nowhere is this mechanism of securing a claim of scientific status through oppositional contrast more plainly visible than in the comparative theology of the late nineteenth century, as we have seen. And nowhere is the illusory character of such politically generated claims of scientific objectivity more apparent.

The phenomenology of religion of Friedrich Heiler provides a more proximate and less obvious—and for that reason all the more instructive—example of a conception of comparative religion whose intellectual legitimacy is maintained by an oppositional contrast with a particular form of theology. Heiler's conception of *Religionswissenschaft* as an inductive science rests on a fine distinction between the discipline's specifically religious presuppositions, such as a reverence for all religions and a capacity for religious feeling,[76] on the one hand, and the a priori attitudes that are to be excluded in order to safeguard the discipline's inductive method, on the other.[77] It is clear that the "apriorism" that Heiler has principally in mind is that of dogmatic, confessional theology.[78] Nothing is more fatal to the science of comparative religion, he writes, than the absolutizing of one's own religion at the expense of others.[79] Heiler implicitly maps the vital distinction between hermeneutically productive presuppositions and data-distorting prejudices onto a distinction between liberal-ecumenical and exclusivist-dogmatic theology, respectively. Thus Nathan Söderblom and Rudolf Otto, two scholars who were quite open about their Christian theological commitments, nevertheless serve for Heiler as models for the comparative study of religion because neither allowed his theological commitments to become rigid and dogmatic.[80] Thus we see that the intellectual legitimacy of Heiler's phenomenology is sustained by essentially the same oppositional contrast between liberal and dogmatic theology that established the comparative theology of the previous century.[81]

So long as the liberal-ecumenical and confessional-dogmatic forms of theology were understood to be discontinuous with each other—a claim that attains its most forceful expression in Hick's "Copernican Revolution in theology"—the notion that hermeneutically productive presuppositions could be neatly separated from data-distorting a priori prejudices seemed plausible enough. From our present perspective, however—a perspective in which, as we have seen, the deep continuities between pluralist and inclusivist theology are clearly visible—the distinction between ecumenical and confessional theology appears more as a matter of degree than a difference in kind. With this change in perspective comes the realization that the relation between productive presuppositions and a priori value judgments is more complex and, consequently, the idea of an interpretive science of religion considerably more elusive, than had previously been acknowledged. Put differently, hermeneutically productive presuppositions cannot be dissociated from a priori value judgments simply by bracketing one's explicit theological commitments (although this may be a good start).

This shift in perspective coincides more generally with the exposure of previously unrecognized forms of theologism—where "theology" is implicitly understood as a cipher for whatever is opposed to "science"—in the comparative study of religion. As alluded to above, the critique of crypto-theologism in comparative religion has elicited two distinct, though not mutually exclusive responses.[82] The one seeks to preserve the Enlightenment tradition of science through a renewed emphasis on a naturalistic, explanatory approach to the study of religion that has lost ground to interpretive, idiographic approaches in anthropology and the history of religions.[83] The other responds to the crisis of the study of religion by assuming a critical stance toward its own categories and presuppositions. This latter is a reflexive response that makes its interpretive categories—that is, elements of the "subjective" apparatus of interpretation—themselves the objects of critical inquiry. Chief among the categories to be subjected to critical scrutiny is the category of religion itself.[84] One could perhaps capture the essential character of this second, "postmodernist" approach by saying that its object is not religion (as in earlier, modernist conceptions of *Religionswissenschaft*) but rather "religion," the quotation marks indicating that religion is taken as a discursive formation rather than as an extra-linguistic phenomenon.

Concomitant with this shift from an objectivist to a discursive understanding of religion has been a thoroughgoing critique and evaluation of the comparative method, itself one of the defining features of the discipline of religious studies.[85] The classic models of comparative religion presupposed the existence of objective and universal structures or principles that the comparative method was thought to uncover. In the evolutionary approach to comparative religion associated with Victorian anthropologists like Tylor, Lang, Marett, and Frazer, the comparative enterprise at once presupposed and provided evidence for supposedly universal laws of human development. In the classic phenomenologies of religion of scholars like van der Leeuw, Otto, and Eliade, the dialectical cum inductive process of comparison was believed to uncover, in a disparate collection of religious data, the putatively invariant "deep structures" of human religiosity.[86] Various critiques associated with postmodern thought have since revealed the putatively universal principles and structures supposedly uncovered by cross-cultural comparison to be little more than ideological projections of the culturally particular and historically contingent presuppositions of the comparativsts themselves. From a postmodernist perspective, the classic, foundationalist systems of comparative religion now appear as exercises in cultural imperialism.

This critique of the traditional models of comparison has itself prompted a range of responses.[87] One of the most promising of these responses is what has been termed, borrowing a felicitous phrase of William E. Paden, the "New Comparativism."[88] The New Comparativism designates a contemporary movement in the academy dedicated to the rehabilitation of the comparative approach in the aftermath of the above-mentioned postmodern critique.[89] It is associated with a rather loosely affiliated group of scholars inspired by Jonathan Z. Smith's seminal, if somewhat elusive, reflections on the comparative method.[90] The New Comparativism takes as its point of departure Smith's provocative characterization of most traditional forms of comparison as "magical" projections of a subjective experience of similarity as "an objective connection through some theory of influence, diffusion, borrowing, or the like."[91] At the same time, however—and again, following Smith's lead—the proponents of the New Comparativism align themselves against a prevalent response to this critique of traditional comparison, namely, to limit the use of comparison to those phenomena for which there are demonstrable historical connections.[92] If I understand him correctly, Smith challenges a basic assumption that the contemporary advocates of "limited" or "controlled" comparison share with the old comparativists, namely, the assumption that comparison depends on some sort of objective connection between the compared phenomena in order to be scientifically valid. In default of a belief in the existence of the universal principles and/or structures presupposed by the traditional models of comparison, the only legitimate (read: objectively based) comparisons recognized by the former group are those based on direct historical relations between the phenomena compared, what Smith terms "genealogical" comparisons. By contrast, those comparisons based merely on a similarity in form or structure between historically unrelated phenomena, what Smith terms "analogical" comparisons, are dismissed as merely impressionistic and hence "unscientific."[93] The New Comparativism dramatically inverts these valuations. The movement can be conveniently understood, in fact, as advocating a paradigm shift from genealogical comparison to analogical comparison as the standard of comparison.[94] Comparison is now understood less as a "scientific" method of uncovering objective facts and more as a pragmatic, rhetorical device to further the task of understanding.[95] The New Comparativists generally accept Smith's understanding of comparison as an imaginative "redescription" of the unfamiliar in terms of the familiar in order to impart intelligibility to the former[96] or, alternatively, as a strategic "defamiliarization" of phenomena the perception of which has been dulled by long familiarity.[97] In an ironic reversal of the standard evaluation of the two forms of comparison, genealogical comparison now comes under suspicion for ideologically masking the interests of the comparativist, effectively disguising what is in fact an active mental operation as a form of passive observation.[98]

In emphasizing the degree to which comparison is a constructive and interested activity, the New Comparativism recognizes and affirms the inherently political nature of the comparative enterprise.[99] Or, as Marsha Hewitt puts it, comparison in the academic study of religion is "*both* a political *and* academic activity simultaneously...it is political because it harbours a dimension of power, which can never be abolished...."[100] According to Hugh Urban, the recognition of this political dimension of comparison calls for "an interested and placed comparison—one that renders the scholar's own political interests as explicit as possible from the outset."[101] Against the widespread—and indeed normative!—view that historians of religion "have no fixed, normative position in relation to their data,"[102] a view he associates, ironically enough, with J. Z. Smith,[103] Urban argues that scholars should forthrightly acknowledge and defend their commitments while at the same time submitting their interpretations to peer criticism and the test of empirical data.[104] What is noteworthy about this proposal for our purposes is that even were we to concede that the particular commitments to be acknowledged are materially distinct from those of theology—Urban's own commitment is to "a basically post-structuralist sociological view of human action" derived from Bourdieu and Foucault[105]—the combination of acknowledgment and openness to corrigibility that Urban advocates is formally identical to the stance of the new generation of comparative theologians. The convergence of this post-Enlightenment model of comparative religion and the new comparative theology becomes all the more striking when we recognize that the commitments to be acknowledged in the former are not necessarily all that different *materially* from those of theology. One can easily cite theologians who theologize with historicist, Marxist, or, for that matter, Bourdieu-influenced sociological commitments.[106] Thus, we see that as scholars of comparative religion begin to recognize the inherently normative and political nature of comparison, the boundary between religious studies and theology appears more arbitrary and tenuous than it did before. With the demise of the Enlightenment myth of disinterested scholarship, those who persist in maintaining a dichotomy between the two disciplines are increasingly forced to rely on a caricatured understanding of theology as an essentially supernaturalistic, dogmatic, and parochial enterprise.[107]

One could argue, in fact, that the new comparative theology serves as the paradigm for this new "interested and placed" comparison. We only have to recall that the older, foundationalist model of comparison that it replaces was sustained in large part by an opposition to confessional theology. Thus the reunification of comparison and theology in the new comparative theology, by deconstructing the projective mechanism that sustained the old comparativism, gives paradigmatic expression to the change in perspective of the new. Comparative theology, in other words, exemplifies the New Comparativism by openly acknowledging the comparativist's own theological and political commitments. For example, Francis Clooney, reflecting on his comparative theological reading of the South Indian Śrivaiṣṇava devotional text, the *Tiruvāymoḻi*, in his book *Seeing Through Texts*, writes:

> In neither my reading nor writing was the goal to be entirely open; it was rather to make sure that our sympathetic reading would go forward with an acute awareness of our strictures of prior

> commitments, beliefs, attachments – according to linguistic community, profession, religion, etc. We have therefore studied *Tiruvāymoḻi* and its reception among the Śrivaiṣṇavas with a growing awareness of our own commitments, imaginations, desires.[108]

More than anything else, it is this willingness to acknowledge its own normative commitments and interests that separates the new comparative theology from its nineteenth-century namesake. A comparison of Clooney's characteristically modest and charitable comparisons to the typically incautious and prejudicial comparisons of a nineteenth-century comparativist like James Freeman Clarke, who was utterly convinced of their fairness and impartiality, provides a striking demonstration of the "postmodern" thesis that the best way to avoid cultural misunderstanding and distortion is through an honest acknowledgment of one's interpretive limitations rather than through an unexamined commitment, however sincerely held, to the ideal of scholarly impartiality and objectivity.

Two Kinds of Acknowledgment

This reflexive, postmodern turn to acknowledgment would appear to be the antidote to the problem of theological hegemonism exemplified by the older comparative theology and the more recent pluralist theology. This is true in an obvious, even banal sense, inasmuch as the defining characteristic of a hegemonic discourse is precisely its unwillingness to acknowledge its own acts of exclusion. It is considerably less clear, however, that the mere acknowledgment of the perspectival character of a given exercise in interreligious theology is an adequate solution to the larger problem of exclusion—the political—in theological discourse. There is a sense in which an appeal to such acknowledgment as the answer simply begs the question—the question, namely, of what one does with the particular aspects of one's perspective once they have been acknowledged. Is a given element of that perspective to be regarded as an ideological bias to be ferreted out or as a legitimate normative commitment to be affirmed and defended? The easy—too easy—answer to this question is that one simply distinguishes between legitimate commitments and illegitimate biases. And yet this answer satisfies only to the extent that one assumes a nonideological, nonpolitical dimension of religious commitment that can be isolated by a faculty of discernment from the more problematic, political-ideological aspects of that commitment—the central presupposition, in other words, of the two-dimensional notion of religion that I questioned in the preceding chapter.[109]

Here, I would like to suggest that the solution to the problem of the political in theology—the problem, that is, of somehow avoiding religious antagonism without falling into the trap of theological hegemonism—is a matter of mediating between two distinct modalities of acknowledgment, each of which carries its own pitfalls if pursued one-sidedly. The first of these is the use of acknowledgment to root out bias. The second is the use of acknowledgment to affirm commitment.[110] The problem with the first, "critical" form of acknowledgment is that it falls short of the acknowledgment needed to annul relations of hegemony between knower and known. The problem with the second, "confessional" form of acknowledgment is that while it does indeed neutralize theological hegemonism, it does so only at the risk of reviving the dubious practice of interreligious apologetics. Such a revival of apologetic theology, at least in its cruder forms, would represent a return of the political in unsublimated form. I shall address each of these points in turn.

A convenient reference point for the first point is the theory of comparison set forth by Robert C. Neville in collaboration with Wesley J. Wildman in the three volumes of their Comparative Religious Ideas Project. Their sophisticated method of comparison is designed to expose and root out bias. It therefore serves as an excellent example of what I am calling critical acknowledgment in the field of religion. Comparison begins with the specification of the respect in which two or more phenomena are to be compared. Neville terms these "respects" of comparison "vague categories"; their vagueness consists in their ability to relate disparate, even contradictory phenomena.[111] The outstanding feature of these vague categories in the context of the overall theory, however, is their vulnerability to correction.[112] Neville and Wildman acknowledge that the initially chosen categories will invariably have a history in a particular tradition of intellectual inquiry and therefore a built-in bias. And yet their method of empirical testing and revision is designed to purify the categories of these antecedent biases.[113] Ideally, this self-correcting procedure of comparison yields a "stable comparative hypothesis" that provide a basis for further empirical research and critique.

Although Neville and Wildman's approach to comparison makes self-criticism an integral part of the comparative process, its self-criticism remains within the scientific framework of representation.[114] Their commitment to the goal of accurate, albeit provisional representation therefore renders their theory of comparison vulnerable to the postcolonialist argument that representation as such, and not simply biased representation, is problematic because it presupposes and perpetuates an asymmetrical power relation between a knowing subject and its objects, in particular, the relation between Western scholarship and the typically non-Western cultures and traditions it represents. Or, as

Tomoko Masuzawa expresses this line of criticism, a comparative method whose self-criticism is confined within an "ethics of science," "ultimately refuses to question the positional structure of the knowing and the known, and thus remains insistently blind to the question of power."[115] Even a perfectly accurate, "scientific" description of a religious tradition is implicated in power relations inasmuch as it contributes to the recognition that sustains the hegemony of the dominant faction(s) over its rivals in that tradition.[116] Whether this critique is fair to Neville and Wildman's complex and nuanced theory of comparison, which I have described here in only the broadest of outlines, is not at all clear.[117] At any rate, it does suffice to illustrate the basic point that a "modernist"[118] comparative project that regards acknowledgment simply as a moment in a scientific program of eliminating bias does not exclude—although I would add that it does not entail[119]—a hegemonic relation between the comparativist and his or her object of study.

We turn now to the second, "confessional" mode of acknowledgment. Above, I noted that simply by acknowledging and affirming the particularity of one's perspective, one ipso facto renounces the universalist pretensions that typically sustain relations of hegemony. And yet this confessional mode of acknowledgment is not without its dangers. To the extent that the comparative theologian acknowledges his or her normative religious commitments only in order to affirm and defend them, comparative theology can devolve into a form of interreligious apologetics. Both Clooney and Fredericks all but concede this point when they affirm an apologetic dimension to the enterprise of comparative theology as a concomitant of its confessional nature.[120] They are quick to reassure us, however, that the apologetics they affirm is well informed and "responsible," and that, at any rate, it is not central to the comparative theological enterprise. One detects in these qualifications a certain anxiety about a potential "return of the political" in the form of old-style Christian apologetics.[121] To the extent that the new comparative theology emphasizes its confessional nature, it reverses the process by which the liberal theological tradition sublimated polemical interreligious relations into hegemonic ones. With this affirmation of apologetic theology, religious antagonism threatens to reappear in more or less unsublimated form.

Comparative theologians keep the antagonistic tendencies of the apologetic dimension of comparative theology firmly in check, however, by balancing the second, confessional aspect of acknowledgment with the first. Confessional comparative theologians like Clooney and Fredericks, no less than Neville and Wildman, stress the self-critical nature of comparison. Using language reminiscent of Karl Popper's "falsificationism" in the philosophy of science, Clooney, for example, notes that even non-comparative theologians "are quite often willing to be tentative in their conclusions, which remain open to revision and correction," and that, accordingly, he will leave his own theological judgments, including fundamental claims regarding the existence and knowability of God, "open to further comparative and dialogical testing."[122] Only by skillfully combining the two forms of acknowledgment are comparative theologians able to negotiate the narrow and perilous path between, on the one side, the theological hegemonism of the liberal tradition of interreligious theology, and, on the other, the illiberal polemics of traditional apologetics.

The tension-filled, dialectical nature of this negotiation is masked somewhat by the presumption of a qualitative distinction between those aspects of religious commitment that motivate and guide the process of mutually transformative interreligious theological encounter and those that block the possibility of a creative transformation of one's theological understanding. Fredericks appears, in fact, to project these latter, ideological aspects of religious commitment onto the pluralist theology of religion serving as the foil to his conception of comparative theology. He contrasts a comparative theology that represents "a more creative way of responding to religious diversity"[123] to a pluralist theology of religion "that does little to equip Christians with the skills necessary for transforming their own religious views in light of the teachings and wisdom of other religious traditions."[124] This contrast implies a sharp distinction between genuine faith, understood to sustain a capacity to respond creatively to religious diversity, and ideology, understood pejoratively as a rigid set of unfalsifiable, a priori theological judgments that insulate the home tradition from the salutary—and potentially transformative—challenge of other faiths. In what might come as a disappointment to those convinced of the unprecedented novelty of the new comparative theology, we note that this implicit distinction between faith and ideology essentially replicates the distinction between hermeneutically productive presuppositions and a priori value judgments that grounded the older phenomenology of religion. As was the case with the latter distinction, the implicit notion of a disjunction between faith and ideology is sustained by an oppositional contrast with an earlier form of theological discourse, in this case, the theology of religions.

Like the homogenization of the fatty and liquid components of milk, comparative theology achieves a measure of consistency by integrating two heterogeneous forms of acknowledgment. As we have just seen, comparative theologians avoid the twin pitfalls of theological hegemonism and polemic by balancing a willingness to revise their theological understanding in light of the teachings of other traditions with affirmations of religious commitment. Inasmuch as comparative theologians tend to be theoretically minimalist, their juxtapositions of expressions of openness and commitment are apt to appear somewhat ad hoc, guided by a more or less intuitive sense of when a receptivity to the teachings of another tradition needs to held in check by an affirmation of commitment, and vice versa. Apart from its dubious use in framing the polemic with the theology of religions, comparative theology's reluctance to theorize reflects a certain practical wisdom. Clooney and Fredericks are acutely aware that a preoccupation with comparative theory and method often serves merely to postpone the rigors of actual comparison. Their theoretical reticence also has the perhaps unintended benefit of avoiding the depoliticizing effects of theory, the tendency, that is, for theory to foster the illusion that the theologian's ultimately political task of negotiating between openness and commitment can be accomplished by following a set of rational procedures.

And yet, this reluctance to theorize the discipline comes at a cost. So long as comparative theology remains an under-theorized discipline, it is difficult to imagine how comparative theologians will be able to persuade the wider theological community that comparison should form an integral part of contemporary theological reflection. The ubiquitous and at times platitudinous appeals to the unprecedented nature of today's situation of religious pluralism are probably not enough to overcome the formidable theological resistances to comparison, much less to persuade other theologians to undertake the onerous, uncertain, and time-consuming task of comparison. To be sure, as Clooney insists, the prospects of comparative theology will ultimately depend—as they should—on how well comparativists actually do their comparisons. And yet, the wider theological community will be less likely to pay attention to those comparisons in the first place if a compelling case is not made for the theological relevance of comparison in general.[125] Put differently, a theological method that successfully integrates comparison is needed to transform what for many otherwise might be mere religious curiosities into vital theological resources. I would therefore argue that a reluctance to theorize the discipline comes at the unwelcome price of its continued marginalization.

In chapter 3, I attempt to meet this challenge by articulating a model of comparative theology that flows from a recognition of the ineluctability of the political in theological discourse. This model seeks to substantiate the claim, somewhat baldly stated in the previous chapter, that a theology that confronts the political as the defining problematic for theology will necessarily have a pronounced comparative or interreligious dimension.

Before I do that, however, I would like to extend and develop the above analysis of the history of modern interreligious theology in terms of Schmitt's inescapability thesis. In the next chapter, I shall argue that the history of modern theology as a whole, and not simply that of specifically interreligious theology, can be illuminatively understood in terms of the problematic of depoliticizing religion. This demonstration will allow me to present the model of comparative theology offered in chapter 3 as a logical endpoint of the theological trajectory sketched out in chapter 2. This narrative style of presentation will lend additional force to the claim that comparison should form an integral part of contemporary theological reflection.

2

The Modern Quest to Depoliticize Theology

> After the hopeless theological disputes and quarrels of the sixteenth century, European society sought a neutral domain in which conflict would cease and where people could come to an understanding, reach an agreement, and convince each other. The disputed concepts and arguments of traditional Christian theology were set aside and a "natural" system of theology, metaphysics, ethics, and law was constructed.
>
> —Carl Schmitt

In this chapter, I propose a reading of the history of modern theology in light of Carl Schmitt's depoliticization thesis. This rereading will bring into focus the underlying problematic of a dominant current in the tradition of modern theology, namely, to dissociate a concept of religion from the principle of political antagonism while still recognizing the importance of the social or communal dimension of religion.

From the Introduction, it will be recalled that Schmitt interprets the history of modern Western society as a series of attempts to realize a domain of human interaction free of social antagonism, the political. The first and most consequential of these attempts was the displacement of traditional Christian theology as the controlling domain of culture.[1] This effort to shift the center of cultural gravity away from religion arose in reaction to the sixteenth-century Wars of Religion and the hopelessly inconclusive theological disputes that ostensibly motivated and justified them.[2] Ultimately, however, the effort to depoliticize society by making a cultural domain previously free of social antagonism the basis of social relations—Schmitt identifies morality and economics as the two favorite refuges of modern liberalism—is a vain endeavor. For, as we have seen, Schmitt regards the political as a fundamental and ineradicable principle of human social relations. Any cultural domain therefore becomes political—that is, becomes the site of a friend-enemy grouping—when it becomes decisive for human thought and action.[3] Thus, whatever cultural sphere becomes the central or controlling cultural domain in a given epoch inevitably becomes a site of political antagonism.[4] For example, the attempt in the twentieth century to depoliticize social relations by basing them on rational economic principles led inexorably to the political antagonism between the rival ideologies of communism and capitalism.[5] There is, then, according to Schmitt's provocative theory, an irresolvable tension at the heart of the project of modern liberalism. The quest to neutralize and depoliticize social relations contradicts the ineradicably political nature of those relations. This inner contradiction sets into motion a dialectic in which one site of social antagonism is displaced only to give rise to another, thereby necessitating another search for a new neutral sphere.[6]

Essentially the same contradiction, I suggest, lies at the heart of in the project of modern theology. The modern theological project of freeing religious conviction from the manifestations of social antagonism can be understood, in fact, as simply a ramification of the larger cultural processes of neutralization and depoliticization of which Schmitt speaks. The tradition of modern theology emerges from the founding gesture of the modern depoliticization project: the displacement of religion as the controlling domain of culture. Like the liberal project of depoliticization described by Schmitt, it was born in reaction to the sixteenth- and seventeenth-century Wars of Religion. The modern theological project of identifying an essence of religion and dissociating this essence from its political excrescences—a project whose various expressions include, as we shall see below, the natural theology of the Enlightenment, Schleiermacher's apology for religion against its "cultured despisers," and the experientialist pluralism of the twentieth century—can be understood as a reflex of the modern differentiation of cultural spheres in which the religious sphere, "came fully into its own, specializing in "its own religious function" and either dropping or losing many other "nonreligious" functions it had accumulated and could no longer meet efficiently."[7]

The modern quest to liberate a putative core of religious conviction from attitudes of chauvinism and intolerance tends to the privatization of religion. Taken to its logical conclusion, this privatizing tendency results in what

Thomas Luckmann calls "invisible religion," that is, a form of religiosity in which a religious way of life is understood in terms of an individual quest for personal meaning. This is, of course, a prevalent religious attitude today, one which is expressed in the popular catchword "spiritual not religious." In its quest to depoliticize religion, however, the tradition of liberal theology has stopped well short of conceding such an attenuated form of religion. Few theologians, including those who freely accept the modern, differentiated model of society and embrace what Bruce Lincoln calls its "minimalist" (as opposed to "maximalist") concept of religion, have been willing to countenance the complete privatization of religion. They are guided by the conviction that religion must have some communal dimension, if not an institutional one as well.

The acknowledgment of a communal dimension to religion did not appear to pose an especially serious challenge to the liberal theological project of depoliticizing religion so long as one assumed the priority of religious experience over its communal expression. As we shall see below when we examine Schleiermacher's conception of religious community, it was possible to imagine a particular form of religious intuition (e.g., Schleiermacher's "sense and taste for the Infinite") expressing itself in an unbounded form of community, a kind of universal brotherhood, that transcended the ordinary dynamics of social groups. In recent decades, however, as theologians have come to recognize that religious experience is more the product than the source of outward cultural and religious forms, and that religious formation, accordingly, must be understood in terms of ordinary processes of socialization, it has become more difficult to dismiss the political aspects of actual religious communities simply as a contingent, empirical matter. For if the religious development of the individual personality is dependent upon the social group of which he or she is a member, then religious formation would appear to be implicated in the political processes by which social groups are formed.

A demonstration of the necessary connection between religious formation and the political constitution of social groups would proceed in three steps.[8] First, one could argue that the capacity of religious discourses and practices to shape personal and communal experience presupposes a structure of authority. Authoritative cultural and religious forms are invested with a power that transcends each of the individuals who recognize those forms as authoritative. And it is thanks to this power that those cultural and religious forms are able to shape the attitudes and understanding, the ethos and worldview (Geertz), of the members of a religious community. Second, this power of authority derives in large part from the social group. One could argue, in fact, following Pierre Bourdieu, that the authority that renders religious discourse efficacious is *constituted* by the recognition of the social group.[9] There would thus appear to be a correlation between the authority of religiously transformative discourse and the cohesiveness of a particular social group. Third and finally, the formation of a cohesive social group presupposes a moment of social exclusion. Social antagonism is the flip-side of social cohesion. Or, as Robert Paul Wolff puts it, "out-group hostility is the natural accompaniment of in-group loyalty."[10]

Post-Enlightenment theology would therefore seem to embody, if not an inner contradiction, at least an unresolved tension between its aspiration to transcend the sphere of antagonistic, political relations, on the one hand, and the irreducibly political nature of the religious community it affirms, on the other. As in Lévi-Strauss's theory of myth, according to which an intractable contradiction gives rise to a succession of variations on a mythical theme, each trying vainly to overcome the contradiction that set the sequence into motion,[11] the history of post-Enlightenment theology reveals a series of compelling but ultimately inconclusive attempts to reconcile the quest to depoliticize religion with an affirmation of religious community. In the pages that follow, I will profile several of the more prominent and influential of these attempts to resolve the problematic of depoliticizing religion. While the following sampling of theological attempts to depoliticize religion can claim to be neither comprehensive nor definitive, it will, I hope, suffice to bring the dimensions of this problematic clearly into view.

Enlightenment Natural Religion

The modern project of depoliticizing religion begins with the quest for so-called "natural religion" in response to the Wars of Religion. As reflected in the respective biographies of two pioneers in this quest, Jean Bodin in the sixteenth century and Herbert of Cherbury in the seventeenth, each of whom served at some point in his life as a professional diplomat, the search for a fundamental and universal religion was motivated by the diplomatic effort to find common ground between warring religious factions.[12] Bodin conceived this fundamental form of religion in terms of originality, Herbert in terms of commonality. But whether "true religion" was conceived as the original religious stem from which the particular faiths branched off as with Bodin, or as the distillation of the creeds of the historical religions in the five essential, "common notions" as with Herbert, the intent was the same: to establish religion on a secure basis lying outside present-day sectarian conflict. In other words, their aim was to formulate a concept of religion transcending relations of political antagonism.

Although one could argue, as does J. Samuel Preus, that these early formulations of natural religion stand at the beginning of a process that would eventually lead to a "paradigm shift" away from a theological to a naturalistic approach to religion,[13] we must recognize that the project of natural religion was originally motivated by genuinely religious concerns and principles.[14] In particular, the quest for a natural religion was motivated and justified by a defense of the justice of God against the exclusivist understandings of salvation propounded by the various Christian sects.[15] That God could condemn the greater part of the human race to perdition seemed inconsistent with the belief in divine beneficence and justice. It is important to note, in this connection, that the concept of nature as it was employed by Herbert, as well as by the group of seventeenth-century theologians and philosophers known as the Cambridge Platonists, was not intended to mark a contrast with that of revelation.[16] As Peter Harrison points out, the contrasting concept of "nature" in this context was not "supernature" but rather "convention."[17] So long as the idea of nature was defined by its contrast with convention, that is, with what human beings arbitrarily agree upon, nature and revelation could even be thought to coincide. The binary opposition of nature and convention, in fact, easily maps onto that of the divine and the human. As contrasted with the idea of arbitrary convention, "nature" referred to what was innate, necessary, and universal, ideas that in no way exclude the idea of revelation. Thus Herbert could maintain that his "five common notions," the distilled essence of the historical religions which comprised the creed of the archetypical religion of humanity, were inscribed upon the human mind by God.[18]

Even when contrasted with the concept of convention, however, the concept of nature nevertheless bears an uneasy and ambiguous relationship to the idea of revelation. An emphasis on the universality of nature can easily overturn the fragile alliance between the two concepts. To be specific, the universality of natural religion invites a contrast with the particularity of the various sectarian creeds mediating traditional claims of revelation. The latter could be easily assimilated to the concept of arbitrary human convention[19]—particularly if one looked at those creeds with a measure of suspicion in light of their role in justifying the religious wars. Still, the concept of revelation by and large retained a positive valence for the proponents of natural religion, most of whom, as I just mentioned, understood their quest in religious terms. In their quest to delegitimize the claims of the warring sects, therefore, these thinkers generally chose to redefine, rather than reject outright, the concept of revelation. As mentioned above, Herbert understood revelation in terms of a direct infusion of divine knowledge into the human mind. For Herbert's eighteenth-century Deist heirs, the faculty of reason was itself a locus of divine revelation, a notion sometimes referred to as "natural revelation" (Locke) or "internal revelation" (Tindal).[20] By thus redefining the traditional concept of revelation, both Herbert and the Deists sought to wrest the concept from its associations with ecclesiastical authority and exclusionary tradition, thereby stripping the warring sects of religious legitimation.[21]

Rational theologians who continued to identify with orthodox Christianity naturally did not go so far as to collapse the distinction between revelation and natural reason. John Locke, for example, continued to recognize, in addition to natural revelation, the presence of a revealed truth in the Bible that was not reducible to what the faculty of reason could discover on its own.[22] And yet, he shared the concern of the more radical theologians in dissociating the concept of divine revelation from the exclusionary claims of the religious sects. Locke makes a sharp distinction between, on the one hand, "the fundamental articles of the Christian faith" revealed by God for our salvation and, on the other, the doctrines differentiating the various churches.[23] Authentic Christian revelation as defined by those fundamental articles—propositions upon which all Christians of good faith could agree—coheres, at least within the Christian frame of reference in which Locke was writing, with the idea of a natural religion of reason transcending sectarian conflict.[24] Locke's argument that Christianity is consistent with (if irreducible to) "natural revelation" leads ineluctably to Matthew Tindal's thesis that natural religion ("internal revelation") differs from revealed religion ("external revelation") "only in its manner of being communicated."[25] In essence (if not in historical actuality) the Christian religion is "the most modest and peaceable religion that ever was."[26] Conflict and controversy enter into Christianity only when the partisans of the various Christian churches, in their sectarian zeal, mistakenly elevate the distinguishing points of their particular communion to the status of fundamental articles of faith essential for salvation.[27]

Fortunately, there was an effective means by which the fundamental articles of faith could be distinguished from the nonessential points of doctrine that served to differentiate one church from another: reason. For when obscurity and contradiction are found in theology, they invariably pertain to the latter.[28] As Hume cynically observed, disputational or scholastic theology "has a kind of appetite for absurdity and contradiction"; in a theological controversy, "whichever opinion is most contrary to plain sense is sure to prevail."[29] At the same time that the obscure subtleties of extra-biblical theology sustain the controversies that divide the Christian churches, they cast a protective aura of mystery over the authoritarian dictates of a corrupt and cynical priesthood. The fundamental articles of Christian faith, by contrast, while they may indeed be "above reason"—that is, underivable from human ratiocination yet nevertheless reasonable[30]—can never be contrary to reason. Thanks to this confidence in the fundamental rationality of Christian truth, then, the rationalist theologians of the Enlightenment believed that Christianity could be liberated from the twin evils of authoritarianism ("priestcraft") and sectarian strife through the instrumentality of reason. That reason could serve as an effective instrument of depoliticization was the great discovery of Enlightenment theology.

Unfortunately, however, the project of depoliticizing Christian theology through rationalization ultimately could not be reconciled with Christian orthodoxy. Submitting claims of revealed truth to the test of reason threatened to render the former superfluous. As we have seen, Locke sought to prevent this possibility, and thus remain on the side of Christian orthodoxy, by affirming a class of propositions "above" reason. And yet, as Locke's self-styled successor John Toland clearly perceived, the distinction between claims "above reason" and those "contradicting reason" could be finessed, leaving an opening for all manner of "absurdities" to reenter Christianity through the back door, as it were.[31] Toland's critique suggests that Locke could stay on the side of Christian orthodoxy only by arbitrarily stopping short of his aim of distilling Christianity down to an essential core of rational truths. By closing off this loophole, Toland effectively collapses the distinction between revelation and reason—and therewith Christian orthodoxy and Deism.

We could perhaps look at this thesis of the incompatibility between a thoroughly rationalized theology and Christian orthodoxy from another angle. The project of rational Christianity threatens to dissolve any concrete notion of Christian community. As Peter Harrison observes in commenting on Herbert's claim that his "common notions" constituted "the only Catholic and uniform Church," the project of paring Christianity down to an essential core of rational propositions effectively replaces the traditional understanding of the church as a historically situated institution of salvation with a body of saving knowledge.[32] It would be the task of the theology of the eighteenth century, particularly in Germany, to reconcile the ideal of a "true church" transcending sectarian division with the historical particularity of Christianity.

Schleiermacher's True Church

The Enlightenment project of depoliticizing religion continues in the work of the great Protestant theologian, Friedrich Schleiermacher (1768–1834). Schleiermacher's approach to the problem of the political in religion, however, differs markedly from that of his Enlightenment predecessors, reflecting as it does the considerable influence of the Romantic critique of Enlightenment rationalism. Instead of abstracting a set of common beliefs from the particular religions, Schleiermacher developed an ideal conception of unbounded religious community that was rooted in a particular religious experience. Since it was better able to affirm the particularity of historical Christianity, Schleiermacher's conception of religion and religious community has proven more successful and influential in shaping the trajectory of liberal theology than has the theological rationalism of the Enlightenment.

Schleiermacher's youthful masterpiece, *On Religion: Speeches to its Cultured Despisers* (first edition, 1799), exemplifies the thesis that the Romantic movement, despite its tendency to define itself in opposition to the rationalism of the Enlightenment, nevertheless preserves many of the Enlightenment's principal interests and concerns.[33] Schleiermacher's chief concern in the *Speeches* is precisely that of his Enlightenment predecessors: to isolate an essence of religion from its political excrescences. Schleiermacher wants to argue that what the "cultured despisers" of religion despise in religion—namely, its tendency to engender strife and persecution—does not properly belong to religion. He shares the despisers' revulsion to the manifestations of the political in religion, but he insists that their criticism strikes at something that is adventitious to religion's essence:

> How wrongly, therefore, do you turn on religion with your reproaches that it is bent on persecution and spitefulness, that it wrecks society and makes blood flow like water. Indict those who corrupt religion, who want to inundate it with philosophy and fetter it to a system. What is it in religion over which men have argued, taken sides, and ignited wars? Sometimes over morals and always over metaphysics, and neither of these belongs to it.[34]

In his effort to identify an essence of religion Schleiermacher, like Locke, seeks to vindicate the Christian religion from its history of persecution and polemic, of authoritarianism and religious war.[35]

Unlike the rationalist theologians of the Enlightenment, however, whose conception of the essence of religion in terms of a set of propositions all but volatilized any concrete notion of religious community, Schleiermacher did not lose sight of the importance of the social dimension of religion in his quest to depoliticize it. Schleiermacher's effort to depoliticize religion attains its clearest expression, in fact, in the often-underappreciated fourth speech, "On the Social Element (*das Gesellige*) in Religion; or, On Church and Priesthhod."[36] There he develops a contrast between "the true church" and the "external religious society" (*die aüssere Religionsgemeinschaft*). Absent from the former is the spirit of exclusion and intolerance characteristic of the latter. The true church embodies a vision of universal brotherhood in which "all distinctions that really exist in religion flow smoothly into one another."[37] To the members of the true church, "the religious world appears as an indivisible whole."[38] The true church and the external religious society thus embody radically heterogeneous principles, the one the principle of reconciliation and unity, the other of antagonism and separation. Like oil and water, these two forms of religious association would naturally separate were it not for corruptive forces from without—in particular, an intrusive state seeking to bring the Church under its influence—that force them together into an artificial unity.[39] Despite its association with religion on the level of empirical reality,[40] the principle of the political—"the malicious spirit of sectarianism and proselytizing (*die gehässige Sekten- und Proselyten-Geist*)"—thus remains far removed from the essence of religion.[41]

Like the Enlightenment's concept of natural religion, then, Schleiermacher's true church embodies a principle of universality that allows it to transcend the parochialism and contentiousness of the established churches.[42] And yet, the universality of the true church is of an entirely different kind than that of natural religion. In setting forth his conception of the true church and the understanding of religion that it embodies, Schleiermacher implicitly appeals to the Romantic notion of poetic universality, a notion that achieves its most eloquent expression in Goethe's famous distinction between poetry and allegory.[43] In contrast to allegory, which abstracts a universal concept from the particulars it subsumes, thereby relegating the latter to the status of mere instances of the former, poetry "beholds the universal *in* the particular."[44] Like poetry according to Goethe's conception, Schleiermacher's concept of true religion is founded on a central intuition that radiates outward into a vision of religious unity. As the efflux of a kind of poetic intuition, Schleiermacher's notion of religion represents the very antithesis to the natural religion of the Enlightenment, which is the product of ratiocination, specifically, the abstraction of a set of common notions from the particular religions.[45]

The concept of poetic universality forms the basis of Schleiermacher's defense of the historical particularity of religious tradition in the fifth of the *Speeches*. The Deist philosophers of the Enlightenment had assumed that religious strife and intolerance were intrinsic to the particular, historical religions. Accordingly, historical or "positive" religion served as the contrasting concept to their notion of natural religion. Against this view, Schleiermacher argues that the advocates of natural religion, in holding positive religion responsible for all the ills of religious history, had mistaken what was in fact an adventitious corrupting tendency for what was essential.[46] Schleiermacher dissociates positive religion from religious exclusion by homologizing the former to the central intuition forming the basis of his expansive vision of religious totality.[47]

Contrasting the formative principle of positive religion with that of sects, he asserts that, "every positive religion, during the time of its formation and flowering..., moves in a completely opposite direction, not concentrating itself and excluding much from itself, but growing towards the outside...."[48] Schleiermacher appeals to the experience of poetic (as opposed to conceptual) apprehension when he goes on to contrast the vitality and concreteness of positive religion to the abstract and lifeless uniformity of natural religion. We see, then, that the Romantic notion of poetic universality plays a vital and essential role in Schleiermacher's effort to reconcile the liberal project of depoliticizing religion with the historical particularity of Christianity.

Schleiermacher's defense of positive religion in the fifth speech, however, qualifies the inclusivity of the true church that he describes in the fourth. As a form of religious community that expands outward from a core of human relationality into open frontiers, the true church is distinct from any association hemmed in by exclusionary boundaries.[49] And yet it is unable to encompass the non-Christian religions. In the fifth speech, Schleiermacher draws a qualitative distinction between the "plurality of the (Christian) churches," on the one hand, and the "plurality of the religions," on the other.[50] Intra-Christian differences differ from interreligious ones in that they are essentially political and not substantive in nature. That is to say, they derive less from objective differences between communities as from what Georg Simmel might call an a priori "spirit of contradiction" (*Widerspruchsgeist*) that exploits and magnifies trivial differences in order to create division where there should be agreement.[51] Were Christian communities to free themselves from this spirit of antagonism, their insubstantial sectarian differences would evanesce in an ecumenical vision of Christian unity. Such is not the case, however, with the various positive religions. These are distinguished from each other by more than a purely formal, political act of exclusion[52]; the differences between them are substantial, essential.[53] Inasmuch as interreligious differences are essential and irreducible, we might therefore expect religious plurality to remain even were religion to be successfully depoliticized, that is, if the "spirit of contradiction" were to be banished from the sphere of religion. Although one could argue that Schleiermacher's evolutionary perspective (entirely typical of his time) ultimately undermines a genuine notion of religious pluralism,[54] one can nevertheless find in Schleiermacher passages like the following which anticipate today's pluralist theology:

> But now, if there will always be Christians, will Christianity for this reason also be infinite in its universal dissemination and rule humanity as the only form of religion? Christianity disdains this

> despotism, . . .; it gladly watches other and younger forms of religion arise from all points outside this corruption, from close beside itself, even from those regions that appear to it as the very outermost and most dubious limits of religion. . . . Let the universe be intuited and worshipped in all ways. Innumerable forms of religion are possible, and if it is necessary that each become real at some time, then it would at least be desirable that one could have an intimation of many at all times.[55]

We see, then, that Schleiermacher's solution to the problem of the political in religion has two dimensions, an ecumenical universalism within Christianity and a kind of Herderian cultural pluralism without. This combination of Christian ecumenism and religious pluralism continues to serve as the basic model for liberal Christianity today.

Drey's Concept of World Religion

Schleiermacher's slightly younger contemporary Johann Sebastian Drey (1777–1853), the founder of the Tübingen School of Catholic theology, also reconciles the idea of universal religion with historical Christianity. Unlike Schleiermacher, however, Drey refuses to qualify his Christian universalism with an acceptance of religious pluralism.

Drey's response to the problematic of religion and the political is a distinction between the religion of a nation and the religion of the world (*Landesreligion* and *Weltreligion*, respectively).[56] The latter refers to the form religion takes when an acknowledgment of the universal sovereignty of God transcends all loyalties to a particular ethnic or national group.[57] The idea of the world religion is embodied, albeit imperfectly, in the Christian—more specifically, the Catholic—Church. The contrasting category of national religion refers, as its name indicates, to those forms of religion in which religious commitment remains bound up with some form of particularistic group loyalty. Drey declares all religions outside of Christianity, both ancient paganisms and contemporary non-Christian religions, to be mere national religions.[58] Predictably, this indictment includes Judaism, which, despite serving providentially as the preparation for the world religion that is Christianity, was itself unable to transcend its partiality for the "chosen people."[59] Drey's category of national religion effectively assimilates the various non-Christian religions, including Judaism, to the forms of tribal religion that paradigmatically exemplify the category. This assimilation of what today would be called the major "world" religions to paganism hearkens back to a premodern form of classification in which most non-Christian religions were indiscriminately subsumed under the tendentious category of "idolatry." Unlike Schleiermacher, Drey recognizes no intrinsic limits to the expansion of the Christian church as it seeks to realize the Kingdom of God on earth.[60]

Apart from its obvious apologetic function, Drey's distinction between world religion and national religion encodes the modern "liberal" project of extricating religion from the political. As the religion of the world, Christianity stands as the antithesis of the political in its twin dimensions of social antagonism and coercive authoritarianism. As for the first of these dimensions of the political, Drey argues that Christianity, inasmuch as it embodies the principle of love and unity, opposes the human tendency toward antagonism and division.[61] The historical appearance of Christianity marks a providential shift in human relations from a divergent tendency—which, in primordial times, providentially allowed humanity to fulfill the biblical commandment to "be fruitful and multiply"—to a convergent one.[62] As evidence for this fundamental shift, Drey cites Christianity's transcendence of national boundaries. He makes the historically dubious claim that Christianity is the first form of religion having no relation to a particular country or people.[63] As for the second dimension of the political, Drey distinguishes the moral authority ideally governing the Church from the coercive authority governing both the state and those religious communities compromised by the political.[64] Ideally the Church renounces a form of authority based on physical coercion, restricting itself to one based on "suasion of faith and love."[65]

Drey correlates his distinction between world religion and national religion to the more familiar distinction between revealed religion and natural religion. In homologizing the categories of world religion and revealed religion, Drey appeals to the commonplace sentiment that human beings are tribalistic by nature.[66] It is only through the action of divine grace that human beings can overcome their parochial attachments to nation, race, and *Volk*.[67] That Christianity was able to transcend its original Jewish cultural matrix in its missionary quest "to make disciples of all nations" testifies to its divine source.[68]

In correlating Christian universalism with revelation, Drey turned the Enlightenment contrast between natural religion and historical-positive religion on its head. Like Schleiermacher, he challenged the Deists' association of Christian claims of historical revelation with sectarian conflict. The concept of revelation now comes to signify the providential divine power working to overcome sectarian division.[69] There are two features of Drey's thought in particular that enable him to invert the arguably more intuitive correspondences that the

Deists had posited between natural religion and universality, on the one hand, and revealed religion and particularity, on the other. The first of these features is Drey's understanding of historical revelation as the continuation of God's original creative activity. Inspired by Schelling's conception of the finite world as the self-expression of the Absolute, Drey redescribes God's original act of creation as a form of self-manifestation or revelation and, conversely, historical revelation as God's ongoing creative activity in the world.[70] Drey's fusion of the concepts of creation and revelation circumvents the Deists' strategy of dichotomizing the concept of nature (i.e., the product of God's creative activity) and historical revelation in order to isolate the latter for criticism.[71] The second feature of Drey's thought that was intended to counteract the Deist effort to discredit the concept of revealed religion was his "scientific" (*wissenschaftlich*) method of theology. According to Drey, the aim of the science of theology is to discern the intelligibility and necessity of the historically given.[72] This understanding of the task of theology presupposes a belief in divine Providence, that is, the conviction that certain historical events unfold in accordance with a purpose that is, at least in principle, intelligible.[73] To the extent that this project is successfully executed, it redeems the concept of historically given or "positive" religion from its association with arbitrariness and contingency—precisely the associations upon which the tendentious Deist contrast between natural religion and positive religion rested.[74]

Understanding the relationship between world religion and national religion in terms of the distinction between the divine and human allows Drey to vindicate the Church from its long history of strife and persecution. The central divine "idea" to be discerned in history in accordance with the scientific method of theology is that of the Kingdom of God (*Reich Gottes*). The Kingdom of God is the great eschatological society in which all persons will be united without regard for ethnicity or race.[75] This divinely willed society transcending the ethnic and the political is only partially and incipiently realized in the Catholic Church.[76] Like Schleiermacher's true church, Drey's *Reich Gottes* is not found in an unmixed, pure state. Drey is painfully aware that the historical church fails to live up to the divine ideal that it nevertheless embodies.[77] And yet he can attribute the elements of antagonism and coercion that hinder the realization of the Kingdom of God to a fallen human nature. The divisive and authoritarian aspects of the Church are therefore merely contingent and—in principle—removable adulterations of Christianity's divine essence.

Drey's conviction that Christianity embodies a divine "idea" that is heterogeneous with the naturalistic aspects of religion places Christianity, strictly speaking, outside the reach of comparison with the other religions, which, as we have seen, represent so many varieties of merely natural, national religion.[78]

Before the categories of national religion and world religion could be used for comparative purposes, they first had to be uncoupled from those of natural religion and revealed religion. This uncoupling took place in the latter part of the nineteenth century, and it established the field of comparative religion or, as it was also sometimes called, comparative theology.

Clarke's Comparative Theology

The work of the American Unitarian theologian James Freeman Clarke (1810–1888) exemplifies the comparative theology of the late nineteenth century. In the introductory chapter of his work, *Ten Great Religions: An Essay in Comparative Theology* (1871), Clarke sets forth the two methodological principles that together define this new theological discipline. The first of these is the classification of religions as either "catholic" (by which he simply means "universal") or "ethnic," a classificatory schema that reproduces Drey's distinction between world religion and national religion.[79] The second methodological principle is the concomitant rejection of the traditional categories of revealed religion and natural religion to describe Christianity's relations with other religions.[80]

Together these two principles establish comparative theology as a new form of theology combining a Christian apologetic task with a comparative method. The distinction between ethnic religion and catholic religion frames what for Clarke is the fundamental question of Christian apologetics:

> Is Christianity, as taught by Jesus, intended by God to be the religion of the human race? Is it only one among natural religions? Is it to be superseded in its turn by others, or is it the one religion which is to unite all mankind?[81]

The proposition that Clarke here somewhat disingenuously presents in the form of an open question is, of course, none other than Drey's notion of Christianity as *the* world religion. Unlike Drey, however, Clarke professes to establish this claim comparatively—that is to say, scientifically[82]—rather than dogmatically. In order to do so, he has to dissociate the notion of Christianity as the world religion from its traditional claims to a supernatural origin. Clarke clearly recognizes that the classification of religions into natural and supernatural precludes a fair and honest comparison of their respective teachings, or, as Clarke puts it, these categories "assume at the beginning what ought to come out at the end, if it comes out at all."[83] With its rejection of the category of revealed religion, comparative theology hearkens back to the concept of natural religion and the Deism of the previous century.[84] In fact, what comparative theology does is to project the Deistic distinction between true Christianity and the warring Christian sects onto the relation between Christianity and the religions of the world.

The two claims forming the twin pillars of comparative theology—first, that Christianity is the true world religion, or, as Clarke puts it, that it "possesses all the aptitudes which fit it to be the religion of the human race"[85]; second, that this claim derives from a fair and impartial study of the religions—appear rather incongruous from our present historical vantage point. And yet, as I argued in the previous chapter, these two claims appear to cohere with one another when seen from the perspective of a nineteenth-century liberal Christian committed to the project of depoliticizing Christianity. From such a perspective, Christian universalism and science each represent, albeit in different ways, the antithesis to the principle of political antagonism. As for the former, we have already seen in our discussion of Drey how the contrast of world religion and national religion encodes the idea of an essence of religion transcending attitudes of religious chauvinism and sectarian hostility. For its part, science, understood as a method of inquiry yielding a body of propositions demanding universal assent, was—and still is—regarded as the very antithesis of traditional theological discourse with its intractable controversies. Thus it is by virtue of sharing the same "constitutive other" that a universalist theology of Christian fulfillment could be sincerely thought to cohere with the ideal of scientific inquiry. This coherence could also be expressed in positive terms. Clarke's contemporary George Matheson expresses the deep affinity between liberal Christianity and scientific inquiry in terms of the concept of unity. Like the secret principle linking the outwardly incongruous terms of a Vedic homology, the concept of unity links the idea of science, understood as the search for universal laws underlying the diverse phenomena of nature, and liberal Christianity, understood to embody a universal essence of religion underlying differences in creed.[86]

Today's reader, of course, is not likely to accept at face value Clarke's claim that his comparative theology is simply a straightforward application of the scientific method to the study of religion—one that just happens to yield conclusions favorable to its author's understanding of Christianity. He or she clearly recognizes that comparison here functions as little more than a rhetorical device fostering a misrecognition of Clarke's theological claims as the natural and unavoidable outcome of an objective comparison of the world's religions.[87]

Clarke's argument begins rather innocently with the uncontroversial observation that some religions have spread outside their original cultural contexts while others have not. Most of the religions that have appeared in human history have been of the latter, "ethnic" variety, that is, they have been closely bound up with the identities of specific peoples or nations—the religion of ancient Greece, Brahmanism in India, Confucianism in China, and so on. A select few, however, have managed to extend their influence beyond the confines of a particular people or nation. Most writers at the time recognized three religions as fitting this definition of what Clarke calls catholic religions and others universal or world religions: Islam, Buddhism, and—of course—Christianity. While conceding all three to have "catholic tendencies," Clarke quickly sets about to challenge the universalist claims of the first two.[88] His argument against the putative understanding of Islam as a catholic religion appeals to the old Christian apologetic representation of Islam as a "religion of the sword." Employing an argument that was entirely typical of the time, Clarke argues that whatever conversions Islam managed to win outside of Arabia were illegitimate because they were achieved through coercive rather than persuasive means.[89] Or, as Clarke himself puts it, Islam failed to attain universality "because it sought to make subjects rather than converts."[90] Islam's alleged recourse to brute force in spreading outside the confines of the Arabic peoples betrays its lack of the essential quality of a true world religion, namely, a capacity to meet the religious needs of humanity.[91] And should this argument fall short of undermining Islam's claim to universality, Clarke has another ready and waiting to fill the gap: whatever genuinely universal qualities are conceded to Islam are to be credited to the Jewish and Christian materials it managed to appropriate.[92] By characterizing Islam as an unoriginal imitator of Christianity, a motif that reaches back to the medieval depiction of Mohammed as a false prophet or imposter, Islam can be harmlessly included among the world religions without threatening what, as we shall see, will be Christianity's exclusive claim to the title.[93]

As for Buddhism, Clarke argues that this religion fails to achieve true catholicity because it remains, despite its international reach, confined to a single "race," namely, the Mongol.[94] What Clarke has done with this argument is simply to "move the goal posts," so to speak, by making a transcendence of the broader category of race, rather than ethnicity and nationality, the criterion of "catholicity."[95] And should finessing the definition of universal or catholic religion in this manner fail to convince, the Christian apologist always has recourse to the argument that Buddhism is not a religion at all, but rather a mere "philosophy," thereby rendering theologically irrelevant any universality it has managed to attain.[96]

We are left, then, with the predictable conclusion that only Christianity is a true "catholic" religion, that is, Christianity is the one religion that, by virtue of its inherent qualities, is entitled to be the religion of humanity. Clarke's comparative theology thus ends up where Drey's apologetic begins, with a dogmatic claim of Christian absolutism. It would appear, then, that a normative-dogmatic claim has insinuated itself into an ostensibly scientific classification between national religions and missionary religions. In this way, Clarke's comparative theology serves as a textbook example of a rhetoric of naturalization, that is, of a discourse that represents a highly partial claim as one that is natural and incontrovertible.

On closer inspection, however, we discover that the initial categories of ethnic and catholic religion are not nearly as innocent as they first appear. It is not the case that Clarke has simply misused a set of valid scientific categories by putting them in the service of a partisan theological agenda. The categories are themselves deeply tendentious. A normative, absolutist claim is implicit in the very concept of "world religion" or "universal religion." As C. P. Tiele observed, "strictly speaking, there can be no more than one universal or world religion."[97] As a category of one member, the concept of world religion anticipates the conclusion that there is but one world religion. But the category of world religion may be tendentious in an even more radical sense than suggested by Tiele's logical point. When we recall the genealogy of the categorical distinction between world religion and national religion in the problematic of isolating an essence of religion from its political accretions, we see that the world religion is not simply one, albeit superior, type of religion, but rather religion itself in its essence. As we have seen, the world religion/national religion distinction encodes Schleiermacher's distinction between the essence of religion and its political adulterations. The national religions, qua national, are not, properly speaking, religions at all. Rather they represent the political dross, the attitudes of in-group chauvinism and out-group hostility, that graft themselves onto genuine religious sentiment and thereby corrupt it. In the final analysis, then, the classification of the religions into catholic and ethnic, like the dogmatic classification of supernatural and natural religion that Clarke rejects,[98] boils down to the age-old apologetic dichotomy between true religion and false religion. The categories of catholic religion and ethnic religion are no less dogmatic, then, than those of revealed religion and natural religion. The only difference is that with the notion of Christianity as the world religion, Christian absolutism takes on a curiously ironic form: essentially what this notion says is that Christianity—or, to be more precise, a liberal interpretation of Christianity[99]—is superior to all other forms of religion because it has transcended the political principle of religious rivalry—a claim that is itself an expression of religious rivalry.

Even at the time, doubts were expressed concerning the scientific usefulness of the categories of universal religion and national religion. In his classic

1884 encyclopedia article on the classification of religions, Tiele is forced to acknowledge a normative, theological sense to the concept of universal or world religion.[100] In order to salvage the national religion/universal religion schema for scientific use, he proposes an abandonment of the term "world" or "universal" religion in favor of "universalistic" religion, the "-ic" suffix conveying the idea of relativity that was supposed to suppress the normative-theological sense of "universal/world religion."[101] And yet, as the tendentious remarks on Buddhism and Islam later on in the very same article suggest, the proposed terminological adjustment was powerless to prevent the intrusion of normative theological judgments into this supposedly neutral classification.

The Transition from Christian Universalism to Religious Pluralism

Tiele's acknowledgment of the pitfalls of the classification of religions into universal and national foreshadows its demise early in the twentieth century. A symbolic marker for this important watershed in the modern study of religion is Ernst Troeltsch's well-known late essay, "The Place of Christianity among the World Religions" (1923). In it, Troeltsch reflects critically on the position he had earlier held on the question of Christianity's claim of absolute validity, a position which he notes had strong affinities with that set forth in Abraham Kuenen's *National and Universal Religions* (1882).[102] He confesses that he is no longer able to justify the basis he (and Kuenen) had earlier claimed for Christianity's superiority over against its rivals, namely, a capacity to transcend the limits of a particular cultural or civilizational matrix. Christianity, he now concedes, is indissolubly wedded to European civilization.[103] For Troeltsch, Christian absoluteness can no longer be based on the claim that Christianity is the universal religion in any objective, empirical sense.[104]

Another important event heralding the transition from Christian universalism to the discourse of religious pluralism that was to replace it was the 1893 World Parliament of Religions in Chicago. What was intended as a demonstration of Christianity's spirit of charity and magnanimity—and thus of its superiority over the religions it deigned to recognize and honor—instead provided a compelling spectacle of religious diversity that would ultimately betray those apologetic intentions.[105] This vision of religious plurality implicitly called into question the distinction between national religions and universal religions forming the basis of the universalist fulfillment theology that the parliament was intended to promote. Thus in an announcement that would soon prove to be prophetic for the study of religion, the Rabbi Emil Hirsch declared at the conclusion of the conference that "[t]he day of national religions is past. The God of the universe speaks to all mankind."[106]

In keeping with the parliament's display of religious pluralism, the classification of religions into national and world religions gave way, in the early decades of the twentieth century, to the familiar notion of seven to ten "world religions." This emergence of the modern pluralist conception of the religions marks a sudden and curious reversal in the nineteenth century tendency to restrict the number of world religions by revoking the universal status of the putatively universal religions of Buddhism and Islam. Now the tendency is to expand the number of world religions in what J. Z. Smith calls a gesture of "pluralistic etiquette."[107] The formerly national religions of Judaism, Hinduism, and the religions of China and Japan are now to be included among the world religions.

Ostensibly this turn from universalism to pluralism marks a shift from, as Tomoko Masuzawa puts it, "the highly selective and frankly evaluative sense (universal religions as opposed to national or ethnic religions) to the avowedly neutral and inclusive sense (any major living religion of the world)."[108] And yet, there is a sense in which the later, more inclusive sense of the term—paradoxically—marks the complete triumph of an evaluative sense over one that was more neutral and descriptive. As we saw in the previous section, the concept of "world religion" originally combined—or better, conflated—two distinct senses, namely, the normative, theological notion of the one religion best equipped to meet the religious needs of all humanity, on the one hand, and the more neutral, empirical notion of a religion that had spread beyond the confines of a particular nation or people, on the other. Though the concepts of world religion and national religion may indeed be unsalvageable as viable descriptive categories, inextricably bound up as they are with normative commitments, we must nevertheless acknowledge that they contained a descriptive element. The discourse of comparative theology, in fact, counted on this descriptive element in order to be rhetorically effective. Now it is precisely this descriptive, empirical sense that has been effaced in the gesture of pluralistic etiquette described by Smith, as evidenced by the characterization of Judaism, the original model of a national religion,[109] as a world religion. When the concept of national religion falls out of currency, the concept of world religion loses its vital link with its original contrasting term, the concept, that is, in relation to which it derived its determinate, logical meaning. Detached from its proper contrasting term, "world religion" ceases to be informative; it becomes little more than a quasi-emotive expression of recognition and respect. Once the designation "world religion" becomes a more or less direct expression of the liberal attitudes of tolerance and respect toward a religion—attitudes that comparativists, including, of course, the comparative theologians of the previous century, had always espoused—it must now be extended to all those religions that one claims to tolerate and respect, including those previously designated as "national" or "ethnic."[110]

We see, then, that when the term "world religion" is uncoupled from the contrasting concept of national religion, the evaluative sense of the term, which had previously coexisted with a more neutral, informative sense in an ambiguous relation, now comes decisively to the fore. But this evaluative sense is promptly sublimated as the term is extended to those religions formerly classified as national or ethnic. The term "world religions" henceforth becomes equivalent to "religions of the world." With this sublimation, the term acquires a semblance of neutrality. And yet, even in this sublimated form, the concept of "world religions" remains implicated in the hegemonic relations that obtain between a now-globalized Western culture and much of the non-Western world. The contemporary pluralistic understanding of "world religions" in the sense of "religions of the world" still preserves an intrinsic reference to the history, identity, and interests of Western civilization. A world religion is, in the words of J. Z. Smith, "a religion like ours,..., a tradition that has achieved sufficient power and numbers to enter our history to form it, interact with it, or thwart it."[111] The contemporary concept of world religion still marks a contrast with the innumerable local or indigenous, "no-name" traditions that have yet to win recognition from a hegemonic global culture still centered in the "West."[112] We see, then, that the contemporary pluralist discourse of "world religions" preserves essentially the same ambiguous relation between an ostensibly neutral, nonpolitical sense ("religions of the world") and an evaluative, inherently political one ("world religions" as opposed to indigenous religions) that we saw in the nineteenth-century concept of world religion. With the transition from nineteenth-century universalism to twentieth-century pluralism, a new equilibrium point between these two senses is reached, but little more than that.[113]

Masuzawa concludes her genealogical analysis of contemporary world-religions discourse with the judgment that "there is no ideological disjuncture between the theological discourse of traditional Christendom and the world religions discourse of today's multicultural world."[114] Christian universalism survives in the contemporary notion of a plurality of "world religions" founded upon a putative unity of religious experience.[115] According to Masuzawa, the form that Christian universalism takes in the twentieth century embodies two strategies that Troeltsch employs in his attempt to reconcile the absolutist claims of Christianity with the principle of historical relativity—the principle on the basis of which he was eventually forced to abandon the idea of Christianity as a universal religion. The first of these strategies is to expand the target of the historical challenge to include "religion in general" and not just Christianity.[116] The second is to find a refuge for Christian absolutism on the level of immediate religious experience, a domain supposedly safely beyond the reach of the principle of historical relativity.[117] Troeltsch's dual strategy exemplifies the larger process by which Christian universalism is transmuted into the contemporary discourse of religious pluralism. Christian universalism goes underground, so to speak, seeking refuge from the relativizing principle of historicity in the sphere of personal experience and concealing its Christian provenance through a strategy of generalization.[118]

The usually obscure link between the Christian universalism of the nineteenth century and the experientialist pluralism of the twentieth is clearly visible in the work of one of the few scholars to carry the categories of national religion and universal religion deep into the twentieth century, the phenomenologist of religion Gustav Mensching.[119] Mensching's work provides a rare glimpse of the crucial intermediate phase in a transition that was elsewhere sudden and nearly imperceptible.[120] To be specific, his conception of universal religion elucidates the logical connection between the nineteenth-century concept of a universal religion, on the one hand, and the concept of personal religious experience forming the basis of the religious pluralism of the twentieth, on the other.

Mensching correlates the distinction between national (or, as he prefers, "ethnic") religions and universal religions to the sociological distinction between *Gemeinschaft* and *Gesellschaft*, respectively. Thus ethnic religions correspond to situations in which the group has priority over the individual.[121] Their chief concern is with preserving the unity and identity of the particular community. Universal religions, by contrast, address the religious needs of individuals. In them "the individual stands as the carrier of the religion at the focal point."[122] In other words, universal religions differ essentially from ethnic religions in that they are rooted in a direct, personal relationship between the individual and the divine.[123] This idea of a personal relationship with the divine bypassing any intermediate, "ethnic" form of collective identity brings us to the threshold of the full-blown pluralism of W. C. Smith, according to whom a generic concept of personal "faith" underlies the manifold expressions of religious belief and practice. Mensching's experientially grounded concept of universal religion and Smith's concept of generic faith each represent a kind of *coincidentia oppositorum* in which liberal individualism coincides with a universalist humanism, more particularistic forms of group identity having precipitated out of the mix, as it were.

Mensching's work provides exemplary support for the thesis that the categories of universal religion and ethnic religion encode the liberal project of depoliticizing religion. His interpretation of these categories places the political element of religion squarely on the side of the ethnic religions. Their overriding concern with maintaining the identity of the group at all costs is the source of religious intolerance and authoritarianism. Ethnic religions embody the principle of what Mensching terms "formal intolerance," that is, the suppression of views solely on the basis of their consequences for the unity of the group without regard for their intrinsic truth value. Since what is socially expedient does not always coincide with what is objectively true, ethnic religions cannot rely on persuasive means to unify the group. A reliance on some degree of coercion is therefore inevitable in ethnic religions.[124] By contrast, universal religion is able to make a clean break with authoritarianism because it renounces any political concern with maintaining the outward form of a particular community.[125] The form of religious community corresponding to universal religion is a purely voluntary association.[126] Nor does universal religion have any need to suppress ethnic religion through force. In addressing its message to the individual, universal religion encounters no competition from ethnic religion. Because the latter is unable to meet the religious needs of individuals, it tends to wither away once universal religion appears on the scene.[127]

Positing an essential difference between ethnic and universal religion allows Mensching to interpret the political features of historical Christianity as adventitious accretions to a universalist essence, a strategy that should be very familiar by now. He notes a regressive tendency of universal religion to take on features of ethnic religion as its members cede responsibility for their salvation to an institutional body.[128] The pronounced "routinization of charisma" theme in Mensching's work gives expression to a thinly veiled anti-Catholic polemic.[129] The unmistakably Protestant character of Mensching's concept of universal religion provides exemplary support for the argument that universalist theologies often fail, despite their pretensions to the contrary, to transcend the particular perspectives of their proponents.

George Lindbeck and the Postliberal Turn

As exemplified by the development of Troeltsch's thinking on the relation between history and theology, liberal theology came to invest more in the concept of personal religious experience as the idea of an objective basis to its universalist claims became increasingly untenable in light of historical criticism. The tradition of liberal theology found itself increasingly relying upon the idea of an irreducible and originary experience of the divine in order to prop up the sagging ideology of liberal universalism, the ideology through which it continued to assert its transcendence over the political. Clearly, the liberal theological tradition had a great deal riding on the concept of religious experience. This reliance probably explains why experiential foundationalism persisted in theological circles deep into the twentieth century, long after historians, anthropologists, and sociologists had recognized the extent to which religious experience, like human experience in general, is shaped by cultural and linguistic factors.[130] With the widening of the gap between theological and non-theological approaches to the study of religion, it was probably only a matter of time before someone figured out how to reconcile a "cultural-linguistic" approach to religion with the particular demands of theology.[131] Such a breakthrough came with the publication of George Lindbeck's *The Nature of Doctrine* (1984), which provided a compelling alternative to the ascendant "experiential-expressivist" approach to the study of religion and theology.[132] Against the "expressivist" tendency to regard a core experience of the self as the creative source of religious discourse and practice, Lindbeck, drawing from the cultural anthropology of Clifford Geertz and the sociology of Peter Berger (among others), presents a theory of religion and doctrine emphasizing the role of the outward features of a religion—its doctrines, sacred narratives, and liturgical practices—in shaping the personal religious experience of its adherents.[133] With genealogical roots in the sociological tradition of Weber and Durkheim,[134] Lindbeck's theory draws an implicit analogy between religious formation and primary socialization.

One might think that Lindbeck's rejection of experiential foundationalism, the final stronghold of liberal universalism, would finally lead to an acknowledgment of the political as an integral part of religion, thus bringing to a close the liberal project of depoliticizing religion. Such a conclusion suggests itself when we look at Lindbeck's theory in terms of Mensching's categories of ethnic religion and universal religion. Lindbeck's emphasis on religious community, and his analogy between religious formation and primary socialization in particular, implies a positive revalorization of Mensching's concept of ethnic religion, which, as we have seen, embodies the political dimension of religion. Religious socialization depends on a well-integrated community whose formation and maintenance would seem to presuppose a political moment of social exclusion.[135]

Lindbeck, however, stops short of recognizing the political as a constitutive dimension of religion, despite affirming aspects of religion that would seem to presuppose it. Perhaps the most striking example of such an aspect of religion that Lindbeck affirms while at the same time refusing to concede its "political" presuppositions is sectarianism. In order to forestall the erosion of Christian identity that he believes threatens Christian churches in an increasingly de-Christianized cultural milieu, Lindbeck calls upon Christians to form small, mutually supportive groups in which they can resist the relativizing pressures of cultural accommodation. Christianity's survival in a post-Christian world, Lindbeck predicts, may depend on Christians banding together in enclaves where they can maintain a distinctively Christian way of life.[136] Such Lindbeckian enclaves foster the kind of social cohesion that is necessary for their members to cultivate the habits of thought and action of a distinctively Christian worldview. But lest one imagine that in advocating a kind of Christian sectarianism he is countenancing the kind of militancy and divisiveness that one typically associates with religious sects, Lindbeck is quick to distinguish the kind of benign, "sociological" or "ecumenical" sectarianism that he has in mind from the reactionary and divisive "theological" sectarianism of religious fringe groups.[137] Lindbeck's Christian enclaves affirm a mainstream, ecumenical interpretation of Christianity and are radically inclusive with regard to race, education, and socioeconomic status.[138] There are reasons to doubt, however, whether these two features of Linbeckian enclaves, namely, their mainstream, ecumenical theology and their social inclusivity, adequately distinguish them from fundamentalist sects. First of all, "mainstream" is only a relative concept, such that whatever theological outlook happens to be adopted by the majority of Christians becomes, by definition, mainstream.[139] Thus, if the fundamentalists were to "inherit the Christian name"[140] in a de-Christianized future, their theological outlook would become, ipso facto, mainstream, and in this new context even "ecumenical," provided the fundamentalist enclaves maintained a basic level of agreement among themselves on theological matters. Furthermore, schismatic, fundamentalist sects are often as inclusive with regard to ethnicity, race, and/or social status as mainline churches.[141] Ultimately the difference between Lindbeck's enclaves and those of a fundamentalist sort has to do with whether the sect in question is actively and inherently oppositional or only reluctantly and accidentally so. The sectarianism Lindbeck endorses is defensive in nature. That is, Lindbeck's sects are primarily concerned with preserving their way of life against forces that actively threaten their survival from without. We can infer from Lindbeck's argument for ecumenical sectarianism that whatever conflict his enclaves experience vis-à-vis the wider culture is the unintended by-product of an innocent effort preserve a traditional way of life against the intrusive pressures of cultural assimilation.[142] The essentially defensive nature of Lindbeck's enclaves contrasts with the inherently oppositional and reactive nature of their fundamentalist counterparts.[143] The sectarianism Lindbeck endorses, then, is a sectarianism stripped of its connotations of active antagonism and oppositional identity—in short, of the political.[144]

Another characteristically "political" aspect of religion that Lindbeck affirms while stopping short of conceding the principle of social antagonism is doctrine, the central topic of his book. Lindbeck makes several observations about doctrine that point to its political function in mobilizing group identity through social opposition. He notes that doctrines can only be understood in terms of what they oppose, that doctrinal significance does not always coincide with what is abidingly significant in terms of Christian belief and practice, and that doctrines are often vaguely formulated so as to be amenable to range of interpretations.[145] Taken together, these observations suggest that the primary way in which doctrines establish Christian identity is by drawing contrasts with rival communities. More specifically, doctrines select certain points of intercommunal difference as being decisive for a group's identity while at the same time glossing over that group's internal differences. The regulative theory of doctrine that Lindbeck presents as a solution to the ecumenical problematic of doctrinal "reconciliation without capitulation," however, fails to acknowledge (though, admittedly, does not exclude) this differential, political function of doctrine. Lindbeck's understanding of doctrines as rules of communal speech and conduct has the effect (whether intended or not) of diverting attention away from their role in establishing group identity by differentiating a group from its rivals. Put differently, by focusing one-sidedly on the way in which doctrines merely regulate, as opposed to constitute, a Christian way of life, the regulative theory gives the misleading impression that the way of life that doctrines regulate has no intrinsic relation to what goes on outside.

What allows Lindbeck to emphasize the communal and doctrinal aspects of religion without conceding the principle of the political is the concept of culture that is implicit in his "cultural-linguistic" theory of religion. Lindbeck's understanding of a religion as "a comprehensive interpretive scheme" or "semiotic system," a conception that he largely appropriates from Clifford Geertz, presupposes the classic anthropological concept of culture as a self-contained, coherent system of belief and practice. This conception of culture as a closed system with its own intrinsic identity, a conception that has retained a remarkable staying power in contemporary discourse despite the many cogent criticisms that have been leveled against it,[146] lends a measure of plausibility to the oxymoronic notion of an inherently non-oppositional, "ecumenical" variety of sectarianism. And with respect to the question of doctrine, the implicit understanding of the religious community to be doctrinally regulated as a self-contained and implicitly reified[147] cultural formation has the effect of subtly eliding the question of how that community is constituted in the first place, the explanation for which would bring the political-oppositional dimension of doctrine to the fore.[148]

There is yet a third respect in which the classic anthropological concept of culture contained in Geertz's understanding of religion spares Lindbeck the obligation to confront the question of the political, and it is the one that is most directly relevant to the narrative I am relating in this chapter. The notion of religions as self-contained "cultural systems" allows Lindbeck to abandon the liberal presupposition of an underlying unity of religions without sacrificing the liberal principles of interreligious tolerance and respect. The understanding of a religion as an essentially self-contained cultural system implies a Herderian vision of religious plurality in which each religious system embodies its own characteristic principle and possesses its own integrity. Lindbeck argues that such a conception fosters the liberal goal of non-prosyletizing interreligious dialogue as well as, if not better than, liberal theologies presupposing a common basis of the religions, whether understood in predominantly metaphysical or experiential terms.[149] There are two implications of this notion of a common basis to the religions that interfere with the goal of interreligious dialogue. First, the presumed common basis or essence is better exemplified in some religions rather than others. In abandoning this notion, then, Lindbeck's postliberalism discourages those invidious comparisons that so often serve to justify subtle and not-so-subtle forms of prosyletization.[150] Second, as Kathryn Tanner observes, the presumption of a common basis of the religions uncritically assumes that similarity is a precondition of religious respect.[151] By abandoning this presumption, Lindbeck's cultural-linguistic understanding of religion clears the way for a genuine respect of religious difference. In this way, postliberalism arguably is in a better position to promote honest and productive forms of interreligious dialogue than is liberal universalism (in either its inclusivist or pluralist forms).[152] In the final analysis, though, Lindbeck's view of "the religions" and that of his liberal pluralist adversaries look rather similar, particularly for two theological outlooks that are supposed to be diametrically opposed. Both claim to acknowledge and affirm religious plurality while eschewing antagonistic relations between the religions.

We have seen, then, that Lindbeck's postliberalism remains, despite its sharp critique of the tradition of liberal universalism, within the broader framework of Enlightenment project of depoliticizing religion. The classic anthropological concept of culture that he appropriates allows him to affirm the communal and doctrinal aspects of religion without having to acknowledge their political presuppositions. With respect to the issue of depoliticization, Lindbeck's postliberalism marks a significant shift in strategy but not a fundamental change in aim. One way of making this point would be to note that the "post" in "postliberalism," like the "post" in similar locutions like "postmodernism" and "postcolonialism," signifies an ambiguous relation with the term it modifies. Postliberalism's announcement of a break with the liberal tradition of theology conceals an underlying continuity of purpose between the two.

Kathryn Tanner's Relational Theory of Christian Identity

The classical anthropological concept of culture that underwrites Lindbeck's postliberal project has scarcely held up better than the experiential foundationalism that he opposes. Against the classical anthropological conception of cultures as self-contained and bounded totalities, each with its own distinctive identity, more recent anthropological and cultural theory views what are conventionally called cultures as contingent social formations that are relationally formed and maintained in a continual process of appropriation, contestation, and negotiation with their surroundings. Cultural identity is no longer understood in terms of a set of intrinsic properties shared by the people socialized into a certain way of life but is rather theorized as something that is actively constructed on the basis of social differences that come to be recognized in the course of social interaction.[153]

In her book *Theories of Culture*, Kathryn Tanner incorporates these recent critiques of the classical anthropological conception of culture into a compelling critique of postliberalism. She argues that the postliberal concern with preserving the distinctiveness of a Christian way of life against outside influence presupposes the very notion that recent cultural theory has shown to be so problematic, namely, that of intrinsic cultural identity.[154] At the same time, she draws creatively from postmodern culture theory to construct a theological account of Christian identity that challenges the assumption, shared by both postliberal and liberal, "correlationist" theologians alike, that Christian identity must be based on something standing apart from Christianity's relations with the wider culture. On both sociological and theological grounds, she argues that a Christian way of life should be understood as internally constituted by the cultural materials that Christians critically appropriate from outside. Against the commonplace assumption that Christian identity is based on an ostensible set of cultural properties intrinsic to a Christian way of life, she argues that a sense of Christian identity is something that emerges out of the distinctive use that Christians make of the beliefs and practices of others.[155] Christian identity is "essentially relational" in the sense that it is constituted by the active relations Christianity maintains with other ways of life.

One might think that this criticism of the classical anthropological concept of culture—the concept which, as we have seen, enabled Lindbeck to emphasize the communal and doctrinal aspects of religion without having to acknowledge their political presuppositions—would finally clear the way for an acknowledgment of the political dimension of religion. Tanner's thesis that Christian identity is essentially relational would seem to oblige her to acknowledge an antagonistic element in Christian identity. Indeed, she appears to do precisely that when she writes that "[a] kind of apologetics or polemics with other cultures is internal, then, to the very construction of Christian sense."[156] And yet, while she duly acknowledges that oppositional relations are logically included in a relational theory of Christian identity,[157] in practice she qualifies that acknowledgment to the point of suppressing the antagonistic, political dimension of Christian identity. While she readily acknowledges opposition with respect to a set of particularly repugnant practices—slavery, infant sacrifice, Nazi genocide, and so on[158]—there is no indication that she is willing to concede what Mensching calls "formal intolerance," that is, opposition toward a belief or practice not because of something inherently objectionable about it, but rather simply because it is non-Christian. A refusal to concede formal opposition can be inferred from one of the arguments she makes against the understanding of Christian identity in terms of a cultural boundary. She argues that the situational nature of cultural boundaries—that what marks a cultural boundary in one context may not in another—disqualifies them from forming the basis of Christian identity.[159] In other words, what argues against a theory of Christian identity in terms of cultural boundaries is that markers of cultural difference do not always line up with matters of central importance for a Christian way of life.[160] What is uniquely Christian in a particular cultural context—she gives the example of Indian Christians eating beef to distinguish themselves from their Hindu neighbors[161]—may not coincide with what is most important in Christianity. Tanner's implicit restriction of legitimate opposition to matters of internal, as opposed to merely external, importance to Christian practice[162] all but excludes the "us" versus "them" discourses that constitute the political dimension of Christian identity. In the final analysis, then, she has not really conceded the antagonistic, "political" dimension of Christian identity after all.

There thus appears to be a tension between, on the one hand, Tanner's insistence, against postliberalism's presumption of intrinsic cultural identity, on the essentially relational nature of Christian identity and, on the other, her reluctance to recognize a legitimate role for oppositional discourses in the formation of Christian identity. We might shed some light on this tension in Tanner's theory of Christian identity, I suggest, by noting a parallel tension in Edward Said's well-known critique of orientalism. According to James Clifford, Said at times speaks of the binary oppositions and essentializing generalizations of orientalist discourse as masking or distorting the underlying human reality of the Orient. When he attacks orientalism's essentialism and its tendency to dichotomize cultures, Said appeals, albeit tentatively and vaguely, to a tradition of liberal humanism and individualism, to universal human experiences and values that are ideologically occluded, abridged, or otherwise distorted by orientalist discourse.[163] Elsewhere, however, he shifts to a more radical line of criticism that takes aim not at certain representations that distort what they purport to represent, but rather at the notion of representation as such, specifically, the duality between discourse and reality implicit in the concept of representation.[164] In this more radical mode of critique, which reflects the "anti-humanist" perspective of Michel Foucault, Said denies the existence of a "real Orient" beyond discourse and representation.[165] This tension in Said's work corresponds nearly exactly to the above-mentioned tension in Tanner's theory of Christian identity.[166] On the one hand, her thesis that Christian identity is essentially relational corresponds to the more radical modality of cultural critique that calls into question the positivistic dichotomy between discourse and reality. The relational character of cultural identity clearly indicates that cultural identity is a matter of discourse, including, of course, discourses of an oppositional nature. Tanner's "relationality" thesis embodies the postmodern critique of the commonsensical notion that cultural identity is based on a set of intrinsic, extra-discursive properties of persons and groups. On the other hand, Tanner qualifies this recognition of the relational nature of Christian identity with the more standard, characteristically Saidian critique of the invidious "dichotomous typifications" that groups use to define themselves over against their ostensible rivals. This implicit qualification of the relationality thesis effectively "depoliticizes" and neutralizes her account of Christian identity by quietly shifting attention away from the role of oppositional discourses in the formation of Christian identity. Almost by default, the cultural process of Christian identity formation becomes primarily a matter of the creative appropriation or "consumption" of the discourses and practices of others. As with the less radical side of Said's orientalism project, Tanner's anti-essentialist critique makes an implicit appeal to a tradition of liberal humanism and individualism. Nowhere is this appeal more apparent than in the argument, found in her earlier work, *The Politics of God*, that the Christian idea of respecting others as God's creatures undercuts the essentialisms and dichotomies of colonialist discourse.[167] Since "God creates each individual directly and not by way of any of the relations that he or she might have with others,"[168] the respect owed to a person as a creature of God takes precedence over any form of group identity which that person might have. This argument that the Christian doctrine of creation serves as an antidote to colonialist discourse trades on a kind of sociological nominalism according to which the differences among individual persons are more real than the differences among social groups.[169] Such a nominalistic presupposition underlies her programmatic thesis that a recognition of the differences among persons confounds the binary oppositions used to mobilize group identity.[170] The individualism implicit in Tanner's conception of creation at the same time implies a universalism: "The community of human beings owed to the rights due creatures of God is a community that includes all people."[171] This notion of the ideal Christian community in which a focus on the individual person coincides with a radical inclusivism recalls Mensching's concept of universal religion. More broadly, it evidences a lingering commitment to the tradition of liberal universalism, despite her rejection of the classic, foundationalist forms of pluralist theology. It would seem, then, that Tanner can evade the "political" implications of her recognition of the inherently relational nature of cultural identity only by making an implicit appeal to that tradition.

Concluding Remarks

Viewing Lindbeck and Tanner in terms of the problematic of depoliticizing religion reveals a curious parallelism between the two theologians. We saw that the former's critique of experiential foundationalism, the most recent incarnation of liberal universalism, placed him on the verge of acknowledging the political as an ineluctable dimension of religious commitment. And yet, Lindbeck finds refuge from the "political" implications of his postliberal project in the classic anthropological concept of culture and its presumption of intrinsic identity. When Tanner attacks that concept of culture, she finds herself in a curiously similar predicament. In her case, however, it was a lingering commitment to the tradition of liberal universalism that forestalled a break with the tradition of depoliticization. The apparent unwillingness of each of these theologians to take their respective critiques of two fundamental presuppositions in the modern project of depoliticization—a concept of an originary religious experience for the one, and a concept of culture as a self-enclosed social formation for the other—to their logical conclusion testifies to the power of the cultural assumptions and commitments that work against the acknowledgment of the principle of the political as an essential, ineluctable dimension of religious commitment. Such an acknowledgment appears to be the theological equivalent of dividing by zero; one can approach this singularity only asymptotically, as it were, whether from the side of liberal universalism or postliberal communitarianism. In the next chapter, however, I will argue that an evasion of the political becomes impossible when Tanner's relational theory of Christian identity is extended to a consideration of Christianity's relations with other religions.[172] On the basis of a critical yet appreciative appropriation of her account of Christian identity, I shall develop a model of comparative theology that reconciles an acknowledgment of the political as a constitutive element of religion with a continuing commitment to the liberal values pluralism and respect for religious difference.

3

From Apologetics to Comparison

Toward a Dialectical Model of Comparative Theology

A kind of apologetics or polemics with other cultures is internal, then, to the very construction of Christian sense. . . .

—Kathryn Tanner

In the preceding chapters, we have seen that the attempt to liberate religious commitment from exclusionary attitudes toward other communities often only results in more subtle and insidious forms of exclusion. The declaration of a break from a tradition of religious exclusion itself constitutes a "political" act of exclusion. This pattern, which I have termed, borrowing from Carl Schmitt, the "inescapability of the political," might lead one to conclude that the Enlightenment project of liberating religious commitment from attitudes of chauvinism and intolerance is ultimately a self-defeating one.

The aim of the present chapter is to challenge such a conclusion by developing a model of theology that acknowledges the ineluctability of the political in theology while at the same time refusing to concede religious intolerance, understood as a refusal to respect religious difference.[1] The theological model I propose is informed by work in political theory that addresses the parallel problem of reconciling recent critiques of classical liberalism with a commitment to pluralism. The work of two theorists in particular has influenced my approach to the problem of reconciling the political dimension of religious commitment with a genuine respect for religious difference.

The first of these influences is Chantal Mouffe's effort to rethink the idea of a pluralistic society in light of Carl Schmitt's critique of liberalism. Although Mouffe's leftist political orientation is diametrically opposed to Schmitt's authoritarianism, she largely accepts the latter's critique of liberalism. That critique begins with the thesis that democratic consensus presupposes a shared sense of social identity, a sense of "we." This sense of "we" in turn presupposes a contrast with a "them."[2] Classic liberalism, whose focus on individual rights presupposes a universalist humanism, refuses to recognize this basic principle of social-political reality. As a result, it is unable to acknowledge the exclusions by which it constitutes itself. We might add, parenthetically, that this incapacity to apprehend the political renders liberalism unable to mobilize itself effectively against the various fundamentalist and anti-liberal movements that threaten it from without.[3]

So far, Mouffe agrees with Schmitt's critique. She goes on to argue, however, that Schmitt fails to acknowledge one implication of this political or antagonistic dimension of social relations, namely, the contingent nature of those relations. Despite his recognition of the ineluctability of the political, Schmitt assumes that political and social identities are empirically given, that in the final analysis the "us" versus "them" distinction is a matter of recognizing already existing social borders.[4] He therefore conceives the political community as a homogeneous formation that is unable to accommodate pluralism without undermining its own integrity.[5] When one recognizes, however, that the political community owes its being to a political act of construction, then one can reconcile an acknowledgment of the ineluctability of the political with the idea of a pluralistic society. Once its contingency and mutability is recognized, the political frontier no longer has to be regarded as an external boundary separating a homogeneous people from a permanent "other," as Schmitt thought, but can be regarded instead as the site of an internal struggle for hegemony.[6] The "them," in other words, is now regarded as a political adversary in a pluralistic political community governed by an ethos of "agonistic respect." In Mouffe's vision of "agonistic pluralism," then, the opponent is considered "not as an enemy to be destroyed, but as an adversary whose existence is legitimate and must be tolerated."[7]

The possibility of transforming potential enemies into tolerated, even respected adversaries rests on a distinction between two moments in the formation of identity that finds particularly eloquent expression in the work of the second theorist who has influenced my approach to the problem of the political in theology, William Connolly. Connolly, who advocates a politics of agonistic pluralism very similar to Mouffe's, also emphasizes the relational nature of identity. In its first, formative moment, identity is mobilized on the basis of differences that come to be recognized in the course of social interaction.[8] Contrary to a common misconception, however, this differential aspect of identity is not inherently problematic. Problems arise only in a second moment, when the essentially relational and contingent nature of identity is disavowed by grounding it in a set of ostensibly inherent cultural properties. This drive to naturalize identity transforms a group's attitude toward the others in opposition to whom it defines itself. Because a group's belief in the intrinsic nature of its identity is threatened by the other upon whom its identity actually depends, such a group tends to assume a hostile attitude toward its proximate rivals.[9] To the extent that one regards one's identity as a natural given, one is apt to construe one's other(s) as somehow unnatural, as deviant.[10] This constitution of the other as deviant is the first and decisive step to dehumanizing them, justifying forms of behavior toward them that would not be permitted toward members of one's own community. Fortunately, however, this second, naturalizing moment in identity formation is neither necessary nor inevitable. The ideal of a democratic society whose inevitable conflicts are governed by an ethos of agonistic respect rests on the possibility of thwarting this naturalizing drive to "convert relations of difference into relations of otherness."[11]

Connolly's distinction between the differential formation of social identity, on the one hand, and its subsequent naturalization, on the other, represents the key to reconciling an acknowledgment of the political dimension of religious commitment with the principle of religious tolerance. The strategy I propose follows Connolly's analysis of identity in pinpointing the source of religious intolerance—again, understood as an unwillingness or an incapacity to respect religious difference—in the naturalization, not the differential formation, of religious identity. As we have just seen, it is only when a group seeks to repress the differences upon which its sense of identity essentially depends that it is tempted to construe the other as somehow deviant and therefore unworthy of respect. Having isolated the second moment in the constitution of religious identity as the locus of religious intolerance, one can safely acknowledge the political dimension of religious identity—the first moment—without conceding the intolerance issuing from the second. This strategy, in other words, shifts the point of critical intervention from the political or differential construction of religious identity to the ideological stabilization or naturalization of that identity.

Many Christian theologians, I suspect, would welcome Mouffe and Connolly's notion of agonistic pluralism as a promising basis for a theory of interreligious relations. Few, however, would be entirely comfortable with affirming the two presuppositions upon which this notion rests, namely, an acknowledgment of the relational and contingent nature of Christian identity, on the one hand, and an acknowledgment of a political moment of exclusion in the constitution of that identity, on the other. At the risk of overgeneralization, we might say that conservative-leaning theologians find it difficult to accept the first of these presuppositions, liberal-leaning theologians the second. The former group tends to adhere to an understanding of the identity-sustaining doctrines of the Christian faith as ontological truth claims, an understanding of doctrine that implicitly grounds Christian identity in an absolute, transcendent dimension of reality. This claim that Christian identity derives from first-order ontological truth claims is difficult to reconcile with an understanding of identity as essentially relational, constructed, and contingent.[12] Liberal theologians, for their part, while open in principle to the notion of relational identity, are nonetheless averse to conceding that Christian identity is founded on a political act of exclusion. To admit such a notion, it is thought, would leave the door open to the kind of unsavory polemics with rival religions and philosophies that offend against the principles of Christian inclusivity and charity.

It is therefore difficult to find a Christian theology that combines a rejection of a metaphysically grounded and implicitly essentialist conception of Christian identity with a willingness to concede the legitimacy of a political dimension of Christian commitment. Prima facie, the postliberal theology of George Lindbeck approaches this ideal with its rejection of a foundationalist (either cognitive or experiential) theory of doctrine and its emphasis on Christian particularism. And yet, as I argued in the previous chapter, postliberalism, despite its antifoundationalist view of religious knowledge and experience, retains the presumption of intrinsic identity. To that extent it fails to break from the paradigm of liberal depoliticization. Its communitarian perspective, no less than the liberal universalism it rejects, represents an evasion of the ineluctability of the political.[13]

Of the theological proposals with which I am familiar, the constructive theory of Christian identity that Kathryn Tanner sets forth in her book *Theories of Culture* comes closest to this ideal of a theology that rejects an essentialist conception of Christian identity while at the same time recognizing the political dimension of Christian commitment.[14] In other words, it is a theological model that embodies the twin presuppositions of the model of agonistic pluralism advocated by theorists like Mouffe and Connolly. As I shall argue below, Tanner's insistence on the essentially relational nature of Christian identity implies a political moment in the construction of identity. At the same time, her effort to deconstruct essentializing contrasts or "dichotomous typifications" between religious communities counters the tendency to naturalize that identity. Thus her theory of Christian identity anticipates the shift in strategy from depoliticization to denaturalization that I propose. It is for this reason that her theory of Christian identity serves as a fruitful starting point for our attempt to formulate a Christian theology that embodies this change in strategy.

It must be acknowledged, however, that Tanner does not really concede the principle of the political in her account of Christian identity.[15] As we saw in the previous chapter, she immediately qualifies the thesis that Christian identity is inherently relational with a critique of essentializing contrasts between cultural formations. This qualification effectively restricts the relational construction of Christian identity to what Tanner, following Michel de Certeau, calls a "creativity of cultural consumption," that is, the creative appropriation of cultural elements inhabiting the cultural spaces in which Christians attempt to work out a distinctive form of life.[16] By focusing her attention on what de Certeau calls the "tactical" dimension of cultural interaction, Tanner all but excludes another, "strategic" dimension of relational identity in which a boundary is drawn between an "us" and a "them."[17] The drawing of such a boundary tends to essentialize inasmuch as it is forced to suppress, at least in part, the internal diversity of the cultural formations being contrasted. It is thus by immediately qualifying a relational conception of Christian identity with a critique of essentialism that Tanner effectively suppresses the former's implication of a political moment of exclusion. One could perhaps say that the critique of essentialism presses in hard upon the thesis of relational identity, preventing her relational conception of Christian identity from revealing its political (in the Schmittian sense) contours.

The political dimension of Christian identity can no longer be suppressed, however, when a relational conception like Tanner's is extended to cultural formations recognized as specifically religious. As I shall argue below, when we enter into the realm of interreligious relations, the formation of Christian identity can no longer be understood primarily in terms of cultural consumption. The recognition of a set of cultural practices as religious presupposes a standpoint from which Christianity's relations to the external world can be managed, that is, Christian identity formation becomes strategic in de Certeau's sense. Some notion of an "us" standing over against a "them" becomes inevitable. The extension of Tanner's theory of Christian identity to the realm of interreligious relations reveals an irreducible tension between, on the one hand, the proposition that Christian identity is essentially relational and, on the other, the critique of dichotomous typification. In an interreligious context, a relational conception of Christian identity therefore takes on a dialectical character. That is to say, it implies a moment in which Christian identity is constructed politically through interreligious contrasts, and another in which those constructions are deconstructed.

Such a conception is precisely one that embodies the change in strategy I propose. That is to say, it is a strategy that shifts its critical focus from the political construction of identity to the ideological stabilization of identity. As these preliminary remarks on Tanner's theory suggest, such a theology will be interreligious in scope and dialectical in character. In the present chapter, I shall describe the two moments that constitute such a theology. To be specific, I first shall describe how Christian identity is constructed "politically" through apologetic contrasts with rival religious communities. Then I shall argue that cross-cultural comparison can be used to "de-essentialize" and partially deconstruct the oppositional contrasts constructed in the first, political moment of identity formation. Before I do either of those two things, however, I would like to examine Tanner's theory of Christian identity more closely, with the aim of showing that a political moment of exclusion is implicit in a relational theory of Christian identity.

The Political Moment in Tanner's Relational Theory of Christian Identity

Tanner develops her relational conception of Christian identity in the context of an effort to rethink theological method. Christian theology in the United States and Europe during the past one hundred years or so has been preoccupied with the question of Christianity's proper relation to the wider culture. Historically, this issue has split theologians into two camps.[18] On the one side are the proponents of the classic liberal project of bringing Christian claims in line with modern forms of knowledge and experience. The predominant concern of this group is to show the relevance of the Christian message to the questions and concerns of the modern world. On the other side are the heirs of the Neo-orthodox movement of Karl Barth. Their principal concern is preserving the distinctiveness of the Christian message against what they regard as liberalism's willingness to compromise that message by subjecting it to the alien standards of meaning and plausibility of the wider culture.[19] Tanner suggests that the debate between these two camps has reached an impasse.[20] The postliberal heirs of Neo-orthodoxy charge their liberal opponents with compromising the distinctiveness of the Christian message in a misguided quest for cultural relevance, while the latter accuse the postliberal camp of making that message culturally irrelevant in a dubious effort to secure ideological purity. The way the debate has evolved suggests that the twin demands of Christian distinctiveness and cultural relevance are fundamentally at odds with one another such that Christianity interacts constructively with the wider culture only at the risk of losing its unique identity, and, conversely, Christianity preserves the distinctiveness of its message only at the high price of rendering itself culturally marginal.[21] Thus, it might seem that Christianity can achieve a degree of cultural relevance without compromising the distinctiveness of its message only by muddling through a series of never fully satisfying, ad hoc compromises.[22]

Tanner proposes a way out of this impasse by challenging the underlying presuppositions of this problematic.[23] It is here that she makes fruitful use of the postmodern shift in the anthropological understanding of culture that we looked at in the preceding chapter. Specifically, she notes that the debate over the proper relation between Christianity and culture presupposes a conception of the two entities that postmodern culture theory has shown to be problematic. Christianity and culture are conceived, like cultures in classic anthropology, as self-contained systems of belief and practice that enter into relation only after they are already more or less fully formed.[24] Against this view, Tanner argues that a distinctively Christian way of life is internally constituted by its relations with the outside culture.[25] Inasmuch as a Christian form of life, like any other cultural formation according to a postmodern theory of culture, is relationally formed, such relations are present from the very beginning, long before there can be any question of a particular type of relation between "Christianity" and "culture" conceived of as two distinct cultural entities.[26] Christians achieve a distinctive sense of identity, Tanner argues, by using or appropriating outside cultural materials in a distinctive way. Thus, it is not by somehow limiting its interaction with the wider culture that Christianity preserves a distinctive sense of identity, as postliberal theologians tend to assume, but quite the contrary, by maintaining active, though often critical, relations with it.

Tanner's understanding of Christian identity in terms of a creative consumption of outside cultural materials involves more than an anthropological or sociological claim about the way cultures, including specifically Christian cultures, are formed. Her theory quite clearly has a normative dimension as well. The normative thrust of Tanner's account is to encourage Christians to engage constructively with the wider culture by disabusing them of the worry that such engagement somehow poses a threat to Christian identity. A specific, albeit unnamed, target of Tanner's proposal might be the kind of Christian sectarianism that George Lindbeck advocates as a part of his postliberal project.[27] Tanner's thesis that a distinctive sense of identity is worked out in the midst of active relations with the wider culture undermines the primary rationale behind the formation of Christian enclaves in which a Christian "cognitive minority" preserves a distinctive way of life against an encroaching, assimilative culture.[28] Stated positively, the theory of Christian identity that Tanner presents in

Theories of Culture coheres with the model of socially engaged Christianity that she advocates in her earlier work, *The Politics of God*.

A normative concern with encouraging an active engagement with the wider culture—or, stated negatively, with undermining the appeal of Christian sectarianism—would explain Tanner's reluctance to recognize forms of Christian identity that involve the formation of cultural boundaries. She argues against an understanding of "Christian identity in virtue of a cultural boundary" on the grounds that cultural boundaries are not natural markers of a highly integrated, self-contained form of life.[29] And yet, as Tanner herself acknowledges, a relational conception of Christian identity does not exclude oppositional relations between Christianity and culture and the formation of cultural boundaries, only the misrecognition of such boundaries as natural markers of self-contained forms of life.[30] Thus she concedes, albeit somewhat reluctantly, that "Christian identity may have to do with the drawing of a boundary" so long as the differences marked by boundaries are understood in a contrastive, relational sense.[31] Despite this acknowledgment, however, Tanner's decision to place her critique of the postliberal conception of Christian identity under the heading of "Christian Identity in Virtue of a Cultural Boundary" gives the impression that boundary formation, even if not excluded by the relational conception of cultural identity that she advocates, is nevertheless somehow peripheral to it.

The overall effect of Tanner's presentation, then, if only on a rhetorical level, is to shift attention away from the oppositional forms of Christian identity that typically express themselves through cultural boundaries. Her theory makes these forms of Christian identity more of a limit case than, as in the postliberal view she criticizes, a paradigm.[32] This marginalization of oppositional forms of Christian identity has the effect of eliding the political, exclusionary moment of Christian identity formation. To the extent that it does so Tanner's conception of Christian identity continues the tradition of liberal depoliticization.

The political dimension of Christian identity comes to the fore, however, when her theory of Christian identity is extended to the realm of interreligious relations. In an interreligious context, a relational conception of Christian identity can no longer be contained within the paradigm of classic liberalism. A convenient, if somewhat facile, way of making this point is to express the thesis that Christian identity is essentially relational in terms of the concept of apologetics. Tanner's claim that Christian theology is intrinsically apologetic in nature[33]—that is, that a theological engagement with the claims of the surrounding culture is integral to the theological task—not only implies the liberal apologetics of the tradition of Schleiermacher, but also the decidedly illiberal, interreligious Christian apologetics recently advocated by Paul Griffiths.[34]

This interreligious dimension of apologetics is integral to the relational conception of Christian identity that Tanner outlines in *Theories of Culture* inasmuch as religion qualifies as a form of culture. An understanding of religion in terms of the concept of culture has been, of course, a widely accepted, even hegemonic view at least since Clifford Geertz's influential essay, "Religion as a Cultural System."[35] Subsequent criticism of Geertz's definition of religion has, if anything, only radicalized Geertz's insight into the intimate connection between religion and culture. Whereas Geertz assumed that specifically religious symbols were distinguished from their nonreligious counterparts by certain intrinsic qualities (specifically, by their reference to a cosmic order), more recent theorists such as Talal Asad, Bruce Lincoln, and Russell McCutcheon have each argued, each in various ways, that the religious character of a given cultural form has more to do with the way it is framed and authorized than with its intrinsic content.[36] These theorists, in other words, view religion as a metadiscursive strategy that constitutes certain cultural contents as somehow transcending the sphere of the merely human and contingent.[37] In principle, practically any cultural content can be classified as religious, and hence authoritative, depending on the particular way cultural meaning is mediated through the structures of power and authority in a given historical context.[38] Specifically religious discourses and practices thus cannot be distinguished from "merely" cultural ones on the basis of any set of intrinsic, context-independent properties. There is therefore no non-arbitrary reason for excluding specifically interreligious relations from a relational theory of Christian identity like Tanner's.[39]

Now whether or not an outside cultural practice is classified as religious will often determine whether one's relation to it will be one of creative appropriation or exclusion.[40] Generally speaking, investing a discourse or practice with authority—especially transcendent authority—encourages an all-or-nothing attitude toward it. Since authoritative discourses and practices typically demand unqualified allegiance, they tend to be either wholly accepted or wholly excluded.[41] In this way religious authorization renders outside discourses and practices resistant to creative appropriation.[42] Once an outside practice or belief is classified as religious, its appropriation, at least in a Christian context, tends to be interpreted negatively, as entailing a syncretistic compromise of Christian identity. In order to render such a practice or belief fit for Christian consumption, then, it must first be reclassified as a nonreligious, merely cultural practice, a strategy of declassification that might be compared to the decision on the part of Nepalese authorities during the 1855 invasion of Tibet to reclassify the yak, a bovine, as a deer in order to provide meat to the Nepalese troops (who were forbidden from eating beef).[43] Thus many Christians freely incorporate the practices of yoga or Zen meditation into their spiritual lives after having first been persuaded that such practices are not "religious" in the sense that, say, offering pūjā to an image of Śiva is. It is important to note, however, that even when the belief or practice associated with another religion is recategorized in this way, that judgment presupposes a position from which relations to outside practices can be consciously managed. Such judgments, in other words, are strategic, and not tactical, in de Certeau's sense of these terms. They presuppose a sense of Christianity as an ideological formation delimited from its surroundings by a cultural boundary, albeit one that is continually being transgressed and renegotiated.

When we enter into the realm of interreligious relations, then, we are forced to recognize another dimension of cultural interaction besides the one foregrounded in Tanner's analysis. The consumption of cultural materials takes place in the context of a series of discursive strategies through which Christians situate themselves in a given cultural-religious milieu by drawing contrasts between themselves and their cultural and/or religious rivals. In highlighting the various ways in which Christians creatively "trope" the cultural discourses and practices of others, Tanner draws our attention to a vital dimension of cultural interaction that easily gets eclipsed in attempts to characterize Christian attitudes toward culture in terms of a single type of relation.[44] Nevertheless, there is reason to doubt that this practical, tactical level of cultural consumption can be easily disengaged from a level of ideological discourse in which Christians draw "us" versus "them" contrasts with others. One could argue, for example, that often what initially motivates one to appropriate otherwise obligatory cultural practices in a distinctive way is a purely formal interest in differentiating one's community from its surroundings.[45] The creative consumption of cultural materials reflects a strategy of differentiation that presupposes an imagined sense of Christian community as a social formation set apart from others. Another way of saying this is that the processes of cultural consumption through which Christians consciously forge a distinctive way of life presuppose a political moment of exclusion.

The Political Moment of Christian Identity: Two Christian Apologetic Constructions of Self and Other

A primary locus for this political, exclusionary dimension of Christian identity is doctrine, a topic that, significantly, receives little explicit attention in Tanner's theory of Christian identity.[46] It would not be difficult to show that, among its various other functions, doctrine forges a sense of group identity by mobilizing differences between religious communities.[47] Doctrine typically selects from a community's discourses and practices those that establish contrasts with its proximate rivals. Those discourses and/or practices deemed doctrinally significant in a given historical context are precisely those that differentiate, say, a particular Christian community from its principal rivals in that context. Because doctrinal significance is determined in part by external, situational factors, what is doctrinally significant does not always coincide with a community's abiding beliefs and orientations.[48] The political dimension of doctrine comes clearly into view when the doctrinal and theological[49] dimensions of Christian teaching fail to coincide. As George Lindbeck observes, the history of doctrinal controversy contains many instances where otherwise-trivial points of difference, such as the infamous iota that separated the Nicene *homoousios* from the *homoiousios* espoused by the followers of Basil of Ancyra, assume life and death importance.[50] What makes these otherwise trivial points of difference doctrinally significant is precisely their role in mobilizing group identity. More often than not, however, this differential aspect of doctrine coincides with a matter of intrinsic theological significance that tends to mask the former.

An excellent example of a Christian doctrine that forged a sense of Christian identity by mobilizing communal difference—and one that therefore exemplifies the political dimension of Christian identity—is a doctrine that, ironically enough, plays a significant role in Tanner's argument against the postliberal understanding of Christian identity in terms of cultural boundaries. This is the doctrine of Jesus Christ as the Word of God. Tanner appeals to this central Christian doctrine in order to challenge the primary rationale behind the formation of cultural boundaries, namely, the concern that outside cultural forms might endanger Christian identity by exercising an undue influence on a Christian way of life.[51] Such a concern, Tanner argues, betrays an essentially idolatrous confusion between God's Word and the various human theological formulations that constitute explicit Christian witness to that Word. Against the postliberal preoccupation with ensuring that Christianity retains the upper hand in its dealings with other cultures, Tanner argues that in certain circumstances faithfulness to the Word of God might actually demand that borrowed materials be allowed to unsettle the established character of Christianity.[52] In this way, faithfulness to the Word of God argues against the formation of sharp cultural boundaries.

Tanner's appeal to the doctrine of the Word of God to justify the transgression of cultural boundaries constitutes what in my view is a compelling theological argument against a sectarian conception of Christian community. And yet, a historical examination of the origins of this doctrine reveals that its relation to the ongoing ideological project of delimiting Christianity from its cultural surroundings is more ambiguous than Tanner's argument might suggest. In his book *Border Lines*, a careful and insightful, if rather provocative study of the historical separation of Judaism and Christianity, Daniel Boyarin shows how the emergence of the doctrine of the Word (or Logos) of God as the defining belief of Christianity, a view that became hegemonic by the fourth century, was inextricably bound up in the contemporary effort to delimit Christianity from Judaism. Boyarin states his main thesis as follows: "Logos theology was not an essential and aboriginal distinguishing mark of Christianity as opposed to Judaism but rather a common theological inheritance that was construed and constructed as such a distinguishing mark by a virtual conspiracy of orthodox theologians on both sides of the new border line—Justin [Martyr] and followers on one side, the Rabbis on the other."[53] Prior to the third century, Boyarin argues, the religious formations that are anachronistically termed Christianity and Judaism were "phenomenologically indistinguishable as entities."[54] At this point the doctrine of binitarianism—that is, the belief in a second divine person or power, whether called Word, Wisdom, or Son—did not differentiate non-Christian Jews from those Jews and non-Jews who were followers of Jesus. There were non-Christian Jews, such as Philo of Alexandria, who held a binitarian theology as well as believers in Jesus who denied any distinction of persons within the Godhead.[55] Between the second and fourth centuries, however, an emerging discourse of Christian orthodoxy redefined the latter group of non-binitarian or monarchian Christians as heretics. This discursive strategy was meanwhile mirrored within Judaism, as an emergent rabbinic orthodoxy, in what Boyarin calls a "virtual conspiracy," did the same to those non-Christian Jews who held some version of what became known in Judaism as the heretical doctrine of "Two Powers in Heaven." Since then the doctrine of the Word of God, identified with the person of Jesus Christ, has been a touchstone for Christian identity while, conversely, the rejection of such a claim has become a defining tenet of Jewish theology.[56] Logos theology, in other words, became the basis of a clear boundary between Judaism and Christianity.[57] Boyarin's historical analysis suggests, then, that the doctrine of Jesus Christ as the Word of God is deeply implicated in the history of Jewish-Christian apologetics and thus inseparable from the issue of Christian boundary formation.

An important component of Boyarin's argument is an analysis of a foundational text in the formation of this discourse of Christian orthodoxy, Justin Martyr's late second-century *Dialogue with Trypho*. Ostensibly the transcript of a conversation between Justin and Trypho, a Jew, in which the former tries to convince the latter to believe in the Logos of God, the *Dialogue*, according to Boyarin's ingenious interpretation, represents an effort to expropriate the

Logos theology for Christianity.[58] At the same time, it disavows Christian monarchianism by projecting this belief onto a Jewish other, represented by the figure of Trypho.[59] Boyarin challenges the traditional presumption that Justin's exchange with Trypho reflects the actual state of Jewish-Christian relations at the time. Rather, he construes the text as an example of hegemonic discourse, that is, as a rhetorical attempt to make what at the time was simply one particular interpretation of Christian belief, namely the Logos theology, normative and representative of Christianity as a whole, while at the same time projecting a competing interpretation of Christianity onto a constructed Jewish other. The text, in other words, constructs what William Scott Green terms a "double metonymy," in which a group "confuses some part of its neighbor with its neighbor, and a piece of itself with itself, and construes each in terms of the other."[60] A text like Justin's *Dialogue* transposes a complex and ambiguous web of cultural relations into an antithesis between isolated features standing in a metonymic, part-whole relation to the cultural formations they each represent.[61] The differential relation between the two selected features is extended, thanks to these metonymical relations, to the relation between their respective wholes.

Such metonymic discourses unavoidably occlude aspects of the social formations they seek to define. Having one part or aspect of a social formation represent that formation as a whole inevitably suppresses much of the internal diversity of the latter. Moreover, the double metonymy, inasmuch as it transfers the differential relation of the selected parts to the relation between their respective wholes, blocks a recognition of the parallels between the two formations that cut across the boundary between them. Such discourses constitute acts of discursive or symbolic violence inasmuch as they are the means through which a particular faction disavows, represses, or, at the very least, refuses to recognize competing interpretations in an effort to secure hegemony.

This repressive dimension of such hegemonic discourses is often concealed, however, by their very success. Such was clearly the case with the *Dialogue with Trypho*. Justin's discourse may not have corresponded to the contemporary sociological reality it purports to describe; Boyarin argues, for example, that a Judaism defined by a denial of Logos theology did not exist at the time Justin wrote. But the larger apologetic discourse of which the *Dialogue* was a constitutive part was effective. Thanks to a set of favorable—or, depending on one's point of view, unfavorable—conditions, Justin's prescriptive characterizations of Christianity and Judaism became reality. A decisive factor in this success, according to Boyarin, was the "complicity" of the rabbis in the Christian expropriation of the Jewish Logos theology. Justin's hegemonic task of making the Logos theology definitive of Christian identity was made considerably easier by the rabbis' willingness, as it were, to cede it to him. This was true in spite of the resistance put up by other contemporary Jewish groups, whose memory has been suppressed thanks to the success of the both Christian and rabbinic orthodoxies in their respective traditions, as well as to the tendency of some historians unwittingly to reproduce rabbinic and Christian orthodox ideology by taking their claims at face value.[62] Often it takes a critical historical analysis like Boyarin's to make these forgotten voices heard once again.

I turn now to a more recent example of a Christian discourse of "double metonymy" whose hegemonic character is more apparent than that of Justin's *Dialogue* precisely because it continues to encounter resistance. This is the apologetic contrast between Christianity, understood as essentially world and life affirming, and various Eastern religions, most notably, brahmanical Hinduism and Buddhism, which are tendentiously understood to be essentially world and life negating.[63] Although the understanding of Christianity as essentially world and life affirming has its roots in the various anti-Gnostic polemics of the early Church, in which Christianity affirmed the inherent goodness of the physical creation and the supremacy of the biblical Creator,[64] it has emerged as a particularly important expression of Christian identity in the modern world. A paradigmatic expression of this contrast is Albert Schweitzer's book, *Indian Thought and Its Development*. In this work, Schweitzer constructs a binary opposition between, on the one hand, a worldview in which "man regards existence as he experiences it in himself and as it has developed in the world as something of value per se," and, on the other, a worldview in which existence is experienced "as something meaningless and sorrowful," leading to a renunciation of "all activity which aims at improvement of the conditions of life in this world."[65] These two worldviews define the thought of the West and of India, respectively. Schweitzer acknowledges that both world and life affirmation and world and life negation can be found side-by-side in each of these cultural contexts. But in the Indian context the latter predominates over the former, while in the West the former predominates over the latter.[66] Thus world and life negation form an essential and aboriginal part of Indian thought; elements of world and life affirmation enter into the Indian tradition only by default, as it were, as the basic demands of human existence—including, most notably, ethical considerations—force it to make concessions to a world-affirming worldview.[67] By contrast, the West has maintained a primary orientation toward world and life affirmation, despite the infusion of elements of world and life negation into the Western cultural tradition during the Hellenistic period. Schweitzer concedes that Christianity in particular contains elements of world and life negation; indeed, it was early Christianity, with its otherworldly orientation, that introduced world and life negation into Western thought.[68] Nevertheless, the Christian form of world and life negation is fundamentally different from that of India. To be sure, the teaching of Jesus takes place in the context of an otherworldly conception of the coming Kingdom of God. And yet this otherworldly eschatology is combined with an active love of neighbor, not with a quietistic quest for spiritual self-perfection in the manner of the sages of India's Upaniṣads.[69] In the Renaissance and the succeeding centuries, the teaching of Christianity is brought completely in line with a world-affirming worldview.[70] The reader is led to infer that Christian teaching, particularly with respect to its ethical dimension, comes into its own when it finds itself expressed in the context of a worldview of world and life affirmation.

Schweitzer justifies his comparison by claiming that Western thought attains a better understanding of its essential nature and an awareness of its current inadequacies when it is brought into relation with the thought of India.[71] One could go further than this, however, and argue that a distinctive sense of cultural identity is not simply *clarified* by such dichotomous characterizations of East and West but is in fact *constructed* through them. In this respect, Schweitzer's text is similar to Justin's. Just as the latter participated in a larger discourse by which something called Christianity constituted itself through a contrast with a constructed Jewish other, so too, as the many critics of "orientalism" have argued, texts like Schweitzer's represent moments in a larger discursive process by which the West has forged and consolidated a distinctive sense of cultural identity through an invidious contrast with a constructed Orient.

Schweitzer's text, perhaps to an even greater degree than Justin's, illustrates the inherent ambiguity of the contrastive process of identity formation. For Schweitzer's work, despite its author's ostensibly modest aim of lending depth to the West's world-affirming worldview by bringing it into a mutually clarifying dialogue with Indian thought,[72] remains for all that an expression of Western cultural superiority. It is hardly surprising that Schweitzer's thesis would provoke a critical response from a prominent Indian writer like Sarvepalli Radhakrishnan. Radhakrishnan takes exception to Schweitzer's tendentious characterization of Indian thought as essentially world and life negating. In his critique of Schweitzer's book, Radhakrishnan points to Indian texts and concepts that argue against this characterization of Indian thought. At the same time, he draws attention to the elements of world and life negation in Christianity that were either overlooked or explained away in Schweitzer's presentation. Radhakrishnan's overall point is that Schweitzer's dichotomy does not hold up against the evidence:

> All immense simplifications of the complicated patterns of reality are misleading. To divide peoples into those who will not accept the world at all and those who will accept nothing else is hardly fair. The many reservations which Schweitzer is obliged to make in applying his scheme of world affirmation and world negation as opposite categories of which one or the other must be denied show that it is not adequate to the facts.[73]

Ultimately, however, Radhakrishnan's critique calls into question not so much Schweitzer's knowledge of the relevant facts as his essentialism. As the reference to Schweitzer's reservations in the quote above indicates, Schweitzer was already aware of many, if not most, of the facts that Radhakrishnan adduces against him. What enables the former to propound his schema in spite of this evidence is the conviction that world affirmation and negation represent essential characteristics of Western and Indian thought, respectively. Essentialism insulates a dichotomous schema against empirical disconfirmation. In an essentialist framework, the exception only serves to prove the rule. In this way, essentialist presuppositions stabilize the notions of cultural identity that such dichotomous characterizations sustain. In order to be effective, however, the proponents of such essentializing contrasts have to figure out some way of neutralizing or containing the voices that such contrasts invariably denigrate, delegitimate, or otherwise marginalize. As we have seen in our discussion of Boyarin's work, Justin Martyr's effort to expropriate the Logos theology owed much of its success to the fortuitous circumstance that his agenda coincided with that of an influential faction in the contemporary Jewish community. By contrast, Schweitzer's dichotomous characterization of Indian thought as essentially world and life negating has generally failed to achieve hegemony precisely because it has failed to win the consent of influential representatives of the Indian cultural tradition like Radhakrishnan.[74]

Comparison as a Technique for Deconstructing Dichotomous Typifications

Our mention of Radhakrishnan's critique of Schweitzer's East-West dichotomy brings us to the second, deconstructive moment in the dialectical model of comparative theology that I propose. At this point, after having acknowledged the political moment of Christian identity formation, our analysis rejoins Tanner's conception of theological method, specifically, her insistence on the need to deconstruct essentializing contrasts between cultures. Following a line of critique characteristic of postmodern approaches to culture, Tanner criticizes the method of cultural self-critique exemplified in Schweitzer's book, namely, the use of qualitative, "we are like this; they like that," contrasts with other cultures to highlight the inadequacies of one's own. Such a strategy of self-criticism unquestioningly accepts the dichotomous typification of other cultures and, to that extent, unwittingly perpetuates the asymmetrical power relations and ethnocentric attitudes that such typifications invariably reflect.[75] As an alternative, Tanner advocates a method of cultural self-criticism that focuses on the differences *within* cultures as opposed to the differences *among* cultures.[76] Such an alternative method, "promotes self-criticism... by uncovering and giving sense to the internal contestations of culture, by disputing the homogeneity and consistency of a culture, by resisting the temptation to assume unified cultural totalities."[77] The recognition of the internal diversity of a cultural formation like Christianity reveals the largely contingent and arbitrary nature of the cultural boundaries delimiting it from its surroundings. For, as our discussion of Boyarin's analysis of the separation of Christianity and Judaism showed, the differentials upon which such boundaries are founded invariably reflect hegemonic relations within each of the delimited formations. Conversely, a demonstration of the contingency and mutability of cultural boundaries attenuates the essentializing characterizations of self and other that interfere with the recognition of the multiplicity of voices within each cultural formation.

In this final section, I will argue that cross-cultural comparison represents one method of unsettling cultural boundaries and deconstructing the essentialized notions of identity that such boundaries typically sustain.[78] It is not the only such method, of course; as Boyarin's work shows, historical or, better, genealogical analysis is another powerful method of anti-essentialist critique. Nevertheless, cross-cultural comparison represents a particularly effective critical method, particularly when it comes to those forms of cultural-religious identity that have been forged or reconstituted in the modern world with its transcultural, global horizons. The comparative juxtaposition of cultural-religious formations sets up resonances between the two whereby prominent features of the one bring to light parallel features of the other that may have been suppressed by various hegemonic discourses, whether those of indigenous orthodoxies or those of Western scholarship. In this way cross-cultural comparison can bring to light parallels that cut across established cultural boundaries, thus revealing the latter's arbitrariness and contingency.

In order to arrive at a proper understanding of how comparison can function as a critical, anti-essentializing discourse, we must first disabuse ourselves of the naive view that such deconstructive criticism is simply a matter of adducing hard facts against an adventitious discourse of ideological mystification and abstraction. To the extent that the dichotomous typifications constructed in the first, political moment of identity formation sustain a sense of cultural identity, they are not airy fictions that can be expected simply to evanesce at the first appearance of countervailing evidence.[79] If such typifications do, in fact, begin their career as fictions, they soon acquire body and substance as they begin to shape the perceptions, attitudes, and behavior of real people. A discursive formation like "Hinduism," for example, may indeed have originally been largely an artificial construct projected onto classical Indian culture by outsiders. Nevertheless, one must recognize that at least since the nineteenth century, this concept has become, whether rightly or wrongly, part of the self-understanding of large numbers of people; it has become, in other words, part of the stock of everyday certitudes grounding the beliefs and actions of many people, Hindus and non-Hindus alike.[80] While this certainly does not mean that the effort to deconstruct a concept like "Hinduism" by challenging its underlying presuppositions is somehow illegitimate, it does mean that we cannot reasonably expect the concept simply to dissolve upon a demonstration of the aspects of classical Indian culture that it distorts or obscures.[81] As Slavoj Žižek observes, only a dying or otherwise attenuated ideology—that is, one that ceases to hold sway over a significant number of people—can be dispelled simply by an appeal to empirical facts.[82]

In order to be effective, such appeals have to be sustained by a counter-ideology. Here I use the term "ideology" in a neutral, as opposed to a critical sense, to use John B. Thompson's helpful distinction.[83] In other words, I am using the concept of ideology to refer broadly to any discourse that functions to mobilize a social group, bracketing a consideration of its often concomitant function in maintaining relations of domination.[84] Thus—to return to my point—an ideological formation like Schweitzer's dichotomy between world and life negation and world and life affirmation can be unsettled or displaced by facts only when these are effectively mobilized by a counter-ideology.[85] In this connection, it is important to recognize that Radhakrishnan does not write as a disinterested scholar of religion—assuming that such a creature exists—but rather as a recognized spokesman for contemporary Hinduism, specifically, the religious ideology dubbed somewhat pejoratively (and to that extent unfairly) as "Neo-Hinduism."

If cross-cultural comparison is going to serve as an effective means of deconstructing dichotomous typifications, then it has to be conceived of as something more than a discourse of mere facts, of objective representation. Here our thesis that comparison can function as a critical method receives support from the recent shift in the theorization of comparison that we discussed at the end of chapter 1. To paraphrase the putative founder of this shift in conceptualization, J. Z. Smith, comparison is to be understood less as a method of discovery—that is, a method of uncovering objective structures of cultural and religious reality—than as a discourse of invention, a work of the imagination.[86] Comparison, according to this new conceptualization, is a kind of rhetorical device, albeit a mode of rhetoric that still leaves space for the discourse of science.[87] This rhetorical dimension of comparison finds expression in one of Smith's most productive insights, namely, that comparison can be fruitfully understood in terms of metaphor.[88] In an often-quoted passage, he describes this metaphorical aspect of comparison as follows:

> Comparison does not necessarily tell us how things "are" . . . ; like models and metaphors, comparison tells us how things might be conceived, how they might be "re-described," in Max Black's useful term. A comparison is a disciplined exaggeration in the service of knowledge. It lifts out and strongly marks certain features within difference as being of possible intellectual significance, expressed in the rhetoric of their being "like" in some stipulated fashion. Comparison provides the means by which *we* "re-vision" phenomena as *our* data in order to solve *our* theoretical problems.[89]

Smith notes that this comparative "re-visioning" of phenomena has a political or ideological dimension.[90] He appeals to an intriguing suggestion made by Karl Mannheim that the holistic and analytical methods of inquiry in the human sciences correspond, respectively, to "right-wing" and "left-wing" political orientations. Looking at his own work in light of Mannheim's distinction between "right-wing" and "left-wing" methodologies, Smith acknowledges that his analytical approach to comparison, in which the comparativist imaginatively decomposes and rearranges phenomena in accordance with his or her theoretical interests, represents a discourse of the "left."[91] Given the intrinsic connection he sees between the activity of comparison, on the one hand, and a particular, politically inflected orientation to the phenomena compared, on the other, Smith argues that comparison must be accompanied by a "a clear articulation of purpose" if it is to be intellectually fruitful.[92]

Other scholars have developed and refined this insight into the pragmatic and political dimension of religious and cultural comparison. One such scholar is Hugh Urban, who, in the context of an appreciative critique of Smith's work, argues that the latter's conception of comparison relies on a problematic theory of metaphor.[93] Specifically, Urban argues that Donald Davidson's pragmatic theory of metaphor allows for a clearer conception of the pragmatic and political dimensions of comparison than the semantic theories of metaphor of Max

Black and Paul Ricoeur upon which Smith relies. Urban appeals to a seminal article by Davidson in which the latter questions the tendency of many theorists to explain the aesthetic effects of metaphor in terms of a special meaning ostensibly generated from the interaction of the metaphor's two terms.[94] Metaphors, Davidson argues, are not to be understood as the bearers of a hidden meaning or message, but rather as pragmatic devices that get us to notice aspects of reality that we did not notice before.[95] Metaphor functions pragmatically to stimulate thought and imagination to attend to previously unnoticed resemblances between things. Metaphor, in other words, makes us look at reality in a new way. Urban suggests that Davidson's pragmatic theory of metaphor serves as a more fitting vehicle for Smith's generally pragmatic and critical approach to the comparative study of religion than the semantic approach to metaphor that Davidson rejects.[96] The latter, Urban notes, has an affinity with an outmoded model of comparative religion, associated with the work of Mircea Eliade, which seeks to uncover the deeper patterns and archetypes allegedly manifest in various religious phenomena. Thus the depth dimension of religious phenomena supposedly revealed through comparison stands in an analogous relation to the hidden meaning allegedly disclosed by metaphor according to a semantic theory.[97] By contrast, Davidson's theory of metaphor, which emphasizes the creativity of the interpreter of metaphor,[98] coheres with a theory of comparison that, like Smith's, regards comparison as a constructive activity integrally related to the scholar's intellectual purposes.

There is reason to doubt, however, that a pragmatic theory of comparison can restrict itself to the "left-wing" mode of metaphorical comparison advocated by Smith. For a theory that recognizes an integral connection between the activity of comparison and the scholar's intellectual purposes implies a range of purposes, and therewith a range of political orientations, potentially served by comparison. These purposes and orientations naturally include those of a more "conservative" nature. Specifically, a pragmatic theory of comparison has to recognize the mode of comparison discussed in the previous section whereby cross-cultural comparison is used to establish and maintain notions of cultural and religious identity. In order to account for these "right-wing" modes of comparison, we must recognize a distinction between metaphor and a trope often confused with it, namely, metonym.[99] Following the insightful analysis of Robert Paine,[100] I would like to argue that metonym and metaphor correspond, respectively, to two forms of political rhetoric, the first aiming at social stability, the second promoting social change. These two forms of rhetoric in turn correspond to two modes of comparison, the first of which is involved in the political construction and stabilization of identity, the second in the critical denaturalization of identity. At the risk of some repetition, which hopefully will be justified by the additional clarity that the metonym/metaphor distinction provides, I shall describe each of these forms of comparison in turn.

Metonymical Comparison in Traditional Apologetics

The dichotomous discourses of identity construction that we saw exemplified by Justin Martyr and Albert Schweitzer can be classed with the forms of political rhetoric associated with metonym. We anticipated this point when we remarked above, following William Scott Green, that the construction of self and other involved a "double metonymy." That is, such comparative discourses cast the relation between two cultural formations in terms of the differential relation that obtains between selected aspects or parts of those formations.

The concept of metonym provides a helpful model for understanding the process of identity formation. To be specific, we can distinguish between two aspects of the metonymical relation between part and whole that correspond, respectively, to the two moments of identity formation that we mentioned at the outset of this chapter, namely, the political mobilization of identity, on the one hand, and the subsequent naturalization of the identity so formed, on the other. Corresponding to the moment of political mobilization is metonym's capacity to render an intangible, complex, or otherwise inaccessible reality in terms of another reality (typically an aspect or part of the former) that is tangible, relatively simple, and therefore accessible. Because social reality is complex and mutable owing to the fact that perceptions of social reality form a constitutive part of that reality,[101] human beings rely on metonymic forms of discourse to apprehend, manage, and modify social relations.[102] Thus the discourses of political mobilization generally have a metonymical structure.

Corresponding to the moment of naturalization is metonym's capacity to occlude problematic aspects of the complex reality that it represents.[103] Metonym's capacity to transpose the intangible into the tangible[104]—precisely the feature that enables it to mediate a consciousness of the otherwise inaccessible reality of social groups—can also be used to transpose a contingent and contestable reality into one that is widely accepted, even self-evident. This aspect of metonym is fully exploited by those forms of political rhetoric that seek to make a particular viewpoint hegemonic. We might cite as examples recent U.S. political slogans like "family values" and "support the troops," which package a highly controversial position—a social platform highlighting a "pro-life" position on abortion, for the first, support for a dubious military enterprise, for the second—in terms of non-controversial, indeed banal, commitments—to the idea of family, to the material support of self-sacrificing soldiers—that are politically unassailable. The Indian context provides another excellent example of metonymic rhetoric with the concept of "Hindutva." This controversial term trades on the ambiguity between, on the one hand, an earlier inclusive and relatively unproblematic cultural meaning and, on the other, a deeply divisive communal-religious one.[105]

This capacity of metonymic discourse to cast a partial and contested perspective in terms of one that is perceived as unproblematic and self-evident corresponds to the naturalizing function typically associated with the concept of ideology. And yet the concept of ideology may not be entirely appropriate for understanding the process of naturalization inasmuch as the term suggests that naturalization is mediated through consciousness and representation. A more adequate concept for understanding the naturalizing function of metonym might be Pierre Bourdieu's concept of doxa.[106] According to Bourdieu, doxa refers to the set of assumptions about the world and society that are so self-evident that they go without saying.[107] The sense of self-evidence conveyed by doxic perceptions of social reality can be regarded as the achievement of metonymic discourse with its reductive capacity to foster the perception that there are fewer possibilities in a given sociopolitical context than there are in fact.[108] It is by suppressing an awareness of alternative political possibilities in this way that metonymic discourse lends stability to existing social arrangements.

The kind of comparison employed in traditional apologetic theology exemplifies this metonymic process of naturalization. Like the social rituals or "rites of institution" analyzed by Bourdieu whereby qualitative social distinctions are fashioned on the basis of preexisting differences between human beings—the way, for example, admission to an elite school confers social status on the basis of examination scores[109]—traditional apologetics seeks to establish a sense of religious distinction—here I use the term "distinction" quite deliberately in order to capture its connotation of a sense of superiority—on the basis of objective differences between communities. When Christian apologists note the differences between Christianity and another religion, they are obviously doing more than simply noting objective differences between two equivalent entities.[110] Their aim is quite clearly to establish the superiority of Christianity—often this conclusion does not even need to be stated explicitly—but in such a way that this sense of distinction, of superiority, is presented as a matter of objective fact. Thus when the Christian apologist notes the "uniqueness" of the doctrine of the Incarnation or the doctrine of prevenient grace, the observation is implicitly understood to demonstrate the superiority of Christianity. This notion of Christian uniqueness, in fact, epitomizes the metonymic nature of traditional apologetics. Like the political slogans mentioned above, this expression plays on the ambiguity between, on the one hand, a normative—and highly contentious—assertion of the absoluteness, definitiveness, and superiority of Christianity and, on the other, the banal fact that Christianity, like any historical datum, is unique.[111] The metonymical grounding of the assertion of Christian superiority in indisputable objective differences between religions shields the former claim from criticism by forcing this criticism to be mediated through a futile argument over factual differences, in much the same way that packaging a policy of military aggression in terms of "supporting the troops" effectively neutralizes criticism of the policy by channeling that criticism through a sham debate over supporting or not supporting soldiers.[112]

Metaphorical Comparison

Understanding the kind of comparison employed in traditional apologetics in terms of the concept of metonym allows its contrast with metaphorical comparison to stand out more clearly. While metonym functions to *contain* thought in order to render a particular perception of social reality self-evident, metaphor *extends* thought in such a way as to render that perception questionable and problematic.[113] So just as metaphor stimulates the imagination by juxtaposing two categorically distant terms,[114] the kind of comparison that J. Z. Smith terms analogical (as opposed to genealogical) generates cognitive insight by bringing together "within the space of the scholar's mind" religious phenomena for which there are no previous causal historical connections, that is, phenomena that are not temporally or spatially contiguous.[115] Like metaphor, this type of comparison allows us to notice aspects of the compared phenomena that we did not notice before.[116] Thus understood, comparison is a technique for breaking from established ways of perceiving cultural and religious reality, from perceptions that invariably reflect the influence of dominant interests, either those originating from within the tradition studied or those bearing on its history of reception from without. Put differently, metaphorical comparison implies a utopian perspective—an exterior standpoint—from which cultural and religious phenomena suddenly appear unfamiliar and questionable.[117]

As Smith observes, this capacity of comparison to challenge the self-evident nature of certain beliefs, customs, and practices can be fruitfully understood in terms of the aesthetic concept of defamiliarization.[118] According to the Russian Formalist critic Victor Shklovsky, the defamiliarizing effects of art counter the tendency for perception to become habitual and automatic.[119] So just as art renews perception by liberating objects from the official concepts of what they are, comparison stimulates critical thought by displacing, even if only temporarily, conventional, taken-for-granted notions of what certain religious phenomena mean. The political implications of the defamiliarization concept, which are largely undeveloped in Shklovsky,[120] become evident when we note the resemblance between the automatization of perception of which Shklovsky speaks and Bourdieu's concept of doxa. In the context of a discussion of Bertolt Brecht's theory of the "estrangement-effect" (*Verfremdung*), Fredric Jameson describes how the aesthetic techniques of defamiliarization function politically to dissolve the doxic illusion of self-evidence that attaches to objects and institutions:

> The effect of habituation is to make us believe in the eternity of the present, to strengthen us in the feeling that the things and events among which we live are somehow "natural," which is to say permanent. The purpose of the Brechtian estrangement-effect is therefore a political one in the most thoroughgoing sense of the word; it is, as Brecht insisted over and over, to make you aware that the objects and institutions you thought to be natural were really only historical: the result of change, they themselves henceforth become in their turn changeable.[121]

Thanks to its defamiliarizing effects, the comparative redescription of one cultural-religious datum in terms of another enhances our awareness of the contingency, and therefore the changeability of religious beliefs, practices, and institutions. This analysis thus supports Smith's remark that metaphorical comparison "is relentlessly an affair of the left."

When thus understood as a technique of defamiliarization, comparison serves as an effective means of intercepting the drive to naturalize notions of religious identity. Put differently, comparison provides one means of partially reversing the reductive process whereby a complex web of intercultural relations is metonymically transposed into a binary opposition between essentialized entities. While the deconstructive effect of metaphorical comparison is not so radical as to completely undo the political moment of boundary formation and therefore dissolve the notions of religious identity that cultural-religious boundaries sustain,[122] it is nevertheless enough to render those boundaries more permeable and flexible than they would otherwise be.[123] Comparison represents a method by which the members of a particular religious community can cultivate what William Connolly terms an "ethos of critical responsiveness" with respect to other religions and cultural movements, that is, a willingness to "revise the terms of self-recognition" as they situate themselves in relation to religious and cultural movements that demand recognition.[124] Inasmuch as comparison serves as a technique for "thawing out" reified notions of identity, it forms an integral part of a Christian theology embodying the change in strategy I propose with respect to the problem of the political in religion, namely, from the "depoliticization" to the "denaturalization" of religious self-understanding.

A good example of the use of comparison to foster an ethos of critical responsiveness vis-à-vis other religions is Francis Clooney's book *Hindu God, Christian God*. In this work, Clooney draws generally unfamiliar parallels in classical Indian thought for several Christian theological arguments and concepts—the cosmological argument for the existence of God, the concept of divine grace, a doctrine of divine embodiment, among others—that have each at some point formed the basis of an assertion of Christian uniqueness. These Indian parallels challenge the claims of Christian distinction that are founded upon a belief in the uniqueness of the corresponding features of Christian belief. By showing that certain central tenets of Christian belief are not unique to Christianity—or, put differently, that substantive theological differences do not always coincide with recognized religious boundaries—Clooney's comparisons destabilize many of the conventional conceptions of Christian identity. In this respect, Clooney's comparative project represents the inverse of the classic apologetic project of inscribing a priori claims of Christian "uniqueness" in selectively adduced objective differences between traditions. And yet, despite its generally critical and revisionist character, his project preserves a relation of continuity with the tradition of Christian apologetics.[125] To the extent that it recognizes a legitimate role for the rhetoric of uniqueness in the articulation of Christian identity,[126] Clooney's project encourages Christian theologians to reexamine their tradition more carefully in order to discern the more subtle ways in which Christianity is distinctive. The aim of Clooney's project is therefore as much constructive as it is critical; clearly, his intention is not simply to undermine and dissolve prevailing concepts of Christian identity but rather to revise and refine them, to re-establish Christian identity claims on the basis of a sound knowledge of the other traditions that inhabit the conceptual world of a now-global Christianity. Such a comparative theology exemplifies the way in which Christian theology can respond creatively and responsibly to the religious traditions and movements that have entered into the historical horizon of contemporary Christianity. Put differently, a comparative project like Clooney's embodies Connolly's principle of critical responsiveness: it implicitly understands that the recognition of religious others entails a revision of the terms of self-recognition. In this respect it also coheres with a relational understanding of Christian identity like Tanner's.

The Inscription of Comparative Theology in an Apologetic Tradition

Clooney's project exemplifies another aspect of the comparative theological enterprise that will figure prominently in the second part of this book, namely, its embeddedness in an apologetic tradition. The topics that structure *Hindu God, Christian God*—the cosmological argument for the existence of God, God's identity, divine embodiment, religion and revelation—all have deep roots in the tradition of Christian apologetics. Although the comparisons that Clooney constructs challenge the corresponding apologetic claims of Christian uniqueness, the particular Indian texts that he profiles nevertheless acquire theological significance for him in relation to the Christian apologetic tradition. In other words, Clooney's choices of what to compare with what are determined in part by Christianity's past attempts to distinguish itself from various rivals. In this respect, the contemporary practice of comparative theology remains inscribed in an apologetic tradition even when the comparative theologian assumes a critical stance vis-à-vis that tradition. We could perhaps say that an exercise in comparative theology is able to focus on the second, deconstructive moment of the dialectic of identity formation only at the price, as it were, of acknowledging its belongingness to a tradition of which the older apologetics forms a constitutive part.

This point regarding the inscription of comparative theology in a tradition of religious apologetics coheres with an emphasis of J. Z. Smith's influential approach to comparison, namely, a recognition of the importance of the history of reception of the phenomena being compared. That is to say, the comparative enterprise must include a description "of how the datum has become accepted as significant for the purpose of argument."[127] This recent emphasis on the importance of reception history is a consequence of the above-mentioned paradigm shift from genealogical to analogical comparison in the study of religion.[128] We recall from our discussion of comparison in chapter 1 that the "new comparativism" inspired by Smith's seminal reflections on comparative method emerges in reaction to a tendency to restrict "legitimate" comparison to those comparisons based on "real," genealogical connections and the concomitant tendency to dismiss merely analogical comparisons as unduly impressionistic and subjective. By abandoning the requirement that comparisons be based on direct, genealogical connections among the compared phenomena, the new model of comparison focuses special attention on the way those phenomena have been received by the second-order scholarly tradition. That is, it heightens the demand for a sensitivity to the historical and contextual factors that have constituted certain phenomena as being of particular significance and concern to the comparativist. It is precisely this history *in front of* the phenomena selected for comparison that the method of genealogical comparison, in its preoccupation with the history *behind* those phenomena, tended to ignore.

When this task of describing the reception history of the phenomena to be compared is undertaken in a theological context, one typically finds that apologetic interests have shaped the reception of the texts and traditions that the comparative theologian finds significant. Thus an exercise in comparative theology invariably finds itself engaging with a tradition of religious apologetics.

In the second part of this book, I shall undertake just such a comparative exercise that understands itself as a self-critical moment within an ongoing apologetic tradition. To be specific, I critically engage the apologetic tradition that we looked at above in our discussion of Schweitzer, namely, the tradition that understands Christianity as world and life affirming over against certain Indian religions invidiously characterized as world and life denying. In the next chapter, I examine a text that brings this apologetic tradition into a convenient focus, Rudolf Otto's comparative study of Meister Eckhart and Śaṅkara, *Mysticism East and West.* In this classic text, Otto appeals to the orientalist world-affirmation/world-denial dichotomy in order to redirect the charges of pantheism, world denial, and quietism for which Eckhart has long been accused onto his Indian counterpart.[129] Otto's specific interest in vindicating Eckhart from heresy, however, complicates this text's relationship with the orientalist and Christian apologetic traditions. Otto's reading of Eckhart suggests the possibility of extending the arguments by which he vindicates Eckhart to Śaṅkara, thereby deconstructing the world and life affirmation versus world and life denial dichotomy. For this reason Otto's text provides a convenient reference point for the comparative theological exercise in Part II, whose aim is to deconstruct the world- and life-affirmation/world- and life-denial dichotomy from within the very tradition that this dichotomy has helped define.

PART II

Mysticism East and West Revisited

4

Mysticism East and West as Christian Apologetic

The perfected human being [according to Meister Eckhart] distances himself entirely from all morals and rules; his entire behavior is completely different. The external world is of no consequence because it belongs to nothingness. All the virtues and means of salvation needed by people who are still striving for perfection no longer have any value for him.

—Carl Schmidt

It is because the background of Sankara's teaching is not Palestine but India that his mysticism has no ethic. It is not immoral, it is a-moral. The Mukta, the redeemed, who has attained ekatā or unity with the eternal Brahman, is removed from all works, whether good or evil. Works bind man. He leaves all activity and reposes in oneness.... With Eckhart it is entirely different. "What we have gathered in contemplation we give out in love." His wonderfully liberating ethic develops with greater strength from the ground of his mysticism.

—Rudolf Otto

In the previous chapter, I presented a dialectical model of comparative theology that acknowledges a political moment of exclusion in the formation of religious community while at the same time using comparison, understood as a technique of defamiliarization, to intercept the drive to naturalize the forms of identity politically formed in that first moment. I further argued that the practice of comparative theology, so understood, represents a self-critical moment in a theological tradition whose identity has been shaped by the oppositional discourses of traditional apologetics. The Christian comparative theologian who reflects critically on his or her choice of materials is apt to discover that apologetic interests have shaped the reception history of those aspects of non-Christian religions that he or she finds theologically significant. At the same time, he or she has the freedom to construct comparisons that qualify and question—or, alternatively, that extend and reinforce—those apologetic discursive traditions.

In part II of this book, I apply this understanding of comparative theology to a particular example. The remaining chapters engage the apologetic tradition, briefly examined in the previous chapter, that has defined Christianity as world and life affirming over against "Eastern" philosophies and religions invidiously represented as world and life denying. The present chapter analyzes a text that exemplifies this apologetic tradition, Rudolf Otto's classic *Mysticism East and West.* Below I show how Otto's comparison of Meister Eckhart and Śaṅkara in this text carries the "East" versus "West" apologetic tradition forward, but in a distinctive way that suggests possibilities for questioning it. Taking Otto's comparison as their point of departure, the subsequent chapters use the technique of mutual redescription to "problematize" the essentializing "East" versus "West" dichotomy that Otto employs.

Otto's Apologetic in *Mysticism East and West*

Mysticism East and West is divided into two parts. In the first, "Part A: Conformity," Otto highlights the many striking parallels between Śaṅkara and Eckhart, "two of the greatest representatives and interpreters of that which is understood by Eastern and Western mysticism."[1] These parallels, which give expression to mystical experiences transcending historical, geographical, and cultural differences,[2] are so close that, "with a little skill it would be possible so to weigh up and present their fundamental teachings that the worlds of the one would read like a translation into Latin or German from the Sanskrit of the other, and vice versa."[3] In the book's second part, "Part B, The Differences: Eckhart versus Śaṅkara," however, Otto will show that these parallels exist only on the level of formal similarity. When one penetrates the surface to discern the special character of each member, one discovers that, "in spite of great formal equalities, the inner core of Eckhart is as different from that of Śaṅkara as the soil of Palestine and of Christian Gothic Germany in the thirteenth century is different from that of India."[4] Despite the universalistic sentiments expressed in Part A—which seem to be retracted in the Herderian rhetoric of cultural distinctiveness in Part B, particularly in the oft-repeated contrast between "the soil of Palestine and the soil of India"[5]—Otto's parallels merely set the stage for the difficult and exacting apologetic task of discerning the specific character and value of each of these mystical expressions.[6] In a procedure that is, if anything, more pronounced in Otto's later study of Śrīvaiṣṇavism, *India's Religion of Grace and Christianity Compared and Contrasted,* Otto will build his apologetic on the basis of the closest—and from the perspective of Christian apologetics most challenging—of parallels.[7] One could perhaps regard this apologetic method as implying a powerful a fortiori argument: if the distinctiveness of Christianity can be demonstrated even in the context of the most striking parallels with its religious rivals, how much more will this be the case in the more familiar situation in which religious differences prevail.

Otto has a more specific aim than simply asserting the superiority of Christian mysticism over the Indian, however. His overriding concern is to dispel long-standing doubts about Eckhart's orthodoxy, specifically, the charge that the German master taught a form of quietistic pantheism. As we shall see in more detail below, Otto's principal purpose in drawing a contrast between Eckhart and Śaṅkara is to shift the charge of pantheism from the former onto the latter. Or, as Richard King puts it, Śaṅkara becomes for Otto "a useful foil, a theological cleansing sponge if you like, which purifies Eckhart of heresy while at the same time absorbing these heretical defects into itself."[8]

The aim and the method of Otto's apologetic—namely, the vindication of Eckhart and the use of Śaṅkara as a foil, respectively—each recapitulate a history of modern scholarship. Otto's interest in vindicating Eckhart reflects a preoccupation with the issue of pantheism in the modern reception of Eckhart, and his use of Śaṅkara as a foil reflects a long orientalist tradition of lifting up Śaṅkara's school of Non-Dualist Vedānta as the epitome or essence of Hinduism. In order to show how each of these figures became significant in the way they did in Otto's intellectual milieu, then, I shall briefly describe each of these reception histories in turn before turning to an analysis of the text of *Mysticism East and West* itself.

The Retrieval of Meister Eckhart and the Question of Pantheism

Eckhart was rediscovered in the context of the nineteenth century intellectual movement of German Idealism.[9] Prior to this time he was known only vaguely and indirectly as the quasi-legendary founder of the tradition of "German mysticism" which was known principally through the more accessible works of Tauler and Suso.[10] A decisive moment in the modern retrieval of Eckhart was

G. W. F. Hegel's claim to have found in the Meister a precursor to his own philosophical program. Hegel saw in Eckhart an anticipation of his own speculative efforts to reconcile belief and knowledge, religion and philosophy.[11] At the same time, Hegel held Eckhart up as a counter example to contemporary theology, which, in its preoccupation with biblical interpretation and the history of doctrine, had reneged on its properly "scientific" task of raising the content of religious belief to the level of conceptual knowledge.[12] This criticism naturally provoked a response from Christian theologians, who challenged Hegel's claim of fidelity to the Christian tradition. Hegel's professed kinship with Eckhart arguably made their polemical task easier, for the long-standing doubts regarding the Meister's orthodoxy could be transferred to the ostensibly cognate Hegelian philosophy.

Such was precisely the agenda of the first modern academic study of Eckhart, that of the Protestant theologian Carl Schmidt in 1839. Schmidt set about to establish that Eckhart's mystical theology was pantheistic, a characterization that encoded the judgment that Eckhart's teaching—and by implication Hegel's—was not genuinely Christian. Schmidt interprets Eckhart's doctrine of the birth of the Son in the soul as a Hegelian process of divine self-realization. Like Hegel's Spirit, the Eckhartian God realizes himself as God—in a process at once intellectual and ontological—only by objectifying himself in his creative Word.[13] This process of divine self-realization, moreover, takes place in and through the intellectual activity of the human soul—God gives birth to his Son in the soul, as Eckhart puts it.[14] Thus, "the human consciousness of God and God's self-consciousness are identical, just as the Hegelian school teaches."[15] Eckhart's teaching is pantheistic inasmuch as it implies a relation of interdependence between God and creation: "God first becomes conscious of himself in the world, and since knowledge is identical with being, God is not [God] without the world, and the world, as his constitutive other (*Andersseyn*) is eternal with him."[16] Toward the end of his study, Schmidt turns his attention explicitly to Hegel, thereby betraying his polemical agenda. Although Hegel rejected the label of pantheism as applied to his speculative philosophy, no other term, Schmidt argues, more aptly describes a philosophical system like Hegel's that identifies the infinite with the finite.[17]

It is clear that Schmidt's judgment of Eckhart as a pantheist was shaped by a concern to establish the boundaries of Christian—specifically Protestant—theology against the philosophy of religion of the Hegelian school.[18] Indeed, Schmidt's monograph on Eckhart was little more than an apologetic for the Christian theology that Hegel attacked.[19] Schmidt's depiction of Eckhart was, accordingly, essentially a projection of Schmidt's understanding of Hegel—"ein verhegelter Eckhart," as Ingeborg Degenhardt aptly puts it.[20] Schmidt's study is significant because it sets the terms for Eckhart's modern reception. Specifically, it exemplifies the way in which the modern retrieval of Eckhart was inextricably bound up in contemporary struggles over the meaning and identity of Christianity.

Although Eckhart's name came to be associated with what from a Christian theological perspective was the damning charge of pantheism,[21] Protestant attitudes toward Eckhart were far from being wholly negative, however. Even those theologians who followed Schmidt in concluding that Eckhart's teaching was pantheistic shared with the German Idealists an admiration for the Meister's originality.[22] Because they were ignorant of Eckhart's Latin corpus, whose discovery would have to await the pioneering research of Heinrich Denifle in the 1880s,[23] German theologians and philosophers in the mid-nineteenth century generally assumed that Eckhart had broken decisively with the scholastic tradition. There were several aspects to Eckhart's alleged break from that tradition, all of them positive from the viewpoint of German Protestants. First, this break was seen as a triumph of genuine religious feeling over the sterile rationalism of scholasticism. The alleged split between mysticism and scholasticism in the late Middle Ages anticipated the Romantic reaction to the one-sided rationalism of the Enlightenment. Second, nineteenth-century German philosophers and theologians saw in Eckhart's break with scholasticism the emergence of a uniquely German form of thought and feeling. Like the Romantic movement that it allegedly foreshadowed, the expression of mystical feeling over scholastic rationalism in the later Middle Ages was believed to have a pronounced nationalist coloring. Reflecting the Romantic doctrine of cultural distinctiveness, the mystical tradition of Eckhart, Tauler, and Suso, with its stress on immediate feeling, was seen as the unique expression of the German spirit.[24] It is hardly accidental, given the inextricable relation that was believed to obtain between a nation's characteristic thought and spirit, on the one hand, and its language, on the other, that Eckhart and his followers would choose to express their thoughts in the German vernacular. While the cosmopolitan Latin of the scholastics may have been a fitting vehicle for a formalistic rationalism lacking in depth and feeling, only the vibrant Middle High German of Eckhart's sermons could adequately express the depth of mystical feeling of "the German soul" or *Gemütsmystik*. Third and finally, German Protestant theologians of the nineteenth century saw in the Meister's alleged break with tradition an anticipation of the Reformation.[25] Protestant admirers of Eckhart saw in the Meister's frequent disparagement of instrumental attitudes in religious practice a spirit of reform anticipating Luther's doctrine of justification by faith.[26]

It was inevitable, in light of the considerable appeal that this image of Eckhart as the father of German piety and as an early precursor to Luther had for German Protestants, that some historians and theologians would reconsider Schmidt's influential judgment that Eckhart's teaching was pantheistic and therefore un-Christian.[27] A number of late nineteenth-century German scholars, including W. Preger, J. Bach, and F. X. Linsenmann, accordingly set about to defend the Meister against the pantheism charge.[28] Otto clearly belongs to this tradition. As mentioned above, his *Mysticism East and West* can be understood as an apology for Eckhart's orthodoxy.[29] Against the widespread prejudice that in Eckhart's mysticism a life of personal faith "is submerged in pale abstractions," Otto repeatedly insists that Eckhart's mysticism rests on a firm theistic foundation, that it is securely grounded in "the simple, Christian belief in God."[30] "Eckhart's mysticism is not to be cut off from the natural foundation of his Christian religion," Eckhart writes; rather, "it bears the special hue of his Christianity and is permeated by it."[31]

What distinguishes Otto's defense of Eckhart is his use of comparison to make his case. The Christian elements of Eckhart's mysticism—the simple piety that animates his speculation and the personal theism that undergirds it—appear in bold relief when profiled against the mysticism of Śaṅkara. As mentioned above, Part B of Otto's study makes an implicit appeal to the orientalist dichotomy between a world-affirming Christian theism, on the one hand, and an illusionistic pantheism ostensibly exemplified by Śaṅkara's Non-Dualist Vedānta, on the other. Although Otto qualifies the orientalist reading of Śaṅkara as we shall see below, his defense of Eckhart nevertheless depends on the "East" versus "West" dichotomy in order to be rhetorically effective. Without it, the differences Otto highlights in Part B would not be sufficient to dispel all doubts concerning the Christian character of Eckhart's mysticism; generally speaking, the contrasts Otto draws are too subtle and qualified for that. The orientalist dichotomy has the effect, at least on a rhetorical level, of magnifying the differences between the two masters, effectively leveraging the complex and often ambiguous teaching of Eckhart over into the Christian camp.

Otto is able to invoke the world-affirmation/world-denial dichotomy simply by choosing Śaṅkara as a conversation partner with Eckhart. In order to understand how this is possible, we need to examine the process by which Śaṅkara's school of Non-Dualist or Advaita Vedānta came to be regarded as the essence or epitome of Hinduism.

The Emergence of Śaṅkara's Vedānta as the Epitome of Hinduism

"Indian philosophy," writes one of the contributors to a recent volume on Advaita Vedānta published in India, "means Vedānta, and Vedānta means the Kevalādvaita ["pure non-dualism"] of Śaṅkara."[32] This understanding of Advaita

Vedānta as the essence of Hinduism—the concept of "philosophy" in the quote above is understood to refer to the essence of religion[33]—is in large part the product of a complex and ambiguous history of cross-cultural interaction between India and the West during the colonial period. An explanation for the modern ascendancy of Advaita must begin with the recognition that Śaṅkara's Vedānta answered to the interests and expectations of Christian missionaries and orientalist scholars. Accordingly, it attained a degree of prominence in the orientalist construction of "Hinduism" that it never had in classical India. In a second moment in the cross-cultural dialectic, the orientalist conception of Advaita Vedānta as the quintessence of Hinduism came to be refracted in Hindu self-understanding, as an influential segment of India's intelligentsia interacted creatively with Western thought. This internalization of the orientalists' "Vedānticized" conception of Hinduism is evident, for example, in Rammohan Roy's program for Hindu reform (the Brahmo Sabha, later the Brahmo Samaj); later in the nationalistically inflected Neo-Vedānta of Swami Vivekanada; and finally in Sarvepalli Radhakrishnan's conception of Neo-Vedānta as the highest expression of a mystical perennial philosophy. Although Otto's introduction of Vaiṣṇava theism to German audiences in his latter works represented an important corrective to the orientalist bias in favor of Śaṅkara,[34] his *Mysticism East and West*, in choosing Śaṅkara as an exemplar of "Eastern mysticism," continued this orientalist tradition of representation.[35]

It would be impossible in the space permitted here to set forth, in detail, this diffuse, varied, and ramified discourse of modern Hinduism with its many inversions, ironies, and ambiguities. All I can do here is to draw attention to two salient features of this discourse, which, as we shall see below, form two fundamental presuppositions of the Christian apologetic discourse that finds expression in Otto's *Mysticism East and West*. The first of these features is an affinity—which with the development of historical linguistics came to be regarded as a genetic relation—between brahmanical and Western thought. The second is an apologetic interest in characterizing Indian thought as essentially pantheistic, world denying, and quietistic. These two features can be conveniently correlated to the two parts of the formula I quoted at the beginning of this section: the putative kinship between brahmanical and Western thought goes a long way in explaining why "Indian philosophy means Vedānta," and the apologetic interest in characterizing Indian thought as a world-negating pantheism in explaining why "Vedānta means the Kevalādvaita of Śaṅkara."

The notion of a kinship between brahmanical and Western thought had its origin in the tendency, present from the beginning of the encounter between India and the West, to privilege the literary tradition of the Brahmins over other aspects of Indian religion. This Western bias in favor of the brahmanical tradition was partly hermeneutical—the Protestant model of religion familiar to Western scholars and missionaries favored the conception of Indian religion as a tradition based on a corpus of sacred texts[36]—and partly pragmatic—Christian missionaries and colonial administrators were able to maximize their influence by forging alliances with the indigenous elites, the Brahmins.[37] No figure better exemplifies these two aspects of Europe's encounter with India, particularly the latter, than the great Jesuit missionary Roberto de Nobili (1577–1646). De Nobili saw in the earliest traditions of the Brahmins evidence for a pristine monotheism, an indigenous natural theology, which would provide a basis for Christian conversion.[38] Christian conversion was thus attractively presented as the means for recovering the knowledge of God preserved in India's own ancient traditions before this knowledge was allegedly overrun by the idolatry and superstition missionaries like de Nobili associated with contemporary Hinduism.[39]

The notion of an affinity between Western and brahmanical thought was to realize its full ideological potential, however, only with the development of modern historical and comparative linguistics in the beginning of the nineteenth century. Specifically, the discovery of a genetic link between the classical and modern languages of Europe, on the one hand, and Sanskrit, on the other—a thesis first formulated by Sir William Jones in a celebrated speech before the newly founded Asiatic Society of Bengal in 1786[40] and later conclusively demonstrated by the linguist Franz Bopp in 1816—was used to support the mythical notion of a cultural and, eventually, racial consanguinity between European peoples and the ancient Indians.[41] This, the notorious Aryan thesis, provided a nascent German nationalism with a seductive myth of cultural origins that would displace Germany's ambivalent and invidious relation with Latin Christendom.[42] At the same time, the notion of a genetic link between Europe and Vedic India also formed the basis of the essentialized contrast between "Aryans" (originally, simply the self-designation of the Vedic Indians but soon to become a racial term) and "Semites," a discourse that emerged in nineteenth century.[43] As is well known, Nazi propagandists used this contrast to mobilize German national identity with great effectiveness and tragic consequences.

Before the Aryan thesis was exploited by German nationalists, it provided ideological support for British colonialism.[44] The notion of a kinship between India and Europe provided a convenient justification for the colonial presence in India when it was combined, via a racial form of evolutionary theory,[45] with the long-standing missiological judgment that contemporary Indian religion and culture was thoroughly debased. According to the resultant narrative, the sublime, spiritual culture of ancient India became corrupted by the gradual infusion of elements of non-Aryan, Dravidian language and culture.[46] Thanks to the purportedly strong genealogical bond between Europe and the Aryan culture of ancient India, the former was in a position to reacquaint a thoroughly benighted contemporary India with the forgotten riches of her own cultural past.[47]

The orientalist myth of India's cultural degeneration and decline accounts for the emergence of the notion of Vedānta as the highest expression of Hinduism. As the indigenous tradition preserving the most direct link with the ancient Vedic tradition, the Vedānta was the one Hindu tradition that had suffered the least from the alleged processes of adulteration and cultural decay. Thus, according to the influential view of Max Müller, the Vedānta was "clearly the native philosophy of India, . . . the first growth of philosophical thought on the ancient soil of India."[48]

But why Śaṅkara's school of Non-Dualist (Advaita) Vedānta? An explanation for this privileging of Advaita over the more numerous theistic and realist interpretations of Vedānta brings us to the second feature of the orientalist discourse mentioned above, namely, an interest in characterizing Indian thought as essentially pantheistic, world denying, and quietistic. As Ronald Inden and Richard King, among others, have argued, the perception of India in terms of an otherworldly mysticism of self-annihilation and moral indifference served as a useful foil to a flattering conception of the West defined by rationality, a spirit of enterprise, and a respect for individual freedom and responsibility.[49] Śaṅkara's Non-Dualist Vedānta, with its unqualified claim of the soul's (*ātman*) identity with Brahman, its doctrine of the world as *māyā* or illusion, and its uncompromising insistence on renunciation as the sole means to liberation, more closely conforms to this orientalist image of brahmanical thought than the various forms of realist and theistic Vedānta. That an image of Indian thought shaped by the ideological concerns of Europe functioned as a principle of selection with respect to Indian culture goes a long way to explaining the emergence of Advaita Vedānta as the paradigmatic form of brahmanical thought in Western representations of India.[50]

As was the case with Eckhart, Vedānta—by which Europeans implicitly understood Advaita Vedānta—becomes a focal point in the lively European debate on the issue of pantheism. The writers and philosophers of the Romantic movement regarded this notoriously vague and ambiguous doctrine as a vital alternative to Enlightenment Christianity and Deism, specifically, to the notion of an abstract Deity presiding ineffectually over the fragmented and disenchanted world of Enlightenment Europe. For the critics of this movement, however, and for Christian theologians in particular, this protean doctrine took on a completely different aspect, as a pernicious teaching stultifying the faculties of rationality, initiative, and moral discernment. As the pantheism debate is taken up in nineteenth-century German Idealism—where the issue is complicated by the fact that "pantheism" becomes something of a derogatory term, forcing the proponents of divine immanence to adopt different terminology[51]—two opposing interpretations of Vedāntic philosophy begin to crystallize. The first of these sees the Vedānta as an underdeveloped or degenerative form of the philosophical and religious thought of the West. Perhaps the most powerful exponent of this position is Hegel, for whom oriental cultures represent petrified and discarded stages of the *Weltgeist*'s ("world spirit") career of historical self-realization. In the impersonal concept of Brahman, the dialectical process of self-realization—that is, the historical process through which the spirit attains self-consciousness by first "othering" itself in various historical forms and then by recognizing itself, in a subsequent moment, in those objectified forms—is truncated and aborted. In Brahman, the absolute fails to cross the vital threshold from being-in-itself to being-for-itself whereby metaphysical substance attains subjectivity. There is lacking, in other words, that decisive moment of self-realization in which spirit recognizes itself in the world.[52] Brahman remains a deficient absolute, an abstract unity devoid of both content and subjectivity.[53] At the same time, Brahman fails to reconcile itself with the world from which it abstracts itself. To the extent that Brahman fails to affirm the individual realities of the world, the Indian "religion of substance" implies an acosmism, that is, a denial of the phenomenal world. On the level of the human individual, Brahman's self-abstraction from finite reality takes the form of a renunciation of "everything that pertains to life and the world, natural and spiritual."[54] Hegel interprets yoga rather uncharitably as an exercise in mental abstraction,[55] which, in emptying the mind of objective content, also empties it, properly speaking, of consciousness itself.[56] Thus understood, Indian yoga is "a stupefaction (*eine Verstumpfung*) that perhaps does not at all deserve the name of mysticism."[57] Hegel, moreover, sees the passivity of yogic meditation as emblematic of an absence of political freedom and a genuine ethical life in India.[58] We thus see that Hegel's interpretation of India, for all the imaginative power and conceptual brilliance of the philosophical system that undergirds it, ultimately rests on the tired and familiar orientalist themes of Eastern quietism and "Oriental despotism."

Diametrically opposed to the Hegelian line of interpretation was the view of Vedānta as a clear and unadulterated expression of a perennial philosophy of idealism. This "perennialist" view of Vedānta finds its inspiration in the philosophy of Schopenhauer and its clearest expression in the work of the Indologist Paul Deussen. According to the latter, the Upaniṣads and the Vedānta, the philosophy of Parmenides and Plato, and, most recently, the philosophy of Kant and Schopenhauer all express the same fundamental philosophical insight, namely, that the empirical world of plurality and change is mere appearance and not reality in itself.[59] Deussen regards this doctrine of idealism—which finds expression in the Vedāntic claim that the Self or *ātman* alone is true reality—as the original and highest philosophy of India; the various other doctrines found in India—pantheism, theism, what Deussen calls cosmogonism, and the atheistic dualism represented by the ancient Sāṃkhya philosophy—only make their appearance as this pure idealism is eventually forced to make concessions to the coarser realist habits of the human mind.[60] As mentioned above, this perennialist line of interpretation was enthusiastically embraced and promoted by the proponents of the so-called Neo-Hinduism in India. For thinkers like Swami Vivekananda and, later, Sarvepalli Radhakrishnan, Vedānta's putative capacity to transcend sectarian division provided a basis, ironically enough, for Indian self-assertion against the provocative cultural presence of Europe in India. The perennialist view of Vedānta as the direct expression of a timeless and universal core of religious insight receives its most succinct formulation in Radhakrishnan's memorable remark that the Vedānta, "is not a religion, but religion itself in its most universal and deepest significance."[61]

Otto's Use of Both the Perennialist and Apologetic Traditions

What makes *Mysticism East and West* a particularly fascinating text is that it makes creative use of *both* of these interpretive traditions. Part A ("Conformity") represents the perennialist tradition, Part B ("The Differences, Eckhart versus Sankara") the apologetic. Otto's juxtaposition of what, from one point of view, are two irreconcilable interpretive perspectives forms part of an ingenious strategy for establishing Meister Eckhart as a legitimate representative of Christian mysticism—the ultimate aim, as I suggested above, of *Mysticism East and West*. The key to understanding this strategy is to recognize that the perennialist and Christian apologetic traditions differ on the question of whether Eckhart is an appropriate choice for East-West comparison.

From the perennialist perspective of Part A, Eckhart is the ideal representative of Christian mysticism. As we have seen, perennialism seeks to isolate a timeless core mystical or philosophical insight from its cultural-historical integument. Its basic presupposition is captured in a famous remark by Schopenhauer: "Buddha, Eckhard [*sic*] and I teach essentially the same thing, Eckhard in the fetters of his Christian mythology. These same thoughts are found in Buddhism, though not stunted (*unverkümmert*) by any such mythology, and are therefore simple and clear, to the extent that a religion can be clear. With me this thought attains its full clarity."[62] Despite the lingering presence of elements of Christian "mythology" in Eckhart's thought, this mythological and doctrinal integument hangs but loosely around the core perennial insight that Schopenhauer will raise to scientific clarity. For perennialist interpreters of Eckhart in the Schopenhauerian tradition, the Meister's distinctive style and his occasional use of unorthodox modes of expression evidence a struggle to liberate a core of mystical insight from its doctrinal husk.[63] Like those metals such as copper and gold that are occasionally found free in nature, Eckhart provides a rare instance of a thinker for whom the process of separating essence from dross was already well under way. Thus for the perennialist tradition, it is precisely the idiosyncratic nature of Eckhart's Christianity—that he seems to be "an extraordinary 'Christian,'" as D. T. Suzuki ironically puts it[64]—that recommends him for comparative study.

From the perspective of the apologetic tradition represented by Part B, by contrast, Eckhart's idiosyncrasy poses something of a liability. For a tradition whose central concern is to highlight the distinctiveness of Christianity with respect to other traditions, the idiosyncratic and controversial nature of Eckhart's teaching makes him a generally poor choice to represent the Christian tradition. Eckhart's work might indeed make for striking parallels with Eastern thought, but his very marginality limits the significance of those parallels for Christianity as a whole. Studies in comparative mysticism belonging to the apologetic tradition typically show a preference for the great fourteenth-century Flemish mystic Jan van Ruusbroec as a representative of the Christian "mysticism of the Ground,"[65] for Ruusbroec's mysticism cannot be so easily disarticulated from basic Christian doctrines like the Trinity as Eckhart's allegedly can.[66]

By deftly integrating this apologetic tradition of comparison with the perennialist perspective of Part A, Otto is able to establish Eckhart as a legitimate representative—indeed the very paradigm—of a distinctly Christian mysticism. Part A with its perennialist perspective establishes Eckhart as an obvious choice to compare with Śaṅkara, who, for his part, is assumed to epitomize the mysticism of the East. The striking parallels Otto develops in Part A have the effect of rendering self-evident Otto's choice of Eckhart as a dialogue partner with Śaṅkara. At no point in Part A is the reader given any reason to doubt the appropriateness of a comparison between the two masters. This sets the stage for the apologetic in Part B, which, in uncovering an essential difference between the two forms of mysticism, has the effect of pulling Eckhart decisively to the Christian side of the divide between Christian mysticism and "oriental" pantheism.[67] The respective mysticisms of Eckhart and Śaṅkara are shown to be as different as Christianity is from Hinduism, as "the soil of Palestine" is from that of India. Thus, we see that what Otto takes from the perennialist tradition is a sense of the obviousness of Eckhart as an appropriate dialogue partner with Śaṅkara, which he then uses to establish the former as a full-fledged representative of a distinctively Christian mysticism.

The Parallels between the Two Masters

There are basically three aspects to the conformity between Eckhart and Śaṅkara. These aspects can be correlated to the categories of God, the soul, and the world, or, using more abstract terminology, theology, soteriology, and cosmology. The theological parallel concerns the relation between the personal and supra-personal aspects of divinity. Śaṅkara makes a distinction between the higher and lower Brahman, the latter with qualities (*saguṇa*), the former without (*nirguṇa*). The lower, *saguṇa* Brahman is associated with Īśvara, the personal God.[68] This distinction between the higher and lower Brahman parallels Eckhart's distinction between God and the Godhead (*gotheit*), the God beyond God. Eckhart's Godhead has "an almost identical relationship to God as that of Brahman to Īśvara."[69] Like *nirguṇa* Brahman, Eckhart's *gotheit* is defined by an absence of determinate properties (*eigenschaften*) and of essential relations with the world. This conception, found in both masters, of the highest aspect of divinity as transcending all relations with the world implies a parallel on the level of cosmology: both masters seem to deny the world any independent truth or reality. There is, in other words, a striking analogy between Śaṅkara's doctrine of *māyā*, or the illusory nature of the world, and Eckhart's repeated claim that all creatures are a "pure nothing" (*pure nihil, lûter nihts*).[70] Finally, both masters share a similar conception of the way to salvation. For both, a salvific knowledge of divinity coincides with a realization of one's innermost self. This innermost core of selfhood—the soul or *gemüet* in Eckhart, the *ātman* in Śaṅkara—is to be found beneath the sensory faculties, the *sensus communis* (the *manas* in Śaṅkara), the discursive intellect (*buddhi*), and the everyday sense of ego (*ahaṃkāra*).[71] For both masters, self-realization presupposes a detachment (*abgescheidenheit; tyāga*) from the things of the world.[72] This practical demand that the soul/*ātman* withdraw itself from both the objects of sense and the objects of thought receives support from the respective cosmological doctrines of the two masters, namely, the doctrine of *māyā* in Śaṅkara and the doctrine of the "nothingness" of creatures in Eckhart.

One of the more perceptive and—as I hope to show in the next chapter—productive of Otto's insights is that Śaṅkara's mysticism rests on a theistic foundation. Against a more conventional interpretation of the Indian master, according to which the personal Lord or Iśvara belongs to a world of *māyā* that is utterly dissolved upon realization, Otto argues that the theistic conception of Brahman remains the basis and presupposition of the conception of the highest Brahman. Otto maintains that there is a relation of continuity between the higher and lower conceptions of Brahman; just as the *via negationis* (way of negation) in Western theology is not the contradiction, but rather the continuation, of the *via eminentiae* (the way of eminence), so too is the higher brahman as the superlative, and not the opposite, of the lower brahman.[73] He argues, quite rightly I believe, that Śaṅkara's argument against the Sāṃkhya doctrine of insentient matter as the world-cause implies a theistic conception of brahman as sentient world-cause.[74] Anticipating the more conclusive research of the Indologist Paul Hacker in the 1950s, Otto notes that Śaṅkara often uses the term Īśvara in contexts where one expects to find the impersonal *nirguṇa* Brahman.[75] For Otto, this apparent terminological inconsistency "is the natural result of the intimate fundamental relationship between the two conceptions."[76] We can infer that, for Otto, this theistic foundation is the source of whatever vitality and "numinosity" Śaṅkara's mysticism possesses, that without it Śaṅkara's system would wither into a stale rationalism.

Otto's insistence on the theistic foundations of Śaṅkara's mysticism not only implies a rejection of the Hegelian conception of Brahman as lifeless substance, but also, concomitantly, challenges Hegel's dubious interpretations of *māyā* as dream or illusion[77] and of yoga as a stultified quietism.[78] Otto's thesis regarding the theistic underpinnings of Śaṅkara, by depriving him of the apologtist's favorite stratagem, the straw man, will make his apologetic task in Part B more difficult. But this thesis is vital for his larger aim of vindicating Eckhart from the suspicions of pantheism. For the parallel between the God-Godhead and Īśvara-Brahman relationships carries the very real danger of reinforcing the long-standing doubts about Eckhart's commitment to Christian theism. Indeed, the parallels Otto develops in Part A come within a hair's breadth of irretrievably capsizing Otto's apologetic project. And yet, by arguing for a relation of continuity between Īśvara and Brahman, Otto deftly transforms an analogy that could easily be fatal to his apologetic program into a powerful a fortiori argument in its favor.[79] If it can be shown that even the non-dualist mysticism of Śaṅkara "maintains a fixed relationship to Indian theism,"[80] how much more is this the case with Eckhart's mysticism, whose theistic elements, as even his fiercest critics would have to concede, are more pronounced?[81]

The Essential Difference between Śaṅkara and Eckhart

The central concept in the apologetic Part B of *Mysticism East and West* is that of "the living God" (*der lebendige Gott*). This theme, which runs throughout

Otto's oeuvre, from his early studies of Luther, through *The Idea of the Holy*, to his later work on Indian religions, forms the basis of the two dimensions of Otto's apologetic, namely, his defense of mysticism in general, on the one hand, and his claim for the superiority of Eckhart's Christian mysticism over that of Śaṅkara, on the other. In the forward to Part B, Otto appeals to the living God theme in his defense of mysticism against the charge of abstraction:

> The reproach is often made against Eckhart and against mysticism in general, that the full, vital, individual life of religion, of personal faith, love, confidence and fear and a richly colored emotional life and conscience, is finally submerged in pale abstractions, in the void and empty formulas of systematized nonentities, . . . As we have seen above, such reproaches are misunderstandings of the experiential content of Indian mysticism. But applied to Eckhart they are simply monstrous. To say that this "Gothic" personality, absolutely permeated and glowing with the urge of a tremendous new life impulse, lived in abstractions is absurd.[82]

Otto quickly moves from this defense of mysticism in general to an assertion of Christian superiority. Two pages later, he uses "the living God" theme to drive a wedge between the mysticisms of Eckhart and Śaṅkara:

> Śankara's Brahman is Sat, Chit and Chaitanyam; is Being and Spirit through and through, utterly opposed to all "deafness" (jada) and all matter. No one can deny the lofty spirituality of this conception of God. But the difference between this and Eckhart's conception is at once palpable, if the question is asked: Is this Brahman a living God? "I am the living God"—that is more than a God who lives.[83]

Otto's allusion in this quotation to Śaṅkara's assertion of Brahman's sentient nature against the Sāṃkhya doctrine of an insentient world-cause—a reference which in turn recalls Otto's earlier discussion of the theistic substructure of Brahman and therewith the parallel with Eckhart's theism—suggests that the apologetic contrast here between Eckhart and Śaṅkara rests not so much on a difference in formal doctrine as on a difference in expressive power. The essential difference between the two masters, in other words, is more rhetorical than doctrinal. More than anything else, what distinguishes Eckhart from his Indian counterpart is his distinctive mode of theological expression, the "imaginative force and daring imagery"[84] of his language, which "glows and sparkles in living colors":[85]

> While Śankara and his school try rather to rationalize the paradoxes of mystical language and even on occasion to reduce them to the

> trivial, thereby transforming the original mystery-filled figures of the Upanishads into abstractions, Eckhart on the contrary excites his listeners by unheard of expressions, and makes the conventional terminology of scholasticism pulsate again with the old mystical meaning. He causes ideas derived from mysticism, but long tamed and reduced to respectable mediocre conceptions, to flame anew with their ancient color and depth.[86]

In this passage and many more like it, Otto appeals to the theme of Eckhart as an "anti-scholastic" thinker, a characteristic feature, as we saw above, of Protestant scholarship on Eckhart.[87] Scholasticism, in both its European and Indian forms, is regarded as manifesting an entropic tendency toward routinization and rationalization that stifles the vitality of religious experience. Otto's appeal to Eckhart's alleged anti-scholasticism betrays a specifically Protestant agenda in this work. Otto's rather heavy-handed effort to establish a kinship between Eckhart and Luther (at one point Otto describes Eckhart's teaching as "nothing more than a doctrine of justification interpreted mystically"[88]), as well as his concomitant attempt to wrest Eckhart from the tradition of his fellow Dominican Thomas Aquinas (who, despite a common doctrinal inheritance, could never have conceived "the immediate impulse to fresh and powerful thought and experience" found in the Meister's works),[89] indicate that Otto's effort to clear Eckhart's name from the charge of pantheism coincides with the more specific aim of laying claim to the Meister's legacy for the Lutheran tradition.[90] Eckhart's conception of the living God expresses itself cosmologically in an affirmative attitude toward creation and ethically in a commitment to a life of intense moral activity. By emphasizing the living God theme, Otto thus seeks to put as much distance between Eckhart and the twin evils of nihilism and quietism long associated with Eckhart's mysticism. These he will effectively project onto Śaṅkara.

Cosmologically, the dynamism of Eckhart's living God expresses itself in creative activity. Implicitly retracting—or qualifying to the point of retraction—his earlier statement that the conception of Brahman as the *māyāvin* (the one rich in the creative power of *māyā*) coheres with "a world of purpose, aim, order, and wisdom,"[91] Otto draws a sharp contrast here in Part B between the creative outflow (MHG: *ûzvluz*; NHG: *Ausfluss*) of Eckhart's dynamic God and the aimless *līla* or divine play of the Indian Godhead.[92] Whereas the *līla* concept signifies an attitude of aloof indifference on the part of the Indian God toward his creation, Eckhart's concept of the divine outflow points to an essential relation between the very nature of the Christian God and his creative activity.[93] In other words, Eckhart's God realizes himself as God in his creative activity.

God's very nature precludes him from remaining in a state of sublime repose like Śaṅkara's Brahman.[94]

The heart of Otto's apologetic, however, lies in the ethical sphere. It is on the level of human behavior that the essential difference between the mysticisms of Śaṅkara and Eckhart become most apparent. The highest goal in Śaṅkara's mysticism is a stilling of all outward works. The spiritual adept who realizes his essential identity with Brahman will naturally share the latter's indifference toward the phenomenal world.[95] By contrast, for the soul that surrenders its will to the living God of Meister Eckhart, mystical rest or quiet represents only a preliminary moment in a dynamic process that reaches its highest fulfillment in outward activity. Such a soul becomes a conduit for a divine life that spontaneously expresses itself in the world. The moral activity of the redeemed soul mirrors the creative activity of God, or, better, is itself an expression of that divine activity. Nowhere is the contrast between this dynamic mysticism of Eckhart and quietism more clearly expressed than in the Meister's novel interpretation of the Lukan parable of Mary and Martha (Lk. 10:38–42).[96] In an ironic reversal of the conventional reading of this passage, Eckhart praises the unwearying activity of Martha, which he takes as an expression of spiritual maturity, over the contemplative quiet of Mary, in which he sees a hint of indolent self-indulgence. Thus interpreted, the story of Mary and Martha can be taken as a parable for the relationship between Śaṅkara's mysticism and Eckhart's.[97]

The bipartite structure of Eckhart's mystical theology, in which the moment of "breakthrough" into the silent unity of the Godhead is followed by that of the "outflow" into activity in the world, readily lends itself to an apologetic in which Śaṅkara's mysticism relates to Eckhart's as the incomplete to the complete.[98] Eckhart's language of divine unity and mystical repose is every bit as radical as Śaṅkara's. But unlike the static rest of the Indian master, Eckhart's repose issues forth in creative activity. In comparison to Eckhart, Śaṅkara's quietistic mysticism appears one-sided and truncated, impoverished and defective. In particular, it is lacking in the full-blooded feeling of moral conscience and the sense of individual responsibility found in the Christian master. Ultimately, Otto's comparison ends in the familiar orientalist dichotomy between an ethical and life-affirming Christianity, on the one hand, and a morally indifferent, life-negating Hinduism on the other:[99]

> It is because the background of Sankara's teaching is not Palestine but India that his mysticism has no ethic. It is not immoral, it is a-moral. The Mukta, the redeemed, who has attained ekatā or unity with the eternal brahman, is removed from all works, whether good

> or evil.[100] . . . Upon Indian soil there could never have developed this inward unceasing preoccupation with the soul's life as a life of Gemüt and conscience, and therewith the "cura animarum" in the sense which is characteristic of, and essential to, Christianity from the earliest days.[101]

The modern reader sensitive to the orientalism issue is apt to be disappointed to encounter the world- and life-affirmation versus world- and life-denial schema here in Part B after Otto seemed to have moved away from it in Part A with what in many ways was a non-stereotypical reading of the Indian master. In particular, Otto's insistence on the theistic substructure in Śaṅkara, a theme noted above, represents a refreshing departure from the orientalist stereotype of Advaita Vedānta as illusionistic pantheism. Seen in light Otto's concluding judgments in Part B, however, even this aspect of his interpretation of Śaṅkara appears to be little more than a lucky accident, the fortuitous product of a wrinkle in his apologetic agenda, namely, his concern to prevent the parallels with Śaṅkara from undermining his defense of Eckhart.[102] Ultimately, Otto's gesture toward a non-stereotypical interpretation of Śaṅkara and his tradition in Part A was unable to displace the apparently irrepressible world-affirmation/world-negation dichotomy.

Otto's apologetic contrast in Part B appears in a somewhat more favorable light, however, when we recall the context of German Indology in which Otto theorized about Indian religion. Above, I argued that Part A makes an implicit appeal to the perennialist approach to the study of religion. Otto bases the parallels developed there on a common religious experience.[103] For Otto's German readers in the late 1920s and '30s, however, the parallels in Part A would have carried a more immediate reference to the "Indo-Germanic" or "Aryan" thesis that I mentioned above in connection with the "Vedānticization" of Hindusim. Thus J. W. Hauer, writing in 1937 at the height of National Socialism in Germany, spoke of the mysticism exemplified in the works of Śaṅkara and Eckhart as "an irrevocable inheritance of the Indo-Germanic spirit."[104] The East-West parallels set forth in Otto's book, moreover, were "the effect not only of the general laws in the world of the human spirit, but in the particular form these common insights assume in the Indo-Germanic world, out of a commonality of blood and spirit" (*aus der Gemeinsamkeit der Blut- und Geistesart*).[105] The Münster Sanskritist Richard Schmidt expressed matters even more bluntly when, in the context of reviewing the relevant section of Hauer's book, he refers to Eckhart and Śaṅkara as "race comrades" (*Rassengenossen*).[106] Otto, of course, can hardly be held responsible for the use, or rather misuse, of his work to support a nativist, racist ideology that he most likely abhorred; Otto, whose political sympathies were democratic and progressive,[107] was no Nazi. As far as I can tell, Otto does not acknowledge an Indo-Germanic dimension to the parallels he draws between Eckhart and Śaṅkara.[108] Nevertheless, one could argue that he contributed, in spite of his personal political convictions, to two discourses—namely, those of German nationalism (evident in his celebration of Eckhart's *Gemütsmystik*) and German Indology—that would feed directly into National Socialist ideology.[109]

When viewed against this backdrop of German Indological discourse, however, Otto's use of the Christian apologetic contrast between world affirmation and world denial takes on, perhaps unexpectedly, a critical, counter-hegemonic function. As I have just noted, the parallels between Eckhart and Śaṅkara in Part A would have evoked the category of the Indo-Germanic on the part of Otto's contemporary readership. This category in turn would have called to mind its contrasting concept, the Semitic. And indeed, the category of the Semitic does appear in Otto's comparison, specifically, in Otto's references, in Part B, to the Palestinian background of Eckhart's Christian faith. But it is easy to misrecognize the antithesis between Aryan and Semite in Otto's syecdochic contrast between "the soil of India" and "the soil of Palestine" because he dramatically inverts the expected valuations of these two categories. As we saw above, Otto valorizes the "Palestinian" aspects of Eckhart's thought—the emphasis on the moral conscience, the longing for righteousness, and the sense of ethical responsibility—precisely those aspects, in other words, that mark the sharpest contrast with his Indian counterpart.[110] In this way, Part B of Otto's text foregrounds the ineradicable tension—indeed contradiction—between Aryan discourse and Christianity, a contradiction perhaps most clearly demonstrated in the failure of the infamous "German-Christian" movement to resolve it. Or perhaps one could view Otto's implicit challenge to the discourse on Aryanism from another angle. Otto's sharp contrast between the German mysticism of Eckhart and the Indian mysticism of Śaṅkara in Part B exposes the tension between the two halves of the composite category of the Indo-German.[111] For, as Richard King shows, one dimension of the East versus West dichotomy that Otto invokes in his comparison of Eckhart and Śaṅkara is a "nationalist" contrast between the former's German and the latter's Indian background.[112]

Otto's Christian apologetic, with its implicit revalorization of the Semitic and its concomitant disarticulation of the concept of the Indo-Germanic, thus disrupts the contingent set of alignments and oppositions constituting the early twentieth-century discourse on Aryanism in Germany. And yet, even if Otto's comparison of Eckhart and Śaṅkara in some ways worked against the grain of an ideological discourse with particularly odious implications and consequences, it nevertheless continues to work with essentialized categories and tendentious dichotomies. In the remaining chapters of this book, I take a fresh look at Eckhart and Śaṅkara with the aim of dismantling the dichotomous world- and life-affirmation/world- and life-denial schema, which, as we have seen, has shaped the modern history of reception of Indian religion and the discourse of comparative mysticism. In this task, Otto's *Mysticism East and West,* despite its use of that schema (and to that extent serving as a negative example), actually provides a helpful point of departure. For, as I hope to show, the analytical and interpretive judgments by which Otto vindicates Meister Eckhart from the charges of pantheism, acosmism, and quietism can be extended to his Indian counterpart.

Each of the following three chapters focuses on a particular aspect of the "East" versus "West" dichotomy that Otto employs in his comparison of Eckhart and Śaṅkara. Chapter 5 critically examines the theological contrast between a dynamic theism and a static pantheism; chapter 6 the cosmological contrast between world affirmation and world denial; and chapter 7 the ethical contrast between activism and quietism. We shall see that Śaṅkara's teaching, when read sympathetically in light of Otto's interpretation of Eckhart, no longer conforms to the orientalist image of Indian master that sustains Otto's Christian apologetic.

5

God and the God beyond God in Eckhart and Śaṅkara

Herein lies the most extraordinary analogy between Eckhart and Śaṅkara: high above the God and the personal Lord abides the "Godhead," having an almost identical relationship to God as that of Brahman to Iśvara.

—Rudolf Otto

One of the most original, though generally underappreciated, aspects of Otto's comparison of Meister Eckhart and Śaṅkara is his thesis that the latter's mysticism rests on a theistic foundation.[1] Like Eckhart's Godhead, Śaṅkara's impersonal concept of Brahman maintains a relation of continuity with God and the personal Lord, Īśvara. With this thesis, Otto challenges the orientalist, specifically, the Hegelian conception of Brahman as a static and lifeless abstraction. By implication, this interpretation of Śaṅkara's theology also challenges the essentializing contrast between a dynamic Christian theism and a static oriental pantheism.

Otto fails to draw out the anti-essentialist implications of his interpretation of Śaṅkara's concept of Brahman, however. As we saw in the previous chapter, Otto's insistence on the "theistic substructure" of Śaṅkara's mysticism is motivated by a specific concern, namely, to prevent the parallel between Śaṅkara's concept of Brahman and Eckhart's concept of God from undermining his project of vindicating Eckhart from the charge of pantheism. In the last analysis, Otto is not interested in radically challenging the essentialist dichotomy between a dynamic Christian theism and a static oriental pantheism. As we have seen, this dichotomy appears in Part B of *Mysticism East and West*.

In this chapter, I would like to develop Otto's insight into the theistic foundation of Śaṅkara's concept of Brahman with the aim of calling this dichotomy into question. By redescribing the relationship between Śaṅkara's Īśvara and *nirguṇa* Brahman in terms of the dialectical relationship between Eckhart's God and Godhead, then, I not only follow Otto in challenging the representation of Śaṅkara's Brahman as a lifeless abstraction, but I also go beyond Otto calling into question the apologetic discourse that this representation of Brahman supports. In challenging the invidious contrast through which Christian apologists have secured a sense of Christian identity—and superiority—over against the religions of the East ostensibly epitomized by Śaṅkara's Vedānta, the comparative exercise undertaken below will exemplify the second, anti-essentializing moment of the dialectical model of comparative theology set forth in chapter 3.

Before examining the Īśvara-Brahman/God-Godhead parallel in detail, however, I would first like to draw attention to an important feature of the comparative process that Otto's discussion of this parallel beautifully illustrates. If comparison is understood as a way of construing or redescribing one thing in terms of another in order to highlight aspects of the former that are of particular interest to the scholar, then it makes a difference which of the two terms is being redescribed and, conversely, which one is providing the redescription. The point of comparative redescription is to transform one's understanding of the former term for a particular purpose. This purpose may be either to overcome the incomprehensibility of an unfamiliar phenomenon, or, alternatively, it may be to unsettle a sense of familiarity that has dulled one's perception of a phenomenon. In either case, it is the phenomenon to be redescribed that represents the primary focus of one's interest, at least at this moment in the comparison. We might say that the term to be redescribed represents the variable and the term forming the redescription the constant in the comparative equation. What this means is that, strictly speaking, comparison is not a symmetrical process. Redescribing A in terms of B is not the same as redescribing B in terms of A. Each direction implies a different purpose. Thus comparison can function as a means of familiarization in one direction (i.e., when the less familiar term is redescribed in terms of the unfamiliar), and as a technique of defamiliarization in the other (when the familiar term is redescribed in terms of the familiar).

In the comparison of Eckhart and Śaṅkara on the question of the relation between the personal and impersonal aspects of the divine, it therefore makes a difference whether Eckhart is redescribed in terms of Śaṅkara or vice-versa.

In other words, the Īśvara-Brahman/God-Godhead parallel can be put to very different purposes depending on which of the two terms of the comparison, Eckhart or Śaṅkara, serves as the focus of comparison. If Eckhart is the focal or variable term in the comparison—that is, if Eckhart represents the term to be redescribed—then the parallel will most likely encourage a pantheistic reading of his theology. Śaṅkara's theology, which in this case is functioning as the constant term in the comparison, is conventionally understood to subordinate the personal Lord, Īśvara, to the impersonal Brahman. Thus the redescription of the God/Godhead relation in Eckhart in terms of the Īśvara-Brahman relation in Śaṅkara tends to focus attention on the difference between the two aspects of divinity to the point of implying a pantheistic denial of the personal God of Christianity. If, on the other hand, Śaṅkara forms the focal or variable term of the comparison, then the parallel serves an entirely different purpose. Here the redescription of the Īśvara-Brahman relationship in Śaṅkara in terms of Eckhart challenges the conventional reading of the former as an abstract monism. It is precisely the second of these options that Otto pursues in Mysticism *East and West*.

In making Śaṅkara the focal point of comparison at this point in his study, Otto is taking strategic advantage of the asymmetrical nature of the comparative process. Given that his primary concern is with Eckhart—specifically, vindicating the German master from the charge of pantheism—one might think that Otto is committed to redescribing Eckhart in terms of Śaṅkara and thus having the Īśvara-Brahman/God-Godhead parallel work against his interpretive interests. In order to prevent this from happening, Otto deftly reverses the direction of comparison so that Śaṅkara provisionally becomes the focus of comparison—that is, he makes Śaṅkara, not Eckhart, the redescribed term at this point in his comparison.

In my reexamination of the Īśvara-Brahman/God-Godhead parallel below, I shall follow Otto in this procedure. Using a non-pantheistic interpretation of Eckhart as the "constant" term of redescription, I shall challenge the conventional interpretation of Śaṅkara, as mentioned above. This procedure requires that we begin with a specification of the God/Godhead relation in Eckhart.

Two Theological Paradigms in Eckhart's Mystical Theology

The suggestion of a "God beyond God" in Eckhart's writings presents both an interpretive and a theological challenge. The central theological question raised by Eckhart's writings is whether Eckhart's Godhead (*gotheit*), the endpoint of the soul's mystical journey, coincides with the first person of the Trinity, God the Father, or, alternatively, lies beyond the Trinity altogether. Louis Dupré articulates this central problem in the interpretation of Eckhart as follows:

> Does Eckhart simply mean that, at some point, in growing toward the Image the soul ends up in darkness, because with the Son she has moved into the dark desert of the Father? Or does he mean that the created mind in its spiritual ascent moves into a divine reality where the distinctions between the Father, Son, and Holy Spirit no longer exist? The latter position is highly controversial from a spiritual as well as a theological viewpoint, and if Eckhart held it, the bishop of Cologne was right to attack it.[2]

In drawing attention to the controversial nature of Eckhart's teaching, Dupré alludes to the charge of pantheism, which, as we saw in the last chapter, has shaped the reception of Eckhart's work.[3]

As indicated by Dupré's use of the conditional in the quote above, however, the question of whether Eckhart taught a God beyond the Trinity is far from unambiguous. One can easily find texts in the Meister's oeuvre supporting a wholly orthodox interpretation of the Godhead as coinciding with the first person of the Trinity. Then again, one can just as easily find others that support a radical interpretation of the Godhead as existing apart from the distinctions of the divine Persons.[4] Thus in his Sermon 15, representing the first, orthodox set of texts, Eckhart writes that "[t]he Father is an origin of the Godhead (*begin der gothait*), for he comprehends himself in himself."[5] As an example of the second, theologically daring group of texts, we may cite a striking passage from Sermon 2: "But as he [God] is simply one, without any manner or properties, he is not Father or Son or Holy Spirit, and yet he is a something that is neither this nor that."[6] The presence of both sets of texts in Eckhart's writings points to an underlying tension between two theological tendencies in the Meister's thought, one orthodox and Trinitarian, the other radical and apophatic.

Following Bernward Dietsche, we can identify two theological paradigms in Eckhart's work corresponding respectively to the orthodox and radical passages. The orthodox passages correspond to what Dietsche terms "the classical Trinitarian model," "which, in accordance with the tradition, takes the first of the three Persons as one with the divine essence without excluding the two other persons."[7] This orthodox theological schema gives way to the second paradigm, which Dietsche calls the "apophatic model," when an emphasis on divine unity reaches the point of tearing the divine essence away from the three Persons.[8] From one perspective, this second, apophatic model implies a kind of unitarianism, inasmuch as it elevates the divine essence above the divine Persons. From another, it implies a kind of quaternity in God, in which the separated essence, variously represented as the Godhead (*deitas, gotheit*) or ground (*grunt*) of God, stands alongside the Father, Son, and Holy Spirit as a kind of fourth principle.

Our particular interest in exploring the parallel with Śaṅkara's distinction between Īśvara and Brahman naturally focuses attention on this second, apophatic model in Eckhart's mystical theology. We must be careful, however, not to allow a preoccupation with the apophatic model to eclipse its intrinsic relation with the Trinitarian. Below I shall argue, following Michael Sells and Shizuteru Ueda (among others), that the Trinitarian and apophatic models represent the two terms of what Sells terms "a discourse of double propositions," that is, a form of theological discourse which, like metaphor, creates meaning out of the tension between its juxtaposed terms.[9] Such a conception of Dietsche's two models as forming a double paradigm forms the basis, in fact, of the redescription of Śaṅkara that I will offer in the next section.

Now the apophatic model assumes different forms in Eckhart's Latin treatises and his German sermons, two bodies of material which, while cohering with each other, nevertheless reflect the particular concerns proper to each genre as well as the different conceptual possibilities of their respective languages.

In the Latin works, the apophatic model takes the form of an uncompromising insistence on the unity of God.[10] There the apophatic model makes its appearance when the unity of God takes precedence over the Trinity of Persons. A central apophatic text in the Latin corpus is a section from Eckhart's *Commentary on Exodus* (nos. 58–72),[11] in which the Meister takes up "that famous and knotty question of whether there is a distinction of attributes in God or only in our intellect's way of grasping."[12] In a passage betraying the substantial influence of the great Jewish scholastic Moses Maimonides (1135–1204), Eckhart answers by declaring unambiguously that the distinction of divine attributes "is totally on the side of the intellect that receives and draws knowledge of such things from and through creatures."[13] Eckhart's unequivocal denial of distinction in God here might be construed as undermining the doctrine of the Trinity because it seems to deny that the Trinitarian distinctions have any basis in the being of God.[14] It is hardly surprising, then, that Eckhart's concluding statement of this paragraph, together with a direct citation from Maimonides, were singled out for condemnation in the Papal Bull *In agro dominico*.[15] Eckhart is himself aware of the tension between his emphasis on the absolute unity of God and a tradition of Trinitarian speculation. This awareness is evident in his acknowledgment, in Paragraph 62, of an apparent contradiction between, on the one hand, his claim that only one of the Aristotelian categories of being, namely substance, exists in God—a specification of his teaching on absolute unity—and, on the other, the teaching of authorities like Augustine and Boethius that there are in fact two such categories in God, namely, substance and relation. Those theologians included relation in the divine being as a way of grounding the Trinitarian distinctions in divine reality. Thus, substance and relation in God correspond to the unity of the divine nature and the Trinity of divine Persons, respectively.[16] Eckhart's effort in the rather technical discussion that follows (Paragraphs 62–72) to reconcile his own teaching with this tradition, however, does little to dispel the concern that Eckhart's emphasis on the absolute unity of God comes at the expense of the Trinitarian distinctions. Indeed, Eckhart interprets the proposition that there are two categories in God in such a way that it supports, rather than qualifies, a theologically questionable prioritization of divine unity over the Trinity of Persons. In his discussion on the categorical distinction between substance and relation in God, Eckhart appeals to a scholastic distinction between relations and other "accidents," such as quality, number, and so on. Unlike those other accidents, relations are not defined by their inherence in a substance (*esse in*), but rather by their reference or "being toward" (*esse ad*) another entity.[17] Whereas the divine attributes (goodness, wisdom, justice, etc.) are absorbed into (*transit*) the divine substance thanks to the *inesse* relation that defines the mode of being of all accidental categories,[18] the divine relations "remain as it were standing outside" (*manet quasi foris stans*) the divine substance.[19] This conclusion, which nearly coincides with the suspect view of Gilbert of Poitiers,[20] contrasts with the orthodox view of Thomas Aquinas that real relations in God—and therefore the three Persons of the Trinity—belong to the divine essence (*quod relatio in Deo est idem quod sua essentia*).[21]

Eckhart's exclusion of the relations from the substance of God can easily be taken to imply a distinction between God as Father and God as substance that is problematic from the standpoint of Christian Trinitarianism. Ueda finds support for such an interpretation in Eckhart's statement that "God is not simply and by the same idea God the Father and God as substance, but he is God as substance by one idea and Father by another."[22] Indeed, he goes even further, arguing that Eckhart's denial of a relation between substance and relation in God implies a separation of God from the essence of God.[23] Bernard McGinn offers an interpretation of this section of the Exodus commentary that, while not going so far as to conclude that Eckhart's exclusion of relations from the divine substance implies a *separation* between God and Godhead, nevertheless agrees with Ueda's in its assessment that this section supports a *distinction* between the two. McGinn suggests that a distinction between God as Trinity and God as hidden Godhead allows one to resolve the apparent contradiction between, on the one hand, Eckhart's denial of distinction in God and, on the other, his affirmation of the distinction between substance and relation in God.[24] We must acknowledge, however, the ambiguity and interpretive uncertainty of this discussion in Eckhart—which, of course, is what we might expect from an attempt to reconcile the negative theology of Maimonides with orthodox Trinitarian speculation (a task that Josef Koch, for one, declares to be impossible[25]). An indication of the interpretive uncertainty of this text is that at least one interpreter of Eckhart, P. L. Reynolds, denies that it supports the notion of a God beyond the Trinity. Challenging McGinn's interpretation in particular, Reynolds argues that Eckhart, in emphasizing that the relations do not pass into the divine substance, probably "wishes to do no more than to affirm that the relations, unlike the attributes, remain multiple."[26] Even if we concede, however, that Eckhart's discussion of substance and relation in God does not demand the God/Godhead distinction as an interpretive hypothesis, it is clear that, at the very least, it does not exclude such an interpretation. This means that even according to a rather cautious interpretation, this discussion can provide corroborative support for a distinction between God as Trinity and God as hidden Godhead if evidence for such a distinction can be found elsewhere in the Meister's oeuvre.

Such evidence is readily found in the Meister's German works, his sermons in particular. Even Reynolds, who argues that a distinction between God as Trinity and as Godhead is not found in the Latin corpus, concedes that such a distinction is unequivocal in the Meister's German sermons.[27] That the God/Godhead distinction finds its clearest expression in the German works suggests that this distinction—and with it Dietsche's "apophatic model"—is motivated by a concern that is, if not specific to, at least definitive of the German sermons. This motivating concern is none other than Eckhart's intention, as a preacher of mysticism, to awaken in his hearers a union, at once rhetorical and experiential, between the soul and God. This mystical concern achieves its most forceful expression in Eckhart's concept of the ground (MHG: *grunt*) of God, a concept that, not coincidentally, is found only in the German works. McGinn describes the *grunt* concept as a "master metaphor" that focuses and organizes the various discourses comprising Eckhart's mystical theology.[28] In particular, the concept of *grunt* unites two ideas that can only be expressed separately in Latin, namely, that of the hidden depth of God, on the one hand, and of the innermost part of the soul, on the other. The first of these aspects of *grunt* finds its nearest parallel in Eckhart's use of the Latin concept of *principium*. *Principium* in Eckhart's theology refers to God as origin and source. But it corresponds to a deeper dimension of God's being than the notion of God as first cause (*causa, causa prima*).[29] Unlike the latter term, which refers to the relation of efficient causality that obtains between God and creation,[30] *principium* denotes the formal presence of God in that of which he is the *principium*. Its primary reference is to the Father as the source and origin of the Son and the Holy Spirit.[31] A good example of Eckhart's use *grunt* in the sense of *principium* as the origin and formal principle of the Trinitarian processions is found in Sermon 69. There Eckhart says that the intellect (MHG: *vernüfticheit*), "never rests, it bursts into the ground from which goodness and truth come forth and perceives it [God's being] *in principio*, in the beginning, where goodness and truth are going out, before it acquires any name, before it bursts forth, . . ."[32]

Unlike Latin *principium*, however, whose reference is limited to the divine realm,[33] *grunt* can also refer to the innermost part of the soul. In this anthropological sense, it corresponds to the Latin *essentia* or *abditum animae* (essence or hidden aspect of the soul).[34] Insofar as *grunt* combines the notion of the hidden essence of the soul and the hidden depth of God, it expresses, in a manner not possible in Latin, the mystical idea that God can be found in the innermost depths of the soul, or, as Eckhart puts it, "the ground of the soul [is] where God's ground and the soul's ground are one ground."[35]

The concept of *grunt*, with its implicit reference to the procession of the divine Persons from the Father, forms the basis of a homology between, on the one hand, the soul in its relation to the three Augustinian faculties of intellect, memory, and will and, on the other, God's essence in relation to the three divine Persons, the Father, Son, and Holy Spirit.[36] Eckhart makes the homology explicit in the opening paragraph of his Sermon 83:

> Augustine says that in the highest part of the soul, which he calls *mens* or disposition, God created together with the soul's being a power, which the authorities call a store or coffer of spiritual forms or formal images. This power makes the soul resemble the Father in his outflowing divinity, out of which he has poured the whole treasure of his divine being into the Son and into the Holy Spirit, differentiating between the Persons, just as the soul's memory pours the treasure of images into the soul's powers.[37]

Theologically, this passage falls within Dietsche's "classical Trinitarian" model. The highest part of the soul corresponds to the Father as *fontalis plenitudo*; God's essence still coincides fully with the Father. In the text immediately following, however, the Trinitarian paradigm quickly gives way to the apophatic:

> But if all images are detached [*abgescheiden werdent*] from the soul, and it contemplates only the Simple One, then the soul's naked being finds the naked, formless being of the divine unity, which is there a

> being above being, accepting and reposing in itself. Ah, marvel of marvels, how noble is that acceptance, when the soul's being can accept nothing else than the naked unity of God![38]

This passage suggests that what initiates the transition from the Trinitarian model to the apophatic is the soul's detachment (*abgescheidenheit*) from all created images. Given the homology between the soul and its powers, on the one hand, and the divine essence and the Persons, on the other, the soul's attempt to tear itself away from its outwardly directed faculties as it seeks to penetrate its hidden ground effects a parallel separation between God's essence and the Persons of the Trinity.[39] As if by an act of sympathetic magic, the soul's detachment on the level of spiritual practice induces an apophasis on the level of metaphysics. A striking passage from Sermon 2 gives expression to this idea:

> This little fortress [*bürgelîn*] is so truly one and simple, and this simple one is so exalted above every manner and every power, that no power, no manner, not God himself may look at it. It is as true that this is true and that I speak truly as that God is alive! God himself never for an instant looks into it, never yet did he look on it, so far as he possesses himself in the manner and according to the properties [*eigenschaft*] of his Persons. It is well to observe this, because this simple one is without manner and without properties. And therefore, if God were ever to look upon it, that must cost him all his divine names and the properties of his Persons;[40] that he must wholly forsake, if he is ever once to look into it. But as he is simply one, without any manner and properties, he is not Father or Son or Holy Spirit, and yet he is a something that is neither this or that.[41]

This passage plays on the ambiguity of MHG *eigenschaft*, which, like English "property," can mean "property" either in the sense of a belonging or a possession or in the sense of a characteristic or a quality.[42] *Eigenschaft*, like the concept of *grunt* itself, unites two discursive realms, those of ascetic practice and metaphysical speculation.[43] Because the soul renounces the possessiveness and possessions (*eigenschaften*) that bind it to a worldly existence, God must divest himself of the properties (*eigenschaften*) that limit the fullness of divine being.[44] Eckhart's use of *eigenschaft* in this sermon exemplifies the way in which Eckhart enacts a mystical homology between the soul and God through the creative use of language.

This passage shows how the soul's quest for radical detachment discloses a hidden aspect of God beyond all relationships, Trinitarian as well as creaturely. At this point we should point out that the notion of a God beyond the

Trinity only arises in connection with one of the two movements that constitute Eckhart's mystical theology, namely, the "breaking through" (*durchbruch*) of the soul to the hidden ground of God. The other, complementary movement, the creative "flowing out" (MHG: *ûzvluz, ûzvliezen*; cf. NHG: *Ausfluss; ausfliessen*) of all things from the divine source, remains, generally speaking, within the Trinitarian paradigm. In the "flowing out," the divine ground coincides with God as the *principium* of the procession of the divine Persons. In other words, God as the source of the creative "boiling" (*bullitio*) that manifests the Persons of the Holy Trinity as well as the "boiling over" (*ebullitio*) of this creative life into the activity of creation proper is the Father as *fontalis plenitudo*. The God of the "outflow" thus is relational: God the Father is constituted by his relation to the Son, and God as creator is defined by his relation to the creation. It is only in the breakthrough, where God is stripped of all his properties and relations as the soul cuts away all its attachments, that Eckhart speaks of God beyond all relationships, whether Trinitarian or creaturely.[45] Nowhere is this distinction between relative and nonrelative aspects of God more clearly or powerfully expressed than in Eckhart's celebrated Sermon 52 on spiritual poverty, *Beati pauperes spiritu* ("Blessed are the poor in spirit"), the locus classicus of the Eckhartian "breakthrough":

> When I stood in my first cause, I then had no "God," and then I was my own cause.... But when I went out from my own free will and received my created being, then I had a "God," for before there were any creatures, God was not "God," but he was what he was. But when creatures came to be and received their created being, then God was not "God" in himself, but he was "God" in creatures.[46]

"If I did not exist," Eckhart declares later in this same sermon, "God too would not be God."[47]

Despite Eckhart's hyperbolic declaration that the relational God and the non-relational Godhead "are as different as heaven and earth,"[48] we must not make the mistake of narrowly identifying the true God with the latter and dismissing the former as an anthropological projection—a mistake, incidentally, that is implicit in the common editorial practice of using either capitalization or quotation marks to distinguish the two aspects of divinity in modern English translations of Eckhart's apophatic passages.[49] One must not, in other words, repeat the mistake of those early interpreters of Eckhart who, in an effort to separate Eckhart from the tradition of Christian scholasticism, focused one-sidedly on the most radical of the Meister's statements while dismissing his (far more numerous) orthodox utterances as mere holdovers from a tradition against which he allegedly struggled to free himself. To isolate the apophatic model in this way as somehow expressive of the "true" Eckhart is to ignore the other "half" of Eckhart's mystical theology, namely, the birth of the Son in the soul and, more generally, the entire movement of the "outflow" of God's creative activity into the world. Even an interpreter like Ueda, who regards the apophatic model as the fulfillment (*Vollendung*) of the Trinitarian, emphasizes the former's dependence on the latter as its necessary presupposition. Appealing to Otto's characterization of Eckhart's mystical theology as a mystical-apophatic superstructure erected upon a base of Christian theism, Ueda argues that the apophatic model can no more be separated from the Trinitarian than the second story of a building can be from the ground floor.[50] Ueda sees this relation of dependence reflected in language: the derivation of the term "*gotheit*" from the word "*got*" signifies this dependence of the apophatic model on the Trinitarian. "Only from God can the ground of God's essence be called 'Godhead.'"[51] A more recent interpreter of Eckhart, Michael Sells, also emphasizes the necessary relation between the two models, but without the hierarchical implications of Ueda's model of base and superstructure. Sells understands the relationship between the two models in terms of a broadened conception of apophatic discourse that includes the discourse that is negated as its necessary presupposition.[52] Apophatic discourse is "an act of unsaying [that] demands or presupposes a previous saying."[53] As the two moments of an act of apophatic discourse, the Trinitarian and apophatic models form a "double paradigm" which, like metaphor, generates meaning from the tension between what is said and unsaid.[54] Together the two models constitute a mode of theological discourse that fights against the reifying tendencies inherent in all language, including its own. And yet Eckhart's apophatic discourse is motivated by something more concrete than simply a kind of postmodern reflex to preempt the occurrence of semantic closure. As the analysis above suggests, what initiates the movement from the Trinitarian model to the apophatic one is an emphasis on radical detachment. We might say that the concern with detachment "stresses" the classic Trinitarian model to the point that it gives way to the apophatic. This understanding of Eckhart's mysticism as a Christian scholasticism strongly inflected by an emphasis on the theme of detachment finds support in Herbert Grundmann's thesis that the distinctive style of "German mysticism" is rooted in the encounter of the theological tradition with the new religious movements of the thirteenth century, particularly the Beguines with their concern with spiritual poverty.[55] From this perspective, Eckhart's emphasis on radical detachment and mystical "releasement" (*Gelassenheit*) represents the interiorization and sublimation of the quest for evangelical poverty that defined Beguine spirituality.[56]

Śaṅkara's Concept of Brahman as a Double Paradigm

In this section, I would like to use this understanding of Eckhart's theology as a "discourse of double propositions" as an interpretive template or paradigm for understanding the relationship between Īśvara and Brahman in Śaṅkara's Advaita Vedānta theology.[57] By redescribing Śaṅkara's theology in terms of Eckhart's concept of God as a double paradigm I would like to challenge a long-standing interpretive tradition that posits a radical break between Īśvara and the highest Brahman. According to this tradition—which, as we shall see, more accurately reflects the teaching of later Advaita than Śaṅkara—Īśvara, the personal lord of the universe, coincides with a lower (*apara*) or "qualified" (*saguṇa*) form of Brahman. As *aparaṃ brahma*, Īśvara is defined by his relation to the world that he creates. Since, according to this interpretation of Advaita, the world with its dualities—including the duality between the world and its divine cause—is ultimately *māyā* or cosmic illusion, Īśvara belongs to the realm of *māyā*. Upon the realization of non-duality, Īśvara-*aparaṃ brahma* is "sublated" (*bādhita*) along with the world. What is revealed is the higher (*para*) Brahman, which is impersonal, non-relational, quality-less (*nirguṇa*), and action-less (*nirkartṛ*).

This interpretation presents problems from both a systematic-philosophical and a historical-philological point of view. From a philosophical point of view, it is problematic because it effectively divorces Brahman from the world. Anantanand Rambachan, writing both as a scholar of Śaṅkara and as an Advaita theologian, gives a particularly eloquent and concise philosophical critique of this conventional hierarchical understanding of the distinction between the two forms of Brahman. Echoing a line of social and political critique of classical Vedānta found in modern Indian thought,[58] Rambachan argues that the separation of the highest Brahman from Brahman as the world-cause has the unfortunate consequence of "reducing the significance of the world and human existence within it."[59] At the same time, this interpretation presents Brahman "as a bland and static reality incapable, unless conjoined with *māyā*, of bringing forth the creation," a description that at once recalls Hegel's tendentious characterization of Brahman as a "an abstract unity without determination" and classical Śākta descriptions of the Absolute separated from the enabling presence of the *śakti* principle.[60] This interpretation of Advaita not only lends support to invidious characterizations of Indian religion as fostering an indifference to the world and its problems, but also, ironically enough, at the same time, forms the basis of an imperialistic Neo-Hindu apologetic that subordinates the various expressions of God in other traditions to the lower form of Brahman.[61]

An interpretation of Śaṅkara's Advaita that neatly separates the higher and lower forms of Brahman and identifies Īśvara with the latter also presents problems from a philological point of view. While it might accurately reflect the teaching of later Vedānta, it fails to harmonize with what is found in Śaṅkara's undisputed works. A line of interpreters of Śaṅkara's authentic works, starting with Colonel G. A. Jacob in 1893 and including, among others, Rudolf Otto and Paul Hacker, have drawn attention to a lack of consistency in Śaṅkara's use of the concepts *īśvara*, *parameśvara* ("highest Lord"), *aparaṃ brahma*, *paraṃ brahma*, as well as *paramātman* ("highest Self").[62] Both Jacob, in the introduction to his edition of Sadānanda's *Vedāntasāra*, and Hacker, in his classic article, "Distinctive Features of the Doctrine and Terminology of Śaṅkara," have cited passages in Śaṅkara's *Brahma-sūtra Bhāṣya* (commentary on the *Brahma-sūtra*) where Śaṅkara uses *īśvara* where one would expect, on the basis of the distinction between conventional (*vyāvahārika*) and absolute (*pāramārthika*) reality that Śaṅkara himself introduces, *paraṃ brahma*, and, converesly, *paraṃ brama* or *paramātman* where would expect *īśvara* or *aparaṃ brahma*. For example, Śaṅkara sometimes speaks of Īśvara as transcending the realm of saṃsāric existence, a distinction that should logically be reserved for the higher Brahman alone.[63] Elsewhere he uses *paraṃ brahma* alongside of *īśvara* to refer to that which is the material and efficient cause of the world, again in apparent disregard of the distinction between the two levels of reality.[64] In short, Śaṅkara uses the terms *paraṃ brahma* and *īśvara* more or less interchangeably. This practice suggests a more exalted view of Īśvara than is justified, strictly speaking, by the conventional understanding of Advaita doctrine. According to this conventional understanding, which is explicit in later Advaita, Īśvara is identified with *aparaṃ brahma*, that is, Brahman associated with *māyā*.[65]

Jacob attributed this terminological inconsistency in Śaṅkara to the influence of a contemporary form of Viśiṣṭādvaita or some other variety of theistic Vedānta. Śaṅkara's mind, he concludes, "was so saturated with their doctrines as to be unable to shake them off even when propounding an antagonistic system."[66] Otto saw more than historical influence behind Śaṅkara's tendency to conflate Īśvara and the highest Brahman. He regarded it instead as evidence for a kind of Christian perennialism, the notion that theism "somehow arises out of the deep necessity of mankind in general."[67] For his part, Hacker prescinds from an investigation of the historical causes for Śaṅkara's terminological inconsistency in his "Distinctive Features," article, a study whose primary aim was establishing criteria for the identification of Śaṅkara's authentic works.[68] However, Hacker apparently cannot resist offering a quasi-psychological explanation of Śaṅkara's terminological inconsistency, attributing it to "an aversion for definitions and a cavalier attitude towards conceptual systematization."[69] Of the three explanatory approaches represented here, the historical, theological, and the psychological, the historical approach is the most plausible. The hypothesis of a theistic, specifically a Vaiṣṇava, context to Śaṅkara's authentic works forms the basis, for example, of J. G. Suthren Hirst's compelling argument that Śaṅkara's distinctive use of Īśvara reflects a teaching strategy that pragmatically draws on his students' Vaiṣṇava background to lead them to Advaitic realization.[70]

In what follows, I would like to suggest a reading of Śaṅkara's *Brahma-sūtra Bhāṣya* (henceforth, BSBh) that supports and complements interpretations like Hirst's that recognize Śaṅkara's creative appropriation of preexisting discourses and practices. Based on a critical analysis of the BSBh,[71] I will argue that Śaṅkara's Advaita is internally constituted by an earlier discourse of theistic, realist Vedānta that is preserved in the BSBh. We will see that this understanding of Śaṅkara's teaching as an instance of what Mikhail Bakhtin might call "double-voiced discourse" accounts for Śaṅkara's terminological inconsistency in a more adequate way than any of the explanations mentioned above. At the same time, it supports an understanding of Śaṅkara's theology of Brahman that is analogous to Eckhart's theology understood as a discourse of double propositions. This understanding of Śaṅkara's concept of Brahman as an Eckhartian double paradigm avoids the main criticisms Rambachan directs against the conventional interpretation of the Advaitic concept of Brahman, specifically, that it fosters an indifferent attitude toward the world and that it conceives of Brahman as a sterile and abstract absolute.

My suggestion that Śaṅkara's Advaita represents a form of double-voiced discourse derives from an appreciation of the richly stratified nature of the BSBh. By this, I mean that the text is not, in all but the most literal and superficial sense, the work of a single author, its teaching the direct expression of the personal religious insight of the individual known as Ādi-Śaṅkara. Rather, it is the product of a creative encounter of multiple "voices" both within and outside of the Vedāntic tradition, an encounter, to be sure, orchestrated and given its final shape by Śaṅkara. Now at one level this multivocality of the text is immediately obvious: the text is a commentary (*bhāṣya*), or more accurately, a meta-commentary. The immediate object of Śaṅkara's commentary (early eighth century CE) is the set of gnomic propositions known as the *Brahma-sūtra* (fifth century CE), traditionally associated with the name Bādarāyaṇa.[72] The *Brahma-sūtra* in turn represents a commentary of sorts on the disparate collection of texts forming the upaniṣadic corpus (the earliest of which date from roughly—very roughly!—the eighth to seventh centuries BCE).[73] But the voices of the tradition are not the only ones that are heard in the text. Included as well are those of the rival teachers and traditions against which the tradition of

Advaita Vedānta defined itself. This second, apologetic dimension of the BSBh's multivocality is also fairly obvious. Even a cursory reading of the text reveals that refutations of rival teachings comprise a large portion of the work.

There is yet a third dimension of the BSBh's multivocality that is more subtle than either its commentarial function or its polemical engagement with rival philosophies. Commentators on Śaṅkara's *Bhāṣya*, both ancient and modern, have noted that Śaṅkara occasionally departs from an earlier, generally realist interpretation of the *Brahma-sūtra* which his text nevertheless preserves. These instances of apparent innovation, which are admittedly exceptional, invariably occur when Śaṅkara introduces his signature teaching of the unreality of the phenomenal world. Later commentators on Śaṅkara's *Bhāṣya* like Vācaspati Miśra (mid-ninth century), Ānandagiri (thirteenth century) and Govindānanda (end of the sixteenth century) attribute the interpretation qualified or overturned by Śaṅkara to a figure they vaguely and enigmatically refer to as the "commentator" (*vṛttikāra*).[74] The Sanskritist D. H. H. Ingalls hypothesized that "the commentator"—Ingalls dubs him the "Proto-commentator" to distinguish him from others[75]—was the author of an earlier, lost commentary on the *Brahma-sūtra*. Both Ingalls and Paul Hacker, working independently of each other, develop this hypothesis of a pre-Śaṅkara *bhāṣya* in order to explain the curious fact that the next oldest extent commentary on the *Brahma-sūtra* after Śaṅkara's, that of Bhāskara (early ninth century), often shows substantial—indeed, sometimes verbatim—agreement with Śaṅkara's text, while at the same time bitterly attacking Śaṅkara's teaching, especially when the latter departs from the realist interpretations of the Proto-commentator.[76] Reasoning that Bhāskara could hardly be expected to reproduce the text of his bitter rival, both Ingalls and Hacker advance the hypothesis, reminiscent of the "Q" hypothesis in New Testament studies, that where the texts of Bhāskara and Śaṅkara agree, they are each drawing from an earlier, no-longer-extant commentary on the *Brahma-sūtra*.[77] Belonging to this common body of text are those passages explicitly attributed to the Proto-commentator by Śaṅkara's later commentators. Thus, Ingalls identifies the Proto-commentator as the author of this hypothetical earlier *Brahma-sūtra* commentary serving as a source document for both Śaṅkara and Bhāskara. Since the texts attributed to the Proto-commentator generally express a realist understanding of the relation between the world and Brahman, so the argument goes, it is not surprising that Bhāskara, who also advocated a realist, specifically a "difference in non-difference" or Bhedābheda interpretation of Vedānta, not only would vigorously defend the Proto-commentator's interpretations against Śaṅkara's innovations, but also would reproduce much of the former's text. Śaṅkara, for his part, preserves the Proto-commentator's text out of a deference to tradition,[78] this despite arguing against a Bhedābheda interpretation of Vedānta both in the BSBh and in other works like his commentary on the Bṛhadāraṇyaka Upaniṣad.[79]

More recent scholarship, however, has raised questions about Ingalls's "Proto-commentator" thesis. In particular, Klaus Rüping, developing earlier criticisms of Ingalls by J. A. B. van Buitenen, has argued on the basis of a careful examination of the textual parallels that Bhāskara is not drawing from a pre-Śaṅkara *Brahma-sūtra* commentary but is rather drawing directly from Śaṅkara's text.[80] Having effectively called into question the use of Bhāskara as evidence for the hypothesis of a common literary source, Rüping goes on to question whether the scattered references to "the commentator" (*vṛttikāra*) in the supercommentaries of Vācaspati, Ānandagiri and Govindānanda justify the inference of a lost, pre-Śaṅkaran *Brahma-sūtra* commentary. Instead of referring to a single teacher and/or text, the various references might simply refer vaguely to various authors who differ from Śaṅkara on the particular interpretative point at issue.[81] Whatever doubts Rüping's analysis casts on the hypothesis of a single, common literary source used by both Śaṅkara and Bhāskara, however, Ingalls's larger point, namely, that Śaṅkara's *Bhāṣya* incorporates much in the way of traditional teaching on the *Brahma-sūtra*, still stands.[82] I therefore see little reason for not following the native tradition in referring to this earlier interpretive tradition on the *Brahma-sūtra*, in a kind of convenient shorthand, as that of the Proto-commentator, provided we recognize that this usage need not imply (though does not exclude) the existence of single author or text as the vehicle of this interpretive tradition.

The claim that Śaṅkara's BSBh records the views of an earlier stratum of the tradition forms a core presupposition of my reading of Śaṅkara's teaching on Brahman as an instance of double-voiced discourse. The Proto-commentator and Śaṅkara represent two distinct voices in the text that correspond to two paradigms of Brahman. The tradition of pre-Śaṅkara Vedānta represented by the Proto-commentator defines Brahman as the material and efficient cause of the world. It does not recognize a distinction between higher and lower forms of Brahman, and it tends to identify Brahman with the highest Lord (*parameśvara*).[83] For this reason, I will term this conception of the highest Brahman as the world-cause the Īśvara paradigm. Those passages that correspond to Śaṅkara's distinctive Advaitic teaching introduce the distinction between the higher and lower Brahman. In its higher, *nirguṇa* form, Brahman transcends its role as world-cause. This paradigm of Brahman I will term, with an obvious allusion to our analysis of Eckhart, the apophatic paradigm.

The Proto-Commentator and the Īśvara Paradigm

The passages in the BSBh that reflect the pre-Śaṅkara tradition of realist Vedānta regard the highest Brahman as both the material and efficient cause of the world. This conception of Brahman as the world-cause defined the tradition of early Vedānta. It was, in fact, the chief means by which Vedānta established itself as an independent tradition with a distinctive sense of identity.

The most fundamental way in which the doctrine of Brahman as the world-cause was used to establish the Vedāntic school was by unifying the disparate texts comprising the upaniṣadic corpus under a single principle. The Upaniṣads extol many metaphysical principles—the vital force (*prāṇa*), consciousness (*vijñāna*), "the indestructible" (*akṣa*), and the "primal man" (*puruṣa*), among others—and it is not immediately obvious that Brahman, which originally denoted the sacral power of the Vedic mantras, was the chief among them.[84] In selecting Brahman from the other possible candidates as the fundamental principle, Bādarāyaṇa and the other early teachers of the Vedānta appealed to the text of Taittirīya Upaniṣad 3.1, which speaks of Brahman as "that from which these beings are born, on which, once born, they live, and into which they pass upon death."[85] The significance of this effort to establish Brahman as the chief purport of the Upaniṣads cannot be underestimated. Nothing less than the integrity of the Vedānta was at stake in this project of harmonizing the Upaniṣads under a single principle. For the Vedānta, as indicated by its very name, was defined by its recognition of the unqualified authority of the Upaniṣads, those texts standing at the end (*anta*) of the Veda.

A second way in which the conception of Brahman as the world-cause established the school of Vedānta was by securing the autonomy of the upaniṣadic corpus vis-à-vis the portions of the Veda concerned with ritual. The school of ritual exegesis or Mīmāṃsā claimed that Vedic authority was based solely on the ritual injunctions of the Veda. Its rationale for this claim was that the Veda was authoritative only to the extent that it constituted an independent means of valid cognition (*pramāṇa*), and that, moreover, only the object of an injunction, "what was to be done" (*kārya*), by virtue of its futurity, was inaccessible to empirical means of knowledge like perception and inference. With this argument, the Mīmāṃsakas maintained that the Upaniṣads were subordinate to the ritual portion or *karma-kāṇḍa* of the Veda. In response the Vedāntins argued that the Upaniṣads could not be subsumed under the injunctive portion of the Veda because their object or referent (*artha*), namely Brahman, was an already-existent reality.[86] At the same time, the Upaniṣads still constituted a nonredundant—and hence authoritative—means of knowledge because

Brahman, as the world-cause, was a transcendent reality inaccessible to the empirical *pramāṇas*, including the various forms of inferential reasoning. In this way, the conception of Brahman as the transcendental world-cause established the Vedānta, also known as the Uttara (later) Mīmāṃsā, as an independent school of Vedic exegesis (*mīmāṃsā*), standing in a complementary relationship with its sister school, the Pūrva (earlier) Mīmāṃsā.

Finally, and most directly relevant for our purposes, the doctrine of Brahman as the world-cause was the means by which early Vedānta defined itself over against the rival school of Sāṃkhya. The Sāṃkhya school had ancient roots in the brahmanical tradition and, accordingly, shared with Vedānta a number of fundamental presuppositions, including the conception of salvation as liberation from rebirth, the view of knowledge (*jñāna*) as the most effective means of liberation, and the recognition upaniṣadic of authority. Precisely by virtue of its proximity to Vedānta, Sāṃkhya most likely constituted early Vedānta's most serious rival.[87] On the basis of the amount of space devoted to a criticism of Sāṃkhya doctrines in both the *Brahma-sūtra* and the BSBh, we might conclude with H. Nakamura that "it was through this criticism that the Vedānta school established itself as an independent philosophical tradition."[88] In other words, the seemingly disproportionate amount of attention devoted to the refutation of Sāṃkhya in these early documents of the Vedāntic school suggests that this polemic was not external to the determination of Vedāntic teaching—that it was not, in other words, simply a matter of defending an already-established Vedānta perspective—but was rather constitutive of the distinctive teaching of the Vedānta. Now, the particular Sāṃkhya doctrine that figures prominently in the BSBh, particularly the first of its four *pāda*s (first level of subdivision), is the doctrine of primary matter or *pradhāna* (literally, "that which is placed before") as the world-cause. The Sāṃkhyas argued that their *pradhāna* principle satisfied the formal definition of the fundamental cosmic principle as the cause of the emergence, continuance, and dissolution of the world (*jagat-utpatti-sthiti-nāśa-kāraṇam*) as well as, in fact better than, the Vedāntic candidate, Brahman.[89] Indeed, the Sāṃkhyas could appeal to one of the most famous upaniṣadic texts in support of their doctrine of *pradhāna* as the world-cause. The celebrated teaching of Uddālaka Āruṇi in the sixth chapter (6.1) of the Chāndogya UpaniṢad likens the supreme epistemological principle—that by which "one hears what has not been heard of before, thinks of what has not been thought of before, and perceives what has not been heard of before"[90]—to the clay out of which clay artifacts are fashioned. The *pradhāna* principle, by virtue of its composite nature, better conforms to this upaniṣadic image of material causality than the simple and unchangeable Brahman proffered by the Vedānta.[91]

Against this argument the BSBh adduces upaniṣadic texts like Chāndogya 6.2 and Aitareya 1.1.1–2 that speak of an act of reflection or visualization (*īkṣā*) preceding the act of creation (*īkṣāpūrvikām*).[92] Such passages draw special attention to the active and deliberative nature of the world-cause.[93] In its polemic against the Sāṃkhya *pradhāna* doctrine Vedānta came to recognize efficient (*nimittika*) causality in Brahman, in addition to the material (*upādāna*) causality deriving from Uddālaka's teaching in Chāndogya Upaniṣad 6.[94] Hence the Vedāntic doctrine of Brahman as both the material (*upādāna*) and efficient (*nimittika*) cause of the world.

Brahman as the efficient cause of the world coincides with Īśvara. The concept of Īśvara highlights precisely that aspect of Brahman's nature that distinguishes him/it from the Sāṃkhya principle of primary matter. We might say that it is precisely in virtue of Brahman's *īśvaratva* (lordship) that early Vedānta cosmogony differs from that of Sāṃkhya. It is hardly surprising, then, that those passages of the BSBh reflecting the perspective of an earlier, formative period of Vedānta, when this tradition was struggling to define itself over and against the Sāṃkhya teaching, would tend to equate Brahman and Īśvara.[95]

Śaṅkara and the Apophatic Paradigm

Those passages where Śaṅkara diverges from the tradition of the Proto-commentator evidence a different polemical concern and, not coincidentally, a different conception of Brahman. Polemically, the main preoccupation of these passages is the refutation of the view that ritual action plays a positive, contributory role in the attainment of liberation. The doctrinal expression of this view is the "doctrine of the coordination of knowledge and works" (*jñāna-karma-samuccaya-vāda*), which Śaṅkara associated with the "difference and non-difference" (Bhadābheda) school of Vedānta.[96] Against this effort to reconcile the Vedāntic quest for emancipatory knowledge with the ritual activity that defined traditional brahmanical society, Śaṅkara insisted upon the need for one to renounce all ritual action (*karma*) in order to attain final liberation from saṃsāric existence.[97] Shortly after Śaṅkara, if not before, this dispute split the brahmanical tradition of renunciation into two factions, the so-called single-staff (*eka-daṇḍa*) and triple-staff (*tri-daṇḍa*) traditions, respectively.[98] The first, represented by Śaṅkara's Advaita followers, defined renunciation—or, to be more precise, its highest and paradigmatic form—in terms of a complete abandonment of ritual activity.[99] The second, represented by Bhāskara and later, by Viśiṣṭādvaita, maintained that a renunciant retained his brahmanical status—and thus ensured the legitimacy of his renunciation—only through a continuing commitment, albeit one greatly reduced, to ritual activity.[100]

Śaṅkara's insistence on the absolute unity of Brahman, together with the corollary view that the powers and functions (*śakti* and *pravṛtti*, respectively) associated with Brahman are adventitious to the divine reality, is motivated in part by this dispute with the Bhedābheda Vedāntins. This correlation between apologetics and theology is clear in BSBh 2.1.14, a text that constitutes an extended argument against *bhedābhedavāda*.[101] Here Śaṅkara presents a Bhedābheda opponent who correlates the aspects of difference and non-difference in Brahman to works and knowledge (*karma* and *jñāna*), respectively. The aspect of difference in Brahman grounds the world of multiplicity—characterized by the distinction between actor, action, and result—which is presupposed in human activity, both social and ritual.[102] Against this view, Śaṅkara insists that unity alone is ultimately real; multiplicity is the product of misapprehension.[103] When the unity of self and Brahman is realized, all those activities presupposing a distinction between actor, means, and result will be revealed to have no basis in reality.[104] Only through the knowledge of Brahman devoid of all distinctions and attributes does one attain liberation.[105] To imagine an aspect of distinction in Brahman in an effort to justify a continuation of ritual activity excludes the possibility of emancipatory knowledge.[106]

Śaṅkara's distinction between the higher and lower forms of Brahman can be understood in terms of this antithesis between emancipatory knowledge and ritual activity (*karman*). The *saguṇa/nirguṇa* distinction invariably appears in the context of a discussion of yogic meditation (*upāsana*), which Śaṅkara, implicitly conceding the analogy between mediation and ritual activity implicit in the Mīmāṃsā concept of "meditative injunctions" (*upāsanāvidhi*),[107] classifies as an action presupposing the "duality" of actor, action, and result. While Śaṅkara affirms the value of *upāsana* as an important means of preparing for liberative knowledge within the realm of conventional (*vyāvahārika*) reality, he ultimately regards it as a merely provisional means that is unable to transcend its dualistic presuppositions.[108] Between meditation and knowledge there is a discontinuity, a caesura; from the perspective of absolute (*pāramārthika*) truth they are seen to be mutually exclusive. The distinction between the two forms of Brahman directly reflects this antithesis between *upāsana*, classified as a form of activity, and liberative *jñāna*; Śaṅkara correlates *saguṇa* and *nirguṇa* Brahman to *upāsana* and *jñāna*, respectively.[109] This correlation suggests that the discontinuity that obtains between *upāsana* and *jñāna* on the anthropological plane also obtains between the two forms of Brahman on the theological or metaphysical plane. Thus, Śaṅkara sometimes speaks of the higher and lower Brahman as two Brahmans (*dve brahmanī paramaparaṃ ca*).[110] It would appear, then, that a concern with marking off a special mode of human comportment motivates the recognition of a distinction with respect to Brahman. And here we see a striking parallel with the above-noted correlation between an ethic of radical detachment and the God beyond God theme in the theology of Meister Eckhart.

We have seen, then, that the two paradigms of Brahman reflect different apologetic concerns. The concept of Brahman as the material and efficient cause of the world—what I have been calling the Īśvara paradigm—was developed with an eye toward distinguishing Vedānta from the teaching of the Sāṃkhya school. And the sharp distinction between the higher and lower Brahman—what I have called the apophatic paradigm—reflects an effort to drive a wedge between knowledge and meditation, two concepts that were not sharply distinguished—indeed, which were often equivalent—in the earlier tradition of the *Brahma-sūtra* and the Proto-commentator.[111] With this distinction between knowledge and mediation, where the latter was defined as a form of action, Śaṅkara extended his critique of Pūrva Mīmāṃsā to include not only Bhedābheda Vedānta but the tradition of Yoga as well.[112]

Usually these two paradigms and the interpretive strata they reflect are not clearly set off from each other in the text of the BSBh. For this reason, the text's stratified, double-voiced character is apt to appear as logical inconsistency, perhaps even suggesting "a cavalier attitude toward conceptual systematization," as Hacker put it.[113] There is one section of the BSBh, however, where this difference in theological perspective stands out in bold relief. This the topical section or *adhikaraṇa* comprising BS 1.1.12–19, which concerns the interpretation of the doctrine of the five sheaths (*kośa*) of the self as set forth in the Taittirīya Upaniṣad. To be specific, the *adhikaraṇa* takes up the question of whether the innermost of the five sheaths, the sheath consisting of bliss (*ānandamaya*), coincides with highest self/Brahman or, alternatively, merely denotes an aspect of the transmigrating self like the previous four. This text is significant because it is one of the few places where Śaṅkara's departure from the earlier tradition breaks out into the open. The Proto-commentator,[114] closely following Bādarāyaṇa, argues that the innermost sheath is nothing other than the highest self that coincides with Brahman (*tasmāt ānanadamaya para evātmā*). At the very end of the sequence of sutras, Śaṅkara abruptly reverses this judgment, arguing instead that the highest Brahman transcends even this innermost sheath as its ground and cause.[115]

This difference in interpretation reflects the respective concerns of the Proto-commentator and Śaṅkara mentioned above. The Proto-commentator's judgment that the bliss sheath is the highest self reflects a concern with refuting the Sāṃkhya *pradhāna* principle. The commentary on BS 1.1.18 makes this connection explicit. There the text draws attention to a cosmogonic text found in the context of the Taittirīya discussion of the five sheaths: "He had this desire: 'Let me be many; let me procreate.'"[116] The mention of desire (*kāma*) in this text excludes the insentient *pradhāna* as either the world-cause or the blissful self (*ānandamaya*).[117] Although the commentary says that the refutation of *pradhāna* in the present discussion is incidental, that task having already been accomplished in BSBh 1.1.5,[118] we can nevertheless infer that this concern was an important motivating factor in the identification of the blissful sheath with the highest *ātman*. For bliss (*ānanda*) is one of the marks of the sentience that distinguishes the world-cause from an insentient principle like *pradhāna*. Given this underlying concern with emphasizing the sentience of Brahman, we should not be surprised that the part of the *adhkaraṇa* developing the preliminary judgment (*uttarapakṣa*) tends to use Īśvara and Brahman interchangeably with respect to the blissful self.[119] Thus the identification of the bliss sheath with Brahman clearly belongs to the Īśvara paradigm of Brahman.

Śaṅkara's reversal of the Proto-commentator's interpretive judgment signifies a shift to an entirely different concern.[120] He announces this shift, in fact, in the *adhikaraṇa*'s prologue. After noting the achievement of the *Bhāṣya* up to this point, namely, establishing the omniscient and omnipotent Īśvara—and not the insentient *pradhāna*—as the upaniṣadic world-cause, Śaṅkara has a rather ingenuous *pūrvapakṣin* ask what the point is of the remaining text of the BSBh. Śaṅkara responds by introducing the distinction between the higher and lower Brahman and a question that this distinction raises: does the emancipatory knowledge of the self, which is imparted with the help of conditioning factors, have the higher or lower Brahman as its object?[121] In the exegetical context of the *adhikaraṇa*, specifically, the interpretation of Taittirīya 2, this question takes the form of whether the innermost sheath consisting of bliss corresponds to the higher or lower Brahman.

Śaṅkara's judgment that the bliss sheath corresponds to the lower, conditioned form of Brahman[122] reflects his specific concern with placing emancipatory knowledge beyond the reach of human experience and motivation. Throughout his works Śaṅkara shows a reluctance to affirm bliss as an essential property of Brahman. This is because he wishes to avoid any suggestion that the non-dual Brahman, like bliss, can be the object of experience or desire.[123] As an object of experience, bliss implies a relation—and hence a dualism—between the experiencer and what is experienced, or, in Śaṅkara's idiom, between the one who enjoys (*bhoktṛ*) and what is enjoyed (*bhogya*). As an object of desire, bliss implies the various forms of activity and behavior having bliss as their goal. This second implication of the identification of the bliss sheath and Brahman—that it seems to countenance goal-directed spiritual activity—

lies at the heart of Śaṅkara's reversal of the Proto-commentator's interpretation. As we have seen, Śaṅkara insists that liberative knowledge is discontinuous with all forms of interested activity, including forms of yogic meditation (*upāsana*). The problem with identifying the highest Brahman with the innermost sheath is that it suggests a relation of continuity between, on the one hand, the forms of interested activity corresponding to the other sheaths and, on the other, the knowledge of Brahman.[124] Ultimately, then, Śaṅkara's decision to place the highest Brahman beyond the five sheaths can be understood in terms of his apologetically motivated dichotomization of knowledge and works.

What is both curious and significant about this section of the BSBh is that it preserves the preliminary judgment of the Proto-commentator. One might wonder why Śaṅkara would preserve in his *Bhāṣya* an interpretive voice that fails to harmonize with his own. I might suggest that Śaṅkara's decision to preserve the Proto-commentator's arguments stems from his awareness that the Advaitic distinction between the higher and lower forms of Brahman, if taken out of context, threatens to undermine the achievement of the *Brahma-sūtra* in establishing Brahman-Īśvara as the upaniṣadic world-cause against the claims of the Sāṃkhya school. Śaṅkara, in fact, acknowledges this danger in BSBh 2.1.14. There a *pūrvapakṣin* asks whether Śaṅkara's insistence on the absolute unity of Brahman, in negating the distinction between the ruler and the ruled (*īśitṛ-īśitavya*) contradicts the Vedāntic teaching of Īśvara as the world-cause.[125] In response Śaṅkara asserts that there is nothing in his Advaitc teaching that contradicts the *Brahma-sūtra*'s teaching of the omniscient and omnipotent Īśvara, and not the insentient *pradhāna*, as the cause of the origin, continuation, and dissolution of the world.[126] Śaṅkara's mention of the *pradhāna* doctrine here is significant. It hints at a specifically apologetic motive behind Śaṅkara's decision to preserve the Proto-commentator's arguments in BSBh 1.1.12–19. To the extent that Śaṅkara's Advaita teaching distinguishes between the highest Brahman and Īśvara, it weakens the Vedāntic case against the Sāṃkhya doctrine of *pradhāna* as the world-cause. An interest in precluding such an attenuation of the *Brahma-sūtra*'s refutation of Sāṃkhya would explain why Śaṅkara announces at the conclusion of his prologue to *adhikaraṇa* 1.1.12–19 that the ensuing theological investigation of the conditioned and unconditioned forms of Brahman will be undertaken concurrently with an elaboration of the refutation of an insentient world-cause.[127]

Whatever may have been Śaṅkara's principal motivation for preserving an earlier stratum of tradition that understood the highest Brahman as the material and efficient cause of the world—whether from an active apologetic concern with preserving the distinctiveness of Vedāntic identity over against Sāṃkhya or simply out of a reverence for an earlier tradition of Vedāntic teaching—one thing, however, is certain: Śaṅkara insists that the Advaitic distinction between the higher and lower Brahman *presupposes* the doctrine of Brahman-Īśvara as the world-cause. The apophatic paradigm therefore does not cancel or replace the Īśvara paradigm. The stratified, multivoiced character of the BSBh, in other words, implies a dialectical relation between the two paradigms of Brahman. Together these two conceptions of Brahman form a double paradigm analogous to the Trinitarian and apophatic models in Eckhart's theology. This analogy suggests that isolating the Advaitic concept of *nirguṇa* Brahman from the "Īśvaric" conception of Brahman as the world-cause distorts Śaṅkara's teaching. It would be an interpretive move analogous to interpreting Eckhart's theology one-sidedly as a pantheisitic denial of the Christian God of creation on the basis of a handful of apophatic passages taken out of context. To sever the Advaitic concept of *nirguṇa* Brahman from the Īśvara paradigm would have the effect of rendering Brahman's sentient nature—the doctrine that, more than any other, distinguishes Vedāntic teaching from that of Sāṃkhya—abstract and tenuous. Brahman would become precisely the "bland and static reality" that an interpreter like Rambachan finds so problematic in the conventional understanding of Advaita. Resisting the systematizing urge to reduce Śaṅkara's "polyphonic" theological discourse to what Michael Sells terms a "discourse of single propositions" may indeed sacrifice something in the way of logical consistency. But it leaves intact a double-voiced conception of Brahman that, even if somewhat "untidy," is, as even Paul Hacker concedes, all the more living.[128]

By calling attention to the dialectical character of Śaṅkara's concept of Brahman, the foregoing comparison with Meister Eckhart has rendered Śaṅkara's Advaita resistant to its subsumption into the apologetic contrast between a dynamic Christian theism and a static and lifeless monism. Put differently, this comparative exercise reverses the constrictive process whereby a complex system of religious thought is streamlined, if not caricatured, in the construction of an invidious cross-cultural dichotomy. The foregoing reading of Śaṅkara constitutes, in fact, something of an a fortiori argument against the essentializing dichotomy that Otto employs: if Śaṅkara's Advaita, the most uncompromising system of non-dualist theology in classical India, fails to conform to the orientalist representation of Vedānta as a lifeless and abstract monism, how much less will the far more typical traditions of theistic Vedānta? In the next chapter, I continue this argument by considering another dimension of Otto's "East" versus "West" apologetic, namely, the question of the ontological status of the phenomenal world.

6

From Acosmism to Dialectic

Śaṅkara and Eckhart on the Ontological Status of the Phenomenal World

If Śaṅkara's philosophy does not treat the world as an illusion, then the very core of the essentialist construction of Hinduism or Brahmanism as a "world renouncing" rather than a "world-accepting" religion is seriously weakened.

—Ronald Inden

The Problem of Acosmism in Śaṅkara and Eckhart

"The Brahmans," writes Pierre Bayle in his *Dictionaire,* "assert that the World is but an illusion, a Dream, a Deceit [. . .]."[1] This statement from the eighteenth century crystallizes the long-standing orientalist prejudice that the doctrine of *māyā* or cosmic illusion associated with Śaṅkara's school of Advaita Vedānta defines brahmanical Hinduism. This teaching that, as a late Advaita Vedānta formula puts it, "Brahman is real and the world is false"[2] finds a striking parallel in Eckhart's deliberately provocative teaching regarding the nothingness of creation. "All creatures are a pure nothing," Eckhart boldly declares, "I do not just say that they are insignificant or are only a little something. They are a pure nothing."[3]

Both expressions of world denial have been controversial in their respective contexts. Śaṅkara's alleged illusionism was rejected and ridiculed by rival teachers in the classical period, including Bhāskara (early ninth century) and, perhaps most famously, the great South Indian teacher of Viśiṣṭādvaita, Rāmānuja (eleventh century). But it has been in the modern period especially that the doctrine of *māyā* has come under fire, particularly for allegedly encouraging an attitude of indifference toward the urgent social and political problems of modern India.[4] Eckhart's teaching that creatures are a "pure nothing" (*pure nihil*) has been no less problematic. This teaching provoked controversy from the very beginning, as evidenced by the fact that the statement from Eckhart's *Sermon* 4 that I quoted in the preceding paragraph wound up on the list of condemned propositions in the Papal Bull *In agro dominico*.[5] Eckhart's alleged acosmism continued to arouse controversy in the modern period, forming as it did a central component of the charge of pantheism, which, as we saw in chapter 4, preoccupied several generations of modern scholars of the German master. More recently, even scholars willing to exonerate Eckhart from the pantheism charge have continued to question whether Eckhart's mystical theology pays adequate regard to the ethical and historical dimensions of human existence.[6]

It is far from clear, however, that the statements of world denial found in each of these thinkers support a nihilistic position when they are read in their respective contexts. Indeed, it is a testament of the complex and protean nature of the work of both Śaṅkara and Eckhart that they have each been read to support theological positions diametrically opposed to a nihilistic denigration of the world. To cite a couple of examples at random for this second interpretive possibility, Śaṅkara provides the primary resource for J. Thatamanil's recent comparative theological project of rethinking the Christian doctrine of creation in order to conceptualize and affirm a more intimate relation between God and the world than has been customary in Christian theology.[7] And Eckhart, for his part, provides a perhaps unexpected source of inspiration for Matthew Fox's "creation spirituality."[8]

In this chapter, I compare Eckhart and Śaṅkara on the question of the ontological status of the phenomenal world with the aim of determining the extent to which—if at all—they can be taken to support a nihilist position. Continuing the analysis of the *Brahma-sūtra Bhāṣya* (BSBh) from the previous chapter, I first show how Śaṅkara reinterprets the realist cosmology of an earlier stratum of Vedānta to emphasize the radical ontological dependency of the world on Brahman. This understanding of Śaṅkara's Advaita as a transformative commentary on realist Vedānta provides a framework for understanding Eckhart's innovative appropriation of the Aristotelian-Thomist doctrine of analogy, the topic of the next section. We shall see that Eckhart, like Śaṅkara, emphasizes the radical ontological dependency of creation on God to the point of undermining the realist presuppositions of the cosmological framework that he inherits from the tradition. At this point analogy gives way to dialectic. In the final section, I examine Śaṅkara's conception of the world of "name and form" in light of Eckhart's understanding of created reality as dialectic of being and nonbeing. By challenging the one-sided orientalist interpretation of Śaṅkara's Advaita as a crude illusionism, the proposed rereading of Śaṅkara challenges the essentialist world-affirmation/world-denial dichotomy that the illusionist interpretation supports.

A Transformative Commentary on Realist Vedānta: Śaṅkara's Reinterpretation of BS 2.1.14

While the association of Śaṅkara and the doctrine of *māyā* has generally gone unquestioned in popular and traditional understandings of the Indian master, the question of whether he actually taught the doctrine has been a subject of debate among Indologists almost from the beginning of his modern reception. In 1827, the great British orientalist T. H. Colebrooke observed that the *māyā* doctrine appears only in post-Śaṅkara Vedānta. "I have remarked nothing which countenances it in the *sútras* of Vyása [i.e., the *Brahma-sūtra*] and the gloss of Śancara [*sic*]," he wrote, "but much concerning it in the minor commentaries and in elementary treatises."[9] Colebrooke's thesis was later (1882) challenged by E. A. Gough, who, perhaps motivated by an ethnocentric commitment to the representation of Indian culture as essentially world denying and amoral, argued for the "primitive antiquity" of the *māyā* doctrine.[10] Concerning Śaṅkara's "gloss" on the *Brahma-sūtra*, in particular, Gough asserts against Colebrooke's observations that "a cursory inspection of the gloss is enough to find the tenet of illusion stated or supposed on every page."[11]

This controversy between Colebrooke and Gough has been taken up by a later generation of scholars, particularly in India. One camp, represented by D. M. Datta and, more recently, S. Rao, essentially takes up the position of Colebrooke, arguing that the doctrine of the unreality of the world is not to be found in the authoritative works of Śaṅkara (and, a fortiori, the *Brahma-sūtra*). In what appears to be an effort to rescue the great name of Śaṅkara from orientalist and Christian apologetic charges of acosmism and quietism, these scholars argue that the *māyā* doctrine only appears only among Śaṅkara's later followers as a distortion of the master's teaching.[12] Another camp, represented by scholars like T. R. V. Murti, argues that the latter tradition of post-Śaṅkara Advaita, in pronouncing the phenomenal world to be unreal and illusory, is in fact being faithful to Śaṅkara.[13] The later Advaitins who explicate the *māyā* doctrine are simply drawing out the logical implications of the latter's authentic teaching.

It should be noted that the more recent form of this debate takes place on a more interpretive, philosophical level than a strictly philological one. Most serious students of Śaṅkara today, I believe, would concede that there are passages in Śaṅkara's BSBh and his other authentic works that lend themselves to a realistic interpretation and others that at least provide a basis for the full-blown illusionism of later Advaita. Even when both types of passages are acknowledged, however, there is a tendency to assume that Śaṅkara taught *either* a realist *or* an illusionist form of Vedānta. Nowhere is this tendency better exemplified than in the work of Paul Hacker, to whom we are indebted for a meticulous elucidation of the criteria by which Śaṅkara's authentic works can be distinguished from those of even his immediate followers.[14] But despite a keen sense of the distinctiveness of Śaṅkara's teaching with respect to the later Advaita tradition, as well as a recognition of the tensions and ambiguities in the master's authentic works, Hacker nevertheless presumes that Śaṅkara's authentic teaching was illusionism. He tends to explain away passages that do not support that interpretation either as concessions to the realist assumptions of his students;[15] as holdovers from an earlier tradition of Vedānta that he continues to honor, particularly in his BSBh;[16] or, finally, as survivals of older habits of thought from the time before he made an alleged conversion from Yoga to Advaita.[17] However compelling such hypotheses may be, though, they do not exclude an alternative, realist interpretation of the same texts.[18] The problem with the assumption that Śaṅkara's "authentic" teaching was illusionist or, alternatively, realist is that one is forced, willy-nilly, to deemphasize or even explain away those passages that do not support one's preferred interpretation.

The understanding of Śaṅkara's *Brahma-sūtra Bhāṣya* suggested in the previous chapter, namely, as internally constituted by an earlier stratum of realist Vedānta, allows us to avoid the interpretive difficulties that inevitably follow from the assumption that Śaṅkara must have taught either a realist or an illusionist form of Vedānta. Viewing the BSBh in this way as an example of Bakhtinian double-voiced discourse—a concept that is particularly appropriate for the commentarial genre of classical Vedānta—shifts attention away from the conventional understanding of Śaṅkara's teaching as the expression of a self-contained, systematic philosophical vision (whether realist or illusionist). Rather, it invites us to understand the distinctiveness of Śaṅkara's teaching as emerging piecemeal out of a series of localized interpretive strategies. A reading of the BSBh that is sensitive to the double-voiced character of Śaṅkara's statements coheres with Francis Clooney's call for a shift from a philosophical to a textual approach to classical Advaita.[19] Abandoning a preoccupation with defending a particular characterization of Śaṅkara's "philosophy" allows us to attend more carefully to the complexity, the "rough texture," of the BSBh text, which resists categorization as either realist or illusionist.

In order to determine the relationship between Śaṅkara's teaching in the BSBh and the doctrine of *māyā*, then, we have to examine how he appropriates the earlier tradition of realist Vedāntic cosmological discourse that is preserved in the text of the BSBh. In keeping with the highly localized nature of Śaṅkara's commentarial method, I will focus mainly on one central text for the relation between Brahman and the world, Śaṅkara's commentary on BS 2.1.14. The *sūtra* itself concerns the relation between the world and its metaphysical cause, Brahman. This relationship it characterizes as one of "non-difference" (*ananyatva*), a characterization that, as we shall see, is open to interpretation. The remainder of the *sūtra* (*ārambhaṇaśabdādibhyaḥ*) alludes to the teaching of Brahman as material cause found in the celebrated sixth chapter of the Chāndogya Upaniṣad.

Śaṅkara's interpretation of this *sūtra* provides a basis for the later Advaita doctrine of *vivarta*, that is, the world as the mere appearance (*vivarta*), rather than a real modification (*pariṇāma*) of Brahman.[20] This conception of the world as *vivarta* or appearance, moreover, coincides with the later doctrine of *māyā*, the world as illusory.[21] After signaling that this, the "*ananyatvam*" *sūtra*, pertains to the level of absolute (*pāramārthika*) rather than everyday (*vyāvahārika*) reality, Śaṅkara interprets the non-difference (*ananyatva*) of cause and effect as follows: the effect—the differentiated world of manifestation (*bahuprapañcaṃ jagat*)—does not exist apart from its cause that is the highest Brahman.[22] Elaborating on the upaniṣadic image of the relationship between clay and pots as a metaphor for the Brahman-world relationship, Śaṅkara notes that the modifications (*vikāra*) of the material cause appear as entities in their own right only through the naming power of language. As linguistically constituted entities—that is, as "the mere products of naming" (*nāmadheyamātram*)—these modifications are ultimately (*paramārthatas*) unreal (*anṛtam*). Śaṅkara adds a couple of images of his own that further emphasize the phenomenal world's lack of substantiality when considered apart from Brahman. He first compares the individual forms of the experienced world to the spaces delimited by containers, spaces which are non-different (*ananya*) from space as such.[23] By thus comparing the differentiation of reality to the delimitation of indivisible space, he underscores the illusory nature of the notion of individuality. Śaṅkara then compares the variegated world of name and form to a desert mirage whose evanescent form (*svarūpa*) eludes description.[24] With these two images, especially the latter, Śaṅkara suggests, though does not conceptualize, what later Advaitins and rival philosophers will call *māyāvāda*.

It is likely that this interpretation of the *ananyatvam sūtra* was innovative. By emphasizing the world's lack of independent existence Śaṅkara was probably departing from the earlier, realist tradition of interpretation on the

Brahma-sūtra that I have been calling, as a kind of shorthand designation, that of Ingalls's Proto-commentator.[25] There are a couple features of Śaṅkara's commentary on BS 2.1.14 that indicate that it belongs to a more recent stratum of interpretation. First of all, it introduces a distinction between conventional and absolute (*vyāvahārika* and *pāramārthika*, respectively) reality, a distinction which is found neither in the *Brahma-sūtra* itself nor in those passages in the BSBh identified by the supercommentators as expressing the view of "the commentator" (*vṛttikāra*) and reproduced by Bhāskara, that is, those passages Ingalls attributes to the Proto-commentator. Integrally connected with the two-truths doctrine is the distinction, unknown to either Bādarāyaṇa or the Proto-commentator, between the higher and lower Brahman.[26] Another indication that we are dealing with a later stage in the tradition is that the main preoccupation of this *sūtra* is a refutation of Bhedābheda Vedānta, and not, as is typically the case with the cosmological passages associated with the earlier interpretive tradition, Sāṃkhya.

Unlike the *adhikaraṇa* on the bliss sheath (BS 1.1.12–19) that we examined in the last chapter, however, the BSBh does not record an earlier interpretation of BS 2.1.14, at least not directly. In order to retrieve that earlier interpretation, then, we must proceed indirectly, first, by noting the use of the term *ananyatva* ("non-difference") in earlier śāstric literature; second, by looking at how Bhāskara understands the term; and, finally, by examining the *sūtras* in the immediate context of BSBh 2.1.14 that most likely reflect the earlier stratum of interpretation that Śaṅkara appropriates.

In a brief but important article on precisely the issue that concerns us, namely, the possible earlier philosophical meaning of term *ananyatva*, M. Hiriyanna draws our attention to the earlier use of this term in the grammatical tradition, specifically, in the third century (CE) grammarian Katyāyana's commentary on Pāṇini's *Aṣṭādhyāyī*. There Katyāyana uses this term in the context of arguing that when Pāṇini mentions a particular sound, it can be taken to represent the larger class of sounds to which it belongs. It is by virtue of the relation of non-difference (*ananyatvāt*) that obtains between the particular sound and its generic class that the latter can be conveyed through the former.[27] Hiriyanna notes that Katyāyana's use of the term to refer to the relation between the universal and particular is relevant to the cosmological discussion of BS 2.1.14 inasmuch as Indian philosophers often theorized about the relation between cause and effect (*kāraṇa* and *kārya*) in terms of the relation between the universal and the particular (*sāmānya* and *viśeṣa*).[28] I might add that Katyāyana's understanding of the *ananyatva* relation, namely, as that by virtue of which a class of sounds can be communicated through a particular instance, dovetails nicely with the upaniṣadic teaching alluded to in BS 2.1.14,

Uddalāka Āruṇi's teaching concerning the epistemological principle by which everything made of clay, for example, can be known (CAU 6.1). That earlier teachers of Vedānta understood the causality of Brahman in terms of the relation between the universal and particular is suggested by the doctrine of Brahman as the great universal (*māhasāmānya*) held by earlier Vedāntins mentioned by Kumārila Bhaṭṭa and Maṇḍana Miśra.[29] The latter, in fact, champions the Advaita doctrine of non-difference (*abhedavāda*) in the context of a discussion of the problem of universals in his *Brahmasiddhi*.[30] Pace Maṇḍana, however, the analogy with the relation between the universal and the particular lends itself most naturally to a *Bhedābheda* (difference in non-difference) understanding of the relationship between Brahman and the world. Hiriyanna suggests that an understanding of the *ananyatvam sūtra* consistent with Katyāyana's usage of the term would exclude the doctrine of absolute difference (*atyanta-bhedatva*), but not the relative difference that obtains between the particular and the universal it instantiates.[31] In other words, according to such an interpretation, the *ananyatvam sūtra* would function minimally to exclude a purely dualistic conception of the relation between the world and Brahman, but would stop short of denying difference altogether in their relation.[32]

Such a conception is precisely what we find in Bhāskara. Bhāskara understands the relation between the material cause and its modifications in terms of the difference-in-non-difference relation between the universal and the particular.[33] All things are non-different (*abhinnam*) by virtue of the fact that they exist and are knowable, but are plural (*bhinnam*) by virtue of their mutual differences as individuals.[34] In his commentary on BS 2.1.14, Bhāskara appeals to the *Bhedābheda* understanding of reality as constituted by both particularity and universality (*sāmānyaviśeṣātmakaṃ vastu*) to defend the reality of difference (*bheda*) against the uncompromisingly non-dualist views of Śaṅkara and Maṇḍana.[35] If Ingalls is correct in his hypothesis that where Bhāskara and Śaṅkara disagree, it is the former that probably expresses the earlier view,[36] then a comparison of Śaṅkara's interpretation of BS 2.1.14 with Bhāskara's would support the hypothesis that the former represents a deliberate "correction" of an of an earlier, realist interpretation of this *sūtra* that construed the Brahman/world relationship in terms of the *Bhedābheda* relation between the universal and particular.[37]

This earlier realist perspective on the *ananyatva* relation between the world and Brahman might in fact be preserved in Śaṅkara's commentary on the immediately preceding *sūtra*, BS 2.1.13.[38] In this *sūtra* the *pūrvapakṣin* argues that the Vedāntic doctrine of Brahman as the world's material cause is invalid because it implies a denial of the everyday experience of a distinction between the enjoyer (*bhoktṛ*) and the objects of enjoyment (*bhogya*).[39] Where the Vedas contradict empirical knowledge, the *pūrvapakṣin* argues, they ought to be interpreted in another, figurative sense.[40] Unlike other passages in the BSBh where Śaṅkara boldly declares everyday experience irrelevant when it contradicts the Advaitic doctrine taught by scripture,[41] the *siddhāntin* here concedes the validity of the *bhoktṛ-bhogya* distinction experienced in the world. Employing a more modest and conciliatory apologetic strategy that we often find in Śaṅkara, the *siddhāntin* denies that this experience conflicts with Vedāntic cosmology. "This distinction is possible in our view as well," he writes,

> because it is seen in the world. For it is like this: we perceive the mutual differences between the waves, foam, and bubbles of the ocean as these combine and separate, even though these modifications of the ocean are non-different (*ananyatve 'pi*) from the ocean itself, [sharing as they do the same] nature of water. [...] It is like this here as well: the enjoyer and the enjoyed do not merge into one another, even though [each] is not different (*na... anyatvam*) from the highest Brahman.[42]

This passage expresses a realist understanding of the relation between Brahman and the things of the world, even if it falls short of the full-blown *bhedābheda* doctrine of Bhāskara inasmuch as it concedes an element of difference only in the relations among the various effects (i.e., between waves and foam; the enjoyer and the enjoyed), not in the relation between each of the effects and their underlying cause (i.e., between the waves, etc. and the ocean itself; between the world and Brahman).[43] Now as Hacker observes, the ocean analogy lends itself to a realist, as opposed to an illusionist, conception of the Brahman-world relationship to the extent that water and foam belong to the same level of reality.[44] What is noteworthy about BSBh 2.1.13 is that it expresses an understanding of "*ananyatva*" that is clearly distinct from that expressed in the following *sūtra*. Here the term describes a variety of non-difference that is compatible with an acknowledgment of the empirical distinction between the enjoyer and the enjoyed. In BSBh 2.1.14, the term takes on a more radical meaning, as Śaṅkara's construal of it implicitly relegates empirical differences to the realm of the unreal. This lack of consistency in the sense of *ananyatva* naturally supports, though admittedly does not prove, the hypothesis that BSBh 2.1.14 represents an innovation, its interpretation of *ananyatva* there a departure from an original understanding. This hypothesis also receives support from the remaining *sūtras* of the *adhikaraṇa* comprising BSBh 2.1.14–20, where *ananyatva* tends to be used in the sense it has in BS 2.1.13. BS 2.1.20, for example, compares the *ananyatva* relation between Brahman and the world to that between the vital force (*prāṇa*) and its various forms, which latter remain, in spite of this shared relation of non-difference to their material cause, distinct from one another.[45] On this hypothesis, the two-truths distinction that bookends BSBh 2.1.14 and justifies the shift in perspective that it expresses appears as a hermeneutical expedient allowing Śaṅkara to introduce a new interpretation of *ananyatva* without effacing the earlier tradition of interpretation.[46] Thus understood, the relationship between 2.1.13 and 14 is analogous to that between the *uttarapakṣa* and the *siddānta* in BS 1.1.12–19, the text we analyzed in the previous chapter. In both texts, Śaṅkara preserves, but renders provisional, an earlier stratum of interpretation.

Śaṅkara's reinterpretation of the *ananyatvam sūtra* thus stands in tension with the discussion of the relation between cause and effect found in the remaining *sūtras* of the *adhikaraṇa*—specifically, their defense of the doctrine of the preexistence of the effect in the cause or *satkāryavāda*.[47] For if in fact the effect has no existence apart from Brahman, as Śaṅkara's interprets the *ananyatvam sūtra*, then one cannot properly speak of a *relation* between cause and effect. As Śaṅkara himself notes in this very *adhikaraṇa*, specifically, in the context of his refutation, in 2.1.18, of the proposal that the Brahman/world relation be understood in terms of the Vaiśeṣika concept of inherence (*samavāya*), one can only speak of a relation between two existing things, not between an existing thing and a non-existent thing.[48] Śaṅkara's reinterpretation of *ananyatva* in BS 2.1.14 thus implicitly explodes the framework of the discussion of causality in BSBh 2.1.15–20 by undermining its presupposition of cause and effect as independent entities. A realist interpretation of *ananyatva* modeled on the difference-in-non-difference (*bhedābheda*) relation between the universal and the particular, by contrast, coheres easily with that discussion because it grants the effect a measure of independent reality.[49]

From Analogy to Dialectic: Eckhart's Reinterpretation of the *Analogia Entis*

Śaṅkara's innovative interpretation of the *ananyatva* relation between the world and Brahman finds an intriguing parallel in Eckhart's idiosyncratic interpretation of the Aristotelian-Thomistic doctrine of analogy. Eckhart's teaching on analogy not only represents the key for understanding his conception of the relation between created and divine being,[50] but also highlights the distinctive way in which he appropriates the theological tradition of his fellow Dominican, Thomas Aquinas. We shall see that Eckhart, much like Śaṅkara, radicalizes the creation's dependence on its Creator to the point of undermining the presuppositions of the doctrine of analogy. In the final analysis, as we shall see,

Eckhart's doctrine of analogy is not, properly speaking, analogy at all, but something else.

The doctrine of analogy was the means by which Thomas solved the problem of theological reference, that is, the problem of how one can speak meaningfully about God without compromising the principle of divine transcendence.[51] Analogous predication represents a middle way between *univocal* predication, according to which words like goodness, wisdom, justice, and the like retain the sense that they have for creatures when they are predicated of God, and *equivocal* predication, according to which these words take on an entirely different sense when they are used in reference to God. On the one hand, if theological predication were univocal, then the wisdom predicated of God would include the inherent limitations of human wisdom; if, on the other hand, theological predication were equivocal, then the "wisdom" of God and the "wisdom" of human beings would be little more than homonyms, that is, words (like "pool" of water and "pool" the game) spelled and pronounced alike but completely different in meaning.[52] Against a theory of univocal predication, Thomas asserts that no word has the same sense when used of God as it has when used of creatures.[53] By denying the univocality of theological discourse, Thomas preserves God's transcendence against the anthropomorphizing tendency of language. At the same time, however, he rejects the theory of equivocal predication on the grounds that it excludes the possibility of drawing theological conclusions from a knowledge of creatures.[54] By refusing to concede equivocation in theological discourse, which would preclude any communication of meaning from the realm of creatures to that of God, Thomas preserves the science of theology against agnosticism.[55]

Words used of both God and creatures, Thomas maintains, are used neither univocally nor equivocally but analogously. Language is being used analogously when the same word is used of two different things by virtue of either a relationship they have to each other or a shared relationship to some third thing.[56] Thomas illustrates the concept of analogical language with Aristotle's example of the word "healthy," which can be used to refer to a man; his diet, as the cause of his heath; and his urine, as a symptom of his health. In analogous predication, a word has a primary reference to one of the terms and a secondary reference to the others by virtue of their relation to this central term.[57] Thus in the example above, "healthy" refers primarily to the health of a healthy living being, and derivatively to the diet as its cause and the urine as its symptom.[58] In a theological context, the central term forming the primary referent of analogical speech is obviously God. Thus "whatever is said both of God and creatures is said in virtue of the order that creatures have to God as to their source and cause (*ut ad principium et causam*) in which all the perfections of things pre-exist transcendentally."[59]

When Eckhart takes up the topic of analogy in his *Sermons and Lectures on Ecclesiasticus* 52–54 (LW II, 280–83), he also defines analogous predication in terms of the reference of each of the analogous terms to one central reality. There he distinguishes analogous predication from univocal and equivocal predication as follows: "Analogous [terms] are not distinguished according to [different] things [as equivocal terms are], nor according to the differences of things [as are univocal terms], but rather according to the modes [*per modos*] of one and the same simple thing."[60] And yet, this definition, with its strong emphasis on a single focal reality as the basis of analogical speech, expresses an understanding of analogy that differs from that of Thomas. The difference between the two becomes readily apparent in Eckhart's explication of the Aristotelian example of health: "For example, the one and the same health that is in an animal is that (and no other) which is in the diet and the urine [of the animal] in such a way that there is no more of health as health in the diet and urine than there is in a stone. Urine is said to be "healthy" only because it signifies the health, the same in number, which is in the animal, just as a circular wreath which has nothing to do with wine in it [signifies] wine."[61] For Thomas, the point of the example was to draw attention to the real connections between the three realities of which the adjective "healthy" was predicated. It is by virtue of those connections that analogical speech differs from merely equivocal speech. For Eckhart, by contrast, the example serves to highlight the fact that analogical predication has its basis in a single reality. A diet or urine sample is called healthy only with reference to the health that inheres in the living person, not to any qualities intrinsic to the diet or the urine itself. In order to underscore the extrinsic nature of the relation between the analogous terms and the focal reality, Eckhart juxtaposes the example of urine as a sign of health to that of the circular wreath that was used to signify the presence of wine in German inns. The example of the wreath, a purely arbitrary sign, serves to eliminate any suggestion that the urine, as a natural sign, functions as a sign of health by virtue of any intrinsic qualities that it might have.[62] Qualified in this way, the example of health illustrates Eckhart's point that, "analogates have nothing of the form according to which they are analogously ordered [*analogantur*] rooted in positive fashion in themselves."[63]

Eckhart uses this understanding of the nature of analogical relations to emphasize the radical dependence of creatures on God. The perfections that are predicated analogously to creatures and to God—goodness, wisdom, justice, and so on—belong entirely to God. The perfections are no more intrinsic to creatures than health is to urine or the presence of wine to a straw wreath. Thus, "goodness and justice and the like [in creatures] have their goodness totally from something outside [*ab aliquo extra*] to which they are analogically ordered, namely, God."[64] Chief among those perfections that come to created beings entirely from without is being or existence (*esse*). And here we come to one of the most distinctive and controversial aspects of the Meister's teaching, namely, his denial of the inherent existence of created reality. Like the sunlight that permeates and illuminates the air but whose effect immediately departs that medium when the sun goes down, the divine act of existence never strikes roots in created reality.[65] Were the presence of the divine source of being to be withdrawn from created reality, even for an instant, the latter would be revealed for what it is in itself—a pure nothing. Being is something that is merely loaned to created beings; it is never something they properly own.[66]

This denial of intrinsic being to created reality marks the essential difference between Eckhart's ontology and Thomas's.[67] Thomas's conception of being (*esse*) as an existential act (*actus essendi*) allows him to recognize a real, existential connection between divine and created reality by virtue of which being is predicated analogously of both. Thomas's conception of finite being as a composite of essence—what it is (*quod est*)—and existence—that by which it is (*quo est*)—implicitly grants a measure of independent being to created reality.[68] Even though the act of being is limited in creatures by their respective essences, they possess an *esse* that is really their own.[69] This contrasts with Eckhart, who, in keeping with an essentialist conception of being (*esse*)—a conception, that is, in which "to be" means "to be something"—restricts the proper sense of being to one member of the analogy, namely, God.[70] As a parallel passage in the *Commentary on Exodus* makes clear,[71] a passage in which Eckhart discusses the doctrine of analogy in terms of the relationship between finite substances and their accidents, Eckhart conceives of God as the *primum analogatum* on the analogy with the substance, the first of the ten Aristotelian categories.[72] Just as the nine categories of accidental being are not, properly speaking, *entia* (beings) but rather *entis*, that is, "of" the one being that is substance, so too are created beings called beings only indirectly (*in obliquo*), that is, with respect to the one unique being that is God.[73] For Thomas, by contrast, the accidents—and, a fortiori, created beings—possess a measure of being, albeit a slight one, thanks to their participation in the same act of existence by which substance exists.[74] Following Dietmar Mieth, we might sum up the essential difference between Thomas and Eckhart's respective understandings of the analogy of being by saying that while for Thomas created beings are a *quasi nihil*, for Eckhart they are a *pure nihil*.[75]

Ultimately the different uses of analogy in Eckhart and Thomas reflect different ethical perspectives.[76] In granting a measure of independence to created reality, Thomas's ontology provides a metaphysical grounding for the cultivation of the virtues and for an active moral life.[77] Eckhart's ontology, by contrast, in stressing the radical indigence of created beings, answers to the demands of a mysticism emphasizing detachment.[78] It supports a mystical vision in which the things of the world are transparent to their divine source. An understanding of analogy that affirmed the independent reality of created realities would distort such a vision by rendering those realities partially opaque to the manifestation of God while at the same time justifying an attitude of attachment to them.[79]

Eckhart's use of the doctrine of analogy to express the ontological indigence of creatures threatens Aquinas's underlying presupposition of an objective order between proportionate terms.[80] When the created order loses its autonomy, the distinctions holding the doctrine of analogy together—namely, those between analogy and equivocation, on the one side, and analogy and univocality, on the other—become uncertain and ambiguous. Ultimately, the loss of these distinctions reveals the inadequacy of the doctrine of analogy for what Eckhart wants to say.[81]

To demonstrate how Eckhart's use of analogy undermines the distinctions constitutive of the concepts of analogy, equivocation, and univocality, we can begin by considering what happens to the distinction between analogy and equivocation. By denying the secondary analogata of any intrinsic qualities linking them with the analogy's primary term, Eckhart brings analogy to the brink of equivocation. If in fact "there is no more of health in the diet and urine than there is in a stone,"[82] then how is the use of the same word with respect to these realities anything more than pure equivocation? As Vladimir Lossky notes, the only way Eckhart can save theological discourse from equivocation is by denying creatures the kind of intrinsic being that would establish them as independent realities, a presupposition of the definition of equivocal terms as "divided according to *different things* that are signified (*dividuntur per diversas res significatas*)."[83] The denial of independent being to creatures that saves the Eckhartian analogy from equivocation, however, brings Eckhart's concept of being perilously close to a monistic theory of pure univocality.[84] Created realities become "modes of one and the same reality" (*modi unius eiusdemque rei simpliciter*), where *modi* here refer not to distinct modes of *being* (as for Thomas), but rather to modes of *presence* of the one simple and unique being that is God.[85] We might say that Eckhart's denial of independent being to creatures has the effect of shrinking the distance between univocality and equivocation—precisely the middle ground occupied by analogy—down to the vanishing point. Thus analogy, which, in Thomas's formulation, represented a middle way between the extremes of equivocation and univocality, now becomes, in Eckhart's hands, something that, like the well-known "duck-rabbit" image, appears as equivocation from one perspective and univocality from another.

Another way of saying this is that with Eckhart, analogy passes over into dialectic, by which I mean a formulation that holds incommensurable terms together in a necessary relation.[86]

The dialectical nature of Eckhart's thought appears most clearly in his distinction between what he calls the virtual being and formal being (*esse virtuale* and *esse formale*) of creatures.[87] These two types of being form two sides of a dialectical conception of created being, as the following passage from the *Commentary on the Book of Genesis* makes clear:

> Every creature has a twofold being (*omnis creatura duplex habet esse*). One is in the causes of its origin, ultimately, in the Word of God; and this being is strong and solid. This is why the knowledge of transitory things is not transitory, but strong and stable; the thing is known in its causes. There is another being of things in nature which things have in their proper form. The first is called virtual being (*esse virtuale*), the second is formal being (*esse formale*) which is generally weak and inconsistent.[88]

Virtual being (*esse virtuale*) refers to the being that creatures have as ideas or *rationes* in the mind of God. As such, the *esse virtuale* of creatures coincides with the being as such (*esse simpliciter*) of God. Formal being (*esse formale*), by contrast, refers to the being that is proper to created beings as individuals. Eckhart does not recognize the *esse formale* of creatures as *esse* proper. In other words, Eckhart, unlike Thomas (or Aristotle), does not recognize a secondary mode of being, that is, a distinct mode of being that is of diminished intensity yet is nonetheless real.[89] The being that creatures have as "this and that" (*esse hoc et hoc*) is formally opposed to the *esse* that properly belongs only to God.[90] Given this relation of formal opposition between the *esse simpliciter* that is proper to God and the *esse hoc et hoc* proper to creatures, if *esse* is affirmed of God, then it must be logically denied to creatures. It is from this perspective that Eckhart declares the latter to be a *pure nihil*. One must add, however, that this relation of formal opposition is reversible such that if *esse* is defined in terms of the *esse formale* of creatures, then God must be beyond being, that is, he becomes, in the most literal sense, a "non-being."[91] Despite this curious capacity of Eckhart's analogy to reverse itself—a feature whose chief appeal for Eckhart, one suspects, was that it allowed him to make shocking statements like "God is a nothing"[92]—Eckhart's usual procedure is to affirm being of God and to deny it of creatures.[93] Ultimately, Eckhart recognizes only one mode of being, which is "other" with respect to creatures as what properly belongs only to God. At the same time, however, this being that is proper to God is intimately present to creatures as that which sustains them in existence. The dialectic of being and nonbeing that describes the "double being" (*esse duplex*) of created reality thus implies a dialectic of divine transcendence and immanence.[94]

Dialectic in the BSBh: The "Double Being" of Śaṅkara's "Name and Form"

In this section, I would like to redescribe Śaṅkara's conception of the world in terms of Eckhart's understanding of created being as a dialectic of being and nonbeing. This will challenge and displace the orientalist reading of Śaṅkara as a crude and, indeed, almost nonsensical, illusionism.

One of the central terms Śaṅkara uses to describe the "world" as it is related to Brahman is *nāma-rūpe*, "name and form." Śaṅkara's usage of *nāma-rūpe* overlaps with that of *māyā* in later Advaita, a term that actually carries relatively little terminological weight in Śaṅkara.[95] And yet when we examine what Śaṅkara says about *nāma-rūpe*, we find that its ontological status is considerably more ambiguous and complex than the illusionism typically associated with the *māyā* concept.[96]

The ambiguity of *nāma-rūpe* is indicated by the formulaic phrase by which it is frequently modified, *tattvānyatvābhyām anirvacanīya*, which at this point we can provisionally translate as "not to be specified (*anirvacanīya*) as either this (*tat*) or as something else (*anya*)."[97] Unfortunately, the "*anirvacanīya*" formula is itself difficult to specify and its interpretation, accordingly, is disputed.[98] Considerations of space prevent me from entering into the details of the scholarly debate here. Suffice it to say that the debate centers around the question of whether or not the "this" (*tat*) in the translation above should be taken to refer to Brahman.[99] Following the native tradition, as well as scholars like Alston[100] and Hirst[101] against Hacker,[102] I believe that the cosmological context in which the formula most often appears, which concerns the causal relation between Brahman and the world, does in fact justify taking the "this" to refer implicitly to Brahman.[103] Thus understood, the formula can be translated as, "not to be specified as either this [Brahman] or as something else."

Now in accordance with the injunctive connotation of the gerundive form of *anirvacanīya*, that is, "not to be spoken of (or specified)," I am inclined to understand the formula in a prescriptive, as opposed to a descriptive sense.[104] Like theological doctrines understood according to a regulative theory of doctrine, the *anirvacanīya* formula can be understood to encapsulate rules for speech about the world of "name and form" in relation to Brahman.[105] To be specific, I would suggest that the formula implicitly contains two such rules, which correspond, respectively, to the two halves of the dual instrumental compound, *tattva-anyatvābhyām*. Corresponding to the second member of the compound, "as something other" (*anyatvena*), is a rule that the world of name and form is not to be spoken of as being other than brahman. This side of the *anirvacanīya* formula refers to the relation of non-difference (*ananyatva*) that obtains between the world and Brahman as its material cause. This rule of Advaitic speech thus coincides with an affirmation of the doctrine of *satkāryavāda*, or the preexistence of the effect in the cause. It refers implicitly to texts like BSBh 2.1.15–20 (but not 2.1.14) that affirm the *ananyatva* relation between cause and effect in the context of a defense of the *satkāryavāda* doctrine.

The "as this" (*tattvena*) portion of the *anirvacanīya* formula corresponds to a rule to the effect that the world of name and form is not to spoken of as the same as Brahman. It is intended to exclude the notion that *nāma-rūpe* and Brahman are identical in such a way that the latter would be implicated in the change and imperfection of the former. This half of the dual *anirvacanīya* formula thus functions as a corrective to the idea of non-difference (*ananyatva*) asserted in the other half. It corresponds to a set of texts that we have not yet considered. These are concerned with defending the impassability of Brahman against the inference that Brahman as the world's material cause must experience change.

One of the most important of these texts is the *adhikaraṇa* comprising BSBh 2.1.26–29. The *adhikaraṇa* begins with the *pūrvapakṣin*'s observation that the transformation (*pariṇāma*) of a non-composite material cause into its effects must be total.[106] In other words, if the material cause does not consist of parts, its transformation cannot leave any remainder. Since the Upaniṣads declare Brahman to be non-composite (*anavayava*), it would follow that Brahman must completely efface itself as it "bodies forth" the world. Transformation is an all-or-nothing proposition for a non-composite reality like Brahman. "If Brahman be partless," the *pūrvapakṣin* reasons, "then either it will not change at all, or else it will change wholly."[107]

Given this choice, Śaṅkara is forced to qualify the conventional understanding of the world as the transformation (*paniṇāma*) of Brahman. The variegated forms of the phenomenal world, which, according to a realist conception of Brahman's material causality, are so many transformations (*vikāra*) of Brahman, are illusory; beneath the changing forms of the world abides the unchanging reality of Brahman in eternal repose.[108] The differences constituted by name and form are imagined products of primordial ignorance (*avidyā*).[109] This understanding of the phenomenal world is formalized in the later Advaita doctrine of the world as the mere appearance (*vivarta*), as opposed to the real transformation (*pariṇāma*), of Brahman.

In BSBh 2.1.28, Śaṅkara gives two examples for this claim that Brahman can create the world without experiencing change. These examples will form the basis for the later doctrine of *māyā*.[110] The first of these is the world of dream, replete with chariots, roads, and animals, that leaves the underlying nature of the dreamer unchanged. The second is the magic illusion (*māyā*) that exerts no effect on the magician (*māyin*) who conjures it up. These same two examples also appear in BSBh 2.1.9, along with the famous Advaitic image of the rope falsely imagined to be a snake at twilight. In the context of BSBh 2.1.9, these "māyic" images answer to a demand for examples (*dṛṣṭānta*) disabusing the *pūrvapakṣin* of the conclusion that Brahman is contaminated by the imperfections of his creation. In both passages, 2.1.28 and 2.1.9, the māyic images support the claim that Brahman is unaffected by the world it brings into being. This is the claim, I suggest, to which the "*tattva*" portion of the *anirvacanīya* formula makes implicit reference.[111]

We have seen, then, that the *anyatva* and *tattva* parts of the *anirvacanīya* formula correspond to two different sets of texts, namely, those defending the doctrine of *satkāryavāda* and those suggesting an illusionistic conception of the world of name and form, respectively. These two sets of texts in turn correspond to the two main "voices" constituting the BSBh, namely, the realist Vedānta of the Proto-commentator, as represented by the texts defending the *satkāryavāda*, on the one hand, and Śaṅkara's illusionistic "voice-over" of the former's Vedāntic cīsmology, on the other. Thus understood, the *anirvacanīya* formula makes implicit reference to the two voices of the BSBh.

This construal of the *anirvacanīya* formula as bringing together the BSBh's two voices suggests that there is an essential connection between the formula and Śaṅkara's reinterpretation of the *ananyatvam sūtra*, BS 2.1.14. For this *sūtra* represents the point of transition between the *satkāryavādic* texts of the Proto-commentator and the māyic texts distinctive of the Śaṅkara school of Advaita. As we have seen, Śaṅkara's innovative interpretation of *ananyatva* pushes the realist cosmology of the *satkāryavāda* in the direction of illusionism—recall the desert mirage as an image for the world apart from Brahman.[112] It welds these two sets of texts together in a dialectical relation, much as Eckhart's idiosyncratic conception of the *analogia entis* brought univocal and equivocal predication—radical immanence and radical transcendence—into a necessary dialectical relation.

Thus, the *tattvanyatvābhyām anirvacanīya* formula, inasmuch as it brings together the two voices of the BSBh, provides the hermeneutical key to BSBh 2.1.14. Like an x-ray, it exposes the dialectic implicit in Śaṅkara's reinterpretation of *ananyatva*.

What I would like to suggest now is that the dialectic embodied in the *anirvacanīya* formula is analogous to the Eckhartian dialectic of virtual being and formal being. This analogy readily suggests itself when we recognize that the māyic texts corresponding to the *tattva* portion of the formula imply a concept of what Eckhart calls *esse formale,* while the "*satkāryavāda*" texts corresponding to the *anyatva* portion of the *anirvacanīya* formula imply a concept of Eckhartian *esse vituale.*

That māyic texts like BSBh 2.1.26–29 and BSBh 2.1.9 express an understanding of the ontological status of "name and form" that is akin to the Eckhartian concept of *esse formale* is almost self-evident. The assertion that Brahman is unaffected by the creation it brings into being—an assertion supported by the māyic images of the dream, the magical illusion, and the rope-snake—presupposes Śaṅkara's reinterpretation, in BSBh 2.1.14, of the *ananyatva* relation, namely, that the effect does not exist apart from its cause. For if the world of name and form were to exercise an effect on Brahman it would have to possess a measure of independent being. The māyic texts suggest that a denial of intrinsic being to "name and form" was the only way of reconciling Brahman's causality with Brahman's changelessness, much as a denial of intrinsic being to creatures was the only way Eckhart could save his conception of analogy from equivocation, as we saw above. The denial of independent being to the world of name and form thus is analogous to Eckhart's denial of intrinsic being to the *esse hoc et hoc* of creatures, that is, to the *esse formale* that is proper to them as individual beings. The māyic texts thus consider the world of name and form under the aspect of *esse formale*—that is, as a *pure nihil.*

That the texts defending the doctrine of *satkāryavāda* imply a concept of virtual being is also clear—tautological in fact—when one recognizes that *satkāryavāda* is equivalent to affirming the preexistence of the effect in the cause.[113] The BSBh explicitly argues for the virtual being of the effect in its cause in 2.1.16. "The effect appearing after creation," it says, "exists in its cause before the creation (*prāg-utpatter*), in identity with the cause."[114] Considered in its aspect of *esse virtuale,* the world exists eternally in Brahman: "Just as the cause that is Brahman does not depart from existence in the three times [past, present, and future—i.e., forever], so too does the effect not depart from existence during the three times of the world."[115] And lest one infer a dualism from this affirmation of the existence of the effect, the text is quick to add, in a formulation reminiscent of Eckhart's reference of analogous terms to the single reality of God, that the existence (*sattva*) affirmed of both cause and effect in the pre-created state is one. Indeed, it is only on the basis of this principle of the unity of being that one can affirm the non-difference of cause and effect.[116]

The following *sūtra,* BSBh 2.1.17, suggests a further dimension of this parallel with the Eckhartian dialectic of *esse virtuale* and *esse formale.* In this *sūtra*, Śaṅkara seeks to reconcile the *satkāryavāda* doctrine with upaniṣadic texts, such as Chāndogya 2.19.1 and Taittirīya 2.7.1, that assert precisely the opposite cosmogonic doctrine, namely, that being came from nonbeing (*asatkāryavāda*).[117] In order to acknowledge those scriptural pronouncements without conceding the rival *asatkāryavāda* doctrine, Śaṅkara introduces a distinction between manifest and unmanifest (*vyākṛta, avyākṛta*) name and form. Unmanifest name and form has a different character (*dharma*) than manifest name and form.[118] By virtue of this different character, unmanifest name and form is sometimes called non-existent, though it nevertheless exists as non-different from its cause.[119] Those upaniṣadic passages expressing the *asatkāryavāda* view reflect an everyday, empirical perspective in which the phenomenal world—manifest name and form—defines what is real (*vastu*).[120] From this perspective, what is not yet manifest in name and form—that is, the world before its creation—is spoken of as non-existent.[121] This text is intriguing because it comes close to suggesting a relationship of formal opposition between empirical and transcendental being like that found in Eckhart. We recall that for Eckhart, if being (*esse*) is identified with the *esse simpliciter* of God, then the being proper to creatures, *esse hoc et hoc*, is declared to be a *pure nihil*. Conversely, if *esse* is defined in terms of the *esse hoc et hoc* of creatures, then God must be declared to be beyond being, literally a nothing (no-thing). Śaṅkara's commentary on BS 2.1.17 suggests a similar reversibility of predication, which can be taken as a telltale mark of a dialectical understanding of created being.[122] If *sat* is identified with the being of Brahman, then one is forced to judge the being proper to name and form to be illusory. This is the perspective expressed in the later doctrine of *māyā*: Brahman is real, the world is illusory (*brahma satyaṃ jagad mithyam*). If, on the other hand, one defines *sat* in terms of the manifestation of name and form, then the *esse virtuale* of non-manifest name and form appears as non-existent or *asat*. From this latter perspective, the mode of being of Brahman is beyond categorical being.[123]

The two perspectives represented by the *satkāryavādic* and the *asatkāryavādic* upaniṣadic passages are not weighted equally, however. The latter represents the perspective of everyday common sense (*vyavahāra*), which, according to the doctrine of the "two truths," is sublated (*bādhita*) upon realization. Ultimately, the perspective reflected in the *satkāryavādic* passages alone reflects the true (*pāramārthika*) nature of reality. To the extent that the relation between these two perspectives or states (*avasthā*) is understood to be hierarchical and unidirectional, Śaṅkara's conception of "name and form" falls short of the dialectic of being and nonbeing that we find in Eckhart's conception of created reality. But perhaps the parallel we have been drawing between the "inexpressibility" of name and form, on the one hand, and Eckhartian dialectic of *esse virtuale et formale*, on the other, invites us to rethink the doctrine of the two truths. Specifically, it invites us to question the tendency to compartmentalize the two states of *vyāvahārika* and *pāramārthika* truth such that everyday experience is utterly innocent of any relativizing perspective while, conversely, the *pāramārthika* perspective dissolves the certitudes of everyday life the way waking experience effaces a dream. Perhaps a recognition of the occasional, indeed almost ad hoc nature of the two-truths distinction in Śaṅkara—that he tends to invoke it on those occasions when he wants to introduce a new interpretive perspective without, however, effacing the prevailing realist perspective of Bādarāyaṇa and the Proto-commentator—justifies a more flexible conception of the relation between conventional and ultimate truth. J. G. Suthren Hirst articulates such a conception when she suggests that we understand the distinction between conventional and ultimate truth in terms of a difference in the way the world is seen and named. "It is not so much that the public conventional world disappears once realization has dawned," she writes, "rather that it is seen in a different way."[124] The parallel with Eckhart's dialectic between formal and virtual being supports this understanding of *pāramārthika* truth as a perspective in light of which the conventional world of experience is relativized through redescription. The parallel with Eckhart's dialectical conception of the *duplex esse* of creatures, a conception that implies the reversibility of the predication of being, suggests that we might understand Advaitic enlightenment in terms of a kind of imaginative agility, an ability to shift freely between a perspective in which the world of name and form appears as real and a perspective in which it appears as "a pure nothing."

The former perspective—the perspective from which the world of name and form appears as real—is suppressed in the construction of the essentializing contrast, à la Schweitzer, between Indian and Western thought in terms of world denial and world affirmation, respectively. This suppression of the realist side of Śaṅkara's dialectical conception of the world of "name and form" can be understood in terms of our analysis of apologetic discourse in chapter 3, namely, as a metonymical reduction of a complex whole to one of its parts. Our redescription of Śaṅkara in terms of Eckhart, therefore, in recovering the dialectic in Śaṅkara's conception of the world, works to undermine the metonymic foundations of the tendentious East versus West dichotomy by which the Christian West has mobilized a sense of identity over and against the religious traditions of India. In this way, the foregoing comparative exercise exemplifies the second, anti-essentializing moment in the model of comparative theology set forth in part I.

In the next chapter, we compare Śaṅkara and Eckhart with respect to the dimension of the pantheism issue forming the basis of Otto's Christian apologetic, namely, the issue of quietism. Up until this point, our comparison of Eckhart and Śaṅkara has basically cohered with Otto's. For Otto himself recognizes the theistic and realist dimension of Śaṅkara's thought,[125] and, to that extent, challenges the orientalist interpretation of Śaṅkara's teaching as illusionistic pantheism. When he turns to the ethical dimension of the pantheism issue in Part B of *Mysticism East and West*, however, the East versus West apologetic appears in full force. In the next chapter, we will therefore be forced to assume a more critical stance toward Otto's study, as we qualify the sharp contrast he draws between Eckhart's activist ethic and Śaṅkara's alleged moral indifference.

7

Liberative Knowledge as "Living without a Why"

The Vedic texts speaking of performance of rites throughout life find their scope among the unenlightened souls who do not long for freedom.

—Śaṅkara

Even though meditation, that is, thinking, is performed mentally, nevertheless it can be done, not done, or done otherwise by a man, for it is dependent on man. But knowledge arises from its valid means (e.g., perception, inference, etc.), and the valid means apprehend the things just as they are. Hence knowledge is not something to be done, not done, or done otherwise, for it is entirely determined by things, and neither by injunctions nor by man.

—Śaṅkara

Some people want to see God with their own eyes, as they see a cow; and they want to love God just as they love a cow. You love a cow because of the milk and cheese and because of your own advantage. This is how all these people act who love God because of external riches or because of internal consolation. They do not love God rightly; rather they love their own advantage.

—Eckhart

In chapter 4, we saw that Otto's apologetic in *Mysticism East and West* rests on an invidious contrast between the dynamism and vitality of

Eckhart's Godhead, on the one hand, and the static repose of Śaṅkara's Brahman, on the other. A concept that plays a central role in this contrast is Eckhart's teaching concerning "living without a why" (*sunder war umbe, âne war umbe*). The idea of "living without a why" links the idea of mystical detachment to the theme of "the living God" that figures so prominently in Otto's apologetic:

> [W]hoever seeks for God without ways will find him as he is in himself, and that man will live with the Son, and he is life itself. If anyone went on for a thousand years asking of life: "Why are you living?" life, if it could answer, would only say: "I live so that I may live." That is because life lives out of its own ground and springs from its own source, and so it lives without asking why it is itself living. If anyone asked a truthful man who works out of his own ground: "Why are you performing your works?" and if he were to a give a straight answer, he would only say, "I work so that I may work."[1]

This notion of "living without a why" encompasses, in a concise formulation, both sides of the Eckhartian dialectic, namely, the "breakthrough" (*durchbruch*) to the silent depths of the Godhead, on the one hand, and the spontaneous outflow (*ûzvluz*) of the divine life into the world, on the other. On the anthropological plane, the formula refers at once to the annihilation of the human will and motivation that places the soul in direct contact with the creative source of divine life and to the spontaneous moral activity of the "just" who embodies that life. With its emphasis on the second moment of the dialectic, the "living without a why" idea marks a contrast between Eckhart's mysticism and those forms of Eastern mysticism, like Śaṅkara's, allegedly lacking an active, ethical dimension. For with the Indian master, the mystical quest comes to a premature end in a passive state of contemplative quiet: "The mukta, the redeemed, who has attained ekatā or unity with the eternal Brahman, is removed from all works, whether good or evil. Works bind man. He leaves all activity and reposes in oneness."[2]

As it appears in the context of Otto's apologetic, Eckhart's teaching concerning the "living without a why" thus calls attention to this one-sidedness of Śaṅkara's mysticism. Having taken on in this context a dimension of differential meaning, this teaching gives concise expression to Otto's Christian apologetic. Inasmuch as it encapsulates both moments of the Eckhartian dialectic, this pregnant formula implies a theology of Christian fulfillment whereby a philosophy of world and life denial finds its fulfillment in Christian mysticism.

Here I shall be putting Eckhart's teaching of "living without a why" to an entirely different use. In keeping with the critical (as opposed to apologetic) model of comparative theology set forth in the preceding chapters, I shall use the "living without a why" idea to "problematize" the standard interpretation of Śaṅkara's teaching as a form of amoral quietism. To be specific, I use this teaching of Eckhart to frame a question to be put to Śaṅkara's teaching concerning the relation between human action and liberative knowledge, namely, what, if any, forms of human action or behavior are compatible with the knowledge of the identity of the Self and Brahman? What we shall see is that when Śaṅkara's teaching on the relation between action and knowledge is "redescribed" in terms of the Eckhartian notion of "living without a why," we uncover dimensions of the action/knowledge relation that have been suppressed not only by the world and life-denial/life-affirmation schema that has shaped the Western reception of Śaṅkara, but also by the polemical and ideological commitments of Śaṅkara himself.

Eckhart's "Living without a Why": Spontaneous Activity from Detachment

As mentioned above, Eckhart's "living without a why" integrates the Meister's emphasis on radical detachment (*abgescheidenheit*) with the notion of spontaneous moral activity. Expressed in negative terms, the formula combines a critique of utilitarian attitudes in religious practice with a critique of quietism. I shall discuss each of these aspects in turn.

A concern with utilitarian forms of religious belief and practice is a theme that runs throughout the Meister's oeuvre. At one point, he likens the religious attitude of those who perform acts and prayers for divine favors to the attitude one has toward a cow from which one gets cheese and milk.[3] Perhaps the most arresting expression of this theme, however, is found in Eckhart's celebrated homily on the cleansing of the temple. In a characteristically bold and innovative reading of the Gospel text (Matthew 21:12–13 and parallels), Eckhart compares those who hope to win something in return for their acts of piety to the "businessmen" (MHG: *koufliute*; cf. NHG: *Kaufleute*) buying and selling in the temple. Such people "want to give one thing in return for another, and thus want to make a business deal with the Lord."[4] Eckhart's critique of instrumental religiosity is not restricted to those cruder forms of religious mercantilism (*koufsmanschaft*) intended to win material benefits from God, however. It extends to those acts of piety motivated by a desire for even the most subtle and rarified forms of spiritual gratification. Eckhart's critique of instrumental forms of piety reflects his relentless quest for true inward poverty, a quest which leads him to exclude any act, religious or otherwise, that can be placed within a framework of motives and ends.[5] Any act that can be conceived in terms of a "why and wherefore," even the most outwardly pious, falls short of the ideal of spiritual poverty. Such a work, Eckhart declares, "is not a divine work and is not performed for God."[6]

With the concept of "living without a why," a fairly conventional, if boldly expressed, critique of instrumental piety ("Some people love God just as they love a cow") opens out into one of the most sublime—and controversial—of the Meister's "mystical" teachings, namely, the annihilation of the created will in God. Eckhart's description of "the just" in his Sermon 6 on Wisdom 5:16 (*Justi vivent in aeternum*), a passage that provides the substance of the eighth of the condemned articles enumerated in the Papal Bull, *In agro dominico*, shows where Eckhart's critique of religious utilitarianism ultimately leads:

> Those who have wholly gone out of themselves, and who do not seek for what is theirs in anything, whatever it may be, great or little, who are not looking beneath themselves or above themselves or beside themselves or at themselves, who are not desiring possessions or honors or ease or pleasure or profit or inwardness or holiness or reward or the kingdom of heaven, and who have gone out from all this, from everything that is theirs, these people pay honor to God, and they honor God properly, and they give him what is his.[7]

As Herbert Grundmann and others in his wake have argued, passages like this one reflect the considerable influence of the thirteenth-century movement of uncloistered women known as Beguines and their quest for spiritual poverty.[8] In particular, the passage quite likely betrays a familiarity with the mystical text *The Mirror of Simple Souls* of Marguerite Porete, the Beguine burned at the stake as a relapsed heretic in Paris in 1310. For Marguerite's *Mirror* also expresses, in nearly identical terms, the idea of the annihilation of the created will in God that we find in Eckhart.[9] The official condemnation of Eckhart's claim that, as the Bull paraphrases the passage above, "those who are not desiring possessions, or honors, or gain, or internal devotion, or holiness, or reward or the kingdom of heaven ... pay honor to God"[10] reflects the Church's long-standing suspicions of the Beguines' quest for spiritual poverty. This quest was believed to serve as a pretext for laziness and moral indifference.[11] Even more troubling, at least from an institutional point of view, was that it threatened to bypass the sacramental life of the Church and the structures of ecclesiastical authority.[12]

Eckhart, of course, was acutely conscious of the suspicions surrounding the Beguine lifestyle and, in particular, the heretical nature of Marguerite's teaching concerning the annihilated soul allegedly no longer subject to the law of virtues. As a theology professor in Paris appointed the year after Marguerite's execution, Eckhart most probably was well informed about the proceedings against the unfortunate Beguine.[13] The theological environment in which Eckhart developed the core themes of his mystical theology was one marked by an acute anxiety over heresy. Given the tense theological atmosphere in which he worked, it is hardly surprising that Eckhart would take measures to dissociate his teaching on detachment and "releasement" (*gelâzenheit*) from the quietism, antinomianism, and antisacramentalism associated, whether rightly or wrongly, with the Beguines and their way of life. It is in the context of this attempt to reconcile the notion of spiritual poverty, the core theme of Beguine spirituality, with the institutional life of the Church and its teaching that we can best understand Eckhart's teaching of "living without a why." The teaching represents a brilliant solution to the problem of integrating the ideas of detachment and the annihilation of will with an activist ethic. It exemplifies the thesis that Eckhart's overall theological mission was to bring the religiously powerful but theologically unrefined ideas and experiences of the thirteenth-century "women's religious movement" (*die religiösen Frauenbewegung*) in line with ecclesiastically orthodox theology.[14]

Nowhere is the second, "activist" aspect of the "living without a why" formula more clearly expressed than in Eckhart's sermon on the Lukan parable of Mary and Martha (Sermon 86, "*Intravit Iesus in quoddam castellum*").[15] A long-standing theological tradition had taken the story of Mary and Martha (Luke 10:38–42) as a parable for the superiority of the contemplative life, represented by the figure of Mary sitting at Jesus' feet, over the active life, represented by Martha, busying herself with household chores. Jesus was understood to be expressing a preference for the contemplative over the active life when he rebukes Martha for her plea to have Mary help her with the household tasks; when he says of Mary that "she has the better part" (Luke 10:42), this was taken to refer to the contemplative life. According to this standard reading, Mary's quiet adoration of Jesus reflects a more refined religious sensibility than Martha's restless activity. The former disposition reflects an inward state of recollection, the latter, of dissipation. In his characteristically audacious and contrarian fashion, Eckhart dramatically inverts the traditional evaluation of the two characters. It is now the active Martha who represents the more mature spiritual outlook. Martha stands so securely in the presence of God that her unity with God cannot be hindered by outward activity.[16] Mary's contemplation, by contrast, "was so fragile and untested that she had to rest at Jesus' feet in order to preserve it."[17] In what amounts to a bold rejoinder to the criticism that his emphasis on perfect detachment implies a withdrawal from outward acts of virtue, Eckhart defines the quietistic form of contemplation represented by Mary as a subtle form of attachment, specifically, to the enjoyment of spiritual consolation.[18] Martha's willingness to work, by contrast, signifies the most perfect form of detachment, one that renounces even the sweet feelings of consolation that accompany an experience of God's presence.[19] Martha is so secure in her knowledge of God's presence that she is able to turn away from a consciously held *experience* of that presence, an experience symbolized by Mary's rapturous meditation at Christ's feet. On Eckhart's reading, Martha does not exhort Mary to get up out of frustration, much less resentment, but rather out of sense of compassionate concern that her younger sister, by lingering at Christ's feet, was clinging to feelings of gratification that were holding up her spiritual progress: "For this reason Martha said, 'Lord, tell her to get up!' because she feared [Mary] would remain in this pleasant feeling and would progress no further."[20] Eckhart interprets Jesus' response to this plea, not as a rebuke, but rather as a kindly reassurance to Martha that Mary's enjoyment of spiritual gratification was only temporary and that she would indeed reach the state of spiritual maturity that Martha herself had already reached.[21]

On Eckhart's reading, Martha's active spirituality stands not as the antithesis, but rather as the fulfillment of Mary's contemplation. Martha represents Mary's spiritual future.[22] That is, when Mary's contemplation reaches maturity, it will naturally express itself in works. In another sermon that Eckhart gives on the same Lukan text (Sermon 2, "*Intravit Iesus in quoddam castellum*"), Eckhart expresses this idea of contemplation fulfilling itself in works with the image of the receptive virgin (representing the annihilated soul) who, in order to be "fruitful," must become a wife.[23] Martha embodies both moments of the Eckhartian dialectic, namely, the breakthrough to the divine ground and the outflow of divine action into the world. In keeping with a long tradition Christian exegesis that sought the hidden ("mystical") meaning in even the seemingly most trivial details of scripture, Eckhart sees in the Jesus' repetition of Martha's name in Luke 10:41 ("Martha, Martha, you are worried and distracted by many things") a veiled reference to these two moments of spiritual perfection. With the first mention of Martha's name, Jesus testifies to her perfection in temporal works; with the second, to the perfection of her unity with God.[24] These two moments of Martha's contemplation in action correspond to a distinction Eckhart draws between "work" (MHG: *werc*) and "activity" (MHG: *gewerbe*). The former refers to outward works of virtue;[25] the latter, to such works "practiced from within, with rational consciousness."[26] This distinction between outer "work" and inner "activity" allows Eckhart to recognize an essential place for the active life without compromising his emphasis on interiority.

It should be clear from this exposition that Eckhart, in extolling Martha as a model of spiritual perfection, is doing something more than simply reversing the traditional ranking of the contemplative and active lives, represented by the figures of Mary and Martha, respectively. By making Martha's active spirituality the fulfillment, and not the antithesis, of the contemplative quiet of Mary, Eckhart overcomes the dualistic schema in which contemplation and action represented alternative modes of Christian life.[27] According to Dietmar Mieth, it was precisely by overcoming this dualism and its attendant ranking that Eckhart was able to recognize the full significance of innerworldly activity in the spiritual life.[28] While earlier theologians like Aquinas had recognized a positive role for the active life in Christian spirituality, they nevertheless remained committed to a schema that privileged the contemplative life over the active. For this schema envisioned the spiritual life as a graduated ascent to a contemplative, even if eschatological, vision of God.[29] Eckhart, writes Mieth, "not only justified the 'Martha-type' over against the 'optima pars' of the Mary-type, as was the case since Augustine, but transformed the former into an ideal of Christian spirituality. The 'vita activa' is not only a provisional necessity for him, but rather realizes a participation in the divine dynamic, in the inter-Trinitarian life, Creation, Salvation, and Consummation in an eternal present."[30] While Eckhart's affirmation of the active life might fall short of recognizing religious significance in the specifically historical character of the works he affirms, still it would be difficult to imagine a conception that more thoroughly integrates human activity into a theological vision than one that envisages a mode of human activity as the site of the presence of God.[31]

Śaṅkara's Antithesis of Action and Knowledge

Eckhart's emphasis on the spirituality of everyday life and his explicit denial of the possibility of achieving freedom from external works[32] mark a stark contrast with Śaṅkara, an uncompromising proponent of the institution of renunciation or *saṃnyāsa* in classical India. One can easily find passages in Śaṅkara's works that seem to support Otto's assertion that "[t]he goal for Śaṅkara is the stilling of all *karmāṇi*, all works, all activity of the will: it is quietism, *tyāga*, a surrender of the will and of doing, an abandonment of good as evil works, for both bind man to the world of wandering."[33] For example, in what could be taken as a direct challenge to Eckhart's understanding of the active "Martha-type" as the ideal for religious life, Śaṅkara declares that "there can be no abiding in the householder's state for one who is inactive and for whom knowledge has dawned."[34] Elsewhere he insists—repeatedly—that the self (*ātman*) has no connection with work (*karma*).[35]

The support that such passages offer to Otto's apologetic contrast between a dynamic mysticism of contemplation-in-action and a quietistic mysticism of world and life denial is somewhat less conclusive than it first appears, however. Otto's contrast rests on the assumption that the "works" (*karmāṇi*) that Śaṅkara claims are excluded by the knowledge of "self-realization" are roughly equivalent to the "works" (*werc*) that Eckhart affirms as an expression of the perfected spiritual life. When we examine Śaṅkara's statements on the relation between work and knowledge in context, however, we find that Śaṅkara's concept of *karma* does not coincide with Eckhart's notion of outward works of virtue (*werc*), much less with the interior activity that such works ideally reflect (*gewerbe*).

To understand what Śaṅkara means by *karma*, it is helpful first to distinguish two basic concepts of *karma* in the context of classical Indian thought. The first corresponds to the understanding of the term in the tradition of brahmanical orthodoxy, epitomized by the school of ritual exegesis or Pūrva Mīmāṃsā; the second to that of the "heterodox" schools in classical Indian philosophy, particularly Buddhism. In the sphere of brahmanical orthodoxy, *karma* was understood primarily in terms of ritual action. The ritual act provided a normative paradigm for human activity in general, although it belonged to a sacral, Vedic (*vaidika*) realm clearly demarcated from the "worldly" (*laukika*) realm. In Mīmāṃsā, the notion of "karmic" effect is understood in terms of the efficacy of ritual, specifically the notion of an unseen power (*apūrva*) linking the correctly performed ritual act with its intended effects.[36] In the heterodox schools of Buddhism and Jainism, which defined themselves over against the brahmanical tradition in general and the institution of Vedic sacrifice in particular, the *karma* concept, accordingly, loses its ritual associations. As it is dissociated from the world of Vedic ritual, the concept of *karma* is universalized and "ethicized."[37] The karmically relevant act is no longer the Vedic rite, correctly executed in accordance with stipulated procedures and social restrictions, but rather the intentional act, the morally relevant act. In this revised concept of *karma*, "moral criteria replace the orientation to ritual correctness."[38] Generally coinciding with this shift in focus from the ritual act to the intentional act is a fusion of the concept of *karma* with the notion of rebirth in the notion of *saṃsāra*.[39] In this soteriological context, the notion of karmically relevant action takes on a decidedly negative connotation that relativizes, indeed undermines, the distinction between good and bad *karma* that held sway in traditional Brahmanism.[40]

Śaṅkara's understanding of *karma* combines these two senses of *karma* in a way that reflects his complicated and ambiguous relationship with the

Mīmāṃsā school. As indicated by its alternative designation as the "Later (Uttara) Mīmāṃsā," Śaṅkara's Advaita Vedānta preserves many of the methodological and epistemological presuppositions of the Earlier (Pūrva) Mīmāṃsā, even as it claims to supersede its predecessor.[41] Śaṅkara's understanding of *karma* reflects this continuity of tradition. Like the Mīmāṃsakas, Śaṅkara "tends to place the [Vedic] rite at the center of his concept of *karma* and to see the Vedic injunctions as the criterion for the karmic quality of actions."[42] In centering his understanding of *karma* on the ritual act, Śaṅkara reveals a conservative tendency, shared by Mīmāṃsakas like Kumārila Bhāṭṭa, to resist and reverse the transformation of meaning that key terms like *karma* and *dharma* experienced under the impact of non-brahmanical movements in classical Indian thought.[43] At the same time, however, Śaṅkara's conception of ritual *karma* reflects his deliberate break from the Mīmāṃsā tradition. In his effort to establish both the autonomy of the upaniṣadic corpus vis-à-vis the ritual portion (*karma-kāṇḍa*) of the Veda and the legitimacy of the institution of renunciation, Śaṅkara is forced to challenge one of the central postulates of the Mīmāṃsā school, namely, that Vedic statements are "meaningful" only to the extent that they enjoin action (*karma*).[44] His strategy in challenging this restriction of Vedic authority to ritual injunctions is to redefine the ritual act—the paradigmic "karmic" action—in terms of desire and ignorance.[45] Commenting on the statement in Bṛhadāraṇyaka Upaniṣad 3.5.1 that the desire for wealth and the desire for worlds (*loka*) are the same inasmuch as they are both desires, Śaṅkara argues that the Vedic rite intended to win a postmortem existence in a heavenly realm (*svarga*) shares the same intentional structure as actions of a more mundane variety. On the basis of this nexus between "the desire for means and the desire for results"[46] in the ritual act, he concludes that "there are neither rites nor ritual instruments for a knower of Brahman."[47] Later on in the same text, Śaṅkara argues that ritual activity, inasmuch as it presupposes the distinctions of act, instrument, and result (*kriyā*, *phala*, and *sādhana*, respectively), betrays an ignorance of the non-dual self, whose nature excludes means and results.[48] Inasmuch as "action, result, and means belong to the sphere of ignorance (*kriyāphalaṃ sādhanaṃ... avidyāviṣayam*)," knowledge and ritual activity exclude each other like light and darkness.[49] By defining ritual in terms of ignorance and desire, Śaṅkara has in effect grafted a Buddhistic conception of *karma* as the intentional act—the second concept of *karma* mentioned above—onto the earlier brahmanical understanding of *karma* as centered in the ritual act. In this hybrid conception of *karma*, ritual activity becomes inextricably entwined within the web of *saṃsāra* and thus diametrically opposed to the liberative knowledge of Brahman.

Śaṅkara's antithesis between (ritual) action and knowledge places him in conflict with an earlier tradition of Vedānta that pursued a less radical strategy for securing the autonomy of the Upaniṣads vis-à-vis the ritual portion (*karma-kāṇḍa*) of the Veda. Śaṅkara engages polemically with this earlier tradition in his lengthy comment on BS 1.1.4. There the principal opponent, whom Śaṅkara's later commentator Govindānanda identifies as the Vṛttikāra—hence Ingalls' "Proto-commentator"—argues that "the Upaniṣads present Brahman in the context of injunction about meditation."[50] This thesis represents a strategy for recognizing the upaniṣadic teaching on Brahman that remains within the basic Mīmāṃsā framework. Specifically, it proceeds from the above-mentioned Mīmāṃsā premise, rejected by Śaṅkara, that Vedic texts must pertain to injunctions in order to be meaningful.[51] The opponent's position, which appears to be consistent with that of Bādarāyaṇa,[52] reflects an earlier stage in the brahmanical tradition in which the two Mīmāṃsās existed in a more or less complementary relationship.[53] According to this earlier conception of Vedānta, the injunctions to engage in meditation (*upāsana*) on Brahman found in the knowledge-portion (*jñāna-kāṇḍa*) of the Veda parallel the injunctions to ritual sacrifice (*yajña*) in the ritual portion (*karma-kāṇḍa*).[54] In this conception, meditation (*upāsana*) represents a bridge of sorts between the world of ritual, on the one hand, and the liberative knowledge that such acts of meditation were instrumental in bringing about, on the other.[55] Although the *pūrvapakṣin* in BSBh 1.1.4 does not make the point explicitly, this earlier notion of meditation as an enjoined act conducive to the knowledge of Brahman coheres with the doctrine of the combination of knowledge and works (*jñāna-karma-samuccaya-vāda*) that Śaṅkara elsewhere strenuously opposes.

It is clear that this earlier Vedāntic paradigm is incompatible with Śaṅkara's dichotomy between ritual action and liberative knowledge. When the conception of meditation and the ritual act as parallel objects of Vedic injunction is subsumed within the framework of Śaṅkara's dichotomy between ritual *karma* and knowledge, the former becomes understood as a ritual act determined by human interests and desires. As such, it stands unambiguously on the *karma* side of the *karma*/knowledge dichotomy:

> Even though meditation, that is, thinking, is performed in the mind, nevertheless it can be done, not done, or done otherwise by a man; for it is dependent on man. But knowledge arises from its valid means (e.g., perception, inference, etc.), and the valid means apprehend the things just as they are. Hence knowledge is not something to be done, not done, or done otherwise, for it is entirely determined by things, and neither by injunctions nor by man.[56]

As an inherently purposeful activity standing in continuity with ritual karmas, meditation is firmly rooted in the conditions of saṃsāric existence. In the introduction to his commentary on the Aitareya Upaniṣad, Śaṅkara states explicitly that the highest aim or result of the meditative act, namely, the entrance or merger into a deity (*devatā-apyaya*), belongs to the realm of *saṃsāra*.[57] This is so despite the fact that some—namely, those rival teachers of Vedānta who advocate the *jñāna-karma-samuccaya* doctrine—mistakenly confuse this saṃsāric state with the highest liberation itself.[58] Śaṅkara,s devaluation of meditation here exemplifies a highly effective strategy of religious polemic that we will examine more closely below, namely, the redescription of a rival conception of the religious ideal as a form of self-interested human activity.

In driving a wedge between meditation and knowledge, Śaṅkara diverges from the viewpoint of the *Brahma-sūtra* itself, which, as alluded to above, most probably held that the former was directly conducive to the latter.[59] This tension between Śaṅkara and Bādarāyaṇa's respective understandings of the relation between meditation and knowledge surfaces in Śaṅkara's interpretation of BS 3.4.26. The *sūtra* itself reads as follows: "[The knowledge of Brahman] depends on all the rites, on the authority of the *śruti* text mentioning sacrifice [BAU 4.4.22]. [These required rites] are like the horse."[60] As P. M. Modi notes, the cryptic mention of the horse here almost certainly refers to the allegorical analysis of the horse sacrifice found in the first chapter of the Bṛhadāraṇyaka Upaniṣad.[61] This allusion suggests that the sacrifices upon which the *sūtra* says the knowledge of Brahman depends are of an allegorical variety, that is, the acts of meditation understood as "internalized quasi-rituals."[62] When interpreted in this way, BS 3.4.26 coheres with the preceding sutra (BS 3.4.25), which states that knowledge does not depend on fire, fuel, and so on, that is, on ritual implements referring synedochecally to the *physical* sacrifice, as opposed to the allegorical sacrifice whose indispensability is affirmed in the following *sūtra*.[63] Śaṅkara, however, in keeping with his refusal to concede a causal link between the activity of meditation and liberative knowledge, interprets the denial of dependence asserted here in *sūtra* 25 in an absolute sense, that is, as applying not only to physical, literal sacrifice but also to allegorical sacrifice—meditation—as well. Thus, when he comes to *sūtra* 26, he finds himself confronted with a text directly contradicting his interpretation. In order to reconcile this verse with his central thesis that liberation is not the result of enjoined activity of any kind, Śaṅkara makes a somewhat specious distinction between the realization of the result (*phalasiddha*) of knowledge, which does not depend on rites, and the emergence (*utpatti*) of knowledge, which does.[64] We see here that when Śaṅkara's back is against the wall, so to speak, he is willing, however reluctantly, to compromise the unity between knowledge and liberation (by speaking of liberation as a result of knowledge) in order to preserve the all-important caesura between human activity and liberative knowledge. Stated negatively, BSBh 3.4.26 reveals a principled refusal to concede a causal link between liberation and even the most sublime human activity, such as meditation.

Śaṅkara's effort to remove the knowledge of Brahman from the realm of human activity encounters a more insidious challenge from the argument that the renunciation of ritual *karma* can itself be considered a kind of act motivated by desire, in this case the desire for liberation. Against such an argument Śaṅkara asserts that the kind of renunciation he has in mind is not something to be done like ritual sacrifice. Rather, it represents the natural expression of the knowledge of Brahman: "Renunciation consists in the mere absence of activity; as something having the nature of reality (*bhāvātmakam*), and it does not have the form of something to be done like sacrifice. And a motive is not to be sought [when] knowledge forms the inherent quality of a man."[65] Elsewhere, specifically in BAUBh 3.5.1, Śaṅkara distinguishes this kind of renunciation from a more mundane variety that is motivated by the desire for religious results like attaining the world of Brahma.[66] The latter's intentional structure betrays an ignorance of the self "which is unrelated to instruments and results."[67] Śaṅkara characterizes this lower form of renunciation as "having the form of an *āśrama*." In other words, it represents an institutionalized form of renunciation belonging to the fourfold system of stations of life (*āśrama*), a central institution in brāhmanical ideology. As such it presupposes an interested agent (*kartṛ*) who is subject to Vedic injunction.[68] By contrast, the higher form of renunciation, which "is characterized by the turning away of desire that contradicts the knowledge of the self" (*ātma-jñāna-virodhy-eṣaṇā-vyutthāna-lakṣaṇam*), lies outside the framework of interest and intentionality. As such, it transcends the *āśramas* (*atyāśrama*), including the fourth that is the lower, instrumental form of renunciation. The knower of *ātman*/Brahman, whom Śaṅkara describes as a *parahaṃsa* renunciant,[69] lies beyond the range of the injunctions that sustain the āśramic system.[70]

Śaṅkara's contrast here between two types of renunciation expresses his polemic with that more conservative current in Vedānta, mentioned above, which held that ritual *karma* played an essential role in the path to liberation.[71] These rival teachers of Vedānta maintained that renunciation, in order to be legitimate, retained a connection, even if a minimal one, with the world of Vedic ritual. This connection was symbolized by three emblems of the renunciant's brahmanical status, namely, the sacrificial cord, the topknot (uncut locks of hair on the renouncer's head), and, above all, the triple-staff (a walking stick made by tying three bamboos together, but most likely originally a tripod used to carry a water pot).[72] Śaṅkara is clearly alluding to this tradition of triple-staff renunciation when he characterizes āśramic meditation as a lower form of religious activity still trapped in the framework of means and ends. Śaṅkara invidiously represents the aim of this form of renunciation as the "world of Brahma," a lower religious goal that, as we saw above, he elsewhere declares to belong to the sphere of *saṃsāra*. This characterization of triple-staff renunciation is surely tendentious. In reality, the aim of the triple-staff renunciants was nothing short of liberation (*mokṣa*) from *saṃsāra*.

Śaṅkara's polemical contrast between *parahaṃsa* renunciation and āśramic, "triple-staff" renunciation makes use of the same contrast that he used to redescribe and devalue the ritual act in his polemic with Mīmāṃsā. Ritual *karma*, we recall, depends essentially on human practice (*puruṣa-vyāpāra-tantra*), whereas the knowledge of Brahman depends on reality itself (*vastu-tantra*).[73] We see that this schema is remarkably versatile. By redescribing both the ritual *karma* of the Mīmāṃsakas and the āśramic renunciation prized by his Vedāntic rivals as expressions of human motive and desire, Śaṅkara is able to place two principal rivals together on the other side of a polemical divide. The apologetic schema with Śaṅkara on one side and his Vedānta and Mīmāṃsā rivals on the other gives dramatic expression to Śaṅkara's claim that those Vedāntic teachers who had argued that the path to liberation fell under the purview of Vedic injunction failed to transcend the Mīmāṃsā framework. We can imagine, of course, that those Vedāntic teachers viewed matters quite differently. Their arguments for recognizing the path to liberation as the object of Vedic injunction were intended to establish, against the resistance of the Mīmāṃsakas, the legitimacy of the celibate *āśrama*s. From their perspective, then, Śaṅkara's claim that the knower of Brahman lies outside the sphere of Vedic injunction threatened to undermine their case against the Mīmāṃsā school and therewith the legitimacy of the Vedāntic project. In this respect, Śaṅkara's distinction between higher and lower forms of renunciation is similar to his distinction between the higher and lower Brahman. Just as his conception of an impersonal Brahman could be seen as weakening Bādarāyaṇa's case against the Sāṃkhya for a conception of the world-cause as a conscious principle, as I suggested in chapter 5, so too could Śaṅkara's claim that the highest form of renunciation lies beyond the range of injunction be seen as undermining Bādarāyaṇa's achievement in winning recognition within the brahmanical tradition for the Vedāntic path to liberation. Śaṅkara's neat schema with the Advaita on one side and the Mīmāṃsakas and rival Vedāntins on the other masks the complexity and delicacy of his polemical task, namely, to supersede the earlier tradition of Vedānta while at the same time not allowing this supersession to undermine the latter's case against the Mīmāṃsā. Śaṅkara's attempt to negotiate this tricky political terrain accounts for much of the well-known ambiguity and inconsistency of his various statements on renunciation.[74]

Enlightened Action in Śaṅkara?

We have seen that Śaṅkara extends his negative characterization of ritual *karma* as self-interested activity to Vedāntic meditation (*upāsana*) and even to āśramically sanctioned renunciation (*saṃnyāsa*). Śaṅkara's extension of his critique of ritual *karma* to include even the ostensible renunciation of ritual karma—an extension, incidentally, that testifies, in an ironic way, to the hegemonic nature of ritual sacrifice in traditional brahmanical thought—raises the question of whether there is *any* form of human activity that escapes this critique. Put differently, are there any forms of human activity that are compatible with the knowledge of *ātman*/Brahman? Or, expressed in terms of our comparative problematic, does Śaṅkara acknowledge any form of human behavior that is analogous, even remotely, to Eckhart's "living without a why"?

If Śaṅkara were inclined to recognize a form of activity consistent with his understanding of liberative knowledge, he would have no better opportunity than in his commentary on the Bhagavad-Gītā. For the Gītā contains Kṛṣṇa's celebrated teaching of *karma-yoga*, of acting without attachment to the fruits of action. It was this teaching that allowed Arjuna to act, and thus fulfill his warrior *dharma*, without fear of suffering adverse karmic consequences. Would not this notion *karma-yoga*, then, a mode of action gutted of self-interested motivation, be precisely the kind of action we are looking for? The Gītā, in fact, even goes beyond simply conceding the possibility of a mode of action compatible with the quest for liberation. In the beginning of Book Five (5:2), for example, Kṛṣṇa declares *karma-yoga* superior to the renunciation of karma (*tayostu karmasaṃnyāsāt karmayogo viśiṣyate*), a claim that suggests an analogy with Eckhart's preference for the active spirituality of Martha over the pure contemplation of Mary. One would think that this verse in particular would invite an affirmation of a form of enlightened activity analogous Eckhart's notion of "living without a why."

One hoping to find such an acknowledgment in Śaṅkara's Gītā Commentary, however, is apt to be disappointed. Śaṅkara's comment on verse 5:2, for example, might even be taken to exemplify Otto's summary judgment that Śaṅkara, "with an appalling persistency and obduracy [...] uses all the powers of his dialectic and his penetrating intellect to cloud and twist the clear meaning of the Gītā."[75] Here Śaṅkara interprets the renunciation of action (*karma-saṃnyāsa*) that Krishna declares inferior to *karma-yoga* as a "mere renunciation" of action, that is, a renunciation devoid of knowledge.[76] In other words, Gītā 5:2 refers to the lower form of renunciation, mentioned above, that remains entwined in the saṃsāric web of motives, means, and results. In the context of the Gītā, this lower form of renunciation would seem to include, if not directly correspond to, the faux renunciation of "hypocrites" (*mithyācārāḥ*) mentioned in Gītā 3:6, who renounce outward actions without the corresponding renunciation of passion and motive.[77] We see, then, that Śaṅkara defines renunciation here in such a way that Kṛṣṇa's stated preference for *karma-yoga* over renunciation in 5:2 leaves Śaṅkara's doctrine of the incompatibility of knowledge and action—a teaching that arguably goes against both the spirit and the letter of the Gītā—unaffected.[78] A couple of verses later (5:5), Śaṅkara appears to go even further in his effort to align the Gītā's teaching on the superiority of *karma-yoga* over *saṃnyāsa* with his doctrine on the incompatibility of knowledge and *karma*. There he suggests that "*yoga* in the highest sense" is nothing other than renunciation that is based on knowledge.[79] Although he leaves the relation between this "*yoga* in a higher sense" and the *karma-yoga* Kṛṣṇa extols in Gītā 5:2 vague, perhaps purposely so, Śaṅkara could be understood here to be mapping his distinction between higher and lower *saṃnyāsa* onto Kṛṣṇa's distinction between (*karma-*) *yoga* and *saṃnyāsa*. Through what might appear from one perspective to be an arbitrary and audacious redefinition of terms—but which we must nevertheless assume stemmed from sincere conviction—Śaṅkara turns the literal sense of Kṛṣṇa's declaration of the superiority of *karma-yoga* over renunciation on its head! An expression of preference for unattached action over renunciation becomes an expression of praise for true renunciation.[80]

Śaṅkara's interpretation of Gītā 5:2 exemplifies his reluctance more generally to concede a form of action that is compatible with the knowledge of *ātman*/ Brahman, a feature of his thought that is all the more conspicuous in the context of the Gītā's teaching of *karma-yoga*. This reluctance can be explained in large part by Śaṅkara's unwillingness to yield ground to the adherents of the doctrine of the combination of knowledge and works (*jñāna-karma-samuccaya-vāda*). A central preoccupation in Śaṅkara's *Gītā* commentary, in fact, is to undermine the appeal these rival Vedāntins made to the Gītā in their effort to deny the Advaita thesis that "liberation is attained through knowledge alone."[81] Śaṅkara's challenge to his opponents' reading of the Gītā centers on the Gītā's teaching of *adhikāra* or eligibility, a notion clearly expressed in Gītā 3:3:

> O unblemished one, I have long taught that there are two kinds of perfection (*niṣṭhā*) in this world: that of the men of knowledge (*sāṃkhyānām*), [which is] attained through the discipline of

> knowledge (*jñānayogena*), and that of the men of discipline (*yoginām*), attained through the discipline of action (*karmayogena*).[82]

Śaṅkara interprets the teaching expressed here of *jñāna-yoga* and *karma-yoga* as alternative means to religious perfection in terms of his distinction between the enlightened and the unenlightened, that is, between those who have overcome the illusion of agency and those who have not.[83] He identifies the "men of knowledge" (*sāṃkhyānām*) who attain perfection through the *yoga* of knowledge with "the renunciants known as the *paramahaṃsas* who are established in Brahman alone."[84] The "perfection through the *yoga* of work," on the other hand, is appropriate for "men of action" (*karmiṇām*), like Arjuna, who are ipso facto unenlightened.[85] By interpreting the two *yogas* in terms of the distinction between knowledge and ignorance, Śaṅkara renders their relation hierarchical and exclusionary.[86] Thus interpreted, the *adhikāra* doctrine expressed in Gītā 3:3 excludes the possibility of one and the same person pursuing the *yoga* of knowledge and the *yoga* of work concurrently. This means that the Gītā contradicts the doctrine of the combination of rites and knowledge in pursuit of liberation.[87]

Śaṅkara's reluctance to acknowledge a mode of activity compatible with the knowledge of *ātman*/Brahman, even when the Gītā text authorizes him to do so, thus becomes intelligible when we recognize the polemical context in which he interprets the Gītā. Śaṅkara's interest in asserting a dichotomy between knowledge and *karma* against his rivals' claim that knowledge and *karma* can be combined serves as a disincentive against an acknowledgment of an enlightened form of activity, for such an admission might be perceived as a fatal concession to his opponents. Nevertheless Śaṅkara does acknowledge such forms of action, although, not surprisingly in view of his polemical concerns, he does so without drawing undue attention to them. The possibility of enlightened forms of activity is implicit in the Gītā's notion of a disjunction between inner and outer action, a teaching concisely and eloquently expressed in the notion of seeing "inaction in action" and "action in inaction" found in verse 4:18.[88] As we saw above, Śaṅkara appeals to the notion of "seeing action in inaction" to call attention to those forms of physical renunciation unaccompanied by a renunciation of the notion of personal agency. In doing so, he is obliged to acknowledge the inverse situation—expressed in the other half of the Gītā's formula, "seeing inaction in action"—of enlightened persons moving about in the world without a deluded sense of personal agency. Śaṅkara says that such an enlightened person, the *jivanmukti*, will still act either to maintain his body[89]—a rather obvious admission, one would think, but a significant qualification of the knowledge/action dichotomy nonetheless—or to prevent people from going astray (presumably to avoid setting an example for antinomian behavior).[90]

As in other areas in his teaching where exegetical, logical, or empirical considerations force him to qualify an Advaita doctrine, Śaṅkara seeks to neutralize the potentially damaging effect of this concession on his polemic by invoking the distinction between absolute and relative truth (*pāramārthika sat* and *vyāvahārika sat*, respectively).[91] Thus the sage who is seen acting in the world—the *jivanmukti*—only appears to act. His action is only a function of the ignorance of those who falsely attribute the idea of agency to his behavior.[92] To convey this idea that the activity of the enlightened sage is only a matter of perspective, Śaṅkara compares his comportment to the trees on a riverbank that appear to move from the perspective of those on a boat sailing downstream.[93] Here we see that Śaṅkara maps the Advaita doctrine of two truths onto the Gītā's distinction between inner and outward action. By thus consigning outward activity to the realm of relative truth, Śaṅkara is able to neutralize his concession of enlightened activity.

Even if we confine ourselves to the perspective of conventional (*vyāvahārika*) truth, it still might appear that the relation between the *jivanmukti*'s action and his outward activity is more or less accidental. He continues to act in the world *in spite of* his realization, for reasons—maintenance of the body and avoidance of leading the unenlightened astray—lacking an intrinsic connection with the truth he has realized.[94] To the extent that the relation between the *jivanmukti*'s enlightened state and his action is accidental, Śaṅkara's concession falls short of the Eckhartian notion of "living without a why." For, as we have seen, the activity of the perfected soul in Eckhart reflects the very nature of his or her union with God. The perfected soul acts because the divine principle that he or she embodies is itself active.

There is, however, a concept found in Śaṅkara's teaching that expresses a more intimate and positive connection between an interior state of transcending desire and motive, on the one hand, and a form of outward activity, on the other. This is the notion of divine play or *līlā* that Hindu theologians have used to affirm the activity of divine creation without imputing motive or need to God (Īśvara). Śaṅkara appeals to the *līlā* concept in his commentary on BS 2.1.33 in order to counter the opponent's argument, voiced in the preceding *sūtra* (BS 2.1.32), that the foundational Vedāntic doctrine of Brahman-Īśvara as the world-cause contradicts the "contentment" (*paritṛptatva*) that the Vedas ascribe to the supreme self (*paramātmā*). All deliberative activity, the opponent argues—including, a fortiori, the exceedingly strenuous activity of world creation—proceeds from a motive (*prayojana*), which in turn presupposes a need, a lack of fulfillment.[95] Against this claim, Śaṅkara argues, on the analogy of kings and other powerful persons who act despite having all their desires fulfilled (*āptaiṣaṇa*), that "the activity of God also has the form of mere sport (*līlā*), arising out of his own nature (*svabhavād eva*) independently of any other motive (*anapekṣya kiṃcitprayojanāntaraṃ*)."[96] Īśvara acts without a motive despite the fact that some people "fancy that sport also has some subtle motive behind it."[97]

As we saw above in chapter 4, Otto dismisses the analogy between *līlā* and Eckhart's understanding of God's creative act as the spontaneous "outflow" (*ûzvluz*) or "boiling over" (*ebullitio*) of the divine life into the world. Concerning the latter, he declares that, "this is no mere *līlā*, no playing of the Godhead, as in India, but the divine life revolving within itself, in which it displays the richness of its own inner life."[98] Despite Otto's peremptory dismissal of the analogy, however, I would argue that Śaṅkara's appeal to the concept of *līlā* here in BSBh 2.1.33 has profound affinities with Eckhart's concept of the ouflow of divine life in the act of creation. The two notions function similarly in their respective contexts to reconcile an affirmation of divine creation (specifically, the Christian doctrine of creation in the one case, the Vedāntic doctrine of Brahman-Īśvara as the world-cause in the other) with the notion of divine perfection. In both cases, elements within common human experience provide intuitive support to the theological claim that God/Brahman can indeed act in the world without that activity betraying a need or want and therefore imperfection. Both notions—not just Eckhart's—express the idea that God's creative activity is the spontaneous expression of the divine nature.[99] On one level, it is not surprising that Otto dismisses the *līlā* analogy so hastily, for the analogy, by affirming an inherent connection between divine activity and divine nature, would compromise the apologetic contrast he wants to draw between the dynamic nature of Eckhart's God and the static and indifferent nature of Śaṅkara's Brahman.

If in fact Śaṅkara comes up short in a comparison with Eckhart when it comes to affirming God's active involvement in the world, it is not, I would suggest, because the concept of *līlā* is somehow lacking in theological gravitas and depth as Otto insinuates.[100] On the contrary, it would be because the concept of *līlā* plays an altogether marginal role in Śaṅkara's teaching, in marked contrast to the central role of the corresponding concepts of the "outflow" and "living without a why" in Eckhart's. Despite the Advaitic doctrine of the identity of *ātman* and Brahman, which would fully justify the use of the concept of *līlā* in relation to human behavior, Śaṅkara appears curiously reluctant to speak of *līlā* in an anthropological context.[101] Moreover, Śaṅkara qualifies, if not undermines, the affirmation of divine activity in the world expressed in the *līlā* concept by denying a literal sense to the cosmological statements of the Veda, relegating the ideas of cosmos and creation to the realm of merely relative truth.[102] Once again, it would appear that a polemical concern in maintaining a dichotomy between action and knowledge was the primary factor in Śaṅkara's marginalization of *līlā*, a form of purposeless activity falling outside Śaṅkara's critique of ritual activity.

We have seen, then, Śaṅkara's overriding concern with refuting the advocates of the *jñāna-karma-samuccaya* doctrine was a major, even determinative, factor in his insistence that the knowledge of Brahman transcends any form of activity that can be correlated with a motive and an aim. In other words, the polemic was conducive to the development, in the Advaita context, of an analogue to the "without a why" part of Eckhart's "living without a why" formula. At the same time, however, that very same polemical concern interfered with an acknowledgment of a form of human activity transcending the realm of human purposes and motives—the "living" part of "living without a why."

The Polemical Dimension of "Living without a Why"

It has become something of a truism—but true nonetheless—that the comparative theological enterprise is justified by its promise of highlighting features of the compared traditions that otherwise might escape notice. In other words, a feature that is conspicuous in one tradition can be used as a heuristic template to focus attention on a parallel feature in another tradition that is either less pronounced or obscured because of the ideological blind spots of its tradition(s) of interpretation. In keeping with this methodological principle, I would like to suggest that our comparison of Śaṅkara and Meister Eckhart in this chapter might serve to focus attention on the polemical dimension of Eckhart's notion of "living without a why," a dimension which is otherwise difficult to discern because it exists in sublimated form.

The polemical dimension of the parallel claim in Śaṅkara—namely, that the knowledge of Brahman has no connection with the world of purposeful activity—is unmistakable. As we have seen, Śaṅkara develops this transcendental conception of *brahmavidyā* in the context of a polemical effort to devalue the central religious institutions of his two principal rivals—namely, the Vedic ritual of the Pūrva Mīmāṃsā, on the one side, and the āśramic renunciation of the Vedāntic advocates of the doctrine of "the combination of rites and knowledge" (*jñāna-karma-samuccaya*), on the other. He does this by redescribing both of these institutions, against the self-understanding of their proponents, as expressions of (merely) human motivation and desire. As we have seen, Śaṅkara's conception of the highest knowledge as grounded in reality (*vastu-tantra*) as opposed to human activity (*puruṣa-vyāpāra-tantra*) can be understood in terms of this effort to assert the superiority of the Advaita school over against its principal brahmanical rivals.[103]

By contrast, it is not immediately obvious that Eckhart's teaching on "living without a why" served a polemical agenda. Eckhart's teaching on "living without a why," in fact, has been interpreted in a way that excludes political considerations a priori. Epitomizing this line of interpretation is Otto, who writes that "such statements about [Eckhart's] 'without a why' do not come to him from speculative thoughts about the wayless Godhead, but rather from the experience of the person united with God...."[104] Otto's interpretation of Eckhart's "without a why" here exemplifies the modern preoccupation with mystical "experience" more generally, a preoccupation which, as we saw in chapter 2, has given expression to the liberal quest to dissociate "religion" from the political. Today such an experientialist approach to the study of mysticism that examines the writings of putative mystics like Eckhart for evidence of extraordinary states of consciousness is thoroughly dated.[105] The general consensus, as I understand it, is that such an experientialist approach to mystical writings must, at the very least, be supplemented by contextual approaches that locate those writings in their historical, theological, literary, and/or sociopolitical contexts.[106]

In keeping with these more recent contextualist approaches, I would argue that if the polemical dimension of the "living without a why" idea is not immediately obvious, this is not because it gives expression to a direct experience bypassing all mundane considerations, including, a fortiori, polemical ones, but rather because its polemical dimension exists in a particularly complex, sublimated form. Above, I suggested that Eckhart's teaching of "living without a why" exemplifies the thesis, advanced by Grundmann, Haas, Ruh, and others, that Eckhart's mystical theology can be understood as an attempt to reconcile the thoughts and experiences of the thirteenth-century women's religious movement with theological orthodoxy.[107] As such, it incorporates two polemical tendencies whose tension it seeks to moderate and transcend. On the one hand, Eckhart's teaching, insofar as it represents the tradition of theological orthodoxy, reflects the Church's response to the challenge that the women's religious movement posed to its authority. In this context, we can understand Eckhart's generally negative attitude towards claims of special religious experience. Grace Jantzen argues that Eckhart's criticism of the contemporary preoccupation with visionary experience expresses a thinly veiled assertion of a patriarchal church against those, typically women, who appealed to such experiences in order to appropriate a measure of religious authority otherwise denied to them. Citing Eckhart's statement that "some people want to see God with their own eyes, as they see a cow,... You love a cow for her milk and her cheese and your own profit," Janzten argues that "there is no room in his thinking for visionary experience based on higher motivation than personal profit, or for claiming authority because of it: in his view all that can be said is that this would make the vision of God equivalent in value to the vision of a cow."[108] By placing Eckhart's critique of visionary experience in the context of the Church's struggle to maintain its authority in face of the religious movements of the thirteenth century, Jantzen presents Eckhart's cow analogy as a particularly striking example of the kind of devaluatory redescription that we saw in Śaṅkara's characterization of Vedic ritual.

Eckhart's critique of instrumental piety, however, cuts both ways. As we have seen, his subordination of the exterior aspect of the morally good act to the interior aspect and his devaluation of petitionary prayer were perceived as a threat to the institutional life of Church.[109] In integrating the idea of spiritual poverty into his speculative theological vision, Eckhart was appropriating an idea with a long history of subversion. The ideal of evangelical poverty provided the basis for a challenge to the Church's authority in a variety of religious movements from the Humiliati and the Waldensians in the twelfth and thirteenth centuries to the Beguines in the thirteenth and fourteenth. Eckhart, supremely confident in his formidable intellectual abilities and the eminent position he held both in his order and the intellectual world,[110] likely believed he was up to the task of integrating an idea with a polemical history behind it into an orthodox theological vision. That several of the fundamental teachings comprising that vision were ultimately judged to be heretical testifies to the power of the history behind the ideas Eckhart appropriated. In light of his official condemnation, it appears that Eckhart badly underestimated the capacity of the ideas he appropriated to reassert their original intention against the new intentionality he sought to impart to them.

The foregoing demonstration of the political dimension of one of Eckhart's most sublime teachings underscores an important point apropos this book's central thesis concerning the ineluctability of the political in religious discourse. That the political goes "all the way down"—that the entirety of religious discourse and practice is implicated, even if only indirectly, in relations of religious rivalry—in no way excludes the capacity of religious discourse to edify and inspire. As someone for whom Eckhart's "living without a why" idea continues to edify, I cannot accept the notion that an acknowledgment of the ideological dimension of a text or practice negates its value and truth. A capacity to live with ambiguity, in fact, may well be a mark of intellectual and religious maturity.

Conclusion

Two Purposes, Two Comparisons

Perhaps more so than any other form of intellectual activity, the practice of comparison is determined by the scholar's interests and motives. What Bruce Lincoln writes about scholarship in general applies, a fortiori, to comparison in particular:

> [S]cholars actively construct that which they study through their selection of evidence, a process in which they systematically disarticulate certain data from their original context while ignoring others, and rearticulate those so chosen within a novel context of their own devising. These novel contexts, moreover, are inevitably, if most often unconsciously, conditioned by the interests of their authors (taking "interests" in its bland, as well as its more pointed meaning)....[1]

Those interests (in both the "bland" and "pointed" senses) will determine the comparativist's partly arbitrary choice of data to compare and, consequently, the conclusions that he or she draws from them. A specification of purpose is therefore integral to both the practice and the assessment of comparison. In light of this point regarding the importance of identifying the comparativist's interests and motives, the larger objectives he or she hopes to achieve through a particular exercise in comparison, it might be helpful at this point to stand back and recall the respective aims of Otto's comparison and mine.

As we saw in chapter 4, Otto's principal aim is to vindicate Eckhart from the charges of mystical "a-theism," acosmism, and quietism, the three dimensions of the charge of pantheism as formulated by the Meister's nineteenth century critics.[2] He seeks to establish Eckhart as a legitimate representative—indeed the exemplar—of Christian mysticism by showing that Eckhart's mystical speculations, for all their daring and sublimity, rest on a firm theistic foundation, "on the simple, Christian belief in God," as he puts it.[3] And the way he highlights this redeeming, theistic dimension of Eckhart's mysticism is by contrasting him with Śaṅkara, a figure who, at least according to a conventional reading, epitomizes the above-mentioned three dimensions of pantheism. With his choice of Śaṅkara as a dialogue partner with Eckhart, Otto invokes the orientalist dichotomy between Christian theism and oriental pantheism. As I argued in chapter 4, this dichotomy plays a crucial role in magnifying the contrasts between the two masters to the point—or at least Otto hopes—of convincing the reader of Eckhart's identity as a full-fledged Christian. To be sure, Otto qualifies the orientalist reading of Śaṅkara in several important respects, basically restricting its validity to the third, ethical dimension of the pantheism charge. Nevertheless, the effectiveness of Otto's defense of Eckhart largely depends on the essentializing contrast between world and life affirmation and world and life denial.

My aim in comparing Eckhart and Otto is essentially the inverse of Otto's. I have not sought to eliminate doubts about Eckhart's orthodoxy or "disambiguate" the characterization of his teaching. In fact, I have presumed and exploited that ambiguity in order to highlight the ambiguity and complexity of his Indian counterpart. By redescribing Śaṅkara in terms of Eckhart, I have sought to highlight the theistic and realist aspects of the former that have been suppressed by the orientalist characterization of his teaching as illusionistic pantheism. This recovery of the dialectical character of Śaṅkara's thought does not simply deprive the essentializing contrast between East and West of one of its most well-known supporting instances. For to the extent that Śaṅkara has served not simply as an instance but as the very exemplar of that essentialist characterization of Indian thought, our reading of Śaṅkara calls into question the dichotomy itself.

One might sum up the essential difference between my comparison and Otto's, then, by saying that whereas his overall aim was to disambiguate Eckhart by making strategic use of the traditional essentializing dichotomy between East and West, mine has been to "ambiguate" Śaṅkara, with the aim of calling that dichotomy into question.

As I have emphasized repeatedly in part II, my comparison, with its overall aim of deconstructing the East versus West dichotomy, exemplifies the second moment of the dialectical model of comparative theology developed in part I of this book. And Otto's, to the extent that it continues the Christian apologetic tradition, represents the first moment of that model. The relation between my comparison and Otto's, then, can be understood in terms of the necessary relation between the two moments of this model of comparative theology. To the extent that my overall purpose has been to question the East versus West apologetic tradition, my comparison only makes sense in relation to a purveyor of that tradition like Otto. My conversation with Otto is integral, then, to my comparison of Eckhart and Śaṅkara.

Two Paradigms of Critical Thought and the Question of the Comparative Method

Having acknowledged and affirmed the constructive and political dimension of the comparative theological enterprise undertaken in part II of this book, I would like to return to the question of the legitimacy of comparison as a scholarly endeavor. Throughout this book, I have sought to justify, indeed, to celebrate, the constructive nature of comparison against what I regard as an understandable but overly reactive tendency in academic circles to restrict comparison to historically contiguous phenomena. Precisely because it is intended as a corrective, however, this affirmation of the constructive dimension of comparison is apt to appear dangerously one-sided if removed from the context of contemporary debates about the use of the comparative method. Prima facie, it would seem that to affirm the constructive aspect of comparison is to concede the projection of the comparativist's own commitments onto the phenomena to be compared.

In order to contextualize my affirmation of the constructive aspect of comparison, I find it helpful to understand the current debate about the legitimacy of comparison in terms of the distinction between what the eighteenth-century Italian humanist Giambattista Vico termed *verum* and *certum*.[4] The former refers to the unchanging, absolute truths of philosophical reason. The latter refers to the everyday certainties (*certa*)—what people in a given historical epoch take to be true—grounding human actions, expressions, and institutions.[5] Corresponding to these two levels of discourse are two paradigms of critical thought. The first of these questions the putative, taken-for-granted certainties of everyday experience in order to access a deeper stratum of reality and truth—Vico's *verum*. This first paradigm corresponds to what is commonly referred to as "critical realism." It refers paradigmatically to those scientific theories that conflict—at least at their inception—with ordinary experience.[6] But this model, with its appeal to two levels of discourse, can be broadened to include those forms of criticism that seek to expose and remove ideological discourses that falsify the underlying human reality these ideologies purport to describe. The second critical paradigm questions the separation, presupposed in the first, between conventional understanding and reality. This more radical mode of critique marks a paradoxical return to conventional experience—Vico's *certa*—as the basis for philosophical reflection and historical understanding. It recognizes that conventional understandings of the world, whatever their intrinsic truth value, themselves have a historical reality.[7] This second paradigm is exemplified by those forms of postmodern thought that question the putative separation between discourse and reality, words and things.

These two paradigms, understood as Weberian ideal types, can shed light on some of the recent scholarly debates over the legitimacy of comparison in the field of religion. The viewpoint of those scholars who reject comparison on the grounds that its cross-cultural categories and generalizations mask, with politically nefarious consequences, the underlying reality of cultural and religious difference can be understood in terms of our first paradigm. According to this line of critique, the classificatory schemes and generalizations of comparative religion exemplify the totalizing schemes and meta-narratives that critics like Adorno and Lyotard identified as discourses of domination. This form of argument implicitly understands the distinction between comparative discourse and the cultural phenomena being compared in terms of the distinction between appearance and reality. Stated crudely, the cross-cultural similarities brought to light by comparison are imagined, whereas the underlying cultural differences are real.[8]

The "New Comparativism," on the other hand, understood in terms of a paradigm shift from genealogical to analogical comparison, can be understood in terms of our second paradigm. It reflects the insight, implicit in Vico's principle that human beings can understand only what they themselves have created,[9] that historical understanding is itself a creative process.[10] Or, put differently, that the understanding of human history itself forms a part of that history. The comparative study of religion exemplifies this principle of the historicity of historical understanding.[11] Scholars of religion have long recognized that the modern comparative study of religion itself constitutes a significant event in the religious history of humankind. As Robert Neville and Wesley Wildman remind us, "comparison is an act that changes things."[12]

This principle of the historicity of comparative discourse leads us to question the first paradigm's dualistic understanding of the relation between the meta-cultural discourse of the comparativist, on the one hand, and the discourses constitutive of the cultural "objects" being compared, on the other. In a particularly insightful defense of the comparative method in anthropology, Greg Urban argues that the activity of comparison is integral to the process of cultural transmission, the process, in other words, by which new experiences are brought into an existing interpretive scheme.[13] Thus, according to Urban, "the tendency to compare grows out of the basic processes of cultural reproduction."[14] This means that the cross-cultural comparisons of the anthropologist and the historian of religions stand in continuity with the culture-internal comparisons by which human beings interpret their social worlds and transmit cultural meanings.[15]

The foregoing comparison of Meister Eckhart and Śaṅkara lends support to this notion that the discourses of comparison are continuous with those of the compared phenomena. In the process of deconstructing the "us" versus "them," "West" versus "East" schema that structures a work like Otto's, our comparison of Śaṅkara and Eckhart uncovered, within each of their respective works, oppositional, "political" discourses of the same basic type. The dialectical character of the teaching of each of these thinkers reflects polemical discourses internal to their respective traditions.

As for Śaṅkara, I have argued that his teaching, at least as presented in the context of his *Brahma-sūtra* Commentary, is internally constituted by the realist and theistic Vedānta of an earlier stratum of the tradition. At the same time that he recognizes and honors this earlier tradition, however, he engages in a vigorous polemic with those teachers who were probably its most faithful contemporary exponents, namely, the Bhedābheda Vedāntins who espouse the doctrine of the coordination of knowledge and works (*jñāna-karma-samuccaya-vāda*). Śaṅkara develops the characteristic features of his Advaitic doctrine—the concept of the impersonal, "qualityless" (*nirguṇa*) Brahman; the concept of the world of "name and form" as unreal; and, most directly, the antithesis between liberative knowledge and action (*karma*)—in the context of this polemic with the *jñāna-karma-samuccaya-vādins*. Precisely because these characteristically Advaitic teachings were developed in a polemical context, they cannot be assimilated to the realist and theistic perspective of that earlier stratum of Vedānta preserved in the BSBh. Śaṅkara's intra-tradition polemic and his concomitant deference to a shared tradition thus together comprise the essential ingredients of a dialectic, by which I mean the juxtaposition of two incommensurable perspectives in a necessary relation.

The dialectical character of Eckhart's mystical theology, for its part, reflects the tension between the two religious perspectives that the Meister sought to reconcile. The Eckhartian "breakthrough" reflects the influence of the doctrine of the annihilation of the created will developed in Beguine circles, the most sublime and radical expression of their ideal of spiritual poverty. The complementary movement of the "outflow" represents the orthodox corrective to the quietist and antinomian tendencies associated with the theme of mystical annihilation. Eckhart's dialectical theology can perhaps be seen, then, as the result of an attempt to recognize and reconcile two opposing theological voices. It represents, in other words, the internalization and sublimation of the tense and at times polemical relation between the Church and the new religious movements of the late Middle Ages.

The foregoing analysis suggests that interreligious comparison has a kind of fractal character. That is to say, cross-cultural comparisons, whether polemical or inclusivistic, often simply replicate relational patterns found within the compared traditions themselves. There is perhaps no clearer illustration of this phenomenon than R. C. Zaehner's comparison of Christianity and Advaita Vedānta in his book *Mysticism, Sacred and Profane.* Zaehner's assessment of Śaṅkara's allegedly monistic mysticism coincides with the fourteenth century mystic Jan van Ruusbroec's negative verdict on the "nature mysticism" associated with the Beghards of medieval Europe:

> This emptiness [the state of emptiness prized by the Beghards] seems to them to be so great that no one ought to hinder them with the performance of any work, however good it be, for their emptiness is of greater excellence than are all virtues. And therefore they remain in mere passivity without the performance of any work directed up towards God or down towards man.[16]

According to Zaehner, this polemical characterization of the annihilated state prized by Ruusbroec's adversaries captures "the essence of the non-dualist Vedānta."[17] It finds a close parallel in the eleventh-century Hindu theist Rāmānuja's polemic against Śaṅkara. In the final analysis, Zaehner's tendentious comparison between theistic and monistic mysticism is modeled on polemical discourses internal to the compared traditions. As comparisons like Zaehner's recede into the past and are themselves folded into the stream of religious history, the boundary between religious discourse and scholarly metadiscourse begins to break down. Cross-cultural comparisons like Zaehner's and Otto's come to be seen as examples of Christian apologetic discourse that are fully continuous with its earlier forms.

Although in this book I have expressed a commitment to the New Comparativism and therefore to the second of the paradigms mentioned above, I would like to conclude by arguing that this paradigm stands in a complementary, rather than an exclusionary, relationship with the first. The first paradigm, with its appeal to two levels of discourse, cannot be caricatured as an outmoded and indefensible positivism that can therefore be set aside. To the contrary, it is only by incorporating the first paradigm with its distinction between representation and represented into the comparative process that one can affirm the constructive aspect of comparison without thereby effacing the religious other.

We can perhaps best demonstrate the value of integrating these two perspectives by recalling our analysis of Kathryn Tanner's theory of Christian identity at the end of chapter 2. There, it will be recalled, I argued that the ambiguity in her theory regarding cultural boundaries could be explained by the co-presence of two critical perspectives corresponding nearly exactly to those being discussed here. The first, a liberal-humanist perspective, sought to deconstruct those essentializing, "we are all one way; they are all another"[18] contrasts between cultures in order to call attention to the underlying intra-cultural differences obscured by such contrasts. The second perspective, implicit in her thesis that Christian identity is essentially relational, recognizes such oppositional discourses to be one of the principal means by which social groups mobilize a sense of identity. From this second, more radical postmodernist perspective, social borders and the oppositional discourses that construct them are as real as the social identities that are formed thereby. In the context of Tanner's theory, the first, humanistic perspective provides an important corrective to the second. As we saw above, it allows Tanner to question the isolationist stance fostered by an intrinsic conception of Christian identity, but without thereby countenancing an understanding of Christian identity in oppositional terms.

Thus understood in terms of a strategic negotiation between two modes of critical thought, Tanner's theory of Christian identity serves as a model for comparative theology. As in Tanner's theory, the first, critical paradigm—here a scientific, representational model of comparison—represents an important corrective to the second, constructive paradigm. But the former, when integrated into a larger process of comparison, is not understood positivistically, as a discourse of absolute truth, but rather pragmatically, as a political discourse of strategic intervention.[19] The scientific paradigm can be strategically invoked at the point that contrastive, political discourse begins to glass over with an essentialist sheen.

Notes

PREFACE

1. Here John Hick's pluralist theology is paradigmatic.

2. My description of this second form of pluralism, like the first, is an ideal type. Two theologians who approximate it are George Lindbeck (see ch. 3 of *The Nature of Doctrine* [Philadelphia: Westminster Press, 1984]) and S. Mark Heim (see the "more pluralistic hypothesis" that he defends in *Salvations* [Maryknoll, N.Y.: Orbis Books, 1995]). It should go without saying that these two theologians defend positions that are considerably more nuanced than the thumbnail description I give here. The same of course can be said of John Hick as a representative of the first, universalistic form of pluralism.

3. See Sheila Greeve Davaney, "Mapping Theologies: An Historicist Guide to Contemporary Theology," in *Changing Conversations*, ed. Dwight N. Hopkins and Sheila Greeve Davaney (New York: Routledge, 1996), 25.

4. As Kathryn Tanner notes, accommodation can also be seen as another type of irrelevance, specifically, "an irrelevance of reduplication or assimilation." See her unpublished article, "Two Kinds of Apologetics," ms. p. 2.

5. Donald Wiebe, in his *The Politics of Religious Studies* (New York: St. Martin's Press, 1999), has made this argument with respect to the work of Müller (ch. 2) and Tiele (ch. 3).

6. On the impact of the so-called theological renaissance on the comparative study of religion (or History of Religions), see Joseph Kitagawa, "The History of Religions in America," in *The History of Religions: Essays in Methodology*, ed. Mircea Eliade and Joseph Kitagawa (Chicago: University of Chicago Press, 1959), 5–6, 11–14, and passim.

7. See, for example, Joachim Wach's characterization of the task of theology as "identifying its own confessional norms, . . . understanding and confirming its own faith." Wach, "The Meaning and Task of the History of Religions (Religionswissenschaft)," in *Understanding and Believing*, ed. Joseph M. Kitagawa (New York: Harper & Row, 1968), 125. A Barthian dogmatic (as opposed to apologetic) method of theology is also presumed in Joseph Kitagawa's remark that "a 'humanistic' historian of religions—unlike a 'theological' historian of religions or philosopher of religion—does not have a speculative purpose, *nor does he resort to an a priori deductive method*" (italics added; "Humanistic and Theological History of Religions with Special Reference to the North American Scene," in *Traditions in Contact and Change*, ed. Peter Slater and Donald N. Wiebe [Waterloo, Ont.: Wilfrid Laurier University Press, 1983], 560).

8. Catherine Bell, "Modernism and Postmodernism in the Study of Religion," *Religious Studies Review* 22:3 (1986): 179–90.

9. J. Samuel Preus, Thomas Lawson and Robert McCauley, and Donald Wiebe represent this first modernist trajectory in the study of religion.

10. Hugh Urban and Tyler Roberts are two scholars who argue eloquently for this approach. See chapter 1 below.

11. See Gregory Alles's introduction to Gregory D. Alles, trans. and ed., *Rudolf Otto: Autobiographical and Social Essays* (Berlin, New York: Mouton de Gruyter, 1996), 3–12.

12. Here I allude to David Tracy's helpful discussion of the three "publics" of the theologian, namely, the church, academy, and the wider society. See *The Analogical Imagination* (New York: Crossroad, 1991), 3–46.

INTRODUCTION

Wilfred Cantwell Smith, *Towards a World Theology* (Philadelphia: Westminster Press, 1981), 115.

1. Caldwell would later regret the "Let all who agree say amen" phrase, which he omitted in the prayer he offered at Bush's second inaugural in 2005. Bill Broadway, "God's Place on the Dias; Use of 'Jesus' in Inaugural Prayers Breeds Some Worry," *Washington Post*, January 27, 2001.

2. Caldwell's benediction prompted the following reaction from Rev. Barry Lynn quoted in the *Washington Post*: "It was an astonishing benediction that is highly exclusionary. It's as if he has created a two tiered system for Americans: those able to say amen—Christians—and those who can't."

3. Representative of the latter group would be the reaction of the Rev. Edward M. O'Flaherty, quoted in the *Boston Globe*: "I feel uncomfortable with prayers that are meant to engage everyone in the audience, so they will all say, 'Amen', but which use words for which people have no feeling or sense of belonging." Michael Paulson, "Debating the Wisdom of Invoking Jesus at Inauguration; Christian Prayer Detracted from Event, Some Say," *Boston Globe*, January 27, 2001.

4. Cathy Lynn Grossman, "Some Call Inaugural Prayers to Jesus Exclusionary," *USA Today*, January 24, 2001.

5. Smith, *Towards a World Theology*, 113–16.

6. Langdon Gilkey, in particular, has argued that Smith, in making this inference, "has confused and identified an unconscious *ignoring* of other forms of thought with a *tolerance* of them." Gilkey, "A Theological Voyage with Wilfred Cantwell Smith," *Religious Studies Review* 7:4 (Oct. 1981): 299; italics in the original.

7. Smith, *Towards a World Theology*, 114, 124 and passim.

8. In his book *Faith and Belief*, Smith qualifies this claim regarding the unity of faith. He stops short of asserting that "faith is everywhere the same." Acknowledging a degree of variation in faith, albeit variation that does not coincide with conventional religious boundaries, Smith asserts more modestly that "the variety of faith seems on the whole less than the variety of forms through which faith has been expressed." Smith, *Faith and Belief* (Princeton, N.J.: Princeton University Press, 1979), 11.

9. Wilfred Cantwell Smith, *The Meaning and End of Religion* (Minneapolis: Fortress Press, 1991), 24–25, 43; cf. 115.

10. See, e.g., *Meaning and End of Religion*, 73.

11. Talal Asad argues that the concept of intolerance is implicit in Smith's concept of reification: "Reading a Modern Classic," *History of Religions* 40 (2001): 211–12. One might correlate the two examples Smith locates at either end of a continuum of increasing reification, namely, Hinduism and Islam, to the concepts of tolerance and intolerance, respectively.

12. See S. Mark Heim, *Salvations: Truth and Difference in Religion* (Maryknoll, N.Y.: Orbis Books, 1995), 55: "The unitary nature of faith and the unitary nature of humanity are two sides of the same coin. . . ."

13. Heim, *Salvations*, 57 and passim.

14. Ibid. 57; cf. 65–66; Asad, "Reading a Modern Classic," 220.

15. Ibid. 55.

16. Wilfred Cantwell Smith, "Comparative Religion: Whither—and Why?" in *The History of Religions: Essays in Methodology*, ed. Mircea Eliade and Joseph M. Kitagawa (Chicago: University of Chicago Press, 1959), 32; *Towards a World Theology*, 43–44.

17. Cf. Kenneth Surin's observation ("A 'Politics of Speech': Religious Pluralism in the Age of the McDonald's Hamburger," in *Christian Uniqueness Reconsidered*, ed. Gavin D'Costa [Maryknoll, N.Y.: Orbis, 1992], 200) that "there is no intractable other for the pluralist."

18. Heim, *Salvations*, 60; Surin, "Politics of Speech," 209 and passim.

19. Kenneth Surin, "Towards a 'Materialist' Critique of Religious Pluralism: An Examination of the Discourse of John Hick and Wilfred Cantwell Smith," in *Religious Pluralism and Belief*, ed. Ian Hammett (New York: Routledge, 1990), 125. For the argument that political liberalism fails to acknowledge its constitutive exclusions, see, e.g., Chantal Mouffe, "Carl Schmitt and the Paradox of Liberal Democracy," in *The Challenge of Carl Schmitt*, ed. Chantal Mouffe (New York: Verso, 1999), 42–46 and passim; William Connolly, *The Ethos of Pluralization* (Minneapolis: University of Minnesota Press, 1995).

20. Surin, "Politics of Speech" 203–4.

21. Surin, "Politics of Speech," 203–4, and passim; Kathryn Tanner, "Respect for Other Religions: A Christian Antidote to Colonialist Discourse," *Modern Theology* 9:1 (Jan. 1993): 1–18. The term "Western cultural hegemonism" comes from Arif Dirlik,

"Culturalism as Hegemonic Ideology and Liberating Practice," *Cultural Critique* 6 (1987): 13–50 (cited in Surin, "Politics of Speech," 203).

22. Roman Jakobson, *On Language*, ed. Linda R. Waugh and Monique Monville-Burston (Cambridge, Mass.: Harvard University Press, 1990), 134–40.

23. Smith's pluralist theology exemplifies Fredric Jameson's argument that hegemonic works embody a utopian impulse. See the latter's *The Political Unconscious* (Ithaca, N.Y.: Cornell University Press, 1981), 286–92.

24. On the application of Benjamin's critique of the "fascist aesthetics of violence" to Schmitt, see Richard Wolin, "Carl Schmitt: The Conservative Revolutionary, Habitus and the Aesthetics of Horror," *Political Theory*, 20:3 (Aug. 1992): 443–44 and passim.

25. The Nazis eventually replaced Schmitt, exemplifying a trend in the life-cycle of totalitarian movements that Hannah Arendt describes as follows: "Totalitarianism in power invariably replaces all first-rate talents, regardless of their sympathies, with those crackpots and fools whose lack of intelligence and creativity is still the best guarantee of loyalty." Arendt, *The Origins of Totalitarianism* (New York: Harvest Books, 1985), 339.

26. There are many forms of liberalism and, accordingly, many definitions, not all of them consistent with one another. For our purposes we might understand the designation in terms of three broad principles: namely, universalism, rationalism, and individualism. Each of these principles, of course, is itself subject to multiple interpretations.

27. Carl Schmitt, *The Concept of the Political*, trans. George Schwab (Chicago: University of Chicago Press, 1996), 25–27, and passim.

28. Schmitt, *Concept of the Political*, 54.

29. Schmitt, *Concept of the Political*, 36, 54; cf. Carl Schmitt, "Das Zeitalter der Neutralisierung und Entpolitisierungen," in *Positionen und Begriffe im Kampf mit Weimar—Genf—Versailles, 1923–1939* (Berlin: Duncker & Humblot, 1988), 132; Paul Edward Gottfried, *Carl Schmitt: Politics and Theory* (New York: Greenwood Press, 1990), 64; Reinhart Koselleck, *Futures Past*, trans. Keith Tribe (Cambridge, Mass.: MIT Press, 1995), 192–93 and passim.

30. Schmitt, "Das Zeitalter der Neutralisierungen," 128.

31. Schmitt, "Das Zeitalter der Neutralisierungen," 125.

32. Schmitt, "Das Zeitalter der Neutralisierungen," 126 and passim.

33. In Smith's terms, Buddhist faith, Islamic faith, etc.

34. On the argument that pluralist theories of religion constitute substantive religious positions in their own right, see Heim, *Salvations*, 141–42 and passim.

35. Gottfried, *Carl Schmitt*, 64–65.

36. Wolin, "Carl Schmitt," 430–35, esp. 432.

37. Schmitt, *Concept of the Political*, 33.

38. See her collection of essays engaging critically with Schmitt's thought contained in the volume *The Return of the Political* (New York: Verso, 1993).

39. Mouffe, *Return of the Political*, 4.

40. Here I am drawing an analogy with Peter Berger's presentation of the Weberian argument that Protestantism prepared the ground for secularization. See

The Sacred Canopy (New York: Anchor Books, 1990), 112. Of course, as we have seen, Smith defines "religion" narrowly, identifying this term with its sociological-historical dimension. Strictly speaking, then, Smith would not speak of a two-dimensional concept of *religion* that includes the transcendental faith dimension.

41. Peter C. Phan, *Being Religious Interreligiously* (Maryknoll, N.Y.: Orbis, 2004), 55; italics in original; see also 56 n. 29.

42. John Hick, *God and the Universe of Faiths* (New York: St. Martin's Press, 1973), 108.

43. The citation by Peter Phan above reflects the influence of Lindbeck's "cultural-linguistic" theory of religion, as Phan himself acknowledges (p. 55 n. 28).

44. Friedrich Schleiermacher, *Über die Religion* (Stuttgart: Reclam, 1969), 151; cf. Richard Crouter's translation, Schleiermacher, *On Religion* (Cambridge: Cambridge University Press, 1996), 91.

45. Kathryn Tanner, *The Politics of God* (Minneapolis: Fortress Press, 1992), 193 and passim. Tanner distinguishes this understanding of tolerance from several other attitudes that commonly go by that name, specifically, those forms of tolerance that "presuppose a position of moral, intellectual, and political superiority," those based on attitudes of indifference to others, and, finally, those forms of tolerance premised on shared norms or beliefs (pp. 195–205). On the critique of understandings of tolerance that presuppose a position of social or political privilege, see also, e.g., Robert Paul Wolff, "Beyond Tolerance," in *A Critique of Pure Tolerance*, ed. Robert Paul Wolff, Barrington Moore, and Herbert Marcuse (Boston: Beacon Press, 1965), 3–52, and Wendy Brown, "Reflections on Tolerance in the Age of identity," in *Democracy and Vision*, ed. Aryeh Botwinick and William E. Connolly (Princeton, N.J.: Princeton University Press, 2001), 99–117.

46. Particularly useful to me have been Mouffe's *Return of the Political* and Connolly's *Ethos of Pluralization*.

47. Connolly, *Ethos of Pluralization*, xxi.

48. We can broaden this point regarding the heuristic power of comparison to include a range of philosophical, theological, and above all ethical issues. As Aaron Stalnaker observes, "religious diversity sharpens questions regarding [among others] ethical universalism and relativism, how to understand and justly order religiously complex communities, and how to navigate multiple and religious and social identities, as well as meta-ethical problems about the nature of moral norms." Stalnaker, *Overcoming Our Evil* (Washington, D.C.: Georgetown University Press, 2006), 3.

49. Cited without reference in Paul Knitter, *Introducing Theologies of Religions* (Maryknoll, N.Y.: Orbis Books, 2005), 205.

50. As an example of this marginality of comparative theology, James C. Livingston and Francis Schüssler Fiorenza's survey of twentieth-century theology (*Modern Christian Thought*, vol. 2, *The Twentieth Century* [Minneapolis: Fortress Press, 2006]) includes no mention of comparative theology, although one chapter is devoted to the Theology of Religions.

51. Exemplifying this understanding of comparative theology as an alternative to the theology of religions is James Fredericks, *Faith among Faiths* (New York: Paulist

Press, 1999). For a lucid overview of the relationship between comparative theology and the theology of religions, see Knitter, *Introducing Theologies of Religion*, 202–14, esp. 203–5. See also Stephen J. Duffy, "A Theology of Religions and/or a Comparative Theology?" *Horizons* 26 (1999): 105–15.

52. Fredericks, *Faith among Faiths*, 8 and passim.

53. On the "Comparative Theology" of the second half of the nineteenth century, see Tomoko Masuzawa, *The Invention of World Religions* (Chicago: University of Chicago Press, 2005), ch. 2, "The Legacy of Comparative Theology."

54. A paradigmatic example of this shift in the understanding of the comparative method is Robert C. Neville's theory of vague comparative categories; see, inter alia, the three volumes of the Cross-Cultural Religious Ideas Project (*The Human Condition, Ultimate Realities, Religious Truth* [Albany: State University of New York Press, 2000]); see also the collection of essays inspired by the work of Jonathan Z. Smith in the volume *A Magic Still Dwells*, ed. Kimberley C. Patton and Benjamin C. Ray (Berkeley and Los Angeles: University of California Press, 2000).

55. Kathryn Tanner, *Theories of Culture* (Minneapolis: Fortress Press, 1997).

CHAPTER 1

F. Max Müller, *Introduction to the Science of Religion* (London: Longmans, Green, and Co., 1882), 146.

Francis X. Clooney, *Theology after Vedānta* (Albany: State University Of New York Press, 1993), 193–194.

1. John H. Berthrong, *All under Heaven* (Albany: State University of New York Press, 1994), 60.

2. John J. Thatamanil, *The Immanent Divine* (Minneapolis: Fortress Press, 2006), 3.

3. As mentioned above in the preface, I suspect that this failure to consider the relevance of the history of comparative religion for the theorization of comparative theology reflects the continuing influence of the Neo-orthodox movement in theology, which effectively delegitimized the role of interreligious comparison in the theological enterprise.

4. See, e.g., Henry Louis Jordan, *Comparative Religion: Its Genesis and Growth* (New York: Charles Scribner's Sons, 1905), 24–28.

5. Eric J. Sharpe, *Comparative Religion: A History* (La Salle, Ill.: Open Court, 1987), 35.

6. Unlike the preferred terms "comparative religion" or the "history of religions," the designation "comparative theology" implicitly limited comparison to the intellectual or doctrinal dimension of religion (Jordan, *Comparative Religion*, 27). C. P. Tiele, for example, writes: "To me, comparative theology signifies nothing but a comparative study of religious dogmas, comparative religion nothing but a comparative study of the various religions in all their branches." Tiele, "On the Study of Comparative Theology," in *A Museum of Faiths*, ed. Eric J. Ziollowski (Atlanta: Scholars Press, 1993), 76. A contemporary example of an understanding of

comparative theology in which theology forms the object of scientific inquiry is Robert C. Neville's Comparative Religious Ideas Project. See Robert Cummings Neville and Wesley J. Wildman, "On Comparing Religious Ideas," in *The Human Condition: A Volume in the Comparative Religious Ideas Project*, ed. Robert Cummings Neville, 9–20 (Albany: State University of New York Press, 2001), 11.

7. For example, Sigurd Hjelde ("The Science of Religion and Theology: The Question of Their Interrelationship," in *Religion in the Making*, ed. Arie L. Molendijk and Peter Pels [Boston: Brill, 1998], 109) notes an ambiguity in Tiele's use of the term theology, whereby the term is used in both a "wider" and a "narrower" sense: "In the first case, Tiele refers to special theologies within the limits of the general, historical study of religion; in the next, the perspective is widened to the effect that the concept of theology actually pertains to the comparative study as well." These two senses of theology, namely, as the subject of comparison and as the object of comparison, can be correlated, respectively, to a distinction between the theologies of Judaism and Christianity, on the one hand, and all other theologies, on the other. Judaism and Christianity, in other words, have tended to be excluded from the history of religions. See Hans H. Penner and Edward A. Yonan, "Is a Science of Religion Possible?" *Journal of Religion* 52:2 (1972): 107; Claude Welch, *Protestant Thought in the Nineteenth Century*, 2 vols. (New Haven, Conn.: Yale University Press, 1985), 132. On the tendency, even today, to exclude Protestant Christianity in particular from the scope of the history of religions and thus from being objectified like other traditions, see also Winnifred Fallers Sullivan, "American Religion is Naturally Comparative," in *A Magic Still Dwells*, ed. Kimberley C. Patton and Benjamin C. Ray, 117–30 (Berkeley and Los Angeles: University of California Press, 2000), 120: "Protestant Christianity has been excluded because it has been thought to be part of the method, a source of theory, not part of the data."

8. Müller, *Introduction to the Science of Religion*, 29.

9. One might object to my decision to include the works of scholars like Müller and Tiele (the widely acknowledged founders of *Religionswissenschaft*) in the same general category as the more openly confessional works of comparative theologians like Clarke and Maurice; such an objection is implicit in the arguments of Donald Wiebe, *The Politics of Religious Studies* (New York: St. Martin's Press, 1999), esp. ch. 2 and 3. Even Tomoko Masuzawa, who in her book *The Invention of World Religions* (Chicago: University of Chicago Press, 2005), 72–104, argues that the latter works have an essential place in the disciplinary history of comparative religion, nevertheless restricts her discussion of "the legacy of comparative theology" to the more openly theological works of comparative theology. I would argue, however, that while one can, of course, distinguish between the two groups of works, a relation of continuity exists between them. As indicated by Müller's acknowledgment, in the preface to his *Introduction to the Science of Religion*, of the works of figures like James F. Clarke, Samuel Johnson, and F. E. Abbot as examples of the "rapidly growing literature of Comparative Theology," both sets of works participate in the same larger discourse of comparative theology, and their differences with respect to Christian commitment are largely a matter of emphasis. Scholars like Müller and Tiele believed that scientific

knowledge and the truth of religion—which for them achieved its fullest expression in Christianity—would ultimately converge. More openly Christian comparative theologians like Clarke, for their part, insisted that their comparative surveys were "fair" and "scientific."

10. James Freeman Clarke, *Ten Great Religions: An Essay in Comparative Theology* (Boston: Houghton Mifflin, [1871] 1899), 14.

11. An example of such an inability to imagine a perspective in which such a claim could be made in earnest might be a comment Timothy Fitzgerald makes on a quote from the historian of religion E. O. James. James claims that the academic study of religion "demands both a historical and scientific approach and a philosophical and theological evaluation." Apparently unable to take James' position at face value, Fitzgerald describes James's statement as "a kind of unconsciously formulated satirical truth." Timothy Fitzgerald, *The Ideology of Religious Studies* (New York: Oxford University Press, 2000), 42.

12. Masuzawa, *Invention of World Religions*, 103–4.

13. Arie L. Molendijk, "Transforming Theology: The Institutionalization of the Science of Religion in the Netherlands," in Molendijk and Pels, *Religion in the Making*, 76 and passim.

14. Hjelde, "Science of Religion and Theology," 107; Molendijk, "Transforming Theology," 81; see also Müller, *Introduction to the Science of Religion*, 8: "But this I will say, that, as far as my humble judgment goes, [the Science of Religion] does not entail the loss of anything that is essential to true religion...."

15. See Carl Schmitt, "Das Zeitalter der Neutralisierungen und Entpolitisierungen," in *Positionen und Begriffe im Kampf mit Weimar—Genf—Versailes* (Berlin: Duncker & Humblot, 1988), 120–32 for the understanding of liberalism in terms of "depoliticization." For the concept of "the political," see Schmitt, *The Concept of the Political*, trans. George Schwab (Chicago: University of Chicago Press, 1996), 25–37 and passim.

16. This second characteristic of confessionalism can be understood as flowing logically from the first. Dogmatism is the inevitable consequence of the formal dimension of political antagonism, what Georg Simmel (*Conflict and the Web of Group-Affiliations*, trans. Kurt H. Wolff and Reinhard Bendix [New York: Free Press, 1955], 29) calls "an abstract impulse to opposition" that is irreducible to whatever material disagreements are cited as justification for the opposition.

17. Hjelde, "Science of Religion and Theology," 106.

18. Pace Donald Wiebe (*Politics of Religious Studies*, 39 and passim), the expressions of theological commitment that one finds in the works of scholars like Müller and Tiele cannot simply be dismissed as accidental holdovers from their authors' cultural-religious backgrounds. Rather, they give expression to the liberal theological commitments that motivate and ground the original project of *Religionswissenschaft*. In defending his thesis, Wiebe appeals to Müller's insistence that theological belief is the result, not the presupposition, of the scientific study of religion (Wiebe, 22). It seems to me, however, that this appeal uncritically buys into Müller's own scientistic ideology, in which the presuppositions of an ostensibly impartial and

objective study are misrecognized as its results—results, in other words, that just happen to coincide with Müller's prior religious commitments.

19. Joachim Wach, "The Meaning and Task of the History of Religions (*Religionswissenschaft*)," in *Understanding and Believing: Essays by Joachim Wach*, ed. Joseph M. Kitagawa (New York: Harper & Row, 1968), 125; cf. Charles Davis, "The Reconvergence of Theology and Religious Studies," *Studies in Religion* 4 (1975): 206.

20. Wach, "Meaning and Task," 130; also 127, 131, 136.

21. Wach, "Meaning and Task," 136. See also p. 137: "Being rooted in a personal faith—a faith which may well blind one to other things but which, in contrast to the opinion of many, need not do so—does not necessarily mean a disadvantage for him who seeks to understand."

22. R. J. Zwi Werblowsky, "The Comparative Study of Religions—A Review Essay," *Judaism* 8:4 (1959): 358.

23. Joseph M. Kitagawa, "Humanistic and Theological History of Religions with Special Reference to the North American Scene," in *Traditions in Contact and Change: Selected Proceedings of the XIVth Congress of the International Association for the History of Religions*, ed. Peter Slater and Donald N. Wiebe (Waterloo, Ont.: Wilfrid Laurier University Press, 1983), 560.

24. Kitagawa, "Humanistic and Theological History of Religions," 554; 558–59; see also Kitagawa, "The History of Religions in America," in *The History of Religions: Essays in Methodology*, ed. Mircea Eliade and Joseph M. Kitagawa (Chicago: University of Chicago Press, 1959). The kinship between *Religionswissenschaft* and liberal theology is even more evident in the phenomenological tradition of Söderblom, van der Leeuw, Otto, and Heiler, scholars who envisioned a more complementary, rather than exclusionary, relationship between the two disciplines.

25. E.g., J. Samuel Preus, *Explaining Religion* (New Haven, Conn.: Yale University Press, 1987); Thomas E. Lawson and Robert N. McCauley, *Rethinking Religion: Connecting Cognition and Culture* (New York: Cambridge University Press, 1990).

26. The theology of religions is better understood diachronically rather than systematically. The limits of the systematic conception of the theology of religions become apparent when one considers the choice of a representative for the exclusivist position. In standard works in the theology of religions, exclusivism is typically represented by the rather idiosyncratic exclusivism of Karl Barth and Heinrich Kraemer, idiosyncratic because, unlike classic Christian exclusivism of the *extra ecclesiam nulla salus* variety, it holds that all "religion," including the Christian, is "unbelief." When the theology of religions discourse is understood in diachronic terms, exclusivism is revealed to be the discourse's other. Thus exclusivism proper does not represent a viable theology of religions position. It is hardly surprising, then, that synchronic presentations that suppress the historical dimension of this discourse are forced to represent exclusivism with theological voices that poorly exemplify it.

27. John Hick, "The Non-Absoluteness of Christianity," in *The Myth of Christian Uniqueness*, ed. John Hick and Paul F. Knitter (Maryknoll, N.Y.: Orbis Books, 1994), 22.

28. See, e.g., S. Mark Heim, *Salvations: Truth and Difference in Religion* (Maryknoll, N.Y.: Orbis Books, 1995).

29. Wolfhart Pannenberg, "Religious Pluralism and Conflicting Truth Claims: The Problem of a Theology of the World Religions," in *Christian Uniqueness Reconsidered*, ed. Gavin D'Costa (Maryknoll, N.Y.: Orbis Books, 1990), 97. Since Hick's proposals have already received extensive and competent attention elsewhere (see, e.g., Heim, *Salvations*, 15–43), I have found it unnecessary to enter into an extended discussion of his oeuvre here. A treatment of the specifically philosophical dimension of his oeuvre, his complex use of philosophers like Wittgenstein and Kant, etc., would unfortunately take the present discussion too far afield.

30. Heim, *Salvations*, 57, 65–66.

31. James Fredericks (*Faith among Faiths* [New York: Paulist Press, 1999], 8) describes this impasse as follows: "the proponents of the pluralistic approach have been very successful in exposing the inadequacies of more traditional views of Christianity in relation to other religions, but, at the same time, their critics have also been successful in exposing the inadequacies of the pluralists."

32. Cited in Paul F. Knitter, *Introducing Theologies of Religions* (Maryknoll, N.Y.: Orbis Books, 2002), 205.

33. Fredericks, *Faith among Faiths*, 109; 111–12 and passim.

34. Fredericks, *Faith among Faiths*, 108–10.

35. Fredericks, *Faith among Faiths*, 167–68; Clooney, *Theology after Vedānta*, 8–9.

36. Clooney, "The Study of Non-Christian Religions in the Post—Vatican II Roman Catholic Church," *Journal of Ecumenical Studies* 28:3 (1991): 488 and passim.

37. Clarke, *Ten Great Religions: An Essay in Comparative Theology*, 1:4ff.; James Freeman Clarke, *Ten Great Religions*, Part II, *A Comparison of All Religions* (Boston: Houghton Mifflin, 1883), 24–25; Müller, *Introduction to the Science of Religion*, 69; George Matheson, *The Distinctive Messages of the Old Religions* (New York: Anson D. F. Randolph, 1894), 38ff.

38. Clarke, *Ten Great Religions: An Essay in Comparative Theology*, 6–7.

39. Clarke, *Ten Great Religions*, Part II: 26–29; Masuzawa, *Invention of World Religions*, 77–78, 108–19; but see Müller, *Introduction to the Science of Religion*, 79–80.

40. Jonathan Z. Smith, *Relating Religion* (Chicago: University of Chicago Press, 2004), 167; cf. 174, 187.

41. Robert Redfield (*The Primitive World and Its Transformations* [Ithaca, N.Y.: Cornell University Press, 1953], 92 and passim) argues that the "us" versus "them" distinction is a fundamental feature of the universal human worldview.

42. The understanding of Christianity as the universal religion can thus be understood as an attempt to establish the hegemony of liberal Christianity within the Christian tradition.

43. See Schmitt, "Das Zeitalter der Neutralisierungen."

44. To characterize nineteenth-century comparative theology as a form of Christian inclusivism is, strictly speaking, an anachronism. One can, in fact, discern pluralistic overtones in the expressions of Christian fulfillment found in these works, particularly when they emphasize that Christianity does not destroy, but rather preserves, the religions it fulfills. See, e.g., Matheson, *Distinctive Messages of the Old Religions*, 328:

But the religion of Christ is not anxious to put things locally together, nor even to make them similar in appearance. It seeks to reconcile them in their differences,—to make them, in the very midst of their diversity, work out one common end. It is not eager for uniformity, not solicitous for the recognition of one mode of government, not desirous that all should think on the same plane; it desires that the air may run through the variations, that the diversity of gifts may enfold a unity of the spirit.

Later (p. 338) Matheson speaks of a Christian dominion, "which extends from sea to sea without destroying the sea—without obliterating the boundaries that now divide, or annihilating the diversities that now distinguish." Such statements would easily find themselves at home in works of pluralist theology written one hundred years later.

45. See, e.g., Clooney, "Study of Non-Christian Religions," 72–75; Kristin Beise Kiblinger, "Relating Theology of Religions and Comparative Theology," in *The New Comparative Theology*, ed. Francis X. Clooney (New York: T & T Clark, 2010).

46. The argument for allying the practice of comparative theology with inclusivism coincides with the justification that is usually given for recognizing a legitimate role for the theology of religions in the contemporary practice of comparative theology. Those who argue for a complementary relationship between the theology of religions and comparative theology justify the former on the grounds that it thematizes the necessary, though provisional, hermeneutical presuppositions of comparative theological study. See Stephen J. Duffy, "A Theology of Religions and/or a Comparative Theology?" *Horizons* 26 (1999): 107 and passim.

47. The distinction between "fulfillment-model" and "acceptance-model" inclusivism is Paul Knitter's. See his *Introducing Theologies of Religions.*

48. One could argue that even Fredericks, who represents those comparative theologians calling for a moratorium on theologies of religion, focuses his criticism on pluralist theologies of religions. As Paul Knitter notes in his review of Fredericks's *Faith among Faiths,* Fredericks devotes four chapters to a critique of pluralism as compared to one chapter each for exclusivism and inclusivism. Knitter, "Review of *Faith among Faiths: Christian theology and Non-Christian Religions,*" *Theological Studies* 62:4 (2001): 874.

49. J. N. Farquhar, *The Crown of Hinduism* (London: H. Milford, 1913), 11.

50. Wilfred Cantwell Smith, "Comparative Religion: Whither and Why?" in Eliade and Kitagawa, *History of Religions,* 32–33.

51. Paul F. Knitter, *No Other Name* (Maryknoll, N.Y.: Orbis Books, 1985), 2–3; Knitter, *Introducing Theologies of Religions,* 5–6.

52. On the present global situation as bringing about a break or rupture with the past, see Arjun Appadurai, *Modernity at Large* (Minneapolis: University of Minnesota Press, 1996), 2–4 and passim.

53. On the virtual oblivion into which the works of comparative theology have fallen, see Masuzawa, *Invention of World Religions,* 72–73.

54. See, e.g., Kathryn Tanner, "Respect for Other Religions: A Christian Antidote to Colonialist Discourse," *Modern Theology* 9:1 (Jan. 1993): 1–18; Kenneth Surin, "A 'Politics' of Speech: Religious Pluralism in the Age of the McDonald's Hamburger," in D'Costa, *Christian Uniqueness Reconsidered,* 192–212.

55. Michael Hardt and Antonio Negri, *Empire* (Cambridge, Mass.: Harvard University Press, 2000), 137–59.

56. Hardt and Negri, *Empire*, 140, 144.

57. Hardt and Negri, *Empire*, 151.

58. Hardt and Negri, *Empire*, 138, 142, and passim.

59. Clooney, "Study of Non-Christian Religions," 489–90.

60. As indicated by the subtitle of his *Hindu God, Christian God* (New York: Oxford University Press, 2001): "How Reason Helps Break Down the Boundaries between Religions." See also his remark on p. 164 of this work: "While there may be some beliefs, practices, and creedal formulations justly recognized as unique to particular traditions, almost all of what counts as theological thinking is shared across religious boundaries."

61. On the vulnerability of the modern nation-state in the present age of globalization, see Appadurai, *Modernity at Large*, 39–40 and passim.

62. Hardt and Negri, *Empire*, 154–55.

63. Hardt and Negri, *Empire*, 150.

64. Fredric Jameson, *Postmodernism, or, the Cultural logic of Late Capitalism* (Durham, N.C.: Duke University Press, 1991), 332.

65. Jameson, *Postmodernism*, 330.

66. Jameson, *Postmodernism*, 405; also 36.

67. Jameson, *Postmodernism*, 334, 405.

68. See, e.g., Clooney, *Theology after Vedānta*, 189. Comparative theology's "modesty" regarding larger interreligious claims might also reflect something analogous to what Jameson calls the "postmodern sublime," that is, the sense of being implicated in a vast, decentralized communicational network whose dimensions exceed the powers of human comprehension and imagination (Jameson, *Postmodernism*, 34–38 and passim). Correlated with the highly localized practice of comparative reading is a rather daunting conception of comparative theology as a large-scale communitarian enterprise in which the extra-biblical theological canon is expanded to include the classics of other faith traditions (Clooney, *Theology after Vedānta*, 203–5). Not unlike postmodern architectural spaces in which the viewer finds it impossible to get his or her bearings (Jameson, *Postmodernism*, 44 and passim), this conception of a discipline whose comprehension, let alone mastery, lies outside the reach of any single theologian is as likely to induce a state of paralysis as of humility (see Clooney, *Hindu God, Christian God*, 175).

69. Clooney, *Theology after Vedānta*, 187–93.

70. James Fredericks (*Buddhists and Christians* [Maryknoll, N.Y.: Orbis Books, 2004], 106–7) somewhat unfairly characterizes the revisionism of pluralists like Hick and Knitter as a "watering down" of traditional Christian belief, as a craven attempt to render those beliefs "more palatable" to their non-Christian dialogue partners. I prefer to regard the pluralist revisionist proposals as sincere attempts to rethink certain Christian beliefs in light of the contemporary situation of religious pluralism.

71. Paul F. Knitter, "Toward a Liberation Theology of Religions," in Hick and Knitter, *Myth of Christian Uniqueness*, 179–200.

72. Even if one concedes Hardt and Negri's thesis that late-stage, global capitalism introduces new and largely unprecedented forms of domination, one must recognize that the transition from "modern sovereignty" to "empire" is a rather uneven and ambiguous process. And to the extent that the older, "modern" forms of domination remain very much in force in today's world, comparative theology's implicit critique of colonialist forms of theological discourse remains quite relevant. Moreover, comparative theologians are by no means blind to the dangers of the present situation of global capitalism. Fredericks's conception of comparative theology, for example, is responsive to the problem of the "commodification of religion as a consumer choice." Fredericks, *Buddhists and Christians*, 101–2.

73. Linell E. Cady, "Territorial Disputes: Religious Studies and Theology in Transition," in *Religious Studies, Theology, and the University*, ed. Linell E. Cady and Delwin Brown (Albany: State University of New York Press, 2002), 111, 113; Catherine Bell, "Modernism and Postmodernism in the Study of Religion," *Religious Studies Review* 22:3 (1996): 183, 187; Paul Griffiths, "On the Future of the Study of Religion in the Academy," *Journal of the American Academy of Religion* 74:1 (2006): 72.

74. Ricoeur's actual statement is: "In fact, however, the epistemological weakness of a general social theory is proportional to the force with which it denounces ideology." Ricoeur, "Science and Ideology," in *From Text to Action*, trans. Kathleen Blamey and John B. Thompson (Evanston, Ill.: Northwestern University Press, 1991), 256.

75. Ricoeur, *From Text to Action*, 256; see also Jorge Larrain, *The Concept of Ideology* (Athens: University of Georgia Press, 1979), 189–99. One could challenge Ricoeur's positivistic conception of natural science, a presupposition of the sharp demarcation he draws between the natural sciences and the humanities. See Paul B. Roscoe, "The Perils of 'Positivism' in Cultural Anthropology," *American Anthropologist* 97:3 (1995): 496–97, who argues that an acknowledgment of the theory-laden character of the empirical data of the natural sciences, and thus of their hermeneutical character, calls into question Ricoeur's sharp distinction between scientific and interpretive method. More generally, the shift from formalist to contextualist approaches in the philosophy of science has tended to break down the separation between the natural sciences and the humanities. See Philip Clayton, *Explanation from Physics to Theology* (New Haven, Conn.: Yale University Press, 1985), 21 and passim.

76. Friedrich Heiler, *Erscheinungsformen und Wesen der Religion* (Stuttgart: W. Kohlhammer, 1949), 17.

77. Heiler, *Erscheinungsformen*, 14; cf. Sharpe, *Comparative Religion*, 244.

78. Included among the apriorisms to be excluded were also be those of a specifically philosophical system, that of Hegel in particular.

79. Heiler, *Erscheinungsformen*, 16; cf. 6.

80. Heiler, *Erscheinungsformen*, 12. See also Heiler, "Die Bedeutung Rudolf Ottos für die vergleichende Religionsgeschichte," in *Religionswissenschaft in neuer Sicht* (Marburg: N. G. Elwert, 1951), 23: "Otto war kein christlicher Apologet, so wenig wie Söderblom."

81. See Heiler, *Erscheinungsformen*, 17: "Dieses Ernstnehmen des religiösen Wirklichkeitsbegriffes ist in gewisser Hinsicht Glaube, aber nicht Glaube im Sinne

eines bestimmten theologischen oder konfessionellen Dogmas. Die grössten Religionsforscher, ein Friedrich Schleiermacher, Max Müller, Nathan Söderblom, sind Männer des Glaubens gewesen, aber Männer eines universalen Glaubens, eines Menschheitsglaubens." Cf. Heiler, *Erscheinungsformen*, 565.

82. In identifying two basic responses, I follow Catherine Bell's distinction between modernist and postmodernist approaches to the study of religion. Bell, "Modernism and Postmodernism in the Study of Religion," 179 and passim.

83. Exemplifying this modernist response is Donald Wiebe (*Politics of Religious Studies*, 181–82, and passim), who argues that the phenomenological approach to religious studies, in abandoning causal explanation (*Erklärung*) in favor of interpretive understanding (*Verstehen*), undermined and "denatured" the Enlightenment idea of science. See also Preus's (*Explaining Religion*, xvii) disapproving characterization of the present state of religious studies in which the question of the cause or origin of religion "is virtually ignored, even demeaned as a futile question or worse." A more balanced and theoretically sophisticated defense of an explanatory approach to the study of religion can be found in Lawson and McCauley, *Rethinking Religion*, 12–31 and passim; Lawson and McCauley, "Crisis of Conscience, Riddle of Identity: Making Space for a Cognitive Approach to Religious Phenomena," *Journal of the American Academy of Religion* 61:2 (1993): 201–23.

84. Fitzgerald, *Ideology of Religious Studies*, 4; Talal Asad, *Genealogies of Religion* (Baltimore: Johns Hopkins University Press, 1993); Russell T. McCutcheon, "A Default of Critical Intelligence? The Scholar of Religion as Public Intellectual," *Journal of the American Academy of Religion* 65:2 (1997): 454.

85. Hugh Urban, "Making a Place to Stand: Jonathan Z. Smith and the Politics and Poetics of Comparison," *Method and Theory in the Study of Religion* 12 (2000): 339–40.

86. Douglas Allen, *Structure and Creativity in Religion* (Paris: Mouton, 1978), 193–95.

87. See Robert A. Segal, "The Postmodernist Challenge to the Comparative Method," in *Comparing Religions*, ed. Thomas A. Idinopulos, Brian C. Wilson, and James C. Hanges, 249–70 (Leiden/Boston: Brill, 2006), 249–70, for a helpful typology of the various responses.

88. See William E. Paden, "Elements of a New Comparison," *Method and Theory in the Study of Religion* 8:1 (1996): 15–20. Here I have taken the liberty of using Paden's designation, "the New Comparativism," to refer to a broader current in the contemporary academy. This usage forces me to dissociate Paden's designation from his more specific proposals, a move, I realize, of which he may not approve.

89. Patton and Ray, *A Magic Still Dwells*, 18 and passim.

90. The New Comparativism can be conveniently associated with the contributors (including William Paden) to the volume *A Magic Still Dwells*, whose title alludes to J. Z. Smith's well-known essay, "In Comparison a Magic Dwells" (in Smith, *Imagining Religion* [Chicago: University of Chicago Press, 1982], 19–35. Smith's essay, which the volume reproduces, serves as a focus and point of departure for the discussion undertaken by the volume's contributors.

91. Smith, *Imagining Religion*, 22.

92. See Smith, *Imagining Religion*, 24.

93. For the distinction between genealogical and analogical comparison, which Smith takes from biology, see his *Drudgery Divine* (Chicago: University of Chicago Press, 1990), 47–52.

94. See Smith, *Drudgery Divine*, 51: "There is nothing 'natural' about the enterprise of comparison. Similarity and difference are not 'given'. They are the result of mental operations. In this sense, *all comparisons are properly analogical*...."

95. The rhetorical nature of comparison finds expression in one of J. Z. Smith's most productive insights, namely, the understanding of metaphor in terms of the metaphorical process, on which see also Fitz Porter Poole, "Metaphors and Maps: Towards Comparison in the Anthropology of Religion," *Journal of the American Academy of Religion* 53:3 (1986): 419–23. We return to the understanding of comparison in terms of the metaphorical process in chapter 3.

96. Smith, *Imagining Religion*, 104–5.

97. Smith, *Imagining Religion*, xiii.

98. Smith, *Drudgery Divine*, 51.

99. See Smith, *Drudgery Divine*, 52–53.

100. Marsha A. Hewitt, "How New Is the 'New Comparativism'? Difference, Dialectics, and World-Making," *Method and Theory in the Study of Religion* 8:1 (1996): 17.

101. Urban, "Making a Place to Stand," 339.

102. Urban, "Making a Place to Stand," 339.

103. Urban, "Making a Place to Stand," 359–70. See also Paul Griffiths's charge that Smith is being "coy" about his own normative commitments ("On the Future of the Study of Religion in the Academy," 72–74). Somewhat less convincingly, Griffiths directs this charge of coyness against Smith's Chicago colleague, Bruce Lincoln, a historian of religions who, despite Griffith's criticism, acknowledges his own normative, specifically Marxist, commitments in numerous publications: see, e.g., the latter's *Discourse and the Construction of Society* (New York: Oxford University Press, 1989), 3–7; Lincoln, *Death, War, and Sacrifice* (Chicago: University of Chicago Press, 1991), xvi-xvii, 244. Urban, in fact, cites Lincoln as a model of a historian of religions who openly acknowledges his own normative stance. (Urban, "Making a Place to Stand," 370–71.)

104. Urban, "Making a Place to Stand," 372–73.

105. Urban, "Making a Place to Stand," 371.

106. Historicism forms a central presupposition of the constructive theology of Gordon Kaufman, for example. Liberation theology, of course, engages constructively with a Marxist critique of society. An example of a theological analysis that proceeds from "a basically post-structuralist sociological view of social action" derived from the work of Pierre Bourdieu is Kathryn Tanner, *Economy of Grace* (Minneapolis: Fortress Press, 2005), 12–22.

107. Tyler Roberts, "Exposure and Explanation: On the New Protectionism in the Study of Religion," *Journal of the American Academy of Religion* 72:1 (2004): 150–51.

108. Francis X. Clooney, *Seeing Through Texts* (Albany: State University of New York Press, 1996), 247.

109. The same ambiguity obtains in the academic study of religion. The combination of revision and defense that Hugh Urban recommends presumes that the problematic, ideological aspects of a scholar's perspective can be isolated from those aspects that he or she will want to defend.

110. I would argue that there is a necessary place for both forms of acknowledgment in both comparative theology and comparative religion. There is a tendency, however, to project the distinction between critical and confessional acknowledgment outward in an effort to draw a sharp distinction between the two disciplines. Thus comparative theology is defined as a confessional enterprise and comparative religion as a critical one. Understanding the distinction between comparative theology and comparative religion in this way carries the danger of caricaturing each. That is, defining comparative theology in confessional terms risks suppressing its critical dimension, while understanding comparative religion in critical terms tends to suppress an acknowledgment of its own normative presuppositions.

111. Neville and Wildman, "On Comparing Religious Ideas," in *The Human Condition*, 14; cf. Neville and Wildman, "On Comparing Religious Ideas," in *Ultimate Realities: A Volume in the Comparative Religious Ideas Project*, ed. Robert C. Neville (Albany: State University of New York Press, 2001), 191–94.

112. See, inter alia, Neville, *Human Condition*, 9–20; *Ultimate Realities*, 187–210.

113. Neville, *Human Condition*, 14–15; *Ultimate Realities*, 206.

114. In other words, their approach "assumes that comparisons aim to be true, in the dyadic sense that locates the truth or falsity of a proposition in the accuracy of interpretation of its subject matter." Wesley J. Wildman, "Comparing Religious Ideas: There's a Method in the Mob's Madness," in Idinopulos et al., *Comparing Religions*, 186.

115. Tomoko Masuzawa, *In Search of Dreamtime* (Chicago: University of Chicago Press, 1993), 6.

116. Neville and Wildman would counter this criticism by arguing that their comparative method, thanks to its self-corrective nature, accommodates a "hermeneutics of suspicion" that criticizes prevailing characterizations of the compared traditions on the behalf of marginalized voices within them. They defend the project of producing stable comparative hypotheses by arguing that, "the only way to make progress in comparison, from the standpoint of the hermeneutics of suspicion, is to have steady and well-formulated hypotheses to criticize." (*Human Condition*, xxv.) In other words, productive criticism must have something with which to work. There does remain a tension, however, between the goal of producing stable representations and the willingness to revise them. Stable representations cannot be politically innocent inasmuch as those representations reinforce indigenous hegemonies.

117. The strategy Neville and Wildman use against the criticism that comparison is an exercise in power, namely, to affirm "the primacy of cognition over will in comparison" (*Ultimate Realities*, 187–88), in presupposing an inverse relation between knowledge and power, does not seem to me an adequate response to the postcolonial critique of representational knowledge as itself an expression of asymmetrical power relations. And yet, in the last analysis, Neville and Wildman's approach to comparison, despite its focus on producing stable comparisons, evades this line of criticism because it does

not presuppose a static, positivistic model of representation. An awareness of the political dimension of representation is implicit in their forthright acknowledgment of the creative, performative dimension of comparison ("Comparison is an act that changes things." *Human Condition*, 17).

118. In his forward to the first volume of the Comparative Religious Ideas Project, Peter Berger emphasizes the modernist—as opposed to postmodernist—character of the Project. According to Berger, comparison presupposes precisely those notions of objective truth and understanding that are currently under attack by various forms of "postmodern" criticism. (Neville, *Human Condition*, xiv.) I might add that the polemical character of Berger's remarks, however, probably reflects more his own personal animus towards postmodern trends in the academy than the ethos of the Project itself, which was marked by an openness to a variety of theoretical approaches in the study of religion.

119. I see no reason why a commitment to accurate representation cannot coexist with the more radical form of self-criticism that extends to the hierarchic relationship between the knower and the known.

120. Clooney, *Hindu God, Christian God*, 11–12; Fredericks, *Buddhists and Christians*, 109, 113–14. Clooney (*Hindu God, Christian God*, 11) makes a distinction between a "confessional" and an "apologetic" theology, but concedes that this distinction becomes "slender" as interreligious differences come to the fore.

121. One could perhaps see such a return in Paul Griffiths's (*An Apology for Apologetics* [Maryknoll, N.Y.: Orbis Books, 1991]) call for a revival of interreligious apologetics, notwithstanding the fact that the apologetics Griffiths recommends is respectful of the religious other and well-informed.

122. Clooney, *Hindu God, Christian God*, 12; Clooney, "Comparative Theology," A Review of Recent Books," *Theological Studies* 56 (1995): 521.

123. Fredericks, *Faith among Faiths*, 167.

124. Fredericks, *Faith among Faiths*, 111. To be fair, Fredericks implicitly qualifies this contrast with his admission of a tension between openness and commitment in comparative theology (*Faith among Faiths*, 169–71).

125. This would be my response to Clooney's ("Comparative Theology," 550) perceptive remark that, "depending on how well comparativists do their comparisons, and depending too on how well the general theological community pays attention to these new resources, we will be able to see in practice whether comparative awareness is to become a central and pervasive feature of comparative studies."

CHAPTER 2

1. Schmitt, "Das Zeitalter der Neutralisierungen," 127.

2. Schmitt, "Das Zeitalter der Neutralisierungen," 127.

3. Carl Schmitt, *The Concept of the Political*, trans. George Schwab (Chicago: University of Chicago Press, 1996), 37, 62.

4. Schmitt, "Das Zeitalter der Neutralisierungen und Entpolitisierungen," in *Positionen und Begriffe im Kampf mit Weimar–Genf–Versailes* (Berlin: Duncker & Humblot, 1988), 127, 132. A cultural domain is neutralized when it ceases to be the central domain. Almost by definition the central domain cannot be a neutral domain.

5. Schnitt, *Concept of the Political*, 37–38; "Das Zeitalter der Neutralisierungen," 125–26.

6. "Das Zeitalter der Neutralisierungen,"128.

7. José Casanova, *Public Religions in the Modern World* (Chicago: University of Chicago Press, 1994), 21. See also Bernd Oberdorfer, *Geselligkeit und Realisierung von Sittlichkeit: Die Theorieentwicklung Friedrich Schleiermachers bis 1799* (Berlin: Walter de Gruyter, 1995), 5, on Schleiermacher's theology in particular as a reflex of the modern differentiation of cultural spheres.

8. I am keenly aware that the following argument for a connection between the oppositional discourses that mobilize and shape moral-religious communities, on the one hand, and the practices of spiritual formation that these communities foster, on the other, is unduly abstract. It needs to be fleshed out with particular historical examples of oppositional discourses that have played a role in authorizing religiously transformative discourses. One such example might be the Buddhist doctrine of "Not-self," a doctrine which was initially motivated by anti-Brahmanical polemical considerations (see Steven Collins, *Selfless Persons* [Cambridge: Cambridge University Press, 1982], 77, 84 and passim) but which has also functioned, through various disciplinary and rhetorical methods of interiorization, to shape characteristically Buddhist ways of life in a variety of historical and cultural contexts. Such detailed empirical studies of the relationship between boundary maintenance and spiritual formation—that is, between the political and ethical dimensions of religious discourse and practice—would obviously hold great interest and significance not only for comparative theologians, but for comparative ethicists as well. Unfortunately, such empirical analyses, ideally undertaken with a comparative approach, lie outside the scope of the present work.

9. Pierre Bourdieu, *Language and Symbolic Power*, trans. Gino Raymond and Matthew Adamson (Cambridge, Mass.: Harvard University Press, 1991), 111–16 and passim. The relation between the social group and its authoritative discourse is reciprocal such that the social group realizes itself and consolidates a sense of identity through this act of collective recognition. David Kelsey presents a functional, as opposed to formalist, account of the authority of Christian scripture that is parallel to Bourdieu's understanding of authority. See the former's *The Uses of Scripture in Recent Theology* (Philadelphia: Fortress Press, 1975), 30, 109, 152.

10. Robert Paul Wolff, "Beyond Tolerance," in *A Critique of Pure Tolerance* (Boston: Beacon Press, 1965), 21–22. In the context of a discussion of the principle of tolerance in a pluralistic society, Wolff makes precisely this argument that primary socialization depends on an in-group/out-group contrast.

11. Claude Lévi-Strauss, *Structural Anthropology*, trans. Claire Jacobson and Brooke Grundfest Schoepf (New York: Basic Books, 1963), 574 and passim. Slavoj Žižek provides an interesting discussion of social antagonism as the "repressed real" (in the Lacanian sense) with reference to Lévi-Strauss. See his essay, "The Spectre of Ideology," in *Mapping Ideology*, ed. Slavoj Žižek (New York: Verso, 1994), 26–27.

12. J. Samuel Preus, *Explaining Religion: Criticism and Theory from Bodin to Freud* (New Haven, Conn.: Yale University Press, 1987), 5, 24.

13. Preus, *Explaining Religion*, xi–xii, and passim.

14. Preus, *Explaining Religion*, 6 (on Bodin); Basil Wiley, *The Seventeenth-Century Background* (New York: Columbia University Press, 1965), 124 (on Herbert); Ivan Strenski, *Thinking about Religion: An Historical Introduction to Theories of Religion* (Malden, Mass.: Blackwell Publishing, 2006), 17, 25.

15. Peter Harrison, *"Religion" and the Religions in the English Enlightenment* (Cambridge: Cambridge University Press, 1990), 45–60; Strenski, *Thinking about Religion*, 25.

16. Harrison, *"Religion" and the Religions*, 32; 40; Preus, *Explaining Religion*, 12–13.

17. Harrison, *"Religion" and the Religions*, 70.

18. Preus, *Explaining Religion*, 28; Wiley, *Seventeenth-Century Background*, 124, 131–32; Peter Byrne, *Natural Religion and the Nature of Religion: The Legacy of Deism* (New York: Routledge, 1989), 31–37.

19. Harrison, *"Religion" and the Religions*, 7.

20. Peter Byrne (*Natural Religion and the Nature of Religion*, 32) argues that one should distinguish Herbert's doctrine of divine inspiration from the later notion of natural revelation. The faculties receiving the five common notions "may be distinguished from reason as such."

21. Preus, *Explaining Religion*, 35–6.

22. John Locke, *The Reasonableness of Christianity*, ed. I. T. Ramsey (Stanford: Stanford University Press, 1958), 65.

23. Locke, *Reasonableness of Christianity*, 71.

24. Locke maintained that revelation was practically necessary to establish claims that human beings would not discover on their own, but which, once having been revealed, would be recognized as self-evidently reasonable (see *Reasonableness of Christianity*, 65; Wiley, *Seventeenth-Century Background*, 286).

25. Matthew Tindal, *Christianity as Old as the Creation* (New York: Garland Publishing, 1978), 3, 67 and passim.

26. John Locke, *Treatise of Civil Government and A Letter Concerning Toleration*, ed. Charles L. Sherman (New York: D. Appleton-Century, 1937), 219 (hereafter, *Letter Concerning Toleration*).

27. Locke, *Reasonableness of Christianity*, 71; *Letter Concerning Toleration*, 222–23.

28. Locke, *Reasonableness of Christianity*, 76. We can perhaps interpret the "l'infame" against which Voltaire railed as nothing other than the political, differential dimension of religion isolated from the moral and cognitive aspects of religious belief.

29. David Hume, *The Natural History of Religion* (Stanford: Stanford University Press, 1956), 54.

30. John Locke, *An Essay Concerning Human Understanding* (Oxford: Clarendon Press, 1924), 354; *Reasonableness of Christianity*, 65–7.

31. John Toland, *Christianity not Mysterious* (New York: Garland Publishing, 1978), 24–25; James C. Livingston, *Modern Christian Thought*, vol. 1, *The Enlightenment and the Nineteenth Century* (Upper Saddle River, N.J.: Prentice Hall, 1988), 21–22.

32. Harrison, *"Religion" and the Religions*, 64.

33. Throughout I cite from the first edition: Friedrich Schleiermacher, *Über die Religion: Reden an die Gebildeten unter ihren Verächtern* (Stuttgart: Reclam, 1985); and

Richard Crouter's translation: Friedrich Schleiermacher, *On Religion: Speeches to its Cultured Despisers,* trans. and ed. Richard Crouter (Cambridge: Cambridge University Press, 1996). On the positioning of Schleiermacher's work between the Enlightenment and Romanticism, see Richard Crouter, *Friedrich Schleiermacher: Between Enlightenment and Romanticism* (New York: Cambridge University Press, 2005), 3–8 and passim.

34. Schleiermacher, *On Religion,* 27–28; *Über die Religion,* 124.

35. See, e.g., Schleiermacher, *On Religion,* 79, 82.

36. A reading of Schleiermacher's project in terms of depoliticization thus focuses particular attention on the often-neglected Fourth Speech. For a critique of the neglect of the Fourth Speech in twentieth-century interpretations of Schleiermacher, see, e.g., Andrew Dole, "The Case of the Disappearing Discourse: Schleiermacher's Fourth Speech and the Field of Religious Studies," *Journal of Religion* 88:1 (Jan. 2008): 1–28.

37. Schleiermacher, *On Religion* 76; cf. *Über die Religion,* 125: "Ich sehe nichts, als dass alles Eins ist und dass Alle Unterschiede, die es in der Religion selbst wirklich gibt, eben durch die gesellige Verbindung sanft ineinanderfliessen."
The true church fosters unity while at the same time preserving the freedom and individuality of its members. The concept of the true church is modeled after Schleiermacher's concept of "free sociability" (*die freie Gesseligkeit*), a social form that combines individuality and "publicness" without subordinating one of these principles to the other. On the concept of free sociability in Schleiermacher, see Bernd Oberdorfer, *Geselligkeit und Realisierung von Sittlichkeit: Die Theorieentwicklung Friedrich Schleiermachers bis 1799* (Berlin: Walter de Gruyter, 1995), 495–502, 523–31. As the fulfillment of free sociability, the true church is neither a mere aggregate of isolated individuals nor a social form that forces its members to conform to a uniform standard. See Oberdorfer, 507–8.

38. Schleiermacher, *On Religion,* 76; cf. *Über die Religion,* 125: "…, je weiter Ihr fortschreitet in der Religion, desto mehr muss Euch die ganze religiöse Welt als ein unteilbares Ganzes erscheinen."

39. Schleiermacher, *On Religion,* 84–8, 80; see also Horst Firsching and Matthias Schlegel, "Religiöse Innerlichkeit und Geselligkeit: Zum Verhältnis von Erfahrung, Kommunikabilität und Socialität—unter besonderer Berücksichtigung des Religionsverständnisses Friedrich Schleiermachers," in *Religion als Kommunikation,* ed. Hartmann Tyrell, Volkhard Krech, and Hubert Knoblauch (Wuürzburg: Ergon Verlag, 1998), 66–68.

40. Schleiermacher nevertheless insists that the true church is not merely an ideal, but a present reality; only a lack of religious sensitivity prevents it from being widely recognized in the world. *On Religion,* 78.

41. Schleiermacher, *On Religion,* 91.

42. Schleiermacher, *On Religion,* 99.

43. In Schleiermacher's work, religion is intimately related to aesthetic experience. On his inability to differentiate clearly between them, see Louis Dupré, "Toward a Revaluation of Schleiermacher's 'Philosophy of Religion,'" *Journal of Religion* 44:2 (Apr. 1964): 109–12.

44. *Conversations with Eckermann*, entry dated October 29, 1823. Cited in David Tracy, *The Analogical Imagination* (New York: Crossroad, 1991), 140 n. 36.

45. Schleiermacher, *On Religion*, 111.

46. Schleiermacher, *On Religion*, 102. Schleiermacher attributes the exclusionary tendency seen in historical religions to "an external, intruding corruption."

47. On the homologizing of positive religion to the intuition of the infinite, see, e.g., Schleiermacher, *On Religion*, 102, where Schleiermacher speaks of a moment "in which this infinite intuition was first established in the world as foundation and focal point of a unique religion."

48. Schleiermacher, *On Religion*, 102.

49. See, e.g., Schleiermacher, *On Religion*, 102.

50. Schleiermacher, *On Religion*, 96–97.

51. George Simmel, *Conflict and the Web of Group-Affiliations*, trans. Reinhard Bendix and Kurt H. Wolff (New York: Free Press, 1955), 28–30.

52. Schleiermacher, *On Religion*, 101.

53. According to Schleiermacher's critique, the Enlightenment overlooked this vital distinction when it tried to abstract a concept of natural religion. Put differently, the Enlightenment philosophers erred in using Christian sectarianism as a model for understanding religious diversity.

54. To be specific, evolutionism undermines pluralism with its assumption that the fully realized essence of religion coincides with the essence of Christianity.

55. Schleiermacher, *On Religion*, 123; cf. *Über die Religion*, 206.

56. Drey sets forth this distinction in his two-part article, "Von der Landesreligion und der Weltreligion," *Tübinger Quartalschrift* (1827): 234–74 and 391–435.

57. Johann Sebastian Drey, *Die Apologetik als wissenschaftliche Nachweisung der Göttlichkeit des Christenthums in seiner Erscheinung*, Bd. 2 (Mainz, 1843), 212; "Von der Landesreligion," 260–61.

58. Drey, *Die Apologetik*, 2:258; cf. *Die Apologetik als wissenschaftliche Nachweisung der Göttlichkeit des Christenthums in seiner Erscheinung*, Bd. 3 (Mainz, 1847), 149.

59. Drey, *Die Apologetik*, 3:148; cf. *Die Apologetik*, 2:215, 259. Drey polemically includes within the category of national religion the national churches of post-Reformation Europe, in which he sees a lamentable regression of the Christian idea of the world religion back to the religious tribalism of ancient heathenism and Judaism ("Von der Landesreligion," 423–24, 426; cf. *Die Apologetik*, 2:215–16).

60. Drey, "Von der Landesreligion," 264.

61. Drey, "Von der Landesreligion,"272.

62. Drey, "Von der Landesreligion," 241–43, 262, 268–69, 273.

63. Drey, "Von der Landesreligion," 260–61; J. S. Drey, *Brief Introduction to the Study of Theology*, trans. Michael Himes (Notre Dame: Notre Dame University Press, 1994), 105, 112. Convergence and divergence, unity and antagonism, are absolute principles for Drey; he distinguishes the principle of unity that the Church, albeit imperfectly, embodies, on the one hand, and the unity achieved through social antagonism, on the other. See "Von der Landesreligion," 412.

64. Drey, *Brief Introduction*, 133, 136; *Die Apologetik als wissenschaftliche Nachweisung der Göttlichkeit des Christenthums in seiner Erscheinung*, Bd. 1 (Mainz, 1838), 97.

65. Drey, *Brief Introduction*, 133.

66. Drey, "Von der Landesreligion," 244.

67. Drey, *Die Apologetik*, 2:258; cf. "Von der Landesreligion," 255.

68. Drey, *Die Apologetik*, 2:259.

69. Drey basically attributes the Wars of Religion to the Protestant repudiation of papal authority; in default of that source of authority, Protestant churches were forced in their conflict with Catholicism to forge compromising alliances with political leaders ("Von der Landesreligion," 420–21). The Protestant challenge in turn forced Catholicism to appear as the state religion of this or that people ("Von der Landesreligion," 427–28).

70. Wayne L. Fehr, *The Birth of the Catholic Tübingen School: The Dogmatics of Johann Sebastian Drey* (Chico, Calif.: Scholars Press, 1981), 30–31.

71. See "Von der Landesreligion," 249, where Drey repudiates the Deistic notion of a God who, like the mechanic with respect to his machine, becomes indifferent to his creation after his original creative work is done.

72. Fehr, *Birth*, 137–41, passim.

73. Fehr, *Birth*, 140.

74. Fehr, *Birth*, 137.

75. Fehr, *Birth*, 205–6, 232, 243.

76. Fehr, *Birth*, 206, 240, passim.

77. Michael J. Himes, "Historical Theology as *Wissenschaft*: Johann Sebastian Drey and the Structure of Theology," in *Revisioning the Past: Prospects in Historical Theology*, ed. Mary Potter Engel and Walter E. Wyman (Minneapolis: Fortress Press, 1992), 209–10.

78. Drey, "Von der Landesreligion," 262.

79. James Freeman Clarke, *Ten Great Religions, An Essay in Comparative Theology* (Boston: Houghton Mifflin, [1871] 1899), 15. In the second volume of this work, which bears the subtitle "A Comparison of all Religions" (1883), Clarke adds the category of "tribal" religions (pp. 26–29). Drey appears to have been the source of the world religion/national religion distinction that figured prominently in the brand new discipline of *Religionswissenschaft* in the late nineteenth century, particularly among the pioneering Dutch scholars Cornelis Petrus Tiele, Abraham Kuenen, and P. D. Chantepie de la Saussaye. these early *Religionswissenschaftler* were reluctant to advertise their indebtedness to Drey, apparently out of a concern that the theological provenance of the classificatory scheme would raise doubts about its scientific usefulness (Masuzawa, 116).

80. Clarke, *Ten Great Religions: An Essay in Comparative Theology*, 4–9; 2:23–26.

81. Clarke, *Ten Great Religions: An Essay in Comparative Theology*, 14.

82. Where "science" is understood in the more familiar empiricist sense, as opposed to the broader, rationalist sense of the term. As we saw in the previous section, Drey understood theology as a "science" (*Wissenschaft*) in the latter sense.

83. Clarke, *Ten Great Religions*, Part II, 26.

84. On the legacy of Deism in the comparative religion of the later nineteenth century, see Peter Byrne, *Natural Religion and the Nature of Religion,* ch. 7 and passim. While acknowledging the scattered references to comparative theology in the work of Max Müller, however, Byrne does not discuss comparative theology per se.

85. Clarke, *Ten Great Religions: An Essay in Comparative Theology,* 14.

86. George Matheson, *The Distinctive Messages of the Old Religions* (New York: Anson D. F. Randolph, 1894), 39–43.

87. Indeed, the illusion of scientific objectivity starts to wear thin early on when Clarke is forced to express the anticipated conclusions of his treatise in conditional form—e.g., "Comparative Theology *will probably show* that the Ethnic Religions are one-sided, each containing a Truth of its own, but defective, . . ."; "Comparative Theology *will probably show* that the Ethnic Religions are arrested, or degenerate, and will come to an End, . . ." (*Ten Great Religions: An Essay in Comparative Theology,* 21, 29. Emphasis added)—an effort to mask the a priori nature of his "conclusions" that is unconvincing in a quaint, almost pathetic sort of way.

88. Clarke, *Ten Great Religions: An Essay in Comparative Theology,* 18–21. Here in the first of the two volumes of his *Ten Great Religions,* Clarke concedes a catholic tendency to Judaism (p. 18), which is probably not all that surprising in view of Judaism's genealogical connection with Christianity. In the second volume (*Ten Great Religions: Part II,* 28-29), he expands the number of putative catholic religions to five, adding Judaism and Zoroastrianism. The expanded list might reflect the influence of W. D. Whitney's distinction between "race religion" and "founded religion." See William Dwight Whitney, "On the So-Called Science of Religion," *Princeton Review* 57 (May 1881): 429–52, esp. 451. Cf. Clarke, *Ten Great Religions*: Part II, 29: "The ethnic religions all grew up without any prophet as their founder; the catholic were each founded by a prophet."

89. E.g., Clarke, *Ten Great Religions: An Essay in Comparative Theology,* 503; see also Abraham Kuenen, *National Religions and Universal Religions* (New York: Charles Scribner's Sons, 1882), 102.

90. Clarke, *Ten Great Religions: An Essay in Comparative Theology,* 19, 503 and passim.

91. On Islam's alleged inability to win over the hearts and minds of its converts, see, e.g., F. D. Maurice, *The Religions of the World and their Relations to Christianity* (London: John W. Parker, 1847), 57.

92. Clarke, *Ten Great Religions: An Essay in Comparative Theology,* 19: "But, correctly viewed, Islam is only a heretical sect, and so all this must be credited to the interest of Christianity."; see also 2:74; Kuenen, *National Religions,* 33, 57; C. P. Tiele, "Religions," in *Encyclopaedia Britannica,* 9th ed. (Edinburgh, 1885), 369.

93. The inclusion of Islam among the universal religions, after it has been represented as a cheap copy of Christianity, allows a scholar like Tiele to maintain a facade of fairness and objectivity. On the Christian/Western representation of Mohammed as an imposter, see Edward Said, *Orientalism* (New York: Vintage Books, 1979), 60, 66, and passim.

94. Clarke, *Ten Great Religions: An Essay in Comparative Theology,* 20, 502. Tiele employs the same argument, only with the difference that he identifies Buddhism with the Aryan, rather than the Mongol race. Tiele, "Religions," 369.

95. Another argument, which is employed by Abraham Kuenen, is that the essential place of monasticism in Buddhism is evidence of its inability to satisfy the religious needs of the laity, and therefore most of humanity. Kuenen, *National Religions*, 305ff., 313.

96. See, e.g., Kuenen, *National Religions*, 304, Barrows, 59.

97. Tiele, "Religions," 368, cf. Chantepie de la Saussaye, 55.

98. Clarke, *Ten Great Religions*: Part II, 24–26.

99. By extolling Christianity as the world religion, comparative theology makes a liberal, inclusivist interpretation of Christianity representative of the Christian tradition as a whole. More doctrinaire, exclusivist forms of Christianity are implicitly classified with the national religions.

100. Tiele, "Religions," 368.

101. Tiele, "Religions," 368–69.

102. Ernst Troeltsch, "The Place of Christianity among the World Religions," in *Christian Thought: Its History and Application*, ed. F. von Hügel (New York: Meridian Books, 1957), 48–51.

103. Troeltsch, "Place of Christianity," 53–54. Against Masuzawa's interpretation of Troeltsch's association of Christianity with European history and civilization as primarily an expression of European cultural hegemony, Amiee Burant Chor argues that the "Place of Christianity" essay—which, significantly, was originally intended as a paper to be delivered at Oxford shortly after the war in 1923—reflects a concern with "promoting European unity in the face of the national enmities fostered not only by the war but also by the bitter peace settlement." Amiee Burant Chor, "Defining 'The Political': Method in the Historiography of Nineteenth-Century Religious Thought," *Papers of the Nineteenth-Century Theology Group* 38 (2007): 92–111.

104. Masuzawa, *Invention of World Religions*, 318.

105. Reflecting on the Parliament several years later, its president, John Henry Barrows, finds it necessary to counter the perception that the Parliament was intended to promote a kind of religious pluralism. Somewhat defensively he writes: "Whoever takes pains to read the proceedings of the Parliament will discover that the meeting "was a great Christian demonstration with a non-Christian section which added color and picturesque effect. . . . The Parliament was not founded on the false theory that all religions are equally good. It was founded on the spirit of Christian courtesy, and also on the rock of absolute sincerity in the maintenance of individual convictions." John Henry Barrows, *Christianity, The World Religion* (Chicago: A. C. McClurg and Company, 1897), 311, 316.

106. Quoted in Diana L. Eck, *Encountering God: A Spiritual Journey from Bozeman to Banares* (Boston: Beacon Press, 1993), 28.

107. Jonathan Z. Smith, "Religion, Religions, Religious," in *Relating Religion* (Chicago: University of Chicago Press, 2004), 191.

108. Masuzawa, *Invention of World Religions*, 310.

109. Smith, "Religion, Religions, Religious," in *Relating Religion*, 191.

110. In other words, one could maintain a liberal attitude of tolerance toward a national religion only so long as "national religion" was regarded as a neutral descriptive term. Once the term lost its neutral descriptive sense it could no longer be

applied to a major religious tradition without betraying the values of liberal tolerance and respect.

111. Smith, "Religion, Religions, Religious," in *Relating Religion*, 192.

112. Smith, "Religion, Religions, Religious," in *Relating Religion*, 192; Masuzawa, *Invention of World Religions*, 114.

113. Masuzawa (*Invention of World Religions*, 114) makes essentially the same point when she suggests that in the contemporary discourse of world religions, Tiele's categorical distinction between universal religions and national religions "survived and simply relocated."

114. Masuzawa, *Invention of World Religions*, 327.

115. This notion of a generalized religious experience underlying the particular forms of religion of course recalls the Enlightenment notion of natural religion underlying the various positive religions or sects.

116. Ernst Troeltsch, "Christianity and the History of Religions," in *Religion in History*, trans. James Luther Adams and Walter F. Bense (Edinburgh: T&T Clark, 1991), 78; see also Masuzawa, *Invention of World Religions*, 312–13.

117. Troeltsch, "Christianity and the History of Religions," 79: "Then the deepest core of the religious history of humanity reveals itself as an experience that cannot be further analyzed, an ultimate and original phenomenon that constitutes, like moral judgment and aesthetic perception and yet with characteristic differences, a simple fact of psychic life. Everywhere the basic reality of religion is the same: an underivable, purely positive, again and again experienced contact with the Deity." See also Masuzawa, *Invention of World Religions*, 314–16.

118. Masuzawa, *Invention of World Religions*, 313–15.

119. Friedrich Heiler and Charles Davis are two other examples twentieth-century scholars who employ some form of the universal religion/national religion distinction. Heiler distinguishes the "high religions" (*Hochreligionen*) from the "lower nationalistic religions of mankind." See Heiler, "The History of Religions as a Preparation for the Co-operation of Religions," in *The History of Religions: Essays in Methodology*, ed. Mircea Eliade and Joseph Kitagawa (Chicago: University of Chicago Press, 1959), 158; see also his *Erscheinungsformen und Wesen der Religion* (Stuttgart: Kohlhammer, 1949), 19, where he cites the distinction between "*die Universal- oder Menschhietsreligion*" and "*die Stammen-, Volks-, Reichsreligion.*" In his essay, "Our New Religious Identity," *Sciences Religieuses/Studies in Religion* 9:1 (1980): 35, Charles Davis draws a contrast between "universalistic personal identity" and "political particularism" which closely corresponds to the distinction between universal religion and national religion. Davis's call for a "post-conventional, universalistic identity" gives particularly clear expression the utopian ideal of a form of religious community transcending the political.

120. On the suddenness of the transition, see Masuzawa, *Invention of World Religions*, 11–12.

121. Gustav Mensching, *Structures and Patterns of Religion*, trans. Hans F. Klimkeit and V. Srinavasa (Delhi: Motilal Banarsidass, 1976), 45.

122. Mensching, *Structures and Patterns*, 323.

123. Mensching, *Structures and Patterns*, 298: "The universal religion appears everywhere in its founders and early communities as a religion of directness. The

rejection of the means and of the mediation of the intercourse with the Godhead and the salvation, which one endeavors, corresponds to the personal and, therefore, direct relationship of the individual to his God or to his godhead as the case may be."

124. Gustav Mensching, *Tolerance and Truth in Religion*, trans. H. J. Klimkeit (Tuscaloosa: University of Alabama Press, 1955), 108.

125. Mensching, *Tolerance and Truth*, 116.

126. Mensching, *Structures and Patterns*, 7 and passim.

127. Mensching, *Structures and Patterns*, 56; cf. *Tolerance and Truth*, 112.

128. Mensching, *Tolerance and Truth*, 117, 141; *Structures and Patterns*, 52.

129. See, e.g., Mensching, *Tolerance and Truth*, 118: "When Christianity was founded and while it was beginning to develop, it was interested only in the individual and in his salvation alone. . . . At this time the Christian church was not in any way a political force in itself." See also *Structures and Patterns*, 52, 297.

130. George Lindbeck, *The Nature of Doctrine* (Philadelphia: Westminster Press, 1984), 25.

131. On the "ghettoization" of theology, see Lindbeck, *Nature of Doctrine*, 25.

132. Lindbeck himself rather modestly downplays the originality of *The Nature of Doctrine* in the forward to the German edition, reprinted in Lindbeck, *The Church in a Postliberal Age*, ed. James J. Buckley (Grans Rapids, Mich.: William B. Eerdmans, 2002), 196–200. There he openly acknowledges the sources—from Clifford Geertz to Bernard Lonergan—of the various ideas he synthesized, as well as precedents for the postliberal perspective on the place of religion in modern society (e.g., Alasdair MacIntyre and Stanley Hauerwas).

133. As David Tracy ("Lindbeck's New Program for Theology: A Reflection," *The Thomist* 4:9 [July 1985]: 465), among others, notes, Lindbeck's cultural-lingusitic theory of religion, specifically its insistence on the priority of the external aspects of religion over the internal, experiential ones, supports a Barthian theology of the revelatory Word addressing the human situation from without.

134. Lindbeck, *Nature of Doctrine*, 20.

135. See the introduction to this chapter above and Wolff, "Beyond Tolerance," 21–22.

136. Lindbeck, *Nature of Doctrine*, 133–34.

137. Lindbeck, "Ecumenism and the Future of Belief," *Una Sancta* 25:3 (1968): 8–9.

138. Lindbeck, "The Sectarian Future of the Church," in *The God Experience*, ed. Joseph P. Whelan, S.J. (New York: Newman Press, 1971), 239; "Ecumenism and the Future of Belief," 11–13.

139. The mainstream status of a doctrine or practice, in other words, is matter of hegemony, rather than of its intrinsic content. See Hugh Nicholson, "The Political Nature of Doctrine: A Critique of Lindbeck in Light of Recent Scholarship," *Heythrop Journal* 48:6 (Nov. 2007): 865.

140. Lindbeck, "Sectarian Future," 240.

141. As a particularly dramatic way of making this point, one could cite the interracial character of the various communities founded by the Reverend Jim Jones,

most notably his Peoples Temple. Jones's churches had a basically fundamentalist orientation and a strong schismatic tendency (culminating tragically in the Jonestown massacre), notwithstanding the fact that the Peoples Temple was affiliated for a time with the Disciples of Christ, a mainline Christian denomination.

142. Note the defensive character of the situation of the Christian community in a secular culture as described by Lindbeck: "Any social grouping whose distinctiveness is imperiled by compromise with alien forces must ultimately become sectarian in the sociological sense of the term in order to preserve its identity" ("Ecumenism and the Future of Belief," 8).

143. In their volume *Strong Religion: The Rise of Fundamentalism around the World*, Gabriel A. Almond, R. Scott Appleby, and Emmanuel Sivan Appleby cite the reactive nature of fundamentalist movements as the most prominent of their defining characteristics: "Religious fundamentalist movements are distinct from other religious movements in that they are inherently interactive, reactive, and oppositional—that is, they are inexorably drawn to some form of antagonistic engagement with the world outside the enclave. In other words, fundamentalisms are inevitably political" (p. 218; see also 93–94 and passim).

144. We could say that the modifier "ecumenical" encodes a liberal denial of social antagonism, and thereby functions to neutralize the negative connotations of the concept of sect.

145. Lindbeck, *Nature of Doctrine*, 75, 95.

146. Patchen Markell, *Bound by Recognition* (Princeton, N.J.: Princeton University Press, 2003), 154 and passim.

147. Cf. Arjun Appadurai's (*Modernity at Large* (Minneapolis: University of Minnesota Press, 1996), 12) observation that the concept of culture (as a noun) carries the problematic implication "that culture is some kind of object, thing, or substance, whether physical or metaphysical."

148. Against Gordon Michalson's claim that the Lindbeck's cultural-linguistic theory of religion "is separable in principle from his postliberal theological interest" ("The Response to Lindbeck," *Modern Theology* 4:2 [January 1988]: 11), or David Tracy's that the regulative theory of doctrine and the cultural-linguistic theory of religion, corresponding to the title and subtitle, respectively, of Lindbeck's book, essentially comprise "two books" ("Lindbeck's New Program for Theology," 462), I would contend that Lindbeck's regulative theory of doctrine (a central concept in his postliberal project) derives crucial support from the theory of religion that he adapts from Geertz. The latter masks the one-sidedness of the former.

149. Lindbeck, *Nature of Doctrine*, 46–63.

150. Lindbeck, *Nature of Doctrine*, 55.

151. Kathryn Tanner, "Respect for Other Religions: A Christian Antidote to Colonialist Discourse," *Modern Theology* 9:1 (Jan. 1993): 1–18, esp. 9–12.

152. Lindbeck, *Nature of Doctrine*, 55 and passim.

153. A good example of current anthropological thinking on the concept of culture—or better, "the cultural"—can be found in Appadurai, *Modernity at Large*, 12–14.

154. Kathryn Tanner, *Theories of Culture* (Minneapolis: Fortress Press, 1997), 104–10 and passim.

155. Tanner, *Theories of Culture*, 110–19 and passim.

156. Tanner, *Theories of Culture*, 116.

157. Tanner, *Theories of Culture*, 110–11.

158. Tanner, *Theories of Culture*, 118; 119.

159. Tanner, *Theories of Culture*, 108–9, 120–21.

160. Cf. Lindbeck, *Nature of Doctrine*, 75.

161. Tanner, *Theories of Culture*, 109; cf. 120.

162. Tanner, *Theories of Culture*, 120–21.

163. James Clifford, *The Predicament of Culture* (Cambridge, Mass.: Harvard University Press, 1988), 258–64 and passim.

164. Clifford, *Predicament*, 264–66.

165. Clifford, *Predicament*, 260.

166. This parallel is hardly coincidental in view of the fact that Tanner's work is informed by postcolonial criticism in general and Said's work in particular.

167. Kathryn Tanner, *The Politics of God* (Minneapolis: Fortress Press, 1992), 208–23; "Respect for other Religions," 12–16.

168. Tanner, "Respect for other Religions," 14; cf. *Politics of God*, 218.

169. Implicit in Tanner's appeal to the doctrine of creation as an antidote to colonialist discourse is an understanding of "political evil" similar to that articulated by George Kateb. Against the commonplace view that the evils perpetuated by governments and political movements can be understood in terms of the moral failings of (individual) human beings, Kateb argues that "much of political evil on a large scale is intimately connected to deep belief in the group and its identity." Kateb, *The Inner Ocean: Individualism and Democratic Culture* (Ithaca, N.Y.: Cornell University Press, 1992), 203; cf. 208. In order to avoid the pathological tendencies of group loyalty, group identity needs to be mitigated by "the doctrine of individual human rights" (Kateb, 209). What William Connolly says about this aspect of Kateb's political theory could perhaps be said of Tanner as well: "[He] sometimes writes as if individual identity is concrete and natural, while group identity is abstract and invented." William E. Connolly, *Why I Am Not a Secularist* (Minneapolis: University of Minnesota Press, 1999), 139. It should be noted, however, that neither Kateb nor Tanner would likely accept this proposition in the crude, unnuanced form in which Connolly states it here, as Connolly himself acknowledges.

170. Tanner, *Politics of God*, 212, 220–21; "Respect for Other Religions," 15; cf. *Theories of Culture*, 58.

171. Tanner, *Politics of God*, 221.

172. To the extent that my model of comparative theology seeks to break the impasse between liberal universalism and postliberal communitarianism by questioning their shared assumptions, it has a certain affinity with, and relevance to, the work of comparative ethicists like Aaron Stalnaker who seek to move beyond the false dichotomy between a "naive universalism" and a "pernicious relativism." (See *Overcoming Our Evil* (Washington, D. C.: Georgetown University Press, 2006), 4–6).

A closer parallel to my project would be Bonnie Honig's effort to move beyond the liberal-communitarian debate in political theory by identifying a tendency to displace politics in the thought of both classic liberals like John Rawls and communitarians like Michael Sandel (Bonnie Honig, *Political Theory and the Displacement of Politics* [Ithaca, N.Y.: Cornell University Press, 1993], 2, 12, 198–99). Unfortunately, I became aware of Honig's work only after I had written this book.

CHAPTER 3

Kathryn Tanner, *Theories of Culture* (Minneapolis: Fortress Press, 1997), 116.

1. As mentioned above, here I follow Kathryn Tanner. Tanner contrasts this understanding of tolerance as a respect for religious difference to a concept of tolerance based on shared presuppositions. See her *Politics of God* (Minneapolis: Fortress Press, 1992), 195–219. Bonnie Honig argues the same basic point in her critique of the communitarianism of Michael Sandel. See her *Political Theory and the Displacement of Politics* (Ithaca, NY: Cornell University Press, 1993), 190–94.

2. Chantal Mouffe, "Carl Schmitt and the Paradox of Liberal Democracy," in *The Challenge of Carl Schmitt*, ed. Chantal Mouffe (New York: Verso, 1999), 40–41.

3. Chantal Mouffe, *The Return of the Political* (New York: Verso, 1993), 1–8 and passim. See also Honig, *Political Theory*, 6, 15, and passim.

4. Mouffe, "Carl Schmitt," 50.

5. Mouffe, "Carl Schmitt," 48.

6. Mouffe, "Carl Schmitt," 51.

7. Mouffe, *Return of the Political*, 4.

8. William E. Connolly, *The Ethos of Pluralization* (Minneapolis: University of Minnesota Press, 1995), xx–xxi.

9. The problematic nature of this "conversion of difference into otherness" is a theme that runs throughout Connolly's work. For a concise discussion of this theme, see, e.g., his *Identity/Difference* (Minneapolis: University of Minnesota Press, 1991), 64–68 and passim.

10. Iris Marion Young, *Justice and the Politics of Difference* (Princeton, N.J.: Princeton University Press, 1990), 59–60.

11. Connolly, *Ethos of Pluralization*, xxi.

12. This tension between a relational conception of Christian identity and a traditional understanding of Christian truth claims is simply a particular instance of a broader tension between an understanding of religious discourses, practices, and institutions as human constructions, on the one hand, and the traditional theological representation of these elements as grounded in eternal, transcendent, and divine reality, on the other.

13. Here I apply Mouffe's criticism of communitarianism to postliberalism. Concerning the communitarian approach, she writes: "Its rejection of pluralism and defence of a substantive idea of the "common good" represents, in my view, another way of evading the ineluctability of antagonism." Mouffe, *Return of the Political*, 7. For a similar—and more elaborate—critique of communitarianism, see

Bonnie Honig's critique of Michael Sandel in her *Political Theory*, 162–99. Honig focuses on Sandel's tendency to displace politics, a tendency he shares with liberals like John Rawls. It should be noted, however, that Honig's concept of the political does not fully coincide with Mouffe's (or Schmitt's). Honig singles out the contingent rather than the antagonistic nature of social relations as the defining characteristic of the political. Thus, she understands depoliticization in terms of the tendency "of certain regimes to stabilize certain practices and subjectivities by opposing them to others against whom they are defined. . . ." (p. 198). According to this definition, Schmitt himself (whom Honig does not reference) would be, ironically enough, the paradigmatic example of a theorist who displaces politics. Ultimately, however, the difference between Honig and Mouffe is largely one of semantics. As we shall see below, Mouffe makes precisely this point in her critique of Schmitt: by conceiving of the political community in substantive terms, Schmitt betrays his own insight regarding the politically constructed nature of political communities. Honig's understanding of the political in terms of contingency rather than antagonism lends the concept a more positive, less ambivalent connotation than that employed here.

14. It is significant that Tanner, despite her critique of postliberalism in *Theories of Culture*, comes from the "Yale school" of nonfoundationalist theology of Frei and Lindbeck. See John E. Thiel, *Nonfoundationalism* (Minneapolis: Fortress Press, 1994), 51–57 and passim.

15. See, e.g., *Theories of Culture* (Minneapolis: Fortress Press, 1997), 55.

16. Tanner, *Theories of Culture*, 112–19. A similar conception of theology inspired by de Certeau's distinction between tactics and strategies is found in Charles E. Winquist's *Desiring Theology* (Chicago: University of Chicago Press, 1995), 127–37.

17. On de Certeau's distinction between strategies and tactics, see Michel de Certeau, *The Practice of Everyday Life* (Berkeley and Los Angeles: University of California Press, 1984), 34–42 and passim.

18. Here I am largely following Tanner's analysis of the debate between liberals and postliberals in her unpublished manuscript, "Two Kinds of Apologetics," which she was kind enough to give me.

19. Tanner, "Two Kinds of Apologetics," 2.

20. Tanner, "Two Kinds of Apologetics," 13.

21. Tanner, "Two Kinds of Apologetics," 3.

22. Tanner, "Two Kinds of Apologetics," 13–14.

23. Tanner, "Two Kinds of Apologetics," 13; 15–16.

24. Tanner, "Two Kinds of Apologetics," 16; *Theories of Culture*, 117.

25. Tanner, *Theories of Culture*, 110–19.

26. Tanner, *Theories of Culture*, 117.

27. Lindbeck advocates what he calls an "ecumenical sectarianism" (as distinct from a theologically divisive, "schismatic" sectarianism) in two articles: "The Sectarian Future of the Church, in *The God Experience*, Joseph P. Whelen, S.J., ed. (New York: Newman Press, 1971) and "Ecumenism and the Future of Belief," *Una Sancta* 25:3, 3–17.

28. Tanner describes the sectarian implications of Lindbeck's postliberalism as follows: "Given the purported discontinuity of kind that separates a Christian way of life from others, Christian identity seems properly maintained by avoiding the influences and alterations that might accrue to it by way of intimate involvement with other ways of doing, feeling and understanding. Christian identity would seem to require, in short, cultural insularity." *Theories of Culture*, 104.

29. Tanner, *Theories of Culture*, 110.

30. Tanner, *Theories of Culture*, 110–11.

31. Tanner, *Theories of Culture*, 108.

32. One could perhaps argue that Tanner's account of Christian identity allows the element of misrecognition to interfere with the identification and ranking of the various forms of relational identity. Thus her theory has difficulty recognizing oppositional forms of Christian identity because these have a tendency to (mis)represent themselves as intrinsic. Meanwhile, it privileges those forms of relational identity whose effectiveness does not depend on such misrecognition, specifically, the ironic troping of outside cultural forms, a procedure whose effectiveness depends, in fact, on preserving traces of the former identity of the appropriated forms.

33. Tanner, *Theories of Culture*, 116.

34. Paul J. Griffiths, *An Apology for Apologetics* (Maryknoll, N.Y.: Orbis Books, 1991). Griffiths is keenly aware that his proposal for a return to the tradition of Christian apologetics offends against liberal sensibilities. In *An Apology for Apologetics* (p. 2), for example, he writes, "To be an apologist for the truth of one religious claim or set of claims against another is, in certain circles, seen as not far short of being a racist."

35. Clifford Geertz, "Religion as a Cultural System," in *Interpretation of Cultures* (New York: Basic Books, 1973), 87–125.

36. Bruce Lincoln, *Holy Terrors* (Chicago: University of Chicago Press, 2003), 6; Talal Asad, "The Construction of Religion as an Anthropological Category," in *Genealogies of Religion* (Baltimore: Johns Hopkins University Press, 1993), 36–39, Russell T. McCutcheon, "Myth," in *Guide to the Study of Religion*, ed. Willi Braun and Russell T. McCutcheon (New York: Cassell, 2000), 199–200.

37. This understanding of "religion" as denoting what certain communities have invested with transcendent authority obviously contrasts with the well-known Neo-orthodox (Barth, Brunner, Kraemer, et al.) redescription of "religion" as the product of human presumption.

We might infer that Tanner's relation to the concept of religion is ambiguous. On the one hand, a Barthian emphasis on the radical transcendence of the Word of God over all products of human choice and initiative, including those conventionally classified as "religious," is central to her theological vision. On the other hand, the Neo-orthodox redescription of non-Christian religious beliefs and practices, against the self-understanding of their adherents, as mere products of human presumption constitutes a blatantly imperialistic gesture that directly offends against the principle of respect for others that is likewise central to her understanding of Christianity.

38. Lincoln, *Holy Terrors*, 6.

39. Tanner all but concedes the arbitrariness of her decision to not to address the "crucial" question of Christianity's relation to other religions in her *Jesus, Humanity, and the Trinity* (Minneapolis; Fortress Press, 2001), xix, a book in which she attempts to state, as concisely and eloquently as possible, "what Christianity is all about."

40. Tanner presupposes this point when she argues against the idea that Christian identity can be established by a religious boundary. The arbitrary nature of the classification of Christian practice as religious extends to the boundary that results from that classification. See *Theories of Culture*, 108.

41. See M. M. Bakhtin, *The Dialogical Imagination*, trans. Caryl Emerson and Michael Holquist (Austin: University of Texas Press, 1981), 343–44. See also Maurice Bloch's analysis of the formalized speech of traditional authority. According to Bloch, the formalization of speech reaches the point where one's response to it is either unqualified acceptance or total rejection. See "Symbols, Song, Dance and Features of Articulation," in *Ritual, History, and Power* (London: Athlone Press, 1989), 29.

42. Bakhtin (*Dialogical Imagination*, 344) argues that authoritative discourse is incapable of being double-voiced. Cf. Tanner's appeal to Bakhtin's concept of double-voiced discourse in *Theories of Culture*, 116.

43. Michael Witzel, *On Magical Thought in the Veda* (Leiden: Universitaire Pers Leiden, 1979), 12.

44. Tanner, *Theories of Culture*, 119.

45. On Tanner's implicit refusal to recognize the legitimacy of a formal, purely differential dimension of Christian identity, see her argument that boundaries do not always reflect matters of internal importance to Christian practice, since they have more to do with "situational factors" (*Theories of Culture*, 108–109; cf. 120–21). See the discussion of this point in chapter 2 above.

This interpretation of cultural consumption as having a formal dimension has a certain affinity with Catherine Bell's understanding of "ritualization" as a strategy of differentiation. See her *Ritual Theory, Ritual Practice* (New York: Oxford University Press, 1992), 88–93 and passim. A good example for this phenomenon in the history of religions might be Buddhism's creative appropriation of the pan-Indian doctrines of karma and rebirth in accordance with its doctrine of "No-self," a doctrine developed in conscious opposition to the brahmanical concept of the transcendental self or *ātman*.

46. In *Theories of Culture*, Tanner does deal with doctrine, but only obliquely, in her critique of the postliberal appeal to the concept of rules as the principle that unifies Christian practices. See *Theories of Culture*, 138–43.

47. I have argued for such a "political" theory of doctrine in the context of a critique of George Lindbeck's *The Nature of Doctrine* in "The Political Nature of Doctrine: A Critique of Lindbeck in Light of Recent Scholarship," *Heythrop Journal* 48:6 (Nov. 2007): 858–77. On the political-sociological dimension of doctrine, see also Alister E. McGrath, *The Genesis of Doctrine* (Oxford: Blackwell, 1990), 37–52.

48. George Lindbeck, *The Nature of Doctrine* (Philadelphia: Westminster Press, 1984), 75; cf. Tanner, *Theories of Culture*, 109, 120–21.

49. On the distinction between the doctrine and theology, see McGrath, *Genesis of Doctrine*, 46.

50. Lindbeck, *Nature of Doctrine*, 75–76.

51. Tanner, *Theories of Culture*, 150–51.

52. Tanner, *Theories of Culture*, 150.

53. Daniel Boyarin, *Border Lines* (Philadelphia: University of Pennsylvania Press, 2004), 28–29.

54. Boyarin, *Border Lines*, 89. For the argument that Christianity emerges from its Jewish matrix as a separate religion much later than is often assumed, see also, e.g., Birger A. Pearson, "The Emergence of Christian Religion," in *The Emergence of the Christian Religion: Essays in Early Christianity* (Harrisburg, Pa.: Trinity Press International, 1997), 7–22, esp. 15–21; James D. G. Dunn, *The Parting of the Ways Between Christianity and Judaism and Their Significance for the Character of Christianity* (London: SCM Press and Trinity Press International, 1991), esp. 230–59.

55. Boyarin, *Border Lines*, 90, 92. On Philo's use of the term "theos" to refer to the Logos of God, see Marianne Maye Thompson, *The God of the Gospel of John* (Grand Rapids, Mich.: Eerdmans, 2001), 35–37.

56. Boyarin, *Border Lines*, 32.

57. Boyarin, *Border Lines*, 93.

58. Boyarin, *Border Lines*, 38, 89.

59. Boyarin, *Border Lines*, 40 and passim.

60. W. S. Green, "Otherness Within: Towards a Theory of Difference in Rabbinic Judaism," in *"To See Ourselves as Others See Us": Christians, Jews, "Others" in Late Antiquity*, ed. J. Neusner and E. S. Frerichs (Chico, Calif.: Scholars Press 1985), 50; cf. 58.

61. Strictly speaking, one cannot speak of two distinct cultural or sociological formations prior to such metonymic transposition. Thus, to continue with our current example, Boyarin argues that one cannot speak of Judaism and Christianity as two distinct entities prior to the discursive "partition" of the "multiform cultural system" he terms Judaeo-Christianity (Boyarin, *Border Lines*, 44). The project of Justin and his followers to make an acceptance of the Logos theology definitive of Christianity was not simply a matter of correctly characterizing an already-existing cultural-religious formation, but was, rather, a vital moment in the actual constitution of the cultural entity known as Christianity.

62. See, e.g., Boyarin, *Border Lines*, 132.

63. On the orientalist contrast between world affirmation and world denial, see, e.g., Ronald Inden, *Imagining India* (Bloomington: Indiana University Press, 1990), 85–108 and passim; Richard King, *Orientalism and Religion* (New York: Routledge, 1999), 118–42; Philip Almond, *The British Discovery of Buddhism* (Cambridge: Cambridge University Press, 1988), ch. 3.

64. See, e.g., Irenaeus of Lyons, *Against the Heresies*, trans. Dominic J. Unger (New York: Paulist Press, 1992).

65. Albert Schweitzer, *Indian Thought and Its Development* (Boston: Beacon Press, 1956), 1–2.

66. Schweitzer, *Indian Thought*, 6; cf. 3.

67. Schweitzer, *Indian Thought*, 7–8.

68. Schweitzer, *Indian Thought*, 4.

69. Schweitzer, *Indian Thought,* 4–5.

70. Schweitzer, *Indian Thought,* 5–6.

71. Schweitzer, *Indian Thought,* v, x, 17.

72. Specifically, Schweitzer's aim is to reconcile the principle of world and life affirmation with mysticism in a kind of cross-cultural synthesis. See Schweitzer, *Indian Thought,* ix–x, 17–18.

73. S. Radhakrishnan, *Eastern Religions and Western Thought* (Oxford: Oxford University Press, 1940), 74.

74. Although it remains true that many orientalist concepts and categories have attained a measure of reality as they have been (unwittingly) internalized by Western educated elites in India.

75. Tanner, *Theories of Culture,* 55.

76. Tanner, *Theories of Culture,* 58.

77. Tanner, *Theories of Culture,* 58.

78. As Aaron Stalnaker (*Overcoming Our Evil* (Washington, D. C.: Georgetown University Press, 2006), 2) notes, "comparative work can be just as effective as historical or 'genealogical' studies in bringing to consciousness the full range of consequences of common contemporary ways of framing ethical issues, and thus calling them into question."

79. A point eloquently made by Edward Said in *Orientalism* (New York: Vintage Books, 1979), 6 and passim.

80. An eloquent statement of the need to recognize the historical reality of those representations and misrepresentations that constitute the worldview of historical actors can be found in Sheldon Pollock's *The Language of the Gods in the World of Men* (Berkeley and Los Angeles: University of California Press, 2006), 2–3, 7, 23, 249, and passim. We return to this point in our Conclusion, below.

81. Indeed, many of the cultural-religious "facts" to which one appeals in an effort to dismantle such ideological formations can be shown to be, on closer analysis, discursive formations of the same basic type. Many of the teachings enshrined in tradition were originally contested interpretations that managed to attain hegemonic status. Only by becoming impacted or sedimented over time do such teachings appear as a bedrock layer of cultural-religious fact in relation to which more recent and more problematic ideological formations can be compared and criticized.

82. Slavoj Žižek, "How Did Marx Invent the Symptom?" in *Mapping Ideology,* ed. Slavoj Žižek (New York: Verso, 1994), 326–27.

83. John B. Thompson, *Studies in the Theory of Ideology* (Cambridge: Polity Press, 1984), 4.

84. Thompson, *Studies,* 4. Karl Mannheim, Clifford Geertz and Paul Ricoeur are examples of influential theorists who argue for a neutral concept ideology. See Mannheim's classic, *Ideology and Utopia,* trans. Louis Wirth and Edward Shils (New York: Harvest Books, 1985); Geertz's "Ideology as a Cultural System," in Geertz, *Interpretation of Cultures,* 193–233; and Ricoeur's essay, "Ideology and Utopia," (which draws from both Mannheim and Geertz) in *From Text to Action,* 308–24.

85. Another way of expressing the point of the preceding paragraphs is to say that the deconstruction of dichotomous typifications cannot be understood in terms of

the specious dichotomy between science and ideology, where ideology is understood as a discourse of falsehood and illusion, and science as a discourse of objective truth. On the science/ideology dichotomy, see Paul Ricoeur, "Science and Ideology," in *From Text to Action*, 246–69. As Slavoj Žižek observes, the science/ideology dichotomy, ironically, constitutes what is perhaps the most effective form of ideological discourse: "'Let the facts speak for themselves' is perhaps the arch statement of ideology...." "The Spectre of Ideology," in Žižek, *Mapping Ideology*, 11 and passim.

86. Jonathan Z. Smith, "In Comparison a Magic Dwells," in *Imagining Religion* (Chicago: University of Chicago Press, 1982), 21; Smith, "The 'End' of Comparison," in *A Magic Still Dwells*, ed. Kimberley C. Patton and Benjamin C. Ray (Berkeley and Los Angeles: University of California Press, 2000), 238–39.

87. Cf. Greg Urban, "The Role of Comparison in the Light of the Theory of Culture," in *Critical Comparisons in Politics and Culture*, ed. John R. Bowen and Roger Petersen (Cambridge: Cambridge University Press, 1999), 106: "To my way of thinking, there is a space for scientific discourse in cultural comparison—and by that I mean a discourse that circulates primarily within the bounds of scholarly communities."

88. An understanding of comparison in terms of metaphor can also be found in Fitz John Porter Poole, "Metaphor and Maps: Towards Comparison in the Anthropology of Religion," *Journal of the American Academy of Religion* 54:3 (Autumn 1986): 420–23 and passim.

89. Jonathan Z. Smith, *Drudgery Divine* (Chicago: University of Chicago Press, 1990), 52.

90. Smith, *Drudgery Divine*, 52.

91. Smith, *Drudgery Divine*, 52–53.

92. Smith, *Drudgery Divine*, 53.

93. Hugh B. Urban, "Making a Place to Take a Stand: Jonathan Z. Smith and the Politics and Poetics of Comparison," *Method and Theory in the Study of Religion* 12 (2000): 339–78, esp. 351–59.

94. Donald Davidson, "What Metaphors Mean," in *Philosophical Perspectives on Metaphor*, ed. Mark Johnson (Minneapolis: University of Minnesota Press, 1981), 217.

95. Davidson, "What Metaphors Mean," 216 and passim.

96. Urban, "Making a Place," 358–59.

97. Urban, "Making a Place," 357–58.

98. See Davidson, "What Metaphors Mean," 200.

99. Robert Paine, for example, notes that there is a tendency to assume that "analogic thought is (only) metaphoric." See his "The Political Uses of Metaphor and Metonym: An Exploratory Statement," in *Politically Speaking: Cross-Cultural Studies of Rhetoric*, ed. Robert Paine (Philadelphia: Institute for the Study of Human Issues, 1981), 187.

100. Paine, "Political Uses."

101. On the reflexive nature of social reality, see Anthony Giddens, *The Consequences of Modernity* (Stanford: Stanford University Press, 1990), 15–17, 36–45. See also Pierre Bourdieu's discussion of what he calls the "theory effect," in *Language and Symbolic Power*, trans. Gino Raymond and Matthew Adamson (Cambridge, Mass.: Harvard University Press, 1991), 133–34 and passim.

102. See, e.g., David I. Kertzer *Ritual, Politics, and Power* (New Haven, Conn.: Yale University Press, 1988), 6–8 and passim; Alfred Schutz, *Collected Papers I: The Problem of Social Reality* (The Hague: Martinus Nijhoff, 1971), 353, 355.

103. A good example is the concealment of the more problematic aspects of the system of capitalism; see Stuart Hall, "The Problem of Ideology—Marxism without Guarantees," in *Marxism: A Hundred Years On*, ed. Betty Matthews (London: Lawrence and Wishart, 1983), 74–75.

104. Paine, "Political Uses," 188.

105. Mark Juergensmeyer, *The New Cold War?* (Berkeley and Los Angeles: University of California Press, 1993), 81.

106. See Žižek, *Mapping Ideology*, 268 and passim, where Terry Eagleton suggests that Bourdieu's concept of doxa is a more adequate concept than ideology.

107. Pierre Bourdieu, *Outline of a Theory of Practice*, trans. Richard Nice (Cambridge: Cambridge University Press, 1977), 184–71.

108. Paine, "Political Uses," 198; Bourdieu, *Outline*, 166.

109. Bourdieu, *Language and Symbolic Power*, 117–26; Bourdieu, *The State Nobility*, trans. Lauretta C. Clough (Cambridge: Polity Press, 1996), 102–15.

110. See J. Z. Smith, "What a Difference a Difference Makes," in *Relating Religion* (Chicago: University of Chicago Press, 2004), 253: "Difference is seldom a comparison between entities judged to be equivalent. Difference most frequently entails a hierarchy of prestige and the concomitant ranking of superordinate and subordinate."

111. In other words, as Paul Knitter observes, the phrase is "mythological" in character. See John Hick and Paul F. Knitter, eds., *The Myth of Christian Uniqueness* (Maryknoll, N.Y.: Orbis Press, 1994), vii.

112. Karl Barth's well-known response to the discovery of a "Protestant" doctrine of divine grace in Jôdo-shin-shû Buddhism might serve as a negative demonstration of the effectiveness of the metonymical conflation of Christian absoluteness and uniqueness. Barth's bald assertion of the a priori nature of his knowledge of Christian superiority—an apriorism rendering irrelevant any formal similarities to Christian teachings that might be found in non-Christian religions—effectively concedes the arbitrary nature of Christian conviction. Barth's response signifies the abandonment of an apologetics of persuasion in favor of dogmatic assertion, a response that perhaps reflects the Barthian dictum that "the best apologetics is a good dogmatics." That even Barth was apparently not content simply to abide in his apriorism, however, undertaking an invidious comparison of Christianity, Vaiṣṇavism, and Jôdo-shin-shû Buddhism on the question of divine grace, testifies to a powerful drive to ground and stabilize a priori assertions of religious distinction in objective religious differences. See the discussion of Barth in Clooney, *Hindu God, Christian God* (New York: Oxford University Press, 2001), 135–38.

113. Paine, "Political Uses," 188. In his book *Rediscovering the Sacred* (Grand Rapids, Mich.: Eerdmans, 1992), 59–81, Robert Wuthnow provides an analysis of religious rhetoric that coheres with Paine's distinction between metaphorical and metonymical political discourse. Wuthnow makes use of Northrop Frye's distinction between "centripetal" and "centrifugal" meaning, which corresponds exactly to Paine's

distinction between metaphor and metonym. Unfortunately, Frye and, following him, Wuthnow do not distinguish between metaphor and metonym, regarding the latter as a species of metaphor.

114. Paul Ricoeur, "The Metaphorical Process," *Semeia*, vol. 4 (Missoula, Mont.: Scholars Press, 1975), 79.

115. Smith, *Drudgery Divine*, 51.

116. Davidson, "What Metaphors Mean," 216.

117. Paul Ricoeur, "Ideology and Utopia," in *From Text to Action*, 320.

118. Smith, *Imagining Religion*, xiii.

119. Victor Schlovsky, "Art as Technique," in *Russian Formalist Criticism: Four Essays*, ed. L. T. Lemon and M. J. Reis (Lincoln: University of Nebraska Press, 1965), 10–13 and passim.

120. Fredric Jameson, *The Prison House of Language* (Princeton, N.J.: Princeton University Press, 1972), 57.

121. Jameson, *Prison House of Language*, 58.

122. This is true inasmuch as the metaphorical effect depends on the juxtaposed terms maintaining their lexical meaning. Otherwise the tension between them would disappear and, with it, the metaphorical effect.

123. To the extent that comparison does not completely dissolve the forms of religious identity constructed in the first moment, this model of comparative theology need not entail what Patchen Markell, referring to the political theory of Ernesto Laclau, calls a political theory "with distinctly Penelopean rhythms," that is to say, a theory that posits the continual fixing and unfixing of identity. See Patchen Markell, *Bound by Recognition* (Princeton, N.J.: Princeton University Press, 2003), 23, 183–84.

124. Connolly, *Ethos of Pluralization*, xv–xix.

125. Clooney, *Hindu God, Christian God*, 11–12. A minor theme running throughout Clooney's book is a generally appreciative, but not naively uncritical, portrayal of the seventeenth-century Jesuit missionary Roberto De Nobili as a model of interreligious reasoning.

126. Clooney, *Hindu God, Christian God*, 165.

127. Smith, "'End' of Comparison," 239.

128. Smith, "'End' of Comparison," 241 n. 9.

129. I am indebted to Richard King (*Orientalism and Religion*, 125–28) for this interpretation of Otto's *Mysticism East and West* as a paradigmatic example of orientalist discourse. While King's interpretation forms the basis of my extended treatment of Otto in the next chapter, I will highlight certain aspects of Otto's text that reveal a more ambiguous relation to the orientalist tradition.

CHAPTER 4

Carl Schmidt, "Meister Eckhart: Ein Beitrag zur Geschichte der Theologie und Philosophie des Mittelalters," *Theologische Studien und Kritiken* 12 (1839): 733: "Er [der vollkommene Mensch] entfernt sich ganz von ihren Sitten und Regeln; sein Thun und Lassen ist ein ganz anderes; das Aeussere ist gleichgültig, denn es gehört der

Nichtigkeit an; alle Tugend- und Heil-mittel, deren die Menschen, die noch im Streben begriffen sind, bedürfen, haben für ihm keinen Werth mehr. . . ."

Rudolf Otto, *Mysticism East and West*, trans. Bertha L. Bracey and Richenda C. Payne (New York: Collier Books, 1962), 225.

1. Otto, *Mysticism East and West*, 14.
2. Otto, *Mysticism East and West*, 13–14, 183.
3. Otto, *Mysticism East and West*, 14.
4. Otto, *Mysticism East and West*, 186, 179; cf. *Vischnu-Nārāyaṇa: Texte zur indischen Gottesmystik* (Jena: Eugen Diederichs, 1923), 218. See also Friedrich Heiler, "Die Bedeutung Rudolf Ottos fuer die Vergleichende Religionsgeschichte," in *Religionswissenschaft in neuer Sicht* (Marburg: N. G. Elwert Verlag, 1951), 23.
5. Otto, *Mysticism East and West*, 185, 223; also 183, 204, 225; note the contradiction between these statements and those which state that differences in mystical doctrine are found within the same cultural context, e.g., p. 14.
6. Cf. Otto, *Vischnu-Nārāyaṇa*, 218: "Und diese Aufgabe wird nicht aufgehoben sondern kehrt in gesteigerter und verfeinerter Form wieder in den Fälle jener noch gesteigerten Homologien und parallelismen, die wir auf die 'Konvergenz der Typen' zurückführen wollten." ("And this task [of apologetics] is not removed, but rather returns in more elevated and refined form in the case of those still more striking homologies and parallels, which we would attribute to the 'convergence of types.'")
7. As suggested by its title, the point of departure of Otto's *India's Religion of Grace* is a striking parallel between forms of devotional Hinduism and Protestant Christianity, a parallel that would seem to challenge the latter's claim to uniqueness as an uncompromising religion of grace. Rudolf Otto, *India's Religion of Grace and Christianity Compared and Contrasted*, trans. Frank Hugh Foster (New York: MacMillan, 1930), 17–18, 65–66; cf. Otto, *Vischnu-Nārāyaṇa*, 4. A closer examination of this parallel between Christianity and Indian *bhakti* religion, however, reveals a qualitative distinction between the two (p. 100), namely, that while the latter revolves around the axis of the goal of liberation through the *ātman* (*ātma siddhi*), the controlling idea of the former is "idea of the Holy," with its emphasis on the consciousness of sin, the feeling of guilt and redemption (90–108; cf. 104: "Christianity is the religion of conscience [*Gewissenreligion*] per substantiam, bhakti-religion per accidens").
8. *Orientalism and Religion* (New York: Routledge, 1999), 127.
9. On the German Idealist philosophers' discovery of Meister Eckhart, see Ernst Benz, *Les Sources Mystiques de la Philosophie Romantique Allemande* (Paris: J. Vrin, 1968), esp. 11–17.
10. Ingeborg Degenhardt, *Studien zum Wandel des Eckhartbildes* (Leiden: E. J. Brill, 1967), 108–9.
11. Degenhardt, *Studien zum Wandel des Eckhartbildes*, 116; Benz, *Les Sources Mystiques*, 13–14.
12. Degenhardt, *Studien zum Wandel des Eckhartbildes*, 116.
13. Schmidt, "Meister Eckhart," 693–94 and passim.
14. Schmidt, "Meister Eckhart,"704.

15. Schmidt, "Meister Eckhart," 705.

16. Schmidt, "Meister Eckhart," 694. According to Schmidt's Hegelian interpretation of Eckhart, the latter taught that the world was eternal (see Schmidt, 69), a position for which he was censured, though not entirely fairly, in the 1329 Papal Bull *In agro dominico*. Eckhart's alleged teaching of the eternity of the world forms the second of the condemned articles set forth in the bull. See Edmund Colledge and Bernard McGinn, eds. *Meister Eckhart: The Essential Sermons, Commentaries, Treatises, and Defense* (Mahwah, NJ: Paulist Press, 1981) (henceforth cited as *Essential Eckhart*), 78. Schmidt apparently fails to recognize the significance of Eckhart's distinction between virtual existence and formal existence of created beings: "[The eternity of the world] concerns not only the ideal being of things in the eternal reason [of God], but the real, objective being in God's most proper essence, [thus] the effective identity of God and world" (p. 697: "Sie betrifft nicht bloss das ideale Seyn der Dinge in der ewigen Vernunft, sondern das reale, objective Seyn derselben in Gottes eigenstem Wesen, die wirkliche Identität Gottes under der Welt"). This failure can be partially excused by the unavailability of Eckhart's Latin corpus in which Eckhart's *inquantum* ("insofar as") principle is clearly stated. For a more recent interpretation similar to Schmidt's in this respect, see Joseph Bernhart, *Die Philosophische Mystik des Mittelalters* (Damstadt: Wissenschaftliche Buchgesellschaft 1967), 184.

17. Schmidt, "Meister Eckhart," 741.

18. Degenhardt, *Studien zum Wandel des Eckhartbildes*, 123.

19. Degenhardt, *Studien zum Wandel des Eckhartbildes*, 123.

20. Degenhardt, *Studien zum Wandel des Eckhartbildes*, 147.

21. Degenhardt, *Studien zum Wandel des Eckhartbildes*, 147.

22. Even Schmidt ("Meister Eckhart," 743) praises Eckhart for his independence from a degenerate tradition of scholasticism and casuistry.

23. Degenhardt, *Studien zum Wandel des Eckhartbildes*, 175–76.

24. Degenhardt, *Studien zum Wandel des Eckhartbildes*, 141. Predictably, the Romantic view of Eckhart as the "German genius" would later have great appeal for ideologues of National Socialism such as Alfred Rosenberg and Hermann Schwarz. See Toni Schaller, "Die Meister Eckhart-Forschung von der Jahrhundertwende bis zur Gegenwart," *Freiburger Zeitschrift für Philosophie und Theologie* 15 (1968): 409–11.

25. Degenhardt, *Studien zum Wandel des Eckhartbildes*, 145; Wilhelm Preger, *Geschichte der deutschen Mystik im Mittelalter* (Leipzig: Doerfling und Franke, 1874), 449; H. Martensen, *Meister Eckhart: Eine theologische Studie* (Hamburg: Friedrich Perthes, 1842), 111; cf. Degenhardt, *Studien zum Wandel des Eckhartbildes*, on Otto, 291–92.

26. E.g., Preger, *Geschichte der deutschen Mystik im Mittelalter*, 450–51; see also Otto, *Mysticism East and West*, 211: "One might be tempted to take the whole of Eckhart's teaching as nothing more than a doctrine of justification interpreted mystically." Cf. also Otto's essay, "Die schlichten Ausgänge bei Eckhart," in *Aufsätze das Numinose Betreffend* (Stuttgart: Friedrich Andreas Perthes, 1923), 94–107.

27. Generally speaking, however, Protestant attitudes toward Eckhart were ambivalent. Their ambivalence placed them in a position intermediate between, on the

one hand, Idealist philosophers who unreservedly extolled Eckhart as the father of German philosophy and, on the other, and Catholic theologians at the time, for whom the Meister's reputation as an iconoclast and proto-reformer understandably had little appeal (see Degenhardt, *Studien zum Wandel des Eckhartbildes*, 147–48). Later, with the aforementioned recovery of Eckhart's Latin works, which evidenced a closer relationship with the tradition, Catholic historians and theologians came to have a newfound, though generally ambivalent, appreciation of Eckhart.

28. See Degenhardt, *Studien zum Wandel des Eckhartbildes*, 150, 152.

29. See King, *Orientalism and Religion*, 126–27.

30. Otto, *Mysticism East and West*, 185, 136.

31. Otto, *Mysticism East and West*, 207.

32. S. R. Talghatti, "Advaita in Marathi," in R. Balasubramanian, ed., *Advaita Vedānta*, vol. 2, part 2 of *History of Science, Philosophy, and Culture in Indian Civilization* (New Delhi: Centre for Studies in Civilizations, 2000), 566.

33. Wilhelm Halbfass, *India and Europe: an Essay in Understanding* (Albany: State University of New York Press, 1988), 293.

34. Hans Rollman, "Rudolf Otto and India," *Religious Studies Review* 5:3 (July 1979): 199. See Otto's *India's Religion of Grace*, 32; also, Otto, *Vischnu-Nārāyaṇa*, 2, 5, 86.

35. As demonstrated by Richard King's analysis of Otto's text in *Orientalism and Religion*, 125–28.

36. King, *Orientalism and Religion*, 101–103.

37. Sheldon Pollock, "Deep Orientalism? Notes on Sanskrit and Power Beyond the Raj," in *Orientalism and the Postcolonial Predicament*, ed. Carol Breckenridge and Peter Van der Veer (Philadelphia: University of Pennsylvania Press, 1993), 101; King, *Orientalism and Religion*, 103–4.

38. Halbfass, *India and Europe*, 40.

39. Halbfass, *India and Europe*, 42. This Christian apologetic contrast between an original Hindu monotheism, on the one hand, and its degradation into a religion of idolatry and superstition, on the other, was later put to quite different purposes. Much to the disappointment of contemporary missionaries, this contrast formed the core of Ram Mohan Roy's program of Hindu reform, while in Europe the idea of a primeval religion of pure monotheism was exploited by the Deists in their polemic against the ritual, doctrinal, and sacerdotal aspects of traditional Christianity. In what Raymond Schwab describes as one of the most delightful ironies of the history of polemics, the allegedly venerable Indian document to which Voltaire appealed in his polemic against Christianity—namely, the spurious *Ezourvedam*, ostensibly a lost Veda that pitted a pure Vedic monotheism against Puranic polytheism and idolatry—most likely was originally, though unbeknownst to Voltaire, a tool of Jesuit propaganda designed to prepare Indians for Christian conversion. Raymond Schwab, *The Oriental Renaissance*, trans. Gene Patterson-Black and Victor Reinking (New York: Columbia University Press, 1984), 155; Halbfass, *India and Europe*, 58; also 46, 49.

40. As Bruce Lincoln shows, Jones's formulation of the Indo-European hypothesis had deep antecedents in a profoundly ambiguous, racially inflected

mythical discourse of European cultural origins. See Lincoln's *Theorizing Myth* (Chicago: University of Chicago Press, 1999), 76–100.

41. Since roughly the first third of the nineteenth century, the Indo-European problematic became intimately bound up with racial theories. The latter purported to provide an explanation for linguistic differences and patterns of development, while linguistic data, for its part, was used as evidence for those theories. This close association between linguistic science and racial ideology lent to the latter an aura of scientific legitimacy. See Ruth Römer, *Sprachwissenschaft und Rassenideologie in Deutschland* (Munich: Wilhelm Fink, 1985), 131–52.

42. Pollock, "Deep Orientalism," 82. On the competitive tendency among German intellectuals to set an idea of Germanic antiquity over against that of Rome, see Römer, *Sprachwissenschaft*, 98–99. The original linguistic theory was that the Indo-Aryans originated from Asia and later migrated westward toward Europe. Eventually, however, as race ideology increasingly influenced historical linguistics, the theory regarding the European and, more specifically, the Nordic origins of the Indo-Aryans gained currency, especially in Germany. Again, see Römer, *Sprachwissenschaft*, 69–71, 134 and passim.

43. Bruce Lincoln gives a lucid and erudite account of the historical formation of this discourse in his *Theorizing Myth*, 47–75; see esp. 74–75.

44. Cf. Pollock, "Deep Orientalism," 83: "The discourse on Aryanism... was, to a degree not often realized, available to the Germans already largely formulated for them at the hands of British scholarship by the middle of the nineteenth century."

45. Thomas R. Metcalf, *Ideologies of the Raj* (New York: Cambridge University Press, 1995), 83.

46. The classic example of this narrative of an original revelation followed by corruption and error is Friedrich Schlegel's seminal *Über die Sprache und Weisheit der Indier* [On the language and wisdom of the Indians], in *The Aesthetic and Miscellaneous Works of Friedrich von Schlegel*, trans. E. J. Millington (London: George Bell and Sons, 1889), 425–526. Schlegel's argument for the thesis of a primeval revelation in India rested on two premises. The first was that the highly inflected nature of the Sanskrit language evidences a high degree of intelligence and religious insight (pp. 454–57 and passim). The second was that the history of language reveals an entropic tendency for inflection to give way to the use of prepositions (p. 451), such that a language's degree of inflection is a mark of its antiquity. Sanskrit's almost perfectly preserved system of inflection—more perfect than even that of Greek or Latin (p. 445)—suggests that the highest intelligence was present at the very origin of language, an inference that could only be explained on the hypothesis of an original revelation. And yet, for Schlegel, writing as a recent convert to Catholicism, the divine truths enshrined in Sanskrit literature can be disentangled from the errors with which they had been adulterated only through the hermeneutic provided by Christianity (p. 518).

47. This audacious European claim to India's ancient past is evident in the tendency of a generation of European Indologists to isolate the Rig Veda—the earliest artifact of Aryan thought—from the later Hindu tradition. For scholars such as M. Müller, R. Roth, W. D. Whitney, and A. B. Keith, the Veda, "seems only to point

backwards to an Indo-European past and not forward to the Hindu context in which it came to stand as the substratum of a tradition of enormous complexity." Herman Tull, "F. Max Müller and A. B. Keith: 'Twaddle', the 'Stupid' Myth, and the Disease of Indology," *Numen* 38:1 (June 1991): 49.

48. F. Max Müller, *The Six Systems of Indian Philosophy* (New York: Longmans, Green, and Co., 1903), 115. On Müller's admiration for the Vedānta, see Johannes H. Voigt, *Max Mueller: The Man and His Ideas* (Calcutta: K. L. Mukhopadhyay, 1967), 32 and passim.

49. Ronald B. Inden, *Imagining India* (Bloomington: University of Indiana Press, 1990), esp. 101–8; King, *Orientalism and Religion*, esp. 118–42.

50. This representation of Indian religious thought is not, however, simply a matter of projection, as an unnuanced construal of Edward Said's "Orientalism" thesis might suggest. Rather, the hermeneutical relation here between East and West can be more accurately understood in terms of what Charles Hallisey terms "intercultural mimesis," that is, the process in which "aspects of a culture of a subjectified people influenced the investigator to represent that culture in a certain manner." Charles Hallisey, "Roads Taken and Not Taken in the Study of Theravāda Buddhism," in *Curators of the Buddha: The Study of Buddhism under Colonialism*, ed. Donald S. Lopez (Chicago: University of Chicago Press, 1995), 33. We can point to several aspects of the precolonial brahmanical tradition that would have influenced European scholars to attach particular importance to Śaṅkara and his tradition. First we should mention the significant institutional presence of the Śaṅkara tradition in the five religious centers or mathas in India with their respective spiritual heads or Śaṅkarācāryas, each of whom stands at the end of a lineage of teachers extending back, as tradition has it, to Śaṅkara himself. Correlated with this institutional expression of the Śaṅkara tradition is a body of hagiographical literature recounting Śaṅkara's *digvijaya* or conquest of rival teachings in the subcontinent. Another aspect of the brahmanical tradition that influenced Western scholars to privilege the Advaita school are the Sanskrit doxographies, or synoptic presentations of the various Indian philosophical schools, which often reflect an Advaita Vedānta perspective. The Advaita doxographies, the best known of which is Mādhava-Vidyāraṇya's *Sarvadarśanasaṃgraha*, present the Advaita school as the apex and fulfillment of the other philosophical systems. The often-uncritical reliance on this literature on the part of Western scholars, most notably the great German orientalist Paul Deussen, tended to validate and reinforce their prior predilections toward the Advaita school. Finally, we should mention the fact that the oldest extant commentary (*bhāṣya*) on Bādarāyaṇa's *Brahma-sūtras*—one of the foundational texts of Vedānta and indeed the most important—is Śaṅkara's *Brahmasūtra-Bhāṣya*. That virtually all subsequent commentators make reference to Śaṅkara's *Bhāṣya*—even those who disagree with his interpretation—enhances his stature as an authoritative interpreter of the Vedānta.

51. Thus Schlegel praises the doctrine of emanation in his *Über die Sprache und Weisheit der Indier*, while Deussen extols the doctrine of idealism.

52. G. W. F. Hegel, *On the Episode of the Mahābhārata known by the name Bhagavad-Gītā by Wilhelm von Humboldt*, ed. and trans. Herbert Herring (New Delhi:

Indian Council of Philosophical Research, 1995), 119–21; Ignatius Viyagappa, S.J., *G. W. F. Hegel's Concept of Indian Philosophy* (Rome: Universita Gregoriana Editrice, 1980), 126.

53. "...nur als die abstrakte Allgemeinheit, als bestimmungslose Substanz." Hegel, *On the Episode of the Mahābhārata*, 112–13.

54. Viyagappa, *G. W. F. Hegel's Concept*, 189.

55. "Abstraktion des Geistes." Halbfass, *India and Europe*, 92.

56. Hegel, *On the Episode of the Mahābhārata*, 104–5.

57. Hegel, *On the Episode of the Mahābhārata*, 64–65; cf. also G. W. F. Hegel, *Lectures on the Philosophy of Religion*, vol. 2, trans. E. B. Speirs and J. Burdon Sanderson (New York: Humanities Press, 1962), 34.

58. Viyagappa, *G. W. F. Hegel's Concept*, 212; Hegel, *Lectures on the Philosophy of Religion*, 45–47.

59. Paul Deussen, *The Philosophy of the Upanishads*, trans. A. S. Geden (New York: Dover Publications, 1966), 41–42, 226–27.

60. Deussen, *Philosophy*, 236–39 and passim.

61. S. Radhakrishnan, *The Hindu Way of Life* (London: George Allen & Unwin Ltd., 1961), 18.

62. Cited in Degenhardt, *Studien zum Wandel des Eckhartbildes*, 158.

63. An excellent example of this perennialist approach to Eckhart is a study by the Schopenhauerian Anton Jonas which enumerates allegedly exact parallels in the Meister's work for the key propositions of Schopenhauer's philosophy. Anton Jonas, "Der transcendentale Idealismus Arthur Schopenhauers und der Mysticismus des Meister Eckhart," *Philosophische Monatshefte*, bd. 2, ed. J Bergmann (Berlin: Nicholaische Verlagsbuchhandlung, 1868–69), 43–74, 161–96. So convinced was Jonas of the adventitious nature of the specifically Christian elements in Eckhart's thought that he felt entirely justified in disregarding whatever in the Meister's teaching was tied to specifically Christian dogma. See p. 196: "Ich habe geflissentlich bei der Darstellung der Eckhartschen Lehre alles übergangen, was an das specifisch christliche Dogma anbindet,...."

64. D. T. Suzuki, *Mysticism: Christian and Buddhist* (New York: Collier Books, 1962), 11.

65. The designation "mysticism of the ground" comes from Bernard McGinn, who argues that it is a more adequate designation for what is more conventionally referred to as "German mysticism." See, e.g., his *The Mystical Thought of Meister Eckhart* (New York: Crossroad, 2001), 35–38.

66. Paul Mommaers and Jan Van Bragt, *Mysticism: Buddhist and Christian* (New York: Crossroad, 1995), 30. The implication of Mommaers and Van Bragt's justification for their preference for Ruusbroec, namely, that Eckhart's mysticism can be disarticulated from basic Christian doctrines with relative ease, is highly questionable, as we shall see in later chapters.

Other examples of studies of comparative mysticism that prefer Ruusbroec to Eckhart as a representative of Christian mysticism are R. C. Zaehner, *Mysticism: Sacred and Profane* (Oxford: Oxford University Press, 1957); Michael Stoeber, *Theo-Monistic*

Mysticism (New York: St. Martin's Press, 1994). Cf. also C. Ullmann, *Reformers before the Reformation*, vol. 2, trans. Robert Menzies (Edinburgh: T&T Clark, 1855), 15–55.

67. We should note that Otto rejects the use of the term "pantheism" in connection with any form of mysticism, Eastern or Western. What is conventionally labeled panthesim, the belief that "God is the All," Otto terms "theopantism" (*Theopantismus*), which is diametrically opposed to pantheism proper, the belief that "The All is God." Having made this distinction, Otto can declare (*Vischnu-Nārāyaṇa*, 85) that "[t]here is no pantheism in India" ("In Indien gibt es Pantheismus überhaupt nicht"). In my exposition of Otto below, however, I will continue to use the term "pantheism" in the more imprecise, conventional sense of Eckhart's (and Śaṅkara's) critics, for this is precisely the interpretation that Otto is countering. Nevertheless, it is important to recognize that Otto, although he eventually associates Śaṅkara's mysticism with acosmism and quietism—two aspects of pantheism as understood by Eckhart's critics—would not use this term to describe Śaṅkara's teaching.

68. Otto, *Mysticism East and West*, 123.

69. Otto, *Mysticism East and West*, 30.

70. Otto, *Mysticism East and West*, 110–11. As we shall see in chapter 6 below, *māyā* is a term that carries less terminological weight in Śaṅkara than interpreters like Otto supposed. For a critique of Otto on this point, see Paul Hacker, "Westöstliche Mystik," in *Kleine Schriften*, ed. Lambert Schmithausen (Wiesbaden: Franz Steiner, 1978), 820.

71. Otto, *Mysticism East and West*, 98–100.

72. Otto, *Mysticism East and West*, 100.

73. Otto, *Mysticism East and West*, 127–28.

74. Otto, *Mysticism East and West*, 123–24.

75. Otto, *Mysticism East and West*, 127, 130, 133. In particular, Otto's observation anticipates the seminal research of Paul Hacker on the distinctive features of Śaṅkara's doctrine and terminology. See chapter 5 below.

76. Otto, *Mysticism East and West*, 127, 174–75.

77. Inasmuch as "Śaṅkara presupposes the whole realistic doctrine of creation." Otto, *Mysticism East and West*, 106.

78. Otto, *Mysticism East and West*, 137–40.

79. Otto, *Mysticism East and West*, 135, 185.

80. Otto, *Mysticism East and West*, 169.

81. Otto, *Mysticism East and West*, 140. Eckhart "is fundamentally a theist despite the highest flights of speculation, and is that neither by concession or exoterically" (p. 153).

82. Otto, *Mysticism East and West*, 185.

83. Otto, *Mysticism East and West*, 187; cf. p. 191, where Otto declares that Śaṅkara "doesn't know the living one."

84. Otto, *Mysticism East and West*, 54.

85. Otto, *Mysticism East and West*, 195.

86. Otto, *Mysticism East and West*, 196.

87. Degenhardt, *Studien zum Wandel des Eckhartbildes*, 138–41.

88. Otto, *Mysticism East and West*, 211; Part B, ch. 5, 211–16; cf. 221, 141. Elsewhere (*Aufsätze das Numinose Betreffend*, 106 n. 1), Otto suggests that Eckhart's true consanguinity lies not with Śaṅkara or Plotinus, but rather with Luther: "Man denke sich das 'in dem ich traut beschlossen bin' im Munde Plotinus oder Śankara's!—Zugleich denke man sich's im Munde Luthers, wo wahre Verwandtschaften sind und wo nicht."

89. Otto, *Mysticism East and West*, 203, 214; cf. also 72, 119, 188, 229. See p. 185: "His master, Thomas Aquinas, is much more abstract, in spite of his correct theism. In comparison with Eckhart, he is looking backward, summing up the results of a preceding period, but not opening up a new era; seriously striving to quadrate the circle, and to amalgamate his Christian heritage of tradition with the rationalism of the Aristotelian system."

90. From the perspective of this more specifically Protestant agenda, Otto's apologetic with Śaṅkara recalls the tradition of "Pagano-papist" apologetics, that is, the assimilation of certain features of the Catholic tradition—in this case, scholasticism—to "pagan" analogues with the aim of casting the former in a negative light. Otto's implicit assimilation of the scholastic nature of Śaṅkara's discourse to that of Aquinas serves as an excellent example of how, as Richard King (*Orientalism and Religion*, 125) puts it, "representations of India functioned as a screen on which European debates could be projected and played out."

91. Otto, *Mysticism East and West*, 135–36.

92. Otto, *Mysticism East and West*, 193; cf. *India's Religion of Grace*, 70.

93. Otto,*Mysticism East and West*, 193; on *līla*, cf. Zaehner, *Mysticism: Sacred and Profane*, 195–96.

94. Otto, *Mysticism East and West*, 187.

95. Otto, *Mysticism East and West*, 191.

96. Bernard McGinn, ed., *Meister Eckhart: Teacher and Preacher* (New York: Paulist Press, 1986), pr. 86, pp. 338–45. On Eckhart's interpretation of this sermon, see chapter 7 below.

97. Otto, *Mysticism East and West*, 194, 152.

98. It is tempting to correlate the two moments of Eckhart's mystical theology with the two parts of Otto's book. Following H. Martensen's (*Meister Eckhart*) admittedly tendentious suggestion that the moment of self-annihilation or breakthrough into the ground of God represents a kind of "night in which all cats are grey" in which the differences between Christian and non-Christian mysticism disappear, we might suppose that this moment corresponds to "Part A: Conformity," where the similarities between Śaṅkara and Eckhart prevail. "Part B: The Differences" would correspond to the moment of "outflow" or the "birth of the Son," in which the differences between the two masters come clearly into view.

99. This contrast between a monism that terminates in a state of divine quiet and a theistic mysticism that expresses itself in ethical action has continued to serve as the interpretive template for non-perennialist studies in comparative mysticism since Otto's. For example, it forms the basis of R. C. Zaehner's comparison of monistic and theistic mysticism in his book, *Mysticism, Sacred and Profane* (1957), a work that clearly belongs,

despite its inclusion of Islamic mysticism in the favored theistic category, to the tradition of Christian apologetics (Zaehner, xv). Zaehner's comparison of Advaita Vedānta and Christian mysticism assimilates Ruusbroec's polemic against nature mysticism to the structurally similar polemic that the great eleventh-century Hindu theist Rāmānuja leveled against Śaṅkara. Zaehner's appeal to Rāmānuja's tradition serves only to mask the ethnocentrism of the world-affirmation/world-denial schema underlying his comparison between theistic and monistic mysticism. It allows Zaehner to assert that the quarrel between theism and monism "cuts clean across the conventional distinctions of creeds" (Zaehner, 205). A similar effort to detach this schema from its orientalist origins can be found in Michael Stoeber's *Theo-Monistic Mysticism* (1994), a work that, in spite of its irenic tone and the nuanced and thoughtful nature of its comparative judgments, belongs to the apologetic tradition of Zaehner. For Stoeber, the categories of monistic and "theo-monistic" mysticism basically serve as Weberian ideal types, which, as in Zaehner's comparison, apply across cultural boundaries. Moreover, these categories, to the extent that they function as ideal types, allow Stoeber to deflect the brunt of the criticism of monistic mysticism away from actual monist mystics, who may only imperfectly conform to the type, onto the type itself. In this way he avoids some of the harshness of Zaehner's critique while still leaving its basic apologetic schema intact (see Stoeber, 96–97). The gap between the ideal type and its ostensible instances allows Stoeber to recognize certain ostensibly "non-theistic monistic mystics" (like Śaṅkara) who evidence lives of undeniable morality and exemplary piety as "anonymous theo-monists" (Stoeber, 98; cf. 49). When we recognize the genealogy of the ostensibly phenomenological distinction between monistic and theo-monistic mysticism in the tendentious apologetic dichotomy between world-affirmation and world-denial, however, the appeal to intra-cultural, indigenous parallels (Rāmānuja; Ruusbroec) and the conversion of cultural stereotypes into ideal types appear as little more than stratagems designed to reconcile a tendentious apologetic tradition with a modern sensitivity to ethnocentrism and a liberal distaste for polemics.

100. Otto, *Mysticism East and West*, 225.

101. Otto, *Mysticism East and West*, 235.

102. It is significant in this connection that both Zaehner and Stoeber, neither of whom share Otto's preoccupation with vindicating Eckhart from pantheism—both use Ruusbroec as the exemplar of Christian mysticism—fall back into the conventional pattern of interpreting Śaṅkara's mysticism as illusionistic pantheism. Thus Zaehner (*Mysticism*, 143) writes, "Those who are new to Śaṅkara's conception of māyā or 'illusion' seem to doubt whether he really means what he says. He does. What we call the phenomenal world he regards as illusion pure and simple, with neither more nor less objective existence than has the stuff of dreams." See also Stoeber, *Theo-Monistic Mysticism*, 47: "Īśvara, the personal deity, is, like any other phenomenon, simply a manifestation of māyā, another aspect of the non-Self, that illusory appearance which hides the Real."

103. See Rudolf Otto, "Parallelisms in the Development of Religion East and West," in *Transactions of the Asiatic Society of Japan* [Yokohama] 40 (1912): 154; cf. Otto, *Siddhānta des Rāmānuja* (Tübingen: J.C.B. Mohr, 1923), 176–77.

104. "So ist auch Mystik in dem eben gekennzeichneten Sinn *ein unverlierbares Erbteil des indogermanischen Geistes.*" J. W. Hauer, *Das Religiöse Artbild der Indogermenen und die Grundtypen der Indo-Arischen Religion* (Stuttgart: W. Kohlhammer, 1937), 93.

105. "Ich möchte an diesen Beispielen zeigen, wie gewisse Erkenntnisse und Einsichten, die in der ostindogermanischen Welt schon sehr früh auftauchen, in bestimmten Entwicklungsstufen auch in der westindogermanischen Welt sichtbar werden, und zwar nicht nur als Wirkung der allgemeinen Gesetzmässigkeit in der Welt des menschlichen Geistes, sondern in der besonderen Form, die sie in der indogermanischen Welt annehmen, aus der Gemeinsamkeit der Blut- und Geistesart." Hauer, *Das Religiöse Artbild*, xi.

106. Richard Schmidt, Review of J. W. Hauer, *Glaubensgeschichte der Indogermanen* (Stuttgart: W. Kohlhammer, 1937), *Orientalistische Literaturzeitung* 8/9 (1939): 548.

107. See John W. Harvey's Introduction to his translation of *The Idea of the Holy* (Oxford, 1958), xi.

108. Although, we should add, he does not disavow it, either. One must admit that the Indo-Germanic dimension of Otto's comparison adds, even if only implicitly, to the self-evidence of the choice of Eckhart and Śaṅkara as subjects of comparison, and thus ultimately to Otto's goal of establishing Eckhart as an appropriate representative of Christian mysticism.

109. Pollock ("Deep Orientalism," 79) gives succinct expression to the enigma of this gap between a scholar's personal politics, on the one hand, and the political character of the larger discourse to which he or she contributes, on the other, when he poses the following question: "How did even those whose overt politics seem to have had little to do with National Socialism come so readily to contribute to precisely the same discourse as officers in the SS?"
We might take the conspicuous title of Otto's 1932 book, *Gottheit und Gottheiten der Arier*, as a convenient symbol for his participation in German Indological discourse. The content of this book is actually more innocent than its title might suggest, however. It is essentially a phenomenology of the numinous (à la *The Idea of the Holy*), largely confined, apart from brief asides such as Otto's excursus on the parallel between Rudra and the Germanic god Wuotan (pp. 58–65), to Vedic materials. To the extent that the use of the term *Arier* is restricted to the ancient Vedic context, it has a measure of legitimacy, for, on the most basic, literal level, "*arya*" was simply the term the Vedic Indians used to refer to themselves. Nevertheless, the author cannot be completely absolved of responsibility for the obvious and far-reaching racial connotations the term had in 1932 Germany. By this time, the term *arisch*, originally a linguistic term, had became a predominantly racial designation. See Römer, *Sprachwissenschaft*, 125 and passim.

110. A revealing illustration of Otto's divergence from the contemporary discourse on Aryanism is the criticism offered by J. W. Hauer in his book, mentioned above, *Das religiöse Artbild der Indogermanen und die Grundtypen der Indo-Arischen Religion* (1937). Although Hauer's assessment Otto's *West-Östliche Mystik* is generally

quite positive, he questions Otto's argument that Eckhart's mysticism is grounded in simple Christian piety (Hauer, 111–12). Against what we have seen is the central thrust of Otto's project, Hauer insists that the underlying presupposition of the doctrine of justification, namely, that of a transcendent God standing over against a sinful and corrupt world, is a "Jewish Christian" conception that is very distant from the Indo-Germanic thought that is exemplified by Eckhart's mysticism (Hauer, 112, 113). In an extraordinary statement that reveals the extent to which Hauer separates Eckhart from the Jewish-Christian (read: Semitic) tradition and, concomitantly, Śaṅkara from the Indo-Germanic, Hauer asserts that "in many places Eckhart displays a much closer kinship to the Upaniṣads and especially the Bhagavad-Gītā than does Śaṅkara." (Hauer, 110) On this point, there could hardly be a sharper contrast between the interpretations of Hauer and Otto. The one seeks to establish Eckhart as a paradigmatic representative of Indo-Germanic religious thought; the other, of Christian spirituality.

111. In his interpretation of Eckhart, Otto emphasizes the distance separating the religious sensibility of Śaṅkara from that of Luther. See the passage quoted in n. 88 (*Aufsätze: Das Numinose Betreffend*, 106) in which Otto asserts that Eckhart's true kinship lies with Luther rather than with Plotinus or Śaṅkara.

112. See King's (*Orientalism and Religion*, 127) helpful table on p. 127, which lays out the various dimensions of Otto's East/West dichotomy. The incompatibility between Otto's Christian apologetic and Indo-German discourse is far from absolute, however. According to a racist construal of the Indo-European hypothesis, the allegedly degenerate character of contemporary Indian culture and society was the unfortunate result of an alleged influx of "nichtarischen" blood from India's native inhabitants. (The distinction between Indians and Indo-Germans naturally becomes even sharper with theories of the European, as opposed to Indic, origins of the original Indo-Aryans.) Thanks to this distinction between Indian and Indo-Aryan, the discourse on Aryanism was able to accommodate the orientalist dichotomy between world affirmation and world denial with ease. Thus, the original Aryan religion was world affirming; world denial only appears in the later, degenerate forms of Indian religion. These latter are, as Hauer (xii) puts it, "the result of a mixing of Aryan culture and Indian spirituality" (das Ergebnis einer Mischung von Ariertum und indischem Seelentum). On this point see Römer, *Sprachwissenschaft*, 83–84.

CHAPTER 5

Epigraph: *Mysticism East and West*, trans. Bertha L. Bracey and Richenda C. Payne (New York: Collier Books, 1962), 30.

1. As acknowledged, for example, by Paul Hacker, "Westöstliche Mystik," in *Kleine Schriften*, ed. Lambert Schmithausen (Wiesbaden: Franz Steiner, 1978), 821. See also Michael Comans's appreciative remarks on Otto's contribution to the study of the Indian master in *The Method of Early Advaita Vedānta* (Delhi: Motilal Banarsidass, 2000), 219.

2. Louis Dupré, *The Common Life* (New York: Crossroad, 1984), 24–25.

3. We should note that, given the standard interpretation of Advaita Vedānta concept of Brahman as an impersonal Absolute, the parallel with the Īśvara-Brahman distinction in Śaṅkara would tend to presuppose, and thereby favor, this second

interpretive possibility that Eckhart's Godhead lies beyond the Trinity. As we shall see, however, the parallel can be turned around to call into question that standard interpretation of Advaita.

4. Bernard McGinn, "The God beyond God: Theology and Mysticism in the Thought of Meister Eckhart," *Journal of Religion* 61:1 (Jan. 1981): 11–12; Edmund Colledge and Bernard McGinn, trans., *Meister Eckhart: The Essential Sermons, Commentaries, Treatises, and Defense* (New York: Paulist Press, 1981), 36–37 (hereafter cited as *Essential Eckhart*).

5. McGinn, "God beyond God," 11–12; cf. *Essential Eckhart*, 192. Other "orthodox" texts: M. O'C. Walshe, trans., *Meister Eckhart: German Sermons and Treatises* (London: Watkins, 1979–83), Sermons 22, 26, and 41. See disagreement between Reynolds and Schürmann on Sermon 26. P. L. Reynolds, "*Bullitio* and the God beyond God. Part II: Distinctionless Godhead and Trinitarian God," *New Blackfriars* 70:827 (May 1989): 238–39; Reiner Schürmann, *Meister Eckhart: Mystic and Philosopher* (Bloomington: Indiana University Press, 1978), 69–74. McGinn, *The Mystical Thought of Meister Eckhart* (New York: Crossroad, 2001)," 85–86, on Sermon 51.

6. *Essential Eckhart*, 181; cf. Dupré, *Common Life*, 25. Other "radical" texts: Sermons 48, 52, and 83.

7. Bernward Dietsche, "Der Seelengrund nach den deutschen und lateinischen Predigten," in *Meister Eckhart der Prediger*, ed. Udo M. Nix and Raphael Öchslin (Freiburg: Herder, 1960), 241.

8. Dietsche, "Der Seelengrund," 203, 207, 239–41.

9. Michael Sells, *Mystical Languages of Unsaying* (Chicago: University of Chicago Press, 1994), 12 and passim.

10. Although some have questioned whether the God beyond God theme that defines the apophatic model can be found in Eckhart's Latin works (Schürmann, *Meister Eckhart*, 116; Reynolds, "*Bullitio* and the God beyond God. Part I: The inner life of God" New Blackfriars 70:826 (April 1989): 177–80), I am persuaded by the analyses of scholars such as Dietsche, Ueda, and McGinn that the model can in fact be discerned in both the Latin treatises and the German sermons.

11. Heribert Fischer, Josef Koch, and Konrad Weiss, ed. and trans., *Magistri Echardi: Expositio Libri Exodi, Sermones et Lectiones super Ecclesiastici Cap. 25, Expositio Libri Sapientiae, Expositio Cantici Canticorum Cap. 1,6.* (Stuttgart: W. Kohlhammer, 1992), nos. 63–75 (hereafter cited as LW II); Bernard McGinn, ed., *Meister Eckhart: Teacher and Preacher* (New York: Paulist Press, 1986), 63–67 (hereafter cited as *Meister Eckhart:Teacher and Preacher*).

12. *Meister Eckhart: Teacher and Preacher*, 63. *Eckhart: Teacher and Preacher*, 63."

13. totaliter est ex parte intellectus accipientis et colligentis cognitionem talium ex creaturis et per creaturis (LW II, no. 64, lines 2–3). But see his qualification, which verges on a retraction, in no. 61: "However, distinct attributions of this kind are not in vain and false because they relate to something that is true and real in God." Trans. McGinn, *Meister Eckhart: Teacher and Preacher*, 64.

14. Thomas rejects Maimonides' teaching in STh 1.13.2; see J. Koch, "Meister Eckhart und die jüdische Religionsphilosophie des Mittelalters," *Jahresbericht der Schlesischen Gesellschaft für vaterländische Kultur 1927*, 100 (1928): 141.

15. The twenty-third article of *In agro dominico* (*Essential Eckhart*, 79). Koch ("Meister Eckhart," 147) asserts that the pope was justified in including the Maimonides quote in the articles of condemnation, for it crystallizes Eckhart's teaching on the absolute unity of God; indeed, Eckhart had made the rabbi's teaching his own (p. 148). We should note, however, that, as McGinn reminds us, these belong to the second category of articles that were merely suspect of heresy and potentially redeemable through qualification (*Meister Eckhart: Teacher and Preacher*, 19).

16. As Boethius puts it in a formulation cited by Eckhart (LW II, no. 75, lines 4–5), "essence preserves the unity, relation brings forth the trinity" (essentia continet unitatem, relatio multiplicat trinitatem).

17. See *Comm. Ex.*, no. 63: "Relation, even though it is an accident, still does not signify in the manner of an accident, because it does not do so as inhering in a subject or substance." (*Meister Eckhart: Teacher and Preacher*, 64; LW II, no. 63, lines 9–11: Relatio autem quamvis sit accidens, non tamen significat per modum accidentis, quia non [per] modum inhaerentis subiecto sive substantiae.

18. *Comm. Ex.*, no. 65: "Now in God Existence Itself is the same as the essence or substance, and therefore in him all the accidental categories are absorbed into the substance according to the genus and manner of predication which they receive from the subject and from their connection with the subject." (*Meister Eckhart: Teacher and Preacher*, 65; LW II, no. 65, lines 13–16: In deo autem idem est et hoc ipsum esse quod essentia sive substantia. Igitur omnia praedicamenta accidentalia in deo transeunt in substantiam secundum genus suum et modum praedicandi, quem sortiuntur a subiecto et ex habitudine ad subiectum. Here Eckhart appeals to the principle that accidental categories change into substance when applied to God. See STh 1.28.2: quidquid autem in rebus creatis habet esse accidentale secundum quod transfertur in Deum habet esse substantiale; nihil enim est in Deo ut accidens in subiecto, sed quidquid est in deo est eius essentia. (Cf. STh 1.28.1.)

19. LW II, 70.

20. Reynolds ("*Bullitio* and the God beyond God," 1:179, 180) argues that Eckhart's use of the qualifier "quasi" indicates a noncommittal attitude on Eckhart's part toward Gilbert's teaching, which he cites, moreover, only because it arises in the context of Thomas's discussion in STh 1.28.2.

21. To the extent that Eckhart regards substantia and essentia as fully equivalent terms (see LW II, no. 65, lines 13–14: In deo autem idem est et hoc ipsum esse quod *essentia sive substantia*, emphasis added), his assertion that relation does not pass into the substantia of God contradicts Thomas's assertion that relation in God is identical to God's essentia.)

The basis of Thomas' argument that the divine relations belong to God's nature or essence is precisely the *inesse* relation that real relations have in common with other accidents. By virtue of the principle that accidental categories change into substance when applied to God, "a relation really existing in God has the same being as the divine nature and is completely identical with it" (relatio realiter existens in Deo habet esse essentiae divinae idem omnino ei existens; Blackfriars trans. slightly modified). Here Aquinas recognizes two constituents of a real (as opposed to a merely logical) relation, namely its accidental mode of being (that is, its inherence in a subject) and its reference or being toward (*ad esse*) another relatum. For a lucid discussion of real relations in Thomas, see Mark G. Henninger, *Relations: Medieval Theories 1250–1325* (Oxford: Oxford University Press, 1989), 13–17; see also 4–6. In STh 1.28.2 Thomas says that Gilbert—and by implication Eckhart as well—erred in considering only the second of these constituents of a real relation. Aquinas's consideration of the first of these constituents—that which distinguishes real relations from logical ones—reflects the importance he attaches to the fact that relations in God are real and not merely logical. For in the preceding article (STh 1.28.1), he argues that relations in God must be real in order to avoid the Sabellian heresy. From this perspective we can appreciate the ambiguity in Eckhart's discussion of divine relations. On the one hand, to the extent that Eckhart assumes that relations in God are real and not logical (an acknowledgment of the reality of divine relations is implicit in his concession in no. 63 that such relations are accidents) he cannot be accused of falling into the Sabellian heresy. On the other hand, however, his failure to consider the accidental mode of being of divine relations implies a neglect of the significance of the specific difference between real and logical relations, and this neglect leads him to make statements that appear to subordinate the Trinity of Persons to the principle of divine unity.

22. Shizuteru Ueda, *Die Gottesgeburt in der Seele und der Durchbruch zur Gottheit* (Gütersloh: Mohn, 1965), 103–4. The citation is from the *Comm. Ex.*, no. 70; *Meister Eckhart: Teacher and Preacher*, 66. LW II, 73, lines 10–12: Et idea non eadem ratione simpliciter est deus pater et deus substantia, sed alia ratione est deus substantia et alia ratione etiam pater.

23. Ueda, *Die Gottesgeburt*, 104: "Zur Beziehungsloskeit zwischen 'substantia' und 'relatio' kommt in der Auffassung der 'relatio' noch ein Moment hinzu, das Eckhart zur Trennung von Gott und dem Wesen Gottes führt."

24. *Meister Eckhart: Teacher and Preacher*, 20.

25. Koch, "Meister Eckhart," 146; cf. 143.

26. Reynolds, "*Bullitio* and the God beyond God," 1:180.

27. P. L. Reynolds, "*Bullitio* and the God beyond God. Part II: Distinctionless Godhead and Trinitarian God," *New Blackfriars* 70:827 (May 1989): 236; cf. Reynolds, "*Bullitio* and the God beyond God," 1:169 and passim.

28. McGinn, *The Mystical Thought of Meister Eckhart* (New York: Crossroad, 2001), 38.

29. McGinn, *Mystical Thought of Meister Eckhart*, 42.

30. Benno Schmoldt, *Die deutsche Begriffssprache Meister Eckharts* (Hedelberg: Quelle & Meyer, 1954), 52.

31. McGinn, *Mystical Thought of Meister Eckhart*, 75.

32. *Meister Eckhart: Teacher and Preacher*, 315; cf. McGinn, *Mystical Thought of Meister Eckhart*, 42.

33. McGinn, *Mystical Thought of Meister Eckhart*, 42–43.

34. Schmoldt, *Die deutsche Begriffssprache Meister Eckharts*, 53–54 McGinn, *Mystical Thought of Meister Eckhart*, 41.

35. Sermon 15, *Essential Eckhart*, 192.

36. Dietsche, "Der Seelengrund," 204–5, 223, 238.

37. *Essential Eckhart,* 206.

38. *Essential Eckhart,* 206.

39. See Dietsche, "Der Seelengrund," 239, on how the apophatic model represents a transfer of a separation between the soul and its faculties, which separation is valid, to the divine realm, where the separation is more problematic.

40. "ez muoz in kosten alle sîn götlîche namen unde sîn persônlich eigenschaft,. . . ." Franz Pfeiffer, ed., *Meister Eckhart* (Leipzig, 1857), 46. Note Eckhart's use here of the metaphor of buying and selling (*koufmanschaft*) in reference to God. Cf. Sermon 1 (*Intravit Iesus in templum dei et ejiciebat omnes vendentes et ementes*); Frank J.Tobin, "Eckhart's Mystical Use of Language: The Contexts of *eigenschaft*," *Seminar* 8:3 (Oct. 1972): 162–63.

41. Colledge's trans. (*Essential Eckhart,* 181) with minor modifications.

42. Tobin, "Contexts of *eigenschaft*," 161.

43. Tobin, "Contexts of *eigenschaft*," 168 and passim; also Tobin, *Meister Eckhart: Thought and Language* (Philadelphia: University of Pennsylvania Press, 1986), 189.

44. On God's self-divestiture of properties, see also John D. Caputo, "Fundamental Themes in Eckhart's Mysticism," *The Thomist* 42 (1978): 213–14 and passim. Also Ueda, *Die Gottesgeburt,* 115, on the *abgescheidenheit gotes.*

45. Ueda, *Die Gottesgeburt,* 114; Caputo, "Fundamental Themes," 211. On the asymmetry between the *durchbruch* and the *ûzvluz,* see Caputo, 217; Reynolds, "*Bullitio* and the God beyond God," 2:242.

46. *Essential Eckhart,* 200; note that the quotations around the word "God" are not found in the original MHG text but are rather added by the translator.
When I subsisted in the ground, in the bottom, in the river and fount of Godhead, no one asked me where I was going or what I was doing: there was no one to ask me. When I flowed forth, all creatures said 'God.'" Trans. Walshe, *Meister Eckhart: German Sermons and Treatises,* 81. MHG text, Pfeiffer, *Meister Eckhart,* 181, lines 1–6: "Got der wirt dâ alle crêatûren. Gotes sprechen dâ gewirt got. dô ich stuont in dem grunt, in dem river und in der quelle der gotheit, dâ frâgte mich nieman, war ich wolte oder was ich tête: dâ enwas nieman, der mich frâgete. Dô ich flôz, dô sprâchen al crêatûren got."

47. *Essential Eckhart,* 203.

48. Walsh, *Meister Eckhart: German Sermons,* 80; Pf. LVI, Pfeiffer, *Meister Eckhart,* 180.

49. Sells, *Mystical Languages,* 1 (on quotation marks); 10 (on capitalization). Among modern translators of Eckhart into English, Blakney uses capitalization; Colledge and Walsh quotation marks.

50. Ueda, *Die Gottesgeburt,* 143.

51. Ueda, *Die Gottesgeburt,* 143: "Nur von Gott her kann der Urgrund als Gottes Wesen Gottheit genannt werden." See also, 114: "Gottheit jedoch ist Gott. . . . " Cf. Dietsche, "Der Seelengrund," 243 on Eckhart's use of the same terminology to refer to the deepest part of the soul in both the Trinitarian and apophatic models.

52. Sells, *Mystical Languages,* 161–62.

53. Sells, *Mystical Languages,* 3.

54. Sells, *Mystical Languages,* 9, 12.

55. Herbert Grundmann, "Die geschichtlichen Grundlagen der deutschen Mystik," in *Altdeutsche und Altniederländische Mystik*, ed. Kurt Ruh (Darmstadt: Wissenschaftliche Buchgesellschaft, 1964), 72–99. See also Kurt Ruh, "Meister Eckhart und die Spiritualität der Beginen," in *Kleine Schriften*, bd. 2, ed. Volker Mertens (Berlin: Walter de Gruyter, 1984), 331 and passim, for the historical observation that Eckhart's mature style of radical discourse coincides with an intense encounter with Beguine piety.

56. Grundmann, "Die geschichtlichen Grundlagen," 86. Ruh ("Meister Eckhart," 329 and passim), following Alois Haas, hypothesizes that Eckhart's mysticism represents an attempt to provide a theological basis for the Beguine themes of spiritual perfection, the love of God, and spiritual poverty.

57. For the characterization of Advaita as "theology" rather than "philosophy," see Clooney, *Theology after Vedānta* (Albany: State University of New York Press, 1993), 26–29 and passim.

58. For a good overview of contemporary Hindu attitudes toward classical Vedānta, see S. L. Malhotra, *Social and Political Orientations of Neo-Vedantism* (Delhi: S. Chand & Co., 1970).

59. Anantanand Rambachan, "Hierarchies in the Nature of God? Questioning the Saguna-Nirguna Distinction in Advaita Vedanta," *Hindu-Christian Studies Bulletin* 14 (2001): 18. See also Rambachan's *The Advaita Worldview* (Albany: State University of New York Press, 2006), 67–86 for a fuller discussion of this problem of interpretation in Advaita. A consideration of this part of Rambachan's critique of the "two Brahmans" understanding of Advaita—namely, that it implies a denigration of the world and the human beings in it—will have to await the next chapter, in which we examine the two paradigms theory from the cosmological, as opposed to the theological perspective.

60. Rambachan, "Hierarchies," 17.

61. Rambachan, "Hierarchies," 14; *Advaita Worldview*, 85.

62. G. A. Jacob, ed., *Vedāntasāra of Sadānanda* (Varanasi: Chaukhamba, 1893), iv–ix, esp. vii–ix; R. Otto, *Mysticism East and West*, 127; Paul Hacker, "Distinctive Features of the Doctrine and Terminology of Śaṅkara," in *Philology and Confrontation*, ed. Wilhelm Halbfass (Albany: State University of New York Press, 1995), 85–96.

63. For example, in BSBh 1.1.16, Śaṅkara speaks of the transmigrating self (*saṃsārī*) as that which is different from Īśvara (*īśvarād anyaḥ saṃsārī jīva ityarthaḥ*), where we would expect *paraṃ brahma* or *paramātman*, who are alone outside of saṃsāric existence (Jacob, *Vedāntasāra*, viii).

64. For example, in BSBh 1.2.1 Śaṅkara describes *paraṃ brahma* as the world cause (*jagatkāraṇam*), where one would expect, on the basis the distinction that Śaṅkara elsewhere makes, either *saguṇa* Brahman or Īśvara (Jacob, *Vedāntasāra*, ix). Similarly in BSBh 2.1.1 *paraṃ brahma* is used alongside of *īśvara* for that which is the material and efficient cause of the world, where one might expect Īśvara to be conjoined with the lower, *apara* or *saguṇa* Brahman (Hacker, "Distinctive Features," 91).

65. Hacker, "Distinctive Features," 94–95.

66. Jacob, *Vedāntasāra*, ix, vii.

67. Otto, *Mysticism East and West*, 140.

68. Hacker, "Distinctive Features," 94.

69. Hacker, "Distinctive Features," 95.

70. J. G. Suthren Hirst, *Śaṃkara's Advaita Vedānta: A Way of Teaching* (New York: Routledge, 2005), 116, 120, 122 and passim.

71. I focus primarily on the BSBh not only for pragmatic reasons (to render a potentially unwieldy comparison somewhat manageable), but also on principle. My decision to restrict my analysis to the BSBh, that is, to bracket a consideration of Śaṅkara's other authentic works, reflects a concern with a text rather than an author. In taking this approach to the study of Śaṅkara's tradition, I largely follow the lead of Francis Clooney, who argues persuasively for a textual, rather than philosophical, approach to Advaita (See *Theology after Vedānta*, 30–32, 214–15 n. 46.). Clooney (pp. 214–15) finds support for his decision to restrict his study of Advaita to the BSBh and its subcommentaries in the Vedāntic commentarial tradition itself, "which never refers to Śaṅkara's upaniṣadic commentaries to explain his UMS Bhāṣya [BSBh]." Unlike Clooney, however, I do not give the subcommentaries on the BSBh as much attention as Clooney's approach recommends, for in this chapter and the next I am concerned with highlighting the theological differences between Śaṅkara and the later Advaita tradition. In this respect, my decision largely to exclude the subcommentaries (and concomitantly, to include a consideration of the Bhedābheda tradition represented by Bhāskara's *Bhāṣya*) reflects the more revisionist, as opposed to traditionalist, approach to Śaṅkara in the present study.

72. But as Hajime Nakamura (*A History of Early Vedānta Philosophy*, part 1, trans. Trevor Leggett, Segaku Mayeda, Taitetz Unno, et al. [Delhi: Motilal Banarsidass, 1983], 406) notes, Bādarāyaṇa cannot be the author of the *Brahma-sūtra*, since the text attempts to lay claim to the authority of former's teaching, indicating its later date. See also 423, 519.

73. See Patrick Olivelle's Introduction to his translation of the Upaniṣads (*Upaniṣads* [New York: Oxford University Press, 1996], xxxvi–xxxvii). Any dates given for the Upaniṣads are extremely rough; as Olivelle notes, "any dating of these documents that attempts a precision closer than a few centuries is as stable as a house of cards" (xxxvi).

74. References to the *vṛttikāra/vṛttikṛt* can be found, e.g., in BSBh 1.1.19, 1.1.23, and 1.1.31. Vācaspati refers to the "Proto-commentator" only in his commentary on BSBh 1.1.31, albeit mentioning him there twice.

75. Daniel H. H. Ingalls, "Śaṅkara's Arguments Against the Buddhists," *Philosophy East and West* 3:4 (Jan. 1954): 293.

76. Ingalls, "Śaṅkara's Arguments against the Buddhists," 293; Paul Hacker, *Vivarta: Studien zur Geschichte der illusionistischen Kosmologie und Erkenntnistheorie der Indier* (Mainz: Akademie der Wissenschaften und der Literatur, 1953), 26; cf. Nakamura, *History of Early Vedānta Philosophy*, 458.

77. Ingalls, "Śaṅkara's Arguments against the Buddhists," 293–94; Hacker, *Vivarta*, 26.

78. Hacker, *Vivarta*, 26; 27; Ingalls, "Śaṅkara's Arguments against the Buddhists," 295 and passim.

79. Arguments against Bhedābhedavāda are more prevalent in Śaṅkara's Bṛhadāraṇyaka Upaniṣad commentary than in the BSBh. See Ingalls, "Śaṅkara's Arguments against the Buddhists," 294.

80. Klaus Rüping, *Philologische Untersuchungen zu den Brahmasūtra-Kommentaren des Śaṅkara und des Bhāskara* (Wiesbaden: Franz Steiner Verlag, 1977). Rüping shows that Bhāskara often deliberately and gratuitously alters the wording of the text he appropriates, a practice that rarely adds anything to the sense of the appropriated text, and indeed often compromises that sense, even when the original text supports his own arguments! (32, 39, 54 and passim). According to Rüping, this procedure indicates that the appropriated text lacked authoritative character for him, which is what we might expect if the text belonged to Śaṅkara, but not if it belonged to an earlier tradition as Ingalls supposed (32–33; cf. 39).

81. Rüping, *Philologische Untersuchungen*, 47.

82. Ingalls, "Śaṅkara's Arguments against the Buddhists," 291. Even if Rüping is correct in supposing that the textual parallels derive from little more than an act of selection on Bhāskara's part, this selection, at the very least, is indicative of a level of doctrinal consistency among these passages. In other words, Bhāskara's act of selection reflects the judgment that these particular passages cohere with Bhāskara's own Bhedābheda perspective, a perspective, incidentally, that is closer to that of the *Brahma-sūtra* than Śaṅkara's.

83. Nakamura, *History of Early Vedānta Philosophy*, 485, 486.

84. Nakamura, *History of Early Vedānta Philosophy*, 104–6, 429.

85. Olivelle, *Upaniṣads*, 190.

86. Śaṅkara's argument for the authority of the Upaniṣads was thus based on an uncompromising realism. Unlike the ritual portion of the Veda, the object grounding upaniṣadic authority is not subject to human choice and initiative. See Madeleine Biardeau, "Quelques Reflexions sur l'Apophatisme de la Śaṅkara," *Indo-Iranian Journal* 3:2 (1959): 87 and passim.

87. On the ascendancy of Sāṃkhya-Yoga in the speculative realm during the formative period of the Vedānta school, see, e.g., Hermann Jacobi, "Über das Verhältnis des Vedānta zum Sānkhya," in *Kleine Schriften*, teil 2, ed. Bernhard Kölver (Wiesbaden: Franz Steiner Verlag, 1970), 361–62.

88. Nakamura, *History of Early Vedānta Philosophy*, 472; cf. also 432, 301.

89. BSBh 1.1.5, J. L. Sasrti, ed. *Brahmasūtra-Śaṅkarabhāṣyam* (Delhi: Motilal Banarsidass, 1996), 101, lines 3–5 (hereafter references to the Sanskrit text of the BSBh will include the page number in the Sastri edition, with the lines following a colon, e.g., 101:3–5): tatra sāṃkhyāḥ pradhānaṃ triguṇam acetanaṃ jagataḥ kāraṇam iti manyamānā āhuḥ—yāni vedāntavākyāni sarvajñasya sarvaśakter brahmaṇo jagatkāraṇatvaṃ darśayantītyavocas tāni pradhānakāraṇapakṣe 'pi yojayituṃ śakyante. ("The Sāṃkhyas—they who maintain that the insentient *pradhāna* with its three qualities is the world-cause—say: 'Those upaniṣadic texts which you claim reveal the omniscient and omnipotent Brahman to be the world-cause also can be taken to support the view that *pradhāna* is the world-cause.' ")

90. Olivelle, *Upaniṣads*, 148.

91. BSBh 1.1.5, 102:8–9: api ca pradhānasyānekātmakasya pariṇāmasaṃbhavāt karanatvopapattir mṛdādivat, nāsaṃhatasyaikātmakasya brahmaṇa iti... ("Because modification is possible for a composite (*anekātmaka*) entity like *pradhāna*, [such an entity] can plausibly be understood as the [world-] cause, like clay and the like. This is not so for an entity like Brahman that is non-composite and one by nature.")

92. BSBh 1.1.5, 103:2–104:1 cites Chāndogya Upaniṣad (CAU) 6.2.3: tadaikṣata bahu syāṃ prajāyeyeti tattejo 'sṛjata. ("And it thought to itself: 'Let me become many. Let me propagate myself.' It emitted heat"; Olivelle, *Upaniṣads*, 149). Śaṅkara responds to the Sāṃkhya argument above simply by asserting that *pradhāna* is not mentioned in the upaniṣadic scriptures: BSBh 108:2–3: yadapyuktaṃ pradhānasyānekātmakatvān mṛdādivat kāraṇatvopapattir nāsaṃhatasya brahmaṇa iti, tatpradhānasyāśabdatvenaiva pratyuktam. ("What was stated above—namely, that *pradhāna* is more plausibly affirmed as the [world-] cause than the non-composite Brahman, on account of the former's composite nature, which likens it to [other material causes] such as clay—is refuted simply because *pradhāna* is not mentioned in the Upaniṣads.")

93. See BSBh 1.1.5, 106:3, where the text defends the appropriateness of ascribing agency (*kartṛtva*) to Brahman, in spite of the absence of an object in relation to which this activity can be directed, in the manner of the sun's intransitive activity of shining. asatyapi karmaṇi savitā prakāśata iti kartṛtvavyapadeśadarśanāt; evam asatyapi jñānakarmaṇi brahmaṇaḥ tad aikṣata iti kartṛtvavyapadeśopapatter na vaiṣamyam. ("When it is said that 'the sun shines,' agency is shown to exist even when there is no direct object of the action. Similarly, when [the Upaniṣad] says, 'It visualized,' agency is being ascribed to Brahman even though there is no object of the act of knowledge. Thus there is no fault [in ascribing omniscience to Brahman even before the creation].") On the active nature of Brahman as the world-cause, see also Nakamura, *History of Early Vedānta Philosophy*, 488.

94. Nakamura, *History of Early Vedānta Philosophy*, 487.

95. Not surpisingly, BSBh 1.1.5 uses Īśvara and Brahman interchangeably. See, e.g., BSBh 104:6–8: tena yaḥ sarvajñaḥ sarvavidyasya jñānamayaṃ tapaḥ, tasmādetadbrahma nāma rūpamannaṃ ca jāyate (Muṇḍaka Upaniṣad 1.1.9) ity evamādīny api sarvajñeśvarakāraṇaparāṇi vākyānyudāhartavyāni. ("He is omniscient and possesses all knowledge; his austerity consists of knowledge. From him this Brahman was born, as well as name, form, and food." [Muṇḍaka Upaniṣad 1.9] Texts such as this one which are chiefly concerned with establishing the omniscient Lord as the world-cause are to be cited.") Note that the BSBh identifies the unnamed subject of the Muṇḍaka text as Īśvara.

See also BSBh 1.1.11, 116:1–3, which equates Brahman and Īśvara in the context of a refutation of the Sāṃkhyan *pradhāna* as the world-cause: svaśabdenaiva ca sarvajña īśvaro jagataḥ kāraṇamiti śrūyate śvetāśvatarāṇāṃ mantropaniṣadi sarvajñamīśvaraṃ prakṛtya sa kāraṇaṃ karaṇādhipo na cāsya kaścijjanitā na cādhipaḥ iti. tasmātsarvajñaṃ brahma jagataḥ kāraṇaṃ, nācetanaṃ pradhānam anyad veti siddham. ("From the very word of scripture we hear that the omniscient Lord is the cause of the world. The verse Upaniṣad of Śvetāśvatara [states], in reference to the omniscient Lord, [that] 'He is the cause, the overlord of the overlord of the senses; he [himself] has neither parent nor overlord.' Therefore, it is established that the omniscient Brahman is the cause of the world, not insentient *pradhāna* or some other [principle].")

As Ingalls ("Bhāskara the Vedāntin," *Philosophy East and West* 17:1/4 [Jan.–Oct. 1967]: 63) notes, Bhāskara also used the terms Īśvara and Brahman interchangeably (along with paramātman), which is what we might expect, given that Bhāskara identifies with an earlier, pre-Śaṅkara interpretation of the Vedānta (see Ingalls, "Bhāskara the Vedāntin," 67).

96. Ingalls, "Śaṅkara's Arguments against the Buddhists," 294. The *jñāna-karma-samuccaya-vāda* was not narrowly restricted to Bhedābheda Vedānta, however. For example, Maṇḍana Miśra defends the doctrine in his *Brahmasiddhi*, which presents an Advaitic interpretation of Vedānta.

97. "For the Advaitin the abandonment of ritual activity is the very definition of renunciation." Patrick Olivelle, *Renunciation in Hinduism: A Medieval Debate*, vol. 1 (Vienna: Institut für Indologie der Universität Wien, 1986), 32.

98. Olivelle, *Renunciation in Hinduism*, 52–53.

99. Olivelle, *Renunciation in Hinduism*, 32.

100. Olivelle, *Renunciation in Hinduism*, 34–35.

101. Ingalls, "Śaṅkara's Arguments against the Buddhists," 294.

102. BSBh 374:6–7–375:1–2: ata ekatvaṃ nānātvaṃ cobhayamapi satyameva, yathā vṛkṣa ityekatvaṃ śākhā iti nānātvam,..., tatraikāṃśena jñānānmokṣavyavahāraḥ setsyati; nānātvāṃśena tu karmakāṇḍāśrayau laukikavaidikavyavahārau setsyata iti. ("Thus both multiplicity and unity are true, just as a tree is a unity qua 'tree' and a multiplicity with respect to its branches.... Thus the state of liberation can be realized from knowledge, by virtue of the aspect of unity [in Brahman], while both worldly and Vedic actions, which are based on the action portion of the Veda, are valid by virtue of the aspect of multiplicity [in Brahman].")

103. BSBh 376:3–4: ekatvamevaikaṃ pāramārthikaṃ darśayati; mithyājñānavijṛmbhitaṃ ca nānātvam. ("It is shown [in the simile of the thief in CAU 6.16] that unity alone is the highest truth, and that multiplicity appears from false cognition.")

104. BSBh 375:8–9: bādhite ca śārīrātmatve tadāśrayaḥ samastaḥ svābhāviko vyavahāro bādhito bhavati yatprasiddhaye nānātvāṃśo 'paro brahmaṇaḥ kalpyeta. ("When one is disabused of the belief that the self is the body, then the entire form of life based on that belief is invalidated; in order to justify this form of life [however], one imagines another aspect of Brahman, one of multiplicity.")

105. BSBh 381:5–6: brahmaprakaraṇe sarvadharmaviśeṣarahitabrahmadarśanād eva phalasiddhau satyāṃ,.... ("In the context of a discussion of Brahman, the result [liberation] is truly attained only from the realization of Brahman devoid of all distinctions and attributes,...)

106. BSBh 376:6–8: na cāsmindarśane jñānānmokṣa ityupapadyate, samyagjñānāpanodyasya kasyacinmithyājñānasya saṃsārakāraṇaatveṇānabhyupagam āt. ubhayasatyatāyāṃ hi kathamekatvajñānena nānātvajñānamapanudyata ity. ("According to the [Bhedābheda] viewpoint no liberation by means of knowledge is possible. For [this viewpoint] does not allow for any kind of false knowledge causing samsāric existence that could be dispelled by right knowledge. For if both [difference

and non-difference] were true, how could the knowledge of multiplicity be dispelled by a knowledge of unity?")

107. Wilhelm Halbfass, *Tradition and Reflection* (Albany: State University of New York Press, 1991), 150.

108. Halbfass, *Tradition and Reflection*, 226, 227.

109. BSBh 118:12–119:1–2: evamekamapi brahmāpekṣitopādhisaṃbadhaṃ nirastopādhisaṃbandhaṃ copāsyatvena jñeyatvena ca vedānteṣūpadiśyata iti. ("In this way the one Brahman is taught in the Upaniṣads either as connected with limiting adjuncts for the purposes of meditation, or as free of limiting adjuncts as something to be known.")

110. BSBh 4.3.14, 889:6–7: kiṃ dve brahmaṇī paramaparaṃ ceti? bāḍhaṃ dve etad vai satyakāma paraṃ cāparaṃ ca brahma yadoṃkāraḥ ityādidarśanāt. ("Are there then two Brahmans, a higher and a lower? Indeed there are two, for there are texts like [in Praśna Upaniṣad 5:2]: "That Brahman, Satyakāma, which is both higher and lower, is the sacred syllabile 'Oṃ.'").

111. Nakamura, *History of Early Vedānta Philosophy*, 520 and passim.

112. Śaṅkara presents his critique of Yoga in BSBh 2.13 (352:1) as an extension of his critique of Sāṃkhya. But as Halbfass (*Tradition and Reflection*, 226–27) notes, it reflects more his critique of the Mīmāṃsā understanding of works.

113. Hacker, "Distinctive Features," 95.

114. Both Govindānanda (BSBh 125:15) and Ānandagiri (BSBh 125:30) identify the *uttarapakṣa* as the "commentator" (*vṛtytikāra*). See also Ingalls, "Śaṅkara's Arguments against the Buddhists," 293 n. 5.

115. BSBh 127:16–128:1: na tvānandamayasya brahmatvam asti, priyaśirastvādibhir hetubhir ity avocāma. ("We say that the sheath consisting of bliss is not Brahman, because [the bliss sheath is spoken of] as having joy as its head, as well for other reasons.")

116. BSBh 124:7: so 'kāmayata bahu syāṃ prajāyeya. From Taittirīya Upaniṣad 2.6; see Olivelle, *Upaniṣads*, 187.

117. BSBh 124:6–8: ānandamayādhikāre ca so 'kāmayata bahu syāṃ prajāyeya iti kāmayitṛtvanirdeśān nānumānikam api sāṃkhyaparikalpitamacetanaṃ pradhānam ānandamayatvena kāraṇatvena vāpekṣitavyam. ("In the section on the blissful one, [Taittirīya 2.6 reads]: 'He desired, "Let me be many, let me be born."' From the mention of desire here, the insentient *pradhāna*, that inferred entity imagined by the Sāṃkhyas, is not to be relied upon [for an understanding] of either the blissful self or the world-cause.") Cf. Bhāskara's comment on this *sūtra*, Vindhyesvarī Prasāda Dvivedin, ed., *Brahmasūtrabhāṣyam Śri Bhāskarācāryaviracitam* (Varanasi: Chowkhamba, 1991), 26, lines 18–19 (hereafter, simply "Bhāskara," e.g., 26:18–19): kāmaścecchā cetanadharmo nācetanasya. ("Desire, or wish, is a property of a sentient being, not of an insentient one.")

118. BSBh 124:9–10: "īkṣater nāśabdam" (BS 1.1.5) iti nirākṛtamapi pradhānaṃ pūrvasūtrodāhṛtāṃ kāmayitṛtvaśrutim āśritya prasaṅgātpunarnirākriyate gatisāmānyaprapañcanāya. ("Having had recourse to the *śruti* text about the desiring one [Taittirīya 2.6] which was alluded to in the earlier *sūtra* [BS 1.1.5] to refute the

pradhāna principle, this [principle] is refuted once again, in passing, in order to elaborate upon the similarity in interpretive procedure.") Cf. Bhāskara, 26:18–19: gatisāmānyasamarthanāyedaṃ prasaṅgād uktam. ("This is mentioned incidentally in order to justify the similarity in procedure.")

119. See, e.g., BSBh 1.1.16, 123:3: itaścānandamayaḥ para evātmā netaraḥ, itara īśvarādanyaḥ saṃsārī jīva ityarthaḥ ("Therefore the [self] consisting of bliss is the highest self, not any other. What is 'other' [than the highest self] is that individual transmigrating soul which is different from the Lord"), a passage cited by Jacob (*Vedāntasāra*, viii). Also BSBh 1.1.17, 124:2–3: parameśvaras tv avidyākalpitāccharīrāt kartur bhaktur vijñānātmākhyād anyaḥ ("The highest Lord is different from the embodied self, the one that acts and experiences, which is imagined through ignorance and which is designated as the self constituted by the intellect."). Here the highest lord (*parameśvara*) is opposed to the previous sheaths, synecdochally represented by the penultimate self of intellect (*vijñānātmā*). When we compare this antithesis between *parameśvara* and the *vijñānātman*, on the one hand, to that between this latter and the highest self (*paramātmā*) expressed two lines later (BSBh 124:5: vijñānātmaparamātmabhedam), we can conclude that *parameśvara* = *paramātman*.

120. Jacobi ("Über das Verhältnis des Vedānta zum Sāṅkhya," 762) suggests that the polemic against Sāmkhya had become a matter of only theoretical interest for Śaṅkara and the later interpreters of Vedānta.

121. BSBh 118:10–12: evaṃ sadyomuktikāraṇam apy ātmajñānam upādiviśeṣa-dvā reṇopadiśyamānam apy avivakṣitopādhisaṃbandhaviśeṣaṃ parāparaviṣayatvena saṃdihyamānaṃ vākyagatiparyālocanayā nirṇetavyaṃ bhavati. ("Even though the knowledge of the Self, the immediate cause of liberation, is imparted with the help of particular conditioning factors, and even though the knowledge as determined by the conditioning factor is not what is intended to be imparted, still it is uncertain whether the object [of this knowledge] is the higher or lower [Brahman]. The issue is to be decided through a consideration of the [Vedāntic] sentences.")

122. BSBh 1.1.19, 127:3–6: api ca ānandamayasya brahmatve priyādyavayavatvena saviśeṣaṃ brahmābhyupagantavyam. nirviśeṣaṃ tu brahma vākyaśeṣe śrūyate, vāṅmanasayor agocaratvābhidhānāt. ("If the one consisting of bliss be Brahman, then it is [only] the conditioned Brahman consisting of parts such as joy, etc. that is to be admitted. However, at the end of the [Taittirīya] text the unqualified Brahman is disclosed, from the statement that [Brahman] is beyond speech and mind.")

123. Halbfass, *Tradition and Reflection*, 255; Andrew O. Fort, "Beyond Pleasure: Śaṅkara on Bliss," *Journal of Indian Philosophy* 16 (1988): 177; Hacker, "Distinctive Features," 86.

124. BSBh 128:4–5: na tasya brahmaviṣayatvam asti; vikārātmanām evānnamayādīnām anātmanām upasaṃkramitavyānāṃ pravāhe paṭhitatvāt. ("This [blissful self] does not refer to Brahman, because it is mentioned in the context of a series of changeable selves, beginning with the self consisting of food, none of which are the self proper.")

125. BSBh 381:9–10: kūtasthabrahmātmavādina ekatvaikāntyādīśitrīśitavyābhāva īśvarakāraṇapratijñāvirodha iti cet. ("Thanks to their insistence on the principle of

absolute unity, the proponents of a changeless Brahman, by effectively denying both the ruler and the ruled, contradict the proposition that the Lord is the world-cause.")

126. BSBh 381:11–382:1: nityaśuddhabuddhamuktasvarūpāt sarvajñāt sarvaśakter īśvarāj jagajjanisthitipralayā nācetanātpradhānād anyasmād vetyeṣo 'rthaḥ pratijñātaḥ 'janmādyasya yataḥ' iti. sā pratijñā tadavasthaiva na tadviruddho 'rthaḥ. ("It was asserted in BS 1.1.2, 'That from which the world has its origin, etc.,' that the origin, continuance, and dissolution of the world comes from the omniscient and omnipotent Lord, who is eternal, pure, intelligent, and free, and not the insentient *pradhāna* or anything else. This proposition still stands; it is not contradicted by [the teaching of absolute unity].")

127. BSBh 119:2–3: yacca gatisāmānyāt ityacetanakāraṇanirākaraṇam uktaṃ tadapi vākyāntarāṇi brahmaviṣayāṇi vyācakṣāṇena brahmaviparītakāraṇaniṣedhena prapañcyate. ("The refutation of an insentient world-cause which was stated in BS 1.1.10, "Because the knowledge is the same," is here being elaborated upon. This is done by rejecting any candidate for the world-cause opposed to Brahman, while at the same time elucidating other upaniṣadic statements that have Brahman as their object.")

128. Hacker, "Distinctive Features," 96.

CHAPTER 6

Epigraph: Ronald B. Inden, *Imagining India* (Bloomington: Indiana University Press, 1990), 108.

1. Pierre Bayle. *The Dictionary Historical and Critical of Mr. Peter Bayle*, 2nd ed., vol. 2 (London, 1735), 118.

2. brahma satyaṃ jagat mitthyam. J. G. Suthren Hirst, *Śaṃkara's Advaita Vedānta: A Way of Teaching* (New York: Routledge, 2005), 89.

3. Sermon 4; Bernard McGinn, ed., *Meister Eckhart: Teacher and Preacher* (New York: Paulist Press, 1986), 250 (hereafter cited as *Meister Eckhart:Teacher and Preacher*).

4. On the problematic of the relation between Vedānta and social action, see, e.g., S. L. Malhotra, *Social and Political Orientations of Neo-Vedantism* (Delhi: S. Chand & Co., 1970). But see Richard King, *Orientalism and Religion* (New York: Routledge, 1999), 133–35, on the role of Advaita Vedānta in mobilizing nationalist sentiment during the colonial period.

5. Specifically, Article 26. See Edmund Colledge and Bernard McGinn, trans., *Meister Eckhart: The Essential Sermons, Commentaries, Treatises, and Defense* (New York: Paulist Press, 1981), 80 (hereafter cited as *Essential Eckhart*).

6. For a thoughtful critique of Eckhart concerning Eckhart's appraisal of the historical dimension of human existence, see Zachary Hayes, "Response to Bernard McGinn," in *God and Creation: An Ecumenical Symposium*, ed. David Burrell and Bernard McGinn (Notre Dame: Notre Dame University Press, 1990), 220–25.

7. See John J. Thatamanil, *The Immanent Divine* (Minneapolis: Fortress Press, 2006), 4–6 and passim. Although Thatamanil's comparative study focuses on Paul Tillich as a dialogue partner with Śaṅkara, he occasionally mentions Eckhart as a Christian thinker "who kept alive a radical sense of divine presence" (p. 9).

8. In citing these two examples, I do not mean to suggest that there is any deeper similarity between them. The two works belong, in fact, to different genres: Thatamanil's is written primarily for a scholarly audience (although Thatamanil writes with admirable lucidity), Fox's for a popular one.

9. H. T. Colebrooke, *Essays on the History, Literature, and Religions of Ancient India*, vol. 1 (New Delhi: Cosmo Publications, 1977), 377.

10. Archibald Edward Gough, *The Philosophy of the Upanishads* (1882; reprint, Delhi: ESS Publications, 1975), 235–68. For Gough's ethnocentrism, see esp. pp. 267–68: "For these [ancient Indian sages] there is no quest of verity and of an active law of righteousness, but only a yearning after resolution into the fontal unity of undifferentiated being;...[The Upanishads] are the work of a rude age, a deteriorated race, and a barbarous and unprogressive community."

11. Gough, *Philosophy of the Upanishads*, 239. In general, I believe that Colebrooke's conclusions are more reliable than Gough's.

12. D. M. Datta, "Some Realistic Aspects of the Philosophy of Śaṃkara," *Recent Indian Philosophy*, vol. 1, ed. Kalidas Bhattacharya (Calcutta: Progressive Publishers, 1963), 241; Srinivasa Rao, "Two 'Myths' in Advaita," *Journal of Indian Philosophy* 24:3 (1996): 266–67, 271.

13. T. R. V. Murti, "The Two Definitions of Brahman in the Advaita," in *Studies in Indian Thought: Collected Papers of Prof. T. R. V. Murti*, ed. Harold G. Coward (Delhi: Motilal Banarsidass, 1983), 75–77 and passim.

14. In particular, his "Distinctive Features of the Doctrine and Terminology of Śaṅkara," in *Philology and Confrontation*, ed. Wilhelm Halbfass (Albany: State University of New York Press, 1995), 57–100.

15. Hacker, "Distinctive Features," 85; Hacker, *Upadeśasahasri: Unterweisung in der All-Einheits-Lehre der Indier* (Bonn, 1949), 19.

16. Paul Hacker, *Vivarta: Studien zur Geschichte der illusionistischen Kosmologie und Erkenntnistheorie der Indier* (Mainz: Akademie der Wissenschaften und der Literatur, 1953), 25–27. This second hypothesis, of course, forms the basic presupposition of the interpretation I have been presenting. Yet there is a subtle yet important distinction between Hacker's approach and mine: whereas I maintain that the realist elements that Śaṅkara appropriates from the earlier tradition form an integral part of his own thought, Hacker tends to assume that these appropriated elements are ultimately external to, and, accordingly, separable from, Śaṅkara's own purportedly illusionistic view.

17. See, e.g., "Śaṅkara the Yogin and Śaṅkara the Advaitin," in *Philology and Confrontation*, 121, 126–27.

18. Jonathan Bader (*Meditation in Śaṅkara's Vedānta* [New Delhi: Aditya Prakashan, 1990], 20, 23) suggests that such developmental theories have the character of myth, understood in the Lévi-Straussian sense of a logical model for overcoming contradiction.

19. Clooney, *Theology after Vedānta* (Albany: State University of New York Press, 1993), 14–32, esp. 31–32.

20. The definitive study on the development of the concept of *vivarta* in Indian philosophy, and in Advaita Vedānta in particular, remains Hacker's *Vivarta*. Among the texts, mentioned by Hacker, in which Śaṅkara anticipates the later distinction between *vivarta* and *pariṇāma* is one from BSBh 2.1.9. In this text Śaṅkara gives a concise statement of the thesis he will develop in BSBh 2.1.14: ananyatva 'pi kāryakāraṇayoḥ kāryasya kāraṇātmatvaṃ na tu kāraṇasya kāryātmatvaṃ ārambhanaśabdādibhyaḥ iti vakṣyāmaḥ. (BSBh 364:6–8; cf. Hacker, *Vivarta*, 28–29). "Even though there is a relation of non-difference between cause and effect, the effect has the nature of the cause, but the cause does not have the nature of the effect. [This thesis] we shall set forth in the 'ārambhanaśabdādibhyaḥ' sūtra [BS 2.1.14]." According to Hacker, this passage leads to the later Advaita doctrine that only the cause is real, or *satkāraṇavāda*, as distinct from the doctrine that the effect preexists in the cause, or *satkāryavāda*. The former corresponds to the later doctrine of *vivartavāda*, the latter to the doctrine of *pariṇāmavāda* (*Vivarta*, 29). The *vivarta/pariṇāma* distinction first becomes explicit in the work of the early thirteenth century Advaitin Prakāśātman, who makes conceptually explicit a distinction that his predecessor Padmapāda had already all but made on the level of usage. See Hacker, *Vivarta*, 36–41. Hacker suggests that early Advaitins like Śaṅkara and Sureśvara avoided the term *vivarta* (understood in a cosmogonic sense) because of its association with Bhartṛhari's school of "word-monism" (*śabdādvaita*; *Vivarta*, 52), if not with Buddhism as well (cf. *Vivarta*, 17).

21. The term *māyā* is not nearly as prominent in Śaṅkara as it is in later Advaita. Moreover, as Hacker observes, "the word *māyā* has for him hardly any terminological weight" ("Distinctive Features," 78).

22. BSBh 373:2: kāraṇāt paramārthato 'nanyatvaṃ vyatirekeṇābhāvaḥ kāryasya. ("From the standpoint of absolute truth, the effect is non-different from its cause [in the sense that] it does not exist apart [from its cause].")

23. BSBh 374:3: tasmādyathā ghaṭakarakādyākāśānāṃ mahākāśānanyatvaṃ,... ("It is like the spaces in puts and jugs, which are non-different from the great space [surrounding them].")

24. BSBh 374:3–5: yathā ca mṛgatṛṣṇikodakādīnām ūṣarādibhyo 'nanyatvaṃ dṛṣṭanaṣṭasvarūpatvāt svarūpeṇānupākhyatvāt, evam asya bhogyabhoktrādiprapañca-jātasya brahmavyatirekeṇābhava iti draṣṭavyam. ("As a mirage is not different from the desert [in which it appears], because it cannot be described in terms of its proper form, since that form is [constantly] appearing and disappearing, in this way it is shown that the variegated world [characterized by the duality] of experiencer and what is experienced does not exist apart from Brahman.")

25. To repeat what I said in the previous chapter apropos Ingalls's "Proto-commentator" thesis, I retain his terminology as a convenient shorthand to refer to an earlier interpretive tradition preserved in the BSBh, but without committing myself to his conclusion that there was a source-text, an earlier *Brahma-sūtra* commentary, that Bhāskara consulted independently of Śaṅkara. Klaus Rüping (*Philologische Untersuchungen zu den Brahmasūtra-Kommentaren des Śaṅkara und des Bhāskara* [Wiesbaden: Franz Steiner Verlag, 1977]) has shown, rather convincingly I believe, that

the former was drawing directly from Śaṅkara's text, not on another, no longer extant *Brahma-Sūtra* commentary. In light of Rüping's arguments, I am willing to concede that the earlier commentarial tradition may have been considerably less determinate than scholars like Ingalls or Hacker supposed (see Rüping, 46–47). Nevertheless, the designation of this earlier interpretive tradition as that of the "commentator" (*vṛttikāra*) or "Proto-commentator"—a designation that follows the native tradition—seems to me as good as any.

26. On the absence of the *saguṇa/nirguṇa* distinction in the Proto-commentator passages, see above, chapter 5. On the absence of the distinction between the two Brahmans in the *Brahma-sūtra*, see Hajime Nakamura, *A History of Early Vedānta Philosophy*, part 1, trans. Trevor Leggett, Segaku Mayeda, Taitetz Unno, et al. (Delhi: Motilal Banarsidass, 1983), 486–87, 488. In his meticulous study of the *Brahma-sūtra* (*A Critique of the Brahmasūtra (III.2.11–IV) with Reference to Śaṅkarācarya's Commentary*, 2 vols. [Baroda: Private Publication], 1956), P. M. Modi argues that Bādarāyaṇa does make a distinction between two aspects of Brahman, the one with form (*rūpavat; sākāra*), the other without (*arūpavat; nirākāra;* 2:xx–xxi and passim). And yet, "the *arūpavat* and the *rūpavat* do not correspond to the *nirguṇa* and *saguṇa* aspects of the Śaṅkara School" (2:3, 20; cf. 2: Introduction, 6). Unlike Śaṅkara's distinction between *saguṇa* and *nirguṇa* Brahman, there is no hierarchical relation between the two aspects of Brahman in the *Brahma-sūtra;* both are conducive to liberation (2:12–13, 18, 20, 54, and passim.). In Śaṅkara, by contrast, liberation results only from the realization of the higher, unqualified Brahman. See, e.g., BSBh 381:5–6: brahmaprakaraṇe sarvadharmaviśeṣarahitabrahmadarśanād eva phalasiddhau satyām,. . . ." ("In the context of Brahman, the fruit [liberation] is only attained from the realization of Brahman devoid of all attributes and distinctions.")

27. Mysore Hiriyanna, "What is Ananyatvam?" in *Festschrift Moriz Winternitz*, ed. Otto Stein and Wilhelm Gampert (Leipzig: Harrassowitz, 1933), 222.

28. Hiriyanna, "What is Ananyatvam?" 223.

29. In his *Ślokavarttika*, Pratyakṣavāda 114, Kumārila alludes to the view held by some that the "great universal" (*mahāsāmānya*) is the object of perception (mahāsāmanyam anyais tu dravyam sad iti cocyate). Maṇḍana, in his *Brahmasiddhi* (S. Kuppuswami Sastri, ed., *Brahmasiddhi of Maṇḍanamiśra* [1937; reprint, Delhi: Sri Satguru, 1984], 37, lines 21–22) similarly refers to "others well-versed in the knowledge of Brahman" who teach that Brahman has the form of the universal (ato 'nyair brahmavidyābhiyuktaiḥ sāmānyarūpaṃ brahma nirūpitam). Kumārila and Maṇḍana are possibly referring here to teachers associated with the school of Bhartṛhāri.

30. See Hugh Nicholson, "Apologetics and Philosophy in Maṇḍana Miśra's *Brahmasiddhi*," *Journal of Indian Philosophy* 30:6 (Dec. 2002): 575–96.

31. Hiriyanna, "What is Ananyatvam?" 224, 222–23.

32. As we shall see below, Bhāskara's commentary on BS 2.1.14 reflects this more modest interpretation of *ananyatva* as excluding absolute, but not relative difference between cause and effect. See Bhāskara, 93, where Bhāskara introduces the Vaiśeṣika view that there is an absolute difference between cause and effect

(kāryakāraṇayor atyantaṃ bhedaḥ) as the view against which the *ananyatvam sūtra* is directed.

33. kāryarūpeṇa nānātvam abhedaḥ kārāṇātmanā / hemātmanā yathābhedaḥ kuṇḍalādyātmanā bhidā (cited in Hiriyanna, "What is Ananyatvam?" 224). "Plurality [exists] by virtue of the form of the effect, non-difference by virtue of the nature of the cause; just as [with respect to objects of gold] there is non-difference by virtue of their nature as gold, difference by virtue of their nature as rings, etc."

34. Bhāskara, 17:3–5: na hyabhinnaṃ bhinnameva vā kvacit kenacid darśayituṃ śakyate. sattā-jñeyatva-dravyatvādi-sāmānyātmanā sarvam abhinnaṃ vyaktātmanā tu parasparavailakṣaṇyād bhinnam. (See trans. in Ingalls, "Bhāskara the Vedāntin," *Philosophy East and West* 17:1/4 (Jan.-Oct. 1967), 66.)

35. See Bhāskara, 98:31–99:2: bhedaṅgīkaraṇaṃ yuktaṃ prāmāṇyatulyatvāt pratyakṣādibhiśca bhedaḥ pratipādyate, na ca sattāmātraṃ pratyakṣasya viṣayaś cakṣurādīnāṃ niyatarūpādiviṣayatvāt. na ca sattā sadbhyo niṣkṛṣya kenacid indriyeṇa viṣayīkriyate, tasmāt sattaivāsiddhāntaviṣaya iti. ("An affirmation of difference is reasonable because [difference] is equally a matter of valid cognition; difference is established through perception and the like. Moreover, being alone is not the object of perception because the eyes [and other sense organs] have determinate forms as their object. Being is not abstracted from beings by some faculty to be made the object [of perception]. Therefore being alone is not the object of established truth.") Here Bhāskara appears to be consciously refuting Maṇḍana's arguments against difference as an object of perception. These can be found in the second chapter (Tarkakāṇḍa) of the latter's *Brahmasiddhi. Bhāskara*, 99:15–16: idam ca vaktavyaṃ sattājñānaṃ, tato vyatiriktam avyatiriktaṃ veti.

36. Ingalls, "Bhāskara the Vedāntin," 67.

37. Additional support for the hypothesis that Bhāskara's Bhedābheda interpretation of BS 2.1.14 is more faithful to Bādarāyaṇa is the former's mention of the Vaiśeṣika teaching of the absolute difference between cause and effect as the view against which the *sūtra* was primarily directed. This understanding of BS 2.1.14 places it in continuity with the other *sūtras* comprising the *adhikaraṇa* (BS 2.1.15–20), which are primarily concerned with a defense of the doctrine of *satkāryavāda* against the *asatkāryavāda* of the Vaiśeṣika.

38. A comparison with the corresponding *sūtra* in Bhāskara's commentary reveals a substantial, indeed at times verbatim, agreement. For a comparison of these two texts, see Rüping, *Philologische Untersuchungen*, 55–57. Compare BSBh 372:2–3: "*syāllokavaditi.* upapadyata evāyam *asmatpakṣe 'pi vibhāgaḥ* evaṃ *loke* dṛṣṭatvāt" to *Bhāskara*, 93:25–26: "*syāllokavat.* bhavet *asmatpakṣe 'py* anayor *vibhāgaḥ*, paramātmanā vā *vibhāgo loke*, ..." The similarity in wording, indicated by italics, is remarkable, but the differences are also significant. Note Bhāskara's addition of the phrase "paramātmanā vā [*sic*] vibhāgo" ("or the difference with the supreme *ātman*"). Bhāskara thus recognizes not only the distinction between the enjoyer and the enjoyed, but also the distinction of both from the supreme *ātman*, which Śaṅkara does not affirm. Also see n. 32 above.

Compare also BSBh 372:3–5: "tathāhi—*samudrād* udakātmano *'nanyatve 'pi* tadvīkīrāṇāṃ *phena*-vīcī-*taraṅga*-buddhudādī*nām* itaretara-*vibhāga* itaretarasaṃśleṣādil akṣaṇaśca vyavahāra upalabhyate," to *Bhāskara*, 26–27: "...*samudreṇa-ananyatve 'pi phenataraṅgādīnāṃ* parasparavibhāgo nābhedāpattir *evam* atrāpi syāt." Here note the distinction Bhāskara draws between *ananyatvam* and *abheda*. (Cf. the Bhāmatī on BSBh 2.1.14, BSBh 373:21: na khalv ananyatvam ity abhedaṃ brūmaḥ.)

39. BSBh 2.1.13, 372:1–2: tasmāt prasiddhasyāsya bhoktṛbhogyavibhāgasyābhāva-prasaṅgād ayuktam idaṃ brahmakāraṇatāvadhāraṇam iti. ("Therefore this affirmation about Brahman as cause is invalid, because it implies the non-existence of the well-known distinction between the enjoyer and the thing enjoyed.")

40. BSBh 371:1–2: yadyapi śrutiḥ pramāṇaṃ svaviṣaye bhavati tathāpi pramāṇāntareṇa viṣayāpahāre 'nyaparā bhavitum arhati. ("Even though scripture is a means of valid cognition for its own characteristic object, it nevertheless must be taken in another sense if it denies something [known] by means of another means of valid cognition.")

41. See, e.g., BSBh 1.4.27, where Śaṅkara, in affirming the material causality of Brahman against the objection that deliberative causality appears in the world only with efficient causes, asserts that arguments from common sense have no applicability.

42. BSBh 372:2–5; 6–7: upapadyate evāyam asmatpakṣe 'pi vibhāgaḥ evaṃ loke dṛṣṭatvāt. tathāhi—samudrādudakātmano ananyatve 'pi tadvikārāṇāṃ phenavīcītaraṅga-budbudādīnām itaretaravibhāga itaretarasaṃśleṣādilakṣaṇaśca vyavahāra upalabhyate. (Cf. Ānandagīri on saṃsleṣādi: viśleṣaparimāṇaviśeṣādi gṛhyate.)...evamihāpi naca bhoktṛbhogyayor itaretarabhāvāpattiḥ, na ca parasmādbrahmaṇo 'nyatvaṃ bhaviṣyati.)

43. As noted by Hacker, *Vivarta*, 27. Compare Śaṅkara here with Bhāskara (92:25–26): anayor [sc. bhoktṛbhogyayor] vibhāgaḥ paramātmanā ca [correction from the *vā* in the text—see Rüping, *Philologische Untersuchungen*, 56–57] vibhāga. ("There is difference between these two [i.e., the subject and object of experience], as well as [between these] and the highest self."). Rüping notes that Bhāskara, in asserting an element of difference between enjoyer/enjoyed and the highest self, departs from the ocean analogy, which speaks only of non-difference (*abheda, ananyatva*) between the ocean and its modifications (pp. 56–57). This observation supports his thesis that Śaṅkara's text, not Bhāskara's, is original (p. 57).

44. Hacker, *Upadeśasahasri*, 19; see also *Vivarta*, 27, where Hacker observes that the analogy of the ocean and waves is characteristic of Bhedābhedavāda. That the Bhedābheda *pūrvapakṣin* in BSBh 2.1.14, 374:7 appeals to the ocean analogy would tend to support this observation.

45. BSBh 393:2–3: naca prāṇabhedānāṃ prabhedavataḥ prāṇād ananyatvaṃ, samīraṇasvabhāvāviśeṣāt. evaṃ kāryasya kāraṇād ananyatvam. ("The different forms of the vital breath, though distinct from one another, are not different from the vital breath itself. Similarly, the effect [that is this entire world, *kṛtsnasya jagato*] is non-different from its cause, [namely, Brahman].")

46. In his study of the doctrine of the "two truths" in the Buddhist context, Matthew Kapstein suggests that "the two truths can plausibly be regarded as originally hermeneutical categories, and not a metaphysical doctrine at all." Kapstein, *Reason's Traces* (Boston: Wisdom Publications, 2001), 214. Kapstein's observation might be

relevant to an appreciation of the hemerneutical dimension of the two-truths doctrine in Śaṅkara, without denying, of course, its obvious, indeed predominant, metaphysical sense in the Advaita context.

47. One clear manifestation of the tension between the tradition of realist Vedānta and Śaṅkara's rereading thereof is Śaṅkara's repeated insistence that the upaniṣadic origination accounts are not to be taken literally, as disclosing information about primeval events, but are rather to be understood as indirect expressions of the teaching of the unity of Brahman and reality/self. In other words, Śaṅkara reads the cosmological texts of the Upaniṣads as *arthavādas*, secondary texts whose interpretation is determined by others that communicate the non-duality of self and Brahman more directly. Hirst, *Śaṃkara's Advaita Vedānta*, 97, 112; Hacker, "Distinctive Features," 77–78; A. J. Alston, *Śaṃkara on the Creation: A Śaṃkara Source-Book*, vol. 2 (London: Shanti Sadan, 1980), 187–98. Śaṅkara's appropriation of the realist tradition of Vedāntic cosmology thus exemplifies the way in which the appropriation of one discourse by another imparts a new intention to the former.

48. BSBh 2.1.18, 390:1–2: sator hi dvayoḥ saṃbandhaḥ saṃbhavati na sadasator asator vā.

49. One of the main arguments for the defense of *satkāryavāda* provides evidence for an affinity between this doctrine and a Bhedābheda understanding of the relation between cause and effect. This argument for the preexistence of the effect in the cause appeals to the fact that one can expect only certain effects to issue from certain causes. For example, curds are produced from milk and not from clay, and, conversely, a clay pot is produced from clay and not milk. See BSBh 2.1.18; Gambhirananda trans., *Brahma-Sūtra-Bhāṣya of Śrī Śaṅkarācārya* (Calcutta: Advaita Ashrama, 1993). It is to be observed that this argument presupposes the empirical differences between the things of the world. A denial of the reality of those differences undermines this argument and, in doing so, weakens the case for the doctrine of *satkāryavāda*.

50. On the importance of the doctrine of analogy for the interpretation of Eckhart, see, e.g., Dietmar Mieth, *Die Einheit von Vita Activa und Vita Contemplativa* (Regensburg: Friedrich Pustet, 1969), 134; Frank Tobin, *Meister Eckhart: Thought and Language* (Philadelphia: University of Pennsylvania Press, 1986), 43.

51. Tobin, *Meister Eckhart*, 35; Paul Ricoeur, *The Rule of Metaphor*, trans. Robert Czerny (Toronto: University of Toronto Press, 1977), 273.

52. This definition of homonym and the example comes from *Webster's Seventh New Collegiate Dictionary* (Springfield, Mass.: G. and C. Merriam Co., 1972), 399.

53. STh 1a.13.5, p. 62: Sed nullum nomen convenit Deo secundum illam rationem, secundum quam dicitur de creatura, ... All page references from Aquinas' *Summa* are from the Blackfriars edition: *Summae Theologiae: Latin Text and English Translation, Introductions, Notes, Appendices, and Glossaries* (Cambridge: Blackfriars, 1964–1981).

54. STh 1a.13.5, p. 64: Sed nec etiam pure aequivoce ut aliqui dixerunt. Quia secundum hoc ex creaturis nihil posset cognosci de Deo, nec demonstrari, ...

55. Ricoeur, *Rule of Metaphor*, 273.

56. STh 1a.13.5, p. 64: Quod quidem dupliciter contingit in nominibus: vel quia multa habent proportionem ad unum,..., vel ex eo quod unum habet proportionem ad alterum,....

57. STh 1a.13.6, p. 68: Dicendum quod in omnibus nominibus quae de pluribus analogice dicuntur, necesse est quod omnia dicantur per respectum ad unum.

58. STh 1a.13.6, p. 68: sicut sanum quod dicitur de animali, cadit in definitione sani quod dicitur de medicina, quae dicitur sana, inquantum causat sanitatem in animali; et in definitione sani quod dicitur de urina, quae dicitur sana inquantum est signum sanitaris animalis.

59. Blackfriars trans., p. 65; Latin text, STh 1a.13.5, p. 64: Et sic quidquid dicitur de Deo et creaturis, dicitur secundum quod est aliquis ordo creaturae ad Deum ut ad principium et causam, in qua praeexistunt excellenter omnes rerum perfectiones.

60. McGinn trans., *Meister Eckhart: Teacher and Preacher*, 178, but with modifications. Heribert Fischer, Josef Koch, and Konrad Weiss, ed. and trans., *Magistri Echardi: Expositio Libri Exodi, Sermones et Lectiones super Ecclesiastici Cap. 25, Expositio Libri Sapientiae, Expositio Cantici Canticorum Cap. 1,6.* (Stuttgart: W. Kohlhammer, 1992), 280 (hereafter cited as LW II): analoga vero non distinguuntur per res, sed nec per rerum differentias, sed per mods unius eiusdemque rei simpliciter. As Josef Koch ("Zur Analogielehre Meister Eckharts," in *Mélanges Offerts a Étienne Gilson* [Toronto: Pontifical Institute of Medieval Studies, 1959], 331) observes, an understanding of Eckhart's conception of analogy, as well as of its distinction from that of Thomas, depends on what he understands here by "modos." Reiner Schürmann, *Meister Eckhart: Mystic and Philosopher* (Bloomington: Indiana University Press, 1978), 178, captures the essential difference between Eckhart and Thomas's understanding of modus when he writes that for Eckhart, "attribution does not refer to a *mode of being* [as with Thomas], but to a *mode of presence* of that single being which is God" (Emphasis added).

61. McGinn, trans., *Meister Eckhart: Teacher and Preacher*, 178. LW II, 280–81: Verbi gratia: sanitas una eademque, quae est in animali, ipsa est, non alia, in diaeta et urina, ita quod sanitatis, ut sanitas, nihil prorsus est in diaeta et urina, non plus quam in lapide, sed hoc solo dicitur urina sana, quia significat illam sanitatem eandem numero quae est in animali, sicut circulus vinum, qui nihil vini in se habet.

62. Koch, "Zur Analogielehre Meister Eckharts," 334; Tobin, *Meister Eckhart*, 45.

63. *Meister Eckhart: Teacher and Preacher*, 178; *Comm. Ecc.* 53, LW II, 282: analogata nihil in se habent positive radicatum formae secundum quam analogantur.

64. McGinn trans., *Meister Eckhart: Teacher and Preacher*, 178. *Comm. Ecc.* 52, LW II, 281:... bonitas et iustitia et similia bonitatem suam habent totaliter ab aliquo extra, ad quod analogantur, deus scilicet.

65. For the metaphor of sunlight, see *Par. Gen.*, nos. 53–54 (*Essential Eckhart*, 101–2). See also *Comm. Jn.*, no. 70 (*Essential Eckhart*, 147).

66. Josef Koch, "Zur Analogielehre Meister Eckharts," 342, 345 and passim. For the metaphor of loan with respect to the effects of divine causality, see *Par. Gen.*, no. 25 (*Essential Eckhart*, 102–3); *Comm. Jn.*, no. 70 (*Essential Eckhart*, 148).

67. Koch, "Zur Analogielehre Meister Eckharts," 344.

68. Put differently, Thomas's "analogy of proportion" is integrally connected to an "existentialist" conception of being. See Vladimir Lossky, *Théologie Négative et Connaissance de Dieu chez Maître Eckhart* (Paris: J. Vrin, 1960), 309–11, 317, and passim.

69. Tobin, *Meister Eckhart*, 58.

70. Lossky argues that Eckhart's analogy of extrinsic attribution is integrally connected with an essentialist conception of divine being, that is to say, "a conception for which 'to be' signifies, above all, 'to be something.'" ("...l'Être divine est ici conçu par une pensée pour laquelle 'être' signifie, avant tout, 'être quelque chose,'" p. 309.) See *Théologie Négative*, 312, 314, 315–16, 318.

71. *Comm. Ex.*, no. 54, LW II, 58–60.

72. But it is important to point out that the relation between the divine being and Aristotelian substance is only analogous. If this point is lost sight of, then Eckhart's mystical theology appears as a pantheism of absolute substance akin to Spinoza's. See Lossky, *Théologie Négative*, 319.

73. *Comm. Ex.*, no. 54, *Meister Eckhart: Teacher and Preacher*, 60–61: "[The ten Aristotelian categories] are in no way the first ten beings, but one thing alone is being, namely, substance. Other things are not really beings, but are what belongs to a being (as *Metaphysics* Book 7 says); they are beings only analogically by relation to the one absolute being which is substance." LW II, 58, lines 7–10: Nequaquam prima decem entia, sed unum ens, substantia scilicet; reliqua vero non sunt entia, sed entis proprie—ex VII Metaphysicae—entia solum analogice ad unum ens absolute, quod est substantia. For a discussion of this section, see, once again, Lossky, *Théologie Négative*, 317, 318.

74. According to Lossky, the key to Thomas's recognition of the intrinsic being of accidents—and, by extension, created reality—is an ontology that places being (*esse*) at a more fundamental level than the Aristotelian substance. See Lossky, *Théologie Négative*, 317 and passim.

75. Mieth, *Die Einheit von Vita Activa*, 136.

76. Koch, "Zur Analogielehre Meister Eckharts," 345–47.

77. Koch, "Zur Analogielehre Meister Eckharts," 345, 347.

78. Lossky, *Théologie Négative*, 317; Koch, "Zur Analogielehre Meister Eckharts," 346.

79. Lossky, *Théologie Négative*, 334.

80. Cf. STh 1a.13.5, p. 64: Dicendum est igitur quod huiusmodi nomina dicuntur de deo et creaturis secundum analogiam, idest, proportionem.

81. Schürmann (*Meister Eckhart*, 176–80, 185–92) emphasizes the insufficiency of the theory of analogy to express Eckhart's understanding of being.

82. *Meister Eckhart: Teacher and Preacher*, 178.

83. My emphasis. Lossky, *Théologie Négative*, 314; cf. 297.

84. Maurice de Gandillac, "La 'Dialectique' de Maitre Eckhart," in *La Mystique Rhénane* (Paris: Presses Universitaires de France, 1963), 85; Lossky, *Théologie Négative*, 297.

85. Schürmann, *Meister Eckhart*, 178.

86. On analogy passing over into or implying a dialectic, see Lossky, *Théologie Négative*, 322; de Gandillac, "Dialectique," 83–86; McGinn, "Meister Eckhart on God as Absolute Unity," in Dominic J. O'Meara, ed. *Neoplatonism and Christian Thought* (Norfolk, VA: International Society for Neoplatonic Studies, 1982), 130–39; Alois M. Haas, "Seinsspekulation und Geschöpflichkeit in der Mystik Meister Eckharts," in *Sein und Nichts in der Abendländischen Mystik*, ed. Walter Strolz (Freiburg: Herder, 1984), 33–34.

87. Haas, "Seinsspekulation," 39–40.

88. From *Comm. Gen.*, no. 77. Tobin, *Meister Eckhart*, 60, trans. Latin text in LW I, 238: Nota quod omnis creatura duplex habet esse. Unum in causis suis originalibus, saltem in verbo dei; et hoc est esse firmum et stabilis; scitur enim res in suis causis. Aliud est esse rerum extra in rerum natura, quod habent res in forma propria. Primum est esse virtuale, secundum est esse formale, quod plerumque infirmum et variabile.

89. Schürmann, *Meister Eckhart*, 178.

90. See McGinn, "Meister Eckhart on God as Absolute Unity," 131.

91. On the reversibility of the predication of being, see McGinn, "Meister Eckhart on God as Absolute Unity," 132 passim; Lossky, *Théologie Négative*, 323, 315; Tobin, *Meister Eckhart*, 44–45. Thus by recognizing the reversible nature of the dialectical relation that obtains between God and creatures, one can reconcile Eckhart's statement in the *Parisian Questions* that God is properly described as an act of understanding above *esse* with the fundamental proposition of the Prologue to the *Work of Propositions* that "God is *esse*" (McGinn, *Essential Eckhart*, 32–33; Lossky, *Théologie Négative*, 320).

92. See, e.g., Sermon 71, *Meister Eckhart: Teacher and Preacher*, 323.

93. McGinn, "Meister Eckhart on God as Absolute Unity," 132.

94. McGinn, "Meister Eckhart on God as Absolute Unity," 133.

95. Hacker, "Distinctive Features," 78.

96. Hacker, "Distinctive Features," 68 and passim.

97. The abstract instrumental (*-tvena*, *-tayā*) in the nominal style of śāstric Sanskrit functions as a predicate nominative. Thus the sentence *hetuḥ liṅgatvena nibadhyate*, to cite an example given by Jacobi, could be translated as: "The reason (*hetuḥ*) is represented (*nibadhyate*) as the mark of the syllogism (*liṅgatvena*). See Hermann Jacobi, "Über den nominalen Stil des wissenschaftlichen Sanskrits," in *Kleine Schriften*, ed. Bernhard Kölver (Wiesbaden: Franz Steiner, 1970), 239–40.

98. This interpretive uncertainty is not really surprising given the formulaic nature of the phrase, for we would not expect an expression used formulaically to mesh perfectly with its context every time it is cited.

99. Hacker, "Distinctive Features," 72.

100. Alston, *Śaṃkara on the Creation*, 2:129–32.

101. Hirst, *Śaṃkara's Advaita Vedānta*, 100–1.

102. Hacker, "Distinctive Features," 72–73.

103. The "*tva*" suffix in the instrumental case denotes the respect in which *nāma-rūpe* is not to expressed. This usage is distinct from the abstractive sense of

tattva as "essence," the second, non-specific sense of the demonstrative "*tat*" that Hacker prefers. It would appear, then, that Hacker, in opting for the non-specific sense of *tattva*, tries to have the "*tva*" suffix perform double-duty.

104. Hacker's interpretation of the *anirvacanīya* formula is essentially descriptive, as this quote from his "Distinctive Features" article (p. 73) indicates: "In a broad sense the expression describes the unsteadiness of that about which one can never sat, 'It is that' or 'It is something else'. . . ."

105. For a regulative theory of doctrine, see, inter alia, Lindbeck, *The Nature of Doctrine* (Philadelphia: Westminster Press, 1984); Nicholas Lash, *Easter in Ordinary* (Charlottesville: University Press of Virginia, 1986).

106. BSBh. 2.1.26, 399:6–7: tataścaikadeśapariṇāmāsaṃbhavāt kṛtsnapariṇāmaprasaktau satyāṃ mūlocchedaḥ prasajyeta. ("Therefore, since it is impossible [for such a non-composite reality] to change only in one place, it follows that it must change completely. This implies an extermination [of that reality] to the very root.")

107. Gambhirananda trans., *Brahma-Sūtra-Bhāṣya*, 355; BSBh. 2.1.27, 401:1: yadi niravayavaṃ brahma syān naiva pariṇameta, kṛtsnam eva vā pariṇameta.

108. BSBh 401:9: pāramarthikena ca rūpena sarvavyavahārātītam apariṇatam avatiṣṭhate. ("In its true form [Brahman] abides unchanged and beyond all conventional forms of experience and action.")

109. avidyākalpitaḥ nāmarūpabhedaḥ.

110. The illusionism suggested by texts like BSBh 2.1.26–20 and 2.1.9 is the product of the tension between the twin claims of Brahman's material causality, on the one hand, and Brahman's impassability, on the other. The idea of the illusory nature of the world of name and form that is suggested by the images of the dream, the magical illusion, and the snake-rope appears as an almost ad hoc solution to the problem of reconciling these two claims. It is almost as if illusionism is the only available—and ultimately self-defeating—way to preserve the idea of Brahman's causality, much as a denial of intrinsic being to creatures was the only way save the Eckhartian analogy from equivocation.

111. The statement upon which Hacker bases his rejection of the *tattvānyatvābhyām anirvacanīya* formula's reference to Brahman, namely, the statement that "[t]he omniscient Lord is different from both [name and form]" (tābhyām anyaḥ sarvajña īśvaraḥ) in BSBh 2.1.14 (382:4), simply expresses this side of the formula. In the immediately preceding sentence, Śaṅkara refers to name and form as Īśvara's power of *māyā* (*māyāśakti*). It is entirely natural for him at this point to stress the difference between Īśvara and his māyic creation along the same lines as his illustration that the *māyin* is not affected by his *māyā* in BSBh 2.1.9 and 2.1.28.

112. Recall also that 2.1.9, a "māyic" text, makes an explicit allusion to BS 2.1.14.

113. One indication of Śaṅkara and Eckhart's shared commitment to a concept of virtual being is that both masters were criticized in their respective contexts for denying the doctrine of creation. Śaṅkara, for his part, was criticized by Bhāskara for denying creation and therefore effectively teaching the Mīmāṃsā doctrine of the

eternality of the world. See Bhāskara, 98:18–19: sargānabhyupagame viyadādi sarvaṃ nityaṃ mīmāṃsakānām iva prasajyate. ("It follows from this [failure] to acknowledge creation that this entire [world], starting with the ether, is eternal, just as it is for the Mīmāṃsakas.") Similarly, but with even less justification, the Papal Bull *In agro dominico*, in its second article, condemned Eckhart for the teaching, heretical in a Christian context, that the world existed from eternity. This charge exemplifies Michael Sells's observation that Eckhart's inquisitors lacked an appreciation for the dialectical nature of the Meister's thought (*Mystical Languages of Unsaying* [Chicago: University of Chicago Press, 1994], 12; 178).

114. BSBh 385:4–5: yatkāraṇaṃ prāgutpatteḥ kāraṇātmanaiva kāraṇe sattvam avarakālīnasya kāryasya śrūyate. ("The existence of the subsequent effect in the cause, as identical with the cause, before creation is taught in the Upaniṣads.")

115. BSBh 385:8–9: yathā ca kāraṇaṃ brahma triṣu kāleṣu sattvaṃ na vyabhicaraty evaṃ kāryam api jagattriṣu kāleṣu sattvaṃ na vyabhicarati. This passage could be taken to support Bhāskara's observation that Śaṅkara's innovative reading of the *ananyatvam sūtra* implies a denial of creation coinciding with the Pūrva mīmāṃsā doctrine of the eternality of the world.

116. BSBh 385:9–10: ekaṃ ca punaḥ sattvamato 'py ananyatvaṃ kāraṇāt kāryasya.

117. The problematic of *satkāryavāda* and *asatkāryavāda* can be traced to the enigmatic Nāsadīya hymn of the Rig Veda (RV 10:129). See Joel P. Brereton, "Edifying Puzzlement: Rgveda 10.129 and the Uses of Enigma," *Journal of the American Oriental Society* 119 (1999): 248–60.

118. BSBh 386:5: vyākṛtanāmarūpatvād dharmād avyakṛtanāmarūpatvaṃ dharmāntaraṃ. . . .

119. BSBh 386:5–6: . . . tena dharmāntareṇāyam asadvyapadeśaḥ prāgutpatteḥ sata eva kāryasya kāraṇarūpeṇānanyasya.

120. BSBh 386:11: nāmarūpavyākṛtaṃ hi vastu sacchabdārhaṃ loke prasiddham. ("For what is manifest through name and form is established in the world as what is real, deserving the name being.")

121. BSBh 386:11–12: ataḥ prāṅnāmarūpavyākaraṇād asad ivāsīd ity upacaryate. ("Therefore [this world] is spoken of, in a figurative sense, as if non-existent before its development into name and form.")

122. McGinn, "Meister Eckhart on God as Absolute Unity," 132; Lossky, *Théologie Négative*, 315, 322–23.

123. Such a perspective is suggested by Śaṅkara's statements elsewhere that Brahman is beyond all class concepts or categories, including being (*sat*). See, e.g., *Gītā-Bhāṣya*, 13:12 (GBh. 434: 5–6): na tu brahma jātimat, ato na sadādiśabdavācyam. ("But Brahman does not belong to any class; hence it is not to be expressed in words such as being.")

124. Hirst, *Śaṃkara's Advaita Vedānta*, 92; cf. 102.

125. "Śaṅkara presupposes the whole realistic doctrine of creation, and presents it over and over again in whole and in part." Otto, *Mysticism East and West*, 106.

CHAPTER 7

Swami Gambhirananda, trans., *Eight Upaniṣads*, vol. 2 (Calcutta: Advaita Ashrama, 1996), 16–17 (commentary on Aitareya Upaniṣad 1.1).

BSBh 83:4–6.

Bernard McGinn, ed., *Meister Eckhart: Teacher and Preacher* (New York: Paulist Press, 1986), 278 (hereafter cited as *Meister Eckhart : Teacher and Preacher*). From Sermon 16b: "*Quasi vas auri solidum ornatum omni lapide pretioso.*"

1. Edmund Colledge and Bernard McGinn, trans., *Meister Eckhart: The Essential Sermons, Commentaries, Treatises, and Defense* (New York: Paulist Press, 1981), 183–84 (hereafter cited as *Essential Eckhart*). From Sermon 5b: "*In hoc apparuit charitas dei in nobis.*"

2. *Mysticism East and West*, trans. Bertha L. Bracey and Richenda C. Payne (New York: Collier Books, 1962), 225.

3. *Meister Eckhart: Teacher and Preacher*, 278. From Sermon 16b: "*Quasi vas auri solidum ornatum omni lapide pretioso.*"

4. *Meister Eckhart: Teacher and Preacher*, 240. From Sermon 1: "*Intravit Jesus in templum et coepit eicere vendentes et ementes.*"

5. Herbert Grundmann, "Die Geschichtlichen Grundlagen der deutschen Mystik," in *Altdeutsche und Altniederländische Mystic*, ed. Kurt Ruh (Darmstadt: Wissenschaftliche Buchgesellschaft, 1964), 94.

6. *Comm. Ex.*, no. 247; *Meister Eckhart: Teacher and Preacher*, 120.

7. *Essential Eckhart*, 185.

8. Grundmann, "Die geschichtlichen Grundlagen." To be more precise, it reflects the influence of a larger movement of religious women in the twelfth and thirteenth centuries, a movement of which the Beguines were just one part, although arguably the most directly relevant to Eckhart and the development of "German mysticism." See Bernard McGinn, "Introduction," in *Meister Eckhart and the Beguine Mystics*, ed. Bernard McGinn (New York: Continuum, 1997), 2–3.

9. On the relation between Eckhart and Porete, see, e.g., Kurt Ruh, "Meister Eckhart und die Spiritualität der Beginen," in *Kleine Schriften*, Bd. 2, ed. Volker Mertens (Berlin: Walter de Gruyter, 1984), 333–35; Maria Lichtmann, "Marguerite Porete and Meister Eckhart: *The Mirror of Simple Souls* Mirrored," in McGinn, *Meister Eckhart and the Beguine Mystics*, 84–85 and passim.

10. *In agro dominico*, article no. 8, *Essential Eckhart*, 78.

11. Herbert Grundmann, *Religious Movements of the Middle Ages*, trans. Steven Rowan (Notre Dame: University of Notre Dame Press, 1995), 147.

12. Grundmann, *Religious Movements*, 157.

13. Ruh, "Meister Eckhart," 329.

14. Ruh, "Meister Eckhart,"329; Grundmann, "Die geschichtlichen Grundlagen," 97–98.

15. This despite the fact that, as McGinn (*The Harvest of Mysticism in Medieval Germany* [New York: Crossroad, 2005], 191) notes, the phrase itself never appears in this sermon.

16. "Marthâ was sô weselich, daz sie ir gewerp niht enhinderte, werk und gewerp leitte sie ze êwiger saelde." *Lectura Eckhardi: Predigten Meister Eckharts von*

Fachgelehrten gelesen und gedeutet, ed. Georg Steer and Loris Sturlese (Stuttgart: Kohlhammer, 1998), 152 (par. 21). See Dietmar Mieth's translation on facing page, 153; cf. also 148–149 (par. 18).

17. John D. Caputo, "Fundamental Themes in Meister Eckhart's Mysticism," *The Thomist* 42 (1978): 204.

18. "Marthâ vorhte, daz ir swester behaftete in dem luste und in der süeze, und begerte, daz si würde als si." *Lectura Eckhardi*, 148–149 (par. 18); cf. also 142–143 (par. 7), cited below.

19. Martha's willingness to work would distinguish her as "good Beguine," as opposed to an undisciplined "bad Beguine" who wanders through the towns, irresponsibly living off of alms. See Grundmann, *Religious Movements*, 147; cf. 141.

20. Meister Eckhart: *Teacher and Preacher*, 339. "Dâ von sprach Marthâ. "herre, heiz sie ûfstân," wan si vorhte, daz si blibe in dem luste und niht vürbaz enkaeme." *Lectura Eckhardi*, 142 (par. 7).

21. "Diz wort ensprach Kristus niht ze Marthen in einer strâfenden wîse, mêr: er antwurte ir und gap ir trôst, daz Marîâ werden sölte als si begerte." *Lectura Eckhardi*, 142-143 (par. 8).

22. Dietmar Mieth, *Die Einheit von Vita Activa und Vita Contemplativa* (Regensberg: Friedrich Pustet, 1969), 189; cf. *Lectura Eckhardi*, 152–153 (par. 21): "Marîâ was ê Marthâ, ê si Marîâ würde."

23. *Essential Eckhart*, 178; Mieth, *Die Einheit*, 155.

24. Mieth, *Die Einheit*, 203. See *Lectura Eckhardi*, 144–145: "An dem êrsten, dô er sprach Marthâ, dô bewîsete er ir volkommenheit zîtlîcher werke. Ze dem andern mâle, dô er sprach Marthâ, dô bewîsete er, allez, daz dâ hœret ze êwiger sælde, daz ir des niht enbræste." ("The first time he said, "Martha," he testifies to her perfection in temporal works. The second time he said, "Martha," he testifies that she lacks nothing that belongs to eternal happiness.") Here I follow Mieth's German translation.

25. More literally, "to works practiced from without, in works of virtue" (*Lectura Eckhardi*, 144: Werk ist, sô man sich üebet von ûzen an werken der tugende, . . .).

26. ". . ., aber gewerbe ist, sô man sich mit redelîcher bescheidenheit üebet von innen." *Lectura Eckhardi*, 144/145; cf. *Meister Eckhart: Teacher and Preacher*, 340. I am inclined to follow Frank Tobin and Bernard McGinn (See *Meister Eckhart: Teacher and Preacher*, 145 n. 6) in interpreting "*werc*" more generally to refer to an outward work of virtue, whether accompanied by a worldly motivation or not. This interpretation contrasts with that of Dietmar Mieth, who appears to understand *werc* in a more restricted sense to refer to works motivated by worldly preoccupations, and thus standing in contrast with divinely motivated activity or *gewerbe*. See Mieth, *Die Einheit*, 204; cf. 155.

27. Mieth, *Die Einheit*, 227.

28. Mieth, *Die Einheit*, 230.

29. Mieth, *Die Einheit*, 197–98.

30. Mieth, *Die Einheit*, 231.

31. Mieth, *Die Einheit*, 232.

32. On the "everydayness" of Eckhart's conception of the spiritual life, see, e.g., Sermon 5b, "*In hoc apparuit charitas dei in nobis*," *Essential Eckhart*, 183: "When people

think that they are acquiring more of God in inwardness, in devotion, in sweetness and in various approaches than they do by the fireside or the stable, you are acting just as if you took God and muffled his head up in a cloak and pushed him under a bench."

Eckhart explicitly denies the possibility of achieving freedom from external works in Sermon 86: Nû wellent etelîche liute dar zuo komen, daz sie werke ledic sîn. Ich spriche: ez enmac niht gesîn. *Lectura Eckhardi*, 152–153 (par. 23).

33. Otto, *Mysticism East and West*, 191.

34. AUBh. 14:2: tato na gārhasthya evākurvata āsanam utpannavidyasya, . . .

35. E.g., BAUBh. 697:8–9: asyātmalokasya karmabhir asaṃbandhāt; 697:12: ātmā karmaphalasādhanāsaṃbandhī, . . .

36. Wilhelm Halbfass, *Karma und Wiedergeburt im indischen Denken* (Munich: Diederichs, 2000), 29.

37. Halbfass, *Karma und Wiedergeburt*, 101–2. See also Richard Gombrich, *Theravada Buddhism: A Social History from Ancient Benares to Modern Colombo* (New York: Routledge, 2001), 66–69.

38. Halbfass, *Karma und Wiedergeburt*, 100.

39. Halbfass, *Karma und Wiedergeburt*, 20 and passim. Halbfass shows that the relation between the concepts of *karma* and rebirth is a contingent one, however well they might cohere with each other in certain philosophical systems in classical India.

40. See BAUBh (on BAU 4.4.23), 700:6–8: taṃ viditvā mahimānaṃ na lipyate na saṃbadhyate karmaṇā pāpakena, dharmadharmalakṣaṇenobhayam api pāpakam eva viduṣaḥ. "Knowing this august one [Brahman], one is not touched or defiled by evil action, for to the knower [of Brahman] both righteous and unrighteous actions are evil."

41. Clooney, *Theology after Vedānta* (Albany: State University of New York Press, 1993), 23–26; Hajime Nakamura, *A History of Early Vedānta Philosophy*, part 1, trans. Trevor Leggett, Segaku Mayeda, Taitetz Unno, et al. (Delhi: Motilal Banarsidass, 1983), 409–13. Nakamura (411–12) argues against a chronological understanding of the relation between the "earlier" and "later" Mīmāṃsās in favor of a logical one: "The Vedānta Mīmāṃsā presupposed the ritual Mīmāṃsā as a precondition."

42. Halbfass, *Karma und Wiedergeburt*, 172. Cf. also 59.

43. On Mīmāṃsā's resistance to the expansion of the semantic fields of key terms like *dharma*, *karma*, and *veda*, see Sheldon Pollock, "The Meaning of *Dharma* and the Relationship of the Two Mīmāṃsās: Appayya Dīkṣita's 'Discourse on the Refutation of a Unified Knowledge System of Pūrvamīmāṃsā and Uttaramīmāṃsā,'" *Journal of Indian Philosophy* 32 (2004): 771–73.

44. Jaimini had argued (Pūrva Mīmāṃsā Sūtra 1.2.1) that, "Since the Vedas are meant to enjoin actions, those portions of them [i.e., the Upaniṣads] that have not this purpose in view are useless." Gambhirananda trans., *Brahma-Sūtra-Bhāṣya*, 20 (on BSBh, 1.1.4, 58:6–59:1: āmnāyasya kriyārthatvād ānarthakyam atadarthānām).

45. Patrick Olivelle, *The Āśrama System: The History and Hermeneutics of a Religious Tradition* (New York: Oxford University Press, 1993), 242.

46. BAUBh 455:28: yā vittaiṣaṇā sā lokaiṣaṇā phalārtheva sā.

47. BAUBh 456:1–2: tasmāt brahmavido nāsti karma karmasādhanaṃ vā.

48. BAUBh 458:7–8: "The self... is to be known as different from results and means." (ātmā... sādhanaphalavilakṣaṇo jñātavyaḥ).

49. "Knowledge and ignorance cannot coexist in one person because they exclude each other like darkness and light." (BAUBh 458:27–459:1: na ca vidyāvidye ekasya puruṣasya saha bhavato virodhāt, tamaḥprakāśāv iva.) In the BSBh (1.1.4), Śaṅkara expresses the antithesis between rites and liberative knowledge in terms of the impermanence of the products of human action and the permanence of the uncreated self: "Had liberation been spoken of in the scriptures as being supplementary to action and had it been asserted as a thing to be achieved, it would become impermanent. In that case liberation would become some sort of an excellent product amidst a horde of above-mentioned products of work standing in a graded order. But all who believe in liberation admit it to be eternal." Gambhirananda trans., *Brahma-Sūtra-Bhāṣya*, 28 (BSBh. 74:2–5: tad yadi kartavyaśeṣatvenopadiśyeta, tena ca kartavyena sādhyaś cen mokṣo 'bhyupagamyeta, anitya eva syāt. tatraivaṃ sati yathoktakarmaphaleṣv eva tāratamyāvisthiteṣv anityeṣu kaścid atiśayo mokṣa iti prasajyeta. nityaśca mokṣaḥ sarvair mokṣavādibhir abhyupagamyate.)

50. "Others object, [arguing that] even if Brahman is known from the *śāstra*, still Brahman is presented by the *śāstra* in the context of injunction about meditation." (BSBh 66:1–2: atrāpare pratyavatiṣṭhante—yadyapi śāstrapramāṇakaṃ brahma tathāpi pratipattividhiviṣayatayaiva śāstreṇa brahma samarpyate.) Govindānanda (end of the sixteenth century) identifies the *pūrvapakṣin* as the *vṛttikāra*. Vācaspati (mid-ninth century), who stands several centuries closer to Śaṅkara, attributes the *pūrvapakṣa* to certain *ācāryadeṣīyāḥ*: "a title used by commentators to scholars or disputants whose statements include only part of the truth and are not entirely correct." (Monier Monier-Williams, *A Sanskrit-English Dictionary* [New York: Oxford University Press, 1992], 131.) On references to the *vṛttikāra* in Vācaspati's *Bhāmatī*, see Klaus Rüping, *Philologische Untersuchungen zu den Brahmasūtra-Kommentaren des Śaṅkara und des Bhāskara* (Wiesbaden: Franz Steiner Verlag, 1977), 46–47.

51. "But if the upaniṣadic sentences do not form parts of injunctions about actions and they refer merely to an entity, there will be no possibility of acceptance or rejection, so ta hey will become certainly useless" Gambhirananda trans., *Brahma-Sūtra-Bhāṣya*, 25 (BSBh 69:6–8: kartavyavidhyananupraveśe vastumātrakathane hāna-upādānāsaṃbhavāt, saptadvīpā vasumatī rājāsau gacchatīty ādīvakyavad, vedāntavākyānām ānarthakyam eva syāt).

52. See BS 3.4.19: "Bādarāyaṇa holds that [the knowledge of or meditation on Brahman is something] to be performed because of the Śruti mentioning the likeness [of nature of the knowledge of Brahman and nature of the action]." P. M. Modi trans., *A Critique of the Brahmasūtra III.2.11–IV*, vol. 1, 260 (anuṣṭheyaṃ bādarāyaṇaḥ sāmyaśruteḥ).

53. Nakamura, *History of Early Vedānta Philosophy*, 409–14.

54. "It being granted that the upaniṣadic sentences have injunctions in view, it stands to reason that just as such means as the Agnihotra sacrifice are enjoined for one who desires heaven, so also the knowledge of Brahman is enjoined for one who hankers after immortality" Gambhirananda trans., *Brahma-Sūtra-Bhāṣya*, 24 (BSBh

68:3–4: sati ca vidhiparatve, yathā svargādikāmasyāgnihotrādisādhanaṃ vidhīyata, evam amṛtatvakāmasya brahmajñānaṃ vidhīyata iti yuktam).

55. Nakamura, *History of Early Vedānta Philosophy*, 519–21.

56. BSBh 83:4–6: dhyānaṃ cintanaṃ yadyapi mānasaṃ, tathāpi puruṣeṇa kartum akartum anyathā vā kartuṃ śakyaṃ, puruṣatantratvāt. jñānaṃ tu pramāṇajanyam. pramāṇaṃ ca yathābhūtavastuviṣayam. ato jñānaṃ kartum akartum anyathā vā kartum aśakyaṃ kevalaṃ vastutantram eva tat. na codanātantram. nāpi puruṣatantram.

57. "The highest result of those rites pertaining to the householder's stage and which are applicable to the knowledge [of the self], the result, namely, of entering into a deity, belongs only to the realm of *saṃsāra*." (AUBh 18:6–19:1: yadvijñānaopayogīni ca gārhasthyāśramakarmāṇi teṣāṃ paraṃ phalam upasaṃhṛtaṃ devatā-apyaya-lakṣaṇaṃ saṃsāraviṣayam eva.)

58. "[Some maintain the following view]: This highest aim of man, characterized by the entrance into a deity, is liberation. This is to be attained by means of the above-mentioned combination of knowledge and rites. There is no higher [state] than this." (AUBh 2:1–2: so 'yaṃ devatāpayalakṣaṇaḥ paraḥ puruṣārthaḥ. eṣa mokṣaḥ. sa cāyaṃ yathoktena jñānakarmasamuccayasādhanena prāptavyo nātaḥ paramastity eke pratipannās, . . .)

59. Nakamura, *History of Early Vedānta Philosophy*, 520.

60. BS 2.4.26: sarvāpekṣā ca yajñādiśruter aśvavat.

61. Modi, *Critique of the Brahmasūtra*, 1:261.

62. Wilhelm Halbfass, *Tradition and Reflection* (Albany: State University of New York Press, 1991), 150.

63. Modi, *Critique of the Brahmasūtra*, 1:262. Note that Modi places *sūtras* 25 and 26 in the same *adhikaraṇa*, whereas Śaṅkara separates them.

64. "Knowledge, once having emerged, does not depend on anything else for effecting its fruit, but it does depend [on others] for its emergence." Cf. Gambhirananda's trans., *Brahma-Sūtra-Bhāṣya*, 783 (BSBh 802:2–3: upannā hi vidyā phalasiddhaṃ prati na kiṃcid anyad apekṣata, utpattiṃ prati tv apekṣate.) Cf. BSBh 3.4.27, "Hence sacrifices etc. and self-control etc., which are the duties of the respective stages of life, are all but means for the emergence of knowledge." Gambhirananda trans., *Brahma-Sūtra-Bhāṣya*, 785.

65. AUBh 13:2–3: kriyābhāvamātraṃ vyutthānaṃ na tu yāgādivad anuṣṭheya-rūpaṃ bhāvātkamaṃ tac ca vidyāvat puruṣadharma iti na prayojanam anveṣṭavyam.

66. "There is, however, another type of renunciation different from the above. This other type constitutes an *āśrama*, and it is a means for obtaining results such as attaining the world of Brahmā." Olivelle trans., *Renunciation in Hinduism: A Medieval Debate*, 89 (BAUBh 460:24–25: tadvyatirekeṇa cāsty āśramarūpaṃ pārivrājyaṃ brahmalokādiphalaprāptisādhanaṃ.)

67. (ātmanaḥ) asādhanaphalarūpasya; cf. BAUBh 694:20–21: na cāsyātmanaḥ sādhyasādhanādi-sarvasaṃsāradharmavinirmuktasya.

68. "He who sees an interest, either in what is desired or not desired by the self, exists in the range of injunction, as is seen in the world." (AUBh 8:5–9:1: iṣṭayogam

aniṣṭaviyogaṃ cātmanaḥ prayojanaṃ paśyaṃs tad upāyārthī yo bhavati sa niyogasya viṣayo dṛṣṭo loke.)

69. BAUBh 462:21.

70. "Opposed to this type of person [subject to injunctions] is one who has realized Brahman, who lies outside the sphere of injunction, as his self." (AUBh 9:1: tadviparīto niyogāviṣayabrahmātmatvadarśī.); cf. also Olivelle, *Renunciation in Hinduism*, 55; Olivelle, *The Āśrama System*, 223, 225.

71. A generation after Śaṅkara, if not before, this debate would be formalized in the sectarian division the so-called single-staff and triple-staff traditions of renunciation. The controversy between the two understandings of renunciation became a point of contention in the division between Viśiṣṭhādvaita, representing the triple-staff tradition, and Advaita, representing the single-staff tradition. (See Olivelle, *Renunciation in Hinduism*, 52–54 and passim.)

72. On these three emblems of brahmanical renunciation, including the argument that the *tridaṇḍa* was originally a tripod, see Olivelle, *Renunciation in Hinduism*, 29–52.

73. "Hence the knowledge of Brahman is not dependent on human action. On what does it depend, then? It is dependent on the thing itself, as in the case of a knowledge of a thing acquired through such valid means as direct perception." Gambhirananda trans., *Brahma-Sūtra-Bhāṣya*, 30 (BSBh I.1.4, 78:4–5: ato na puruṣa-vyāpāratantrā brahmavidyā. kiṃ tarhi? pratyakṣādipramāṇaviṣaya-vastujñānavad vastutantrā.); see also BSBh 83:4–6, cited above.

74. On Śaṅkara's inconsistency on the question of renunciation, see, e.g., Olivelle *The Āśrama System*, 226–27; Roger Marcaurelle, *Freedom through Inner Renunciation* (Albany: State University of New York Press, 2000), 141, 142.

75. Otto, *Mysticism East and West*, 225.

76. "You asked, with respect to the mere renunciation of action and discipline-in-action (*karmayoga*), which of the two was better. My response to this was that, disregarding knowledge, the discipline-in-action was to be preferred over the renunciation of action." (GBh 191 [on Gītā 5:5]: tvayā pṛṣṭaṃ kevalaṃ karmasaṃnyāsaṃ karmayogaṃ ca abhipretya tayoḥ anyataraḥ kaḥ śreyān iti. tadanurūpaṃ prativacanaṃ mayā uktaṃ karmasanyāsāt karmayogaḥ viśiṣyate iti jñānaṃ anapekṣya.) See also GBh 188, on Gīta 5:2; cf. GBh 104–5, on Gītā 3:4.

77. GBh 106; see also GBh 150 [on Gītā 4:18]: "He who sees the action in this inaction—namely, the view, caused by egotism, that 'I am happly sitting quietly, doing nothing,"—is wise [...]." (tūṣṇīṃ akurvan sukhaṃ āse iti ahaṃkārābhisandhihetutvāt tasmin akarmaṇi ca karmaḥ yaḥ paśyet..., sa buddhimān.)

78. Karl H. Potter, *Encyclopedia of Indian Philosophies*, vol.3, *Advaita Vedānta up to Śaṃkara and His Pupils* (Delhi: Motilal Banarsidass, 1981), 45.

79. GBh 191 (on Gītā 5:5): "Renunciation that is based on knowledge is what I mean by '*sāṃkhya*.' And it is precisely this that is yoga in the highest sense. But that yoga which is Vedic karmayoga is figuratively called 'renunciation' because [it has] the same meaning." (jñānāpekṣas tu saṃnyāsaḥ sāṃkhyamiti mayā abhipretaḥ. paramārthayogaśca sa eva. yastu karmayogaḥ vaidikaḥ sa ca tādarthyāt yogaḥ saṃnyāsaḥ iti ca upacaryate.) See also GBh 101 (on Gītā 3:3).

80. This interpretation of 5:2 that is found in 5:5 is only implied, not stated. Śaṅkara's comment on 5:2 itself suggests a more modest interpretation, namely, that for the unenlightened Arjuna, *karma-yoga* better than the only form of *saṃnyāsa* available to him, viz., the lower form accompanied by the idea of agency.

81. See GBh 20 (on Gītā 2:10): "On this point some argue as follows: The absolute oneness cannot be attained merely by a knowledge of the self that is preceded by the renunciation of action. But then what? The established point of the entire Gītā is that the attainment of the state of absolute oneness comes from knowledge combined with the rites enjoined by the Veda and the tradition such as the fire sacrifice." (atra kecit āhuḥ—sarvakarmasaṃnyāsapūrvakāt ātmajñānaniṣṭhāmātrāt eva kevalāt kaivalyaṃ na prāpyate eva. kiṃ tarhi? agnihotrādiśrautasmārtakarmasahitāt jñānāt kaivalyaprāptiḥ iti sarvāsu gītāsu niścitaḥ arthaḥ iti.) See also GBh 93 (introduction to Gītā, ch. 3).

82. Gītā 3:3: loke 'smin dvividhā niṣṭhā purā proktā mayā 'nagha; jñānayogena sāṃkhyānāṃ karmayogena yoginām.

83. GBh 21 (on Gītā 2:10): "The two states corresponding, respectively, to the ideas of knowledge and of practice have been spoken of by the Lord himself, who saw that a single person cannot be committed to both knowledge and works—based as these are on the [contradictory] notions of non-agency and agency, unity and plurality, respectively—at the same time." (evaṃ sāṅkhyabuddhiṃ yogabuddhiṃ ca āśritya dve niṣṭhe vibhakte bhagavatā eva ukte jñānakarmaṇoḥ kartṛtvākartṛtvaikatvā nekatva-buddhyāśrayoḥ yugapat ekapuruṣāśrayatvāsaṃbhavaṃ paśyatā.) Cf. GBh 62 (on Gītā 2:39).

84. GBh 101 (on Gītā 3:3): jñānayogena sāṃkhyānām] paramahaṃsaparivrājakānāṃ brahmaṇi eva avasthitānāṃ niṣṭhā proktā.

85. GBh 101: tena karmayogena yogināṃ karmiṇāṃ niṣṭhā proktā ityarthaḥ.

86. GBh 181 (introduction to Gītā, ch. 5): "These two, the performance of action and the renunciation of action, being mutually exclusive like rest and motion, cannot both be undertaken by a single person." (tayoḥ ubhayośca karmānuṣṭhānakarmasaṃn yāsayoḥ sthitigativat parasparavirodhāt ekena saha kartuṃ aśakyatvāt.)

87. GBh 25 (on Gītā 2:10): "Therefore, the clear intent of the Gītā's teaching is that liberation is attained only from a knowledge of reality, and not from [knowledge] combined with rites." (tasmāt gītāśāstre kevalāt eva tattvajñānāt mokṣaprāptiḥ, na karmasamuccitāt iti niścitaḥ arthaḥ.) See also GBh. 102–103 (on Gītā 3.3); GBh 21 (on Gītā 2:10).

88. Gītā 4:18: karmaṇyakarma yaḥ paśyed, akarmaṇi ca karma yaḥ; sa buddhimān manuṣyeṣu, sa yuktaḥ kṛtsnakarmakṛt.

89. GBh 155 (on Gītā 4:19): "He who sees inaction in action is, simply by virtue of this seeing of inaction, inactive, a renunciant. His movements serve merely to maintain his [physical being]; nevertheless, he does not engage in action." (yastu karmādau akarmādidarśī saḥ akarmādidarśanāt eva niṣkarmā saṃnyāsī jīvanamātrārthaceṣṭhaḥ san karmaṇi na pravartate.)

90. GBh 145 (on Gītā 4:15): "If [you] do not have knowledge, [act] in order to purify the self. If, on the other hand, [you] know the truth, then [act] in order to protect

the world, as was done long ago by the ancients, Janaka and others." (yadi ajñaḥ tadā ātmaśuddhyartham; tattvavit cet lokasaṃgrahārthaṃ pūrvaiḥ janakādibhiḥ pūrvataraṃ kṛtaṃ....) See also GBh 155 (on Gītā 4:19); Gbh 192 (on Gītā 5:7).

91. See, e.g., GBh 144 (glossing Gītā 4:13): "Even though I am an agent of this work according to the conventional understanding in the sphere of *māyā*, know me to be a non-agent from the standpoint of highest truth." (yadyapi māyāsaṃvyavahāreṇa tasya karmaṇaḥ kartāram api santaṃ māṃ paramārthataḥ viddhi akartāram.)

92. GBh 160 (on Gītā 4:22): "But when agency is ascribed [to him] by ordinary people by virtue of the similarity [between his behavior and] everyday behavior in the world, he becomes the agent of actions like wandering about begging." (lokavyavahāra-sāmānyadarśanena tu laukikaiḥ āropitakartṛtve bhikṣāṭanādau karmaṇi kartā bhavati.)

93. GBh 150 (on Gītā 4:18): "Therefore in the action which is believed by the entire world to be inherent in the Self in the same way that trees standing on a riverbank are perceived to move in a direction opposite [to the boat], [the wise man] sees inaction, like the one that realizes that there is no motion in the trees." (ataḥ ātmasamavetatayā sarvalokaprasiddhe karmaṇi nadīkūlastheṣu iva vṛkṣeṣu gatiprātilomyena akarma karmābhāvaṃ gatyabhāvam iva vṛkṣeṣu yaḥ paśyet.)

94. A significant exception to this characterization would be the teaching role he assumes upon liberation. Anantanand Rambachan argues constructively for an extension of this teaching role to other forms of compassionate service in the world. See his *The Advaita Worldview* (Albany: State University of New York Press, 2006), 107–8.

95. "It is a matter of common experience that an intelligent man whose engagement in work is preceded by forethought, does not start any activity, easy of performance though it be, unless it is conductive to his purpose. What to speak of an undertaking requiring stupendous effort?... Even if this effort be imagined to be conducive to some purpose of the conscious supreme Self, then the mention in the Vedas of Its contentment will be contradicted. Alternatively, if there is no purpose, then there will be no activity." Gambhirananda trans., *Brahma-Sūtra-Bhāṣya*, 360.

96. BSBh 406: 2–3: īśvarasyāpy anapekṣya kiṃcit prayojanāntaraṃ svabhāvād eva kevalaṃ līlārūpā pravṛttir bhaviṣyati. There is a tension between, on the one hand, this and similar statements denying motive to Brahman and, on the other, those texts, discussed in ch. 5 above, highlighting the intentional nature of creation in order to refute the Sāṃkhya doctrine of spontaneous generation from an insentient first principle. Citing the latter set of texts, Rambachan (*Advaita Worldview*, 93–96) argues that the concept of *līlā* does not exclude a certain kind of desire in Brahman-Īśvara's creative activity, only limitation.

97. Gambhirananda trans., *Brahma-Sūtra-Bhāṣya*, 361. (BSBh 406: 6: yadi nāma loke lokāsvapi kiṃcitsūkṣmaṃ prayojanam utprekṣyeta,...) See also above, GBh 160 (4:22), on people ascribing motive to the *jivanmukti*.

98. Otto, *Mysticism East and West*, 193. Against Otto, I concur with the following statement of Rambachan (*Advaita Worldview*, 93): "The point of the analogy, we want to suggest, is not to trivialize creation or liken the creativity of Brahman to human diversion, but to indicate the possibility of action as celebrative self-expression and action that does not spring from self-limitation."

99. On Śaṅkara, see once again Rambachan, *Advaita Worldview*, 91–93. Rambachan (91; cf. 92) argues more constructively for an understanding of creation as "an expression of the nature of Brahman," a view he sees suggested in Gauḍapāda's statement, *devasya esaḥ svabhāvaḥ ayam*.

100. In dismissing the *līlā* concept, Otto unfairly transfers the element of disanalogy (present in all theological concepts) in the *līlā* concept—namely, the lack of seriousness or childishness associated with human play—to the Indian conception of God.

101. Although a later Advaita text like the *Vivekacūḍāmaṇi* is bolder in describing the spontaneous comportment of the *jivanmukti*.

102. "And yet the Vedic statement of creation does not relate to any reality, for it must not be forgotten that such a text is valid within the range of activities concerned with name and form called up by ignorance, and it is meant for propounding the fact that everything has Brahman as its Self." Gambhirananda trans., *Brahma-Sūtra-Bhāṣya*, 361.

103. This analysis of Śaṅkara's polemic can perhaps be generalized. I suspect that *any* form of human activity, even the most noble and generous, can ultimately be (re)described in terms of self-interest. Given the vulnerability of virtually any form of religious activity to such devaluatory redescription, it is not surprising to find the invidious contrast between selfless and self-interested behavior a staple of religious polemic. A paradigmatic example would be the Mahāyāna Buddhist characterization of the Theravāda *arhat* as proud and selfish.

104. Rudolf Otto, "Meister Eckhart's Sunder Warumbe," in *Aufsätze: Das Numinose Betreffend*, (Stuttgart: Friedrich Andreas Perthes, 1923), 134–35. Otto's formulation ("sondern aus der Erfahrung des gotteinigen Menschen, der, wenn er dieses ist, kein warumbe... braucht") leaves the question of whether Eckhart's statements concerning the "living without a why" originate from Eckhart's own personal experience somewhat vague, however.

105. For a good critique of this tradition of interpretation, see, e.g., Grace Jantzen, *Power, Gender and Christian Mysticism* (New York: Cambridge University Press, 1995), 1–25. For a discussion of the concept of mystical experience in relation to Eckhart more specifically, see, e.g., Frank Tobin, *Meister Eckhart: Thought and Language* (Philadelphia: University of Pennsylvania Press, 1986), 185–92; Richard Kieckhefer, "Meister Eckhart's Conception of Union with God," *Harvard Theological Review* 71:3/4 (July–Oct. 1978): 203–25.

106. The concept of experience is a still valid analytical concept, but it is understood less in terms of psychological states than in terms of literary effects. See, for example, Michael Sells's understanding of mystical discourse as a "meaning event" (*Mystical Languages of Unsaying* [Chicago: University of Chicago Press, 1994], 9–10 213–17); also Amy Hollywood, *The Soul as Virgin Wife* (Notre Dame: University of Notre Dame Press, 1995), 21; Tobin, *Meister Eckhart*, 187. See also Paul Rabbow's thesis (*Seelenführung: Methodik der Exerzitien in der Antike* [Munich: Kösel, 1954], 55–90) regarding the origins of Ignatius of Loyola's *Spiritual Exercises*, and of the Western discipline of meditation more generally, in the rhetorical tradition.

107. Ruh, "Meister Eckhart," 329.
108. Jantzen, *Power, Gender,* 188.
109. Bernard McGinn, "Theological Summary," in *Essential Eckhart,* 58–59.
110. Ruh, "Meister Eckhart," 332.

CONCLUSION

1. Bruce Lincoln, "Kings, Rebels, and the Left Hand," in *Death, War, and Sacrifice* (Chicago: University of Chicago Press, 1991), 244. Cross-cultural comparison differs from more conventional historical research in that the construction of the new context must be undertaken more or less consciously.

2. H. L. Martensen, for example, in his *Meister Eckhart: Eine Theologische Studie* (Hamburg: Friedrich Perthes, 1842), explicitly identifies acosmism (33–40) and "atheism" (in the sense of a denial of the God of creation) (40–44) as two sides of the doctrine of pantheism. The third, quietism, is implicit (see, e.g., 39).

3. *Mysticism East and West,* trans. Bertha L. Bracey and Richenda C. Payne (New York: Collier Books, 1962), 136.

4. In the following discussion I have been inspired by Sheldon Pollock's use of Vico's *verum/certum* distinction to illustrate the historiographical method he follows in his book *The Language of the Gods in the World of Men* (Berkeley: University of California Press, 2006), 2–3. Pollock also correlates the *verum/certum* distinction to the distinction in Indian philosophy between *pāramārthika* and *vyāvahārika sat,* respectively.

5. Here I follow Erich Auerbach's exposition of Vico in *Gesammelte Aufsätze zur Romanischen Philologie* (Munich: Francke Verlag, 1967), 238, 245, 264–65.

6. On the conflict between scientific theory and ordinary experience, see, e.g., Louis Dupré, *Passage to Modernity* (New Haven: Yale University Press, 1993), 76–77; Paul Feyerabend, *Against Method* (New York: Verso, 1993), 79, 110, 117 and passim.

7. On this point, see Pollock, *Language of the Gods,* 7, 23, 249.

8. Kimberley C. Patton, "Juggling Torches: Why We Still Need Comparative Religion," in *A Magic Still Dwells,* ed. Kimberley C. Patton and Benjamin C. Ray (Berkeley: University of California Press, 2000), 155.

9. Auerbach, *Gesammelte Aufsätze,* 239, 259, 252.

10. Auerbach, *Gesammelte Aufsätze,* 260; elsewhere (p. 259) Auerbach argues that for Vico, "there is no cognition without creation."

11. This principle of the historicity of everyday understandings of the world can also be used to justify the study of religion against those critics (Asad, McCutcheon, Fitzgerald, et al.) who question the continued use of religion as an analytical category on the grounds that "religion" does not name a transhistorical reality or essence. Even when one concedes their point that the concept of religion is part and parcel of discourses characteristic of Western modernity, the discipline of religious studies is justified to the extent that religion remains, for good or for ill, a powerful discourse in today's world. It therefore has a place in an approach that recognizes the certitudes grounding everyday belief and action as a basis for historical

understanding. Such an approach, however, calls for a more pragmatic and critical conception of the discipline of religious studies than has been the case in the past. That is to say, it is an approach that takes as its point of departure concepts like "religion" that are in wide circulation and then, through the intellectual discipline of critical reflection, proceeds to uncover the hidden, unexamined assumptions that render such concepts self-evident objects of discourse.

12. Robert C. Neville and Wesley J. Wildman, "On Comparing Religious Ideas," in *The Human Condition: A Volume in the Comparative Religious Ideas Project*, ed. Robert C. Neville (Albany: State University of New York Press, 2001), 17.

13. Greg Urban, "The Role of Comparison in Light of the Theory of Culture," in *Critical Comparisons in Politics and Culture*, ed. John R. Bowen and Roger Peterson (Cambridge: Cambridge University Press, 1999), 102 and passim.

14. Urban, "Role of Comparison," 107.

15. Urban, "Role of Comparison," 99 and passim.

16. R. C. Zaehner, *Mysticism, Sacred and Profane* (Oxford: Oxford University Press, 1957), 171.

17. Zaehner, *Mysticism*, 170.

18. *Theories of Culture* (Minneapolis: Fortress Press, 1997), 55.

19. Somewhat ironically, the point here is the inverse of Tanner's argument (*Politics of God* [Minneapolis: Fortress Press, 1992], 220–21) that essentialism can be tactically, but provisionally, deployed.

Bibliography

TEXTS AND TRANSLATIONS OF SANSKRIT SOURCE MATERIALS

Aitareyopaniṣad: saṭippaṇa-saṃskṛta-hindī-ṭīkā-dvaya-saṃvalita-śāṅkarabhāṣya-sametā. Edited by Umeśānanda Śāstri and Svarṇalāla Tulī. Hṛṣīkeśa, UP: Śrī Kailāsa Vidyā Prakāśana, 1999. (Cited as *Aitareya Upaniṣad-Bhāṣya*.)

Bhagavad-Gītā with the Commentary of Śaṅkarācārya. Translated by Swāmī Gambhīrānanda. Calcutta: Advaita Ashrama, 1995.

Brahma-Sūtra-Bhāṣya of Śrī Śaṅkarācārya. Translated by Swāmī Gambhīrānanda. Calcutta: Advaita Ashrama, 1993.

Brahma-Sūtra-Śāṅkarabhāṣyam with the Commentaries: Bhāṣyaratnaprabhā of Govindānanda, Bhāmatī of Vācaspatimiśra, and Nyāyanirnaya of Ānandagiri. Edited by J. L. Sastri. 1980. Reprint, Delhi: Motilal Banarsidass, 1996.

Brahmasiddhi by Acharya Maṇḍanamiśra with Commentary by Saṅkhapāṇi. Edited by S. Kuppuswami Sastri. 1937. Reprint, Delhi: Sri Satguru, 1984.

Brahmasūtrabhāṣyam Śri Bhāskarācāryaviracitam. Edited by Vindhyesvarī Prasāda Dvivedin. Varanasi: Chowkhamba, 1991.

Bṛhadāraṇyakopaniṣat, ānandagiri-kṛta-ṭīkā-saṃvalita-śāṃkara-bhāṣya-sametā. ˜Edited by Kāśinātha Śastrī Āgāśe. Puṇyākhyapattane: Ānandāśramasaṃsthā, 1982. (Cited as Śaṅkara, *Bṛhadāraṇyaka Upaniṣad-Bhāṣya*.)

Eight Upaniṣads. Vol. 2, *Aitareya, Muṇḍaka, Māṇḍūkya and Kārikā, and Praśna, with the Commentary of Śaṅkarācārya*. Translated by Swāmī Gambhīrānanda. Calcutta: Advaita Ashrama, 1996.

Śrīmad Bhagavad Gītā Bhāṣya of Śaṃkarācārya. Translated and edited by A. G. Krishna Warrier. Madras: Sri Ramakrishna Math, 1983.

Upaniṣads. Translated by Patrick Olivelle. New York: Oxford University Press, 1996.

TEXTS AND TRANSLATIONS OF MEISTER ECKHART AND THOMAS AQUINAS

Lectura Eckhardi: Predigten Meister Eckharts von Fachgelehrten gelesen und gedeutet. Edited by Georg Steer and Loris Sturlese. Stuttgart: W. Kohlhammer, 1998.

Meister Eckhart. Edited by Franz Pfeiffer. Leipzig, 1857.

Magistri Echardi: Expositio Libri Exodi, Sermones et Lectiones super Ecclesiastici Cap. 25, *Expositio Libri Sapientiae, Expositio Cantici Canticorum Cap.* 1,6. Translated and edited by Heribert Fischer, Josef Koch, and Konrad Weiss. Stuttgart: W. Kohlhammer, 1992. (Cited as LW II.)

Magistri Echardi: Expositio Sancti Evangelii Secundum Iohannem. Translated and edited by Karl Christ, Bruno Decker, Josef Koch, Heribert Fischer, Loris Sturlese, and Albert Zimmermann. Stuttgart: W. Kohlhammer, 1994. (Cited as LW III.)

Meister Eckhart: German Sermons and Treatises. 3 vols. Translated by M. O'C. Walshe. London: Watkins, 1979–83.

Meister Eckhart: Teacher and Preacher. Edited by Bernard McGinn. New York: Paulist Press, 1986.

Meister Eckhart: The Essential Sermons, Commentaries, Treatises, and Defense. Translated by Edmund Colledge and Bernard McGinn. New York: Paulist Press, 1981.

Summae Theologiae: Latin Text and English Translation, Introductions, Notes, Appendices, and Glossaries. Cambridge: Blackfriars, 1964–81.

GENERAL

Allen, Douglas. *Structure and Creativity in Religion: Hermeneutics in Mircea Eliade's Phenomenology and New Directions.* Paris: Mouton, 1978.

Alles, Gregory D., ed. and trans. *Rudolf Otto: Autobiographical and Social Essays.* Berlin, New York: Mouton de Gruyter, 1996.

Almond, Gabriel A., R. Scott Appleby, and Emmanuel Sivan. *Strong Religion: The Rise of Fundamentalism around the World.* Chicago: University of Chicago Press, 2003.

Almond, Philip. *The British Discovery of Buddhism.* Cambridge: Cambridge University Press, 1988.

Alston, A. J. *Śaṃkara on the Creation: A Śaṃkara Source-Book.* Vol. 2. London: Shanti Sadan, 1980.

Appadurai, Arjun. *Modernity at Large.* Minneapolis: University of Minnesota Press, 1996.

Arendt, Hannah. *The Origins of Totalitarianism.* New York: Harvest Books, 1985.

Asad, Talal. *Genealogies of Religion: Discipline and Reasons of Power in Christianity and Islam.* Baltimore: Johns Hopkins University Press, 1993.

———. "Reading a Modern Classic." *History of Religions* 40 (2001): 205–22.

Auerbach, Erich. *Gesammelte Aufsätze zur Romanischen Philologie.* Munich: Francke Verlag, 1967.

Bader, Jonathan. *Meditation in Śaṅkara's Vedānta.* New Delhi: Aditya Prakashan, 1990.

Bakhtin, M. M. *The Dialogical Imagination.* Trans. Caryl Emerson and Michael Holquist. Austin: University of Texas Press, 1981.

Barrows, John Henry. *Christianity, The World Religion.* Chicago: A. C. McClurg, 1897.

Bayle, Pierre. *The Dictionary Historical and Critical of Mr. Peter Bayle.* 2nd ed. Vol. 2. London, 1735.

Bell, Catherine. "Modernism and Postmodernism in the Study of Religion." *Religious Studies Review* 22:3 (1986): 179–90.

———. *Ritual Theory, Ritual Practice.* New York: Oxford University Press, 1992.

Benz, Ernst. *Les Sources Mystiques de la Philosophie Romantique Allemande.* Paris: J. Vrin, 1968.

Berger, Peter. *The Sacred Canopy.* New York: Anchor Books, 1990.

Bernhart, Joseph. *Die Philosophische Mystik des Mittelalters.* Damstadt: Wissenschaftliche Buchgesellschaft, 1967.

Berthrong, John H. *All Under Heaven.* Albany: State University of New York Press, 1994.

Biardeau, Madeleine. "Quelques Reflexions sur l'Apophatisme de la Śaṅkara." *Indo-Iranian Journal* 3:2 (1959): 81–101.

Bloch, Maurice. "Symbols, Song, Dance and Features of Articulation." In *Ritual, History, and Power,* 19–45. London: Athlone Press, 1989.

Bourdieu, Pierre. *Outline of a Theory of Practice.* Translated by Richard Nice. Cambridge: Cambridge University Press, 1977.

———. *Language and Symbolic Power.* Translated by Gino Raymond and Matthew Adamson. Cambridge, Mass.: Harvard University Press, 1991.

———. *The State Nobility.* Translated by Lauretta C. Clough. Cambridge: Polity Press, 1996.

Boyarin, Daniel. *Border Lines.* Philadelphia: University of Pennsylvania Press, 2004.

Brereton, Joel P. "Edifying Puzzlement: Rgveda 10.129 and the Uses of Enigma." *Journal of the American Oriental Society* 119 (1999): 248–60.

Broadway, Bill. "God's Place on the Dias; Use of 'Jesus' in Inaugural Prayers Breeds Some Worry." *Washington Post,* January 27, 2001.

Brown, Wendy. "Reflections on Tolerance in the Age of Identity." In *Democracy and Vision,* edited by Aryeh Botwinick and William E. Connolly, 99–117. Princeton, N.J.: Princeton University Press, 2001.

Burant, Aimee. "Defining 'The Political': Method in the Historiography of Nineteenth-Century Religious Thought." *Papers of the Nineteenth-Century Theology Group* 38 (2007): 92–111.

Byrne, Peter. *Natural Religion and the Nature of Religion: The Legacy of Deism.* New York: Routledge, 1989.

Cady, Linell E. "Territorial Disputes: Religious Studies and Theology in Transition." In *Religious Studies, Theology, and the University,* edited by Linell E. Cady and Delwin Brown, 110–25. Albany: State University of New York Press, 2002.

Caputo, John D. "Fundamental Themes in Meister Eckhart's Mysticism." *The Thomist* 42 (1978): 197–225.

Casanova, José. *Public Religions in the Modern World.* Chicago: University of Chicago Press, 1994.

Chantepie de la Saussaye, P. D. *Manual of the Science of Religion.* Translated by Beatrice S. Colyer-Fergusson. London: Longmans, 1891.

Clarke, James Freeman. *Ten Great Religions. An Essay in Comparative Theology*. Boston: Houghton Mifflin Company, [1871] 1899.

———. *Ten Great Religions*. Part II, *A Comparison of all Religions*. Boston: Houghton Mifflin Company, 1883.

Clayton, Philip. *Explanation from Physics to Theology*. New Haven, Conn.: Yale University Press, 1985.

Clifford, James. *The Predicament of Culture*. Cambridge, Mass.: Harvard University Press, 1988.

Clooney, Francis X. "The Study of Non-Christian Religions in the Post–Vatican II Roman Catholic Church." *Journal of Ecumenical Studies* 28:3 (1991): 482–94.

———. "Comparative Theology: A Review of Recent Books." *Theological Studies* 56 (1995): 521–50.

———. *Theology after Vedānta*. Albany: State University of New York Press, 1993.

———. *Seeing Through Texts*. Albany: State University of New York Press, 1996.

———. *Hindu God, Christian God*. New York: Oxford University Press, 2001.

Colebrooke, H. T. *Essays on the History, Literature, and Religions of Ancient India*. Vol. 1. New Delhi: Cosmo Publications, 1977.

Collins, Steven. *Selfless Persons*. Cambridge: Cambridge University Press, 1982.

Comans, Michael. *The Method of Early Advaita Vedānta*. Delhi: Motilal Banarsidass, 2000.

Connolly, William E. *Identity/Difference*. Minneapolis: University of Minnesota Press, 1991.

———. *The Ethos of Pluralization*. Minneapolis: University of Minnesota Press, 1995.

———. *Why I am Not a Secularist*. Minneapolis: University of Minnesota Press, 1999.

Crouter, Richard. *Friedrich Schleiermacher: Between Enlightenment and Romanticism*. New York: Cambridge University Press, 2005.

Datta, D. M. "Some Realistic Aspects of the Philosophy of Śaṃkara." In *Recent Indian Philosophy*, vol. 1, edited by Kalidas Bhattacharya, 341–50. Calcutta: Progressive Publishers, 1963.

Davaney, Sheila Greeve. "Rethinking Theology and Religious Studies." In *Religious Studies, Theology, and the University*, edited by Linell E. Cady and Delwin Brown, 140–54. Albany: State University of New York Press, 2002.

Davidson, Donald. "What Metaphors Mean." In *Philosophical Perspectives on Metaphor*, edited by Mark Johnson, 200–20. Minneapolis: University of Minnesota Press, 1981.

Davis, Charles. "The Reconvergence of Theology and Religious Studies." *Studies in Religion* 4 (1975): 205–21.

———. "Our New Religious Identity." *Sciences Religieuses/Studies in Religion* 9:1 (1980): 25–39.

De Certeau, Michel. *The Practice of Everyday Life*. Berkeley and Los Angeles: University of California Press, 1984.

De Gandillac, Maurice. "La 'Dialectique' de Maitre Eckhart." In *La Mystique Rhénane*, 59–94. Paris: Presses Universitaires de France, 1963.

Degenhardt, Ingeborg. *Studien zum Wandel des Eckhartbildes*. Leiden: E. J. Brill, 1967.

Deussen, Paul. *The Philosophy of the Upanishads*. Translated by A. S. Geden. New York: Dover Publications, 1966.

Dietsche, Bernward. "Der Seelengrund nach den deutschen und lateinischen Predigten." In *Meister Eckhart der Prediger*, edited by Udo M. Nix and Raphael Öchslin, 200–58. Freiburg: Herder, 1960.

Dirlik, Arif. "Culturalism as Hegemonic Ideology and Liberating Practice." *Cultural Critique* 6 (1987): 13–50.

Dole, Andrew. "The Case of the Disappearing Discourse: Schleiermacher's Fourth Speech and the Field of Religious Studies." *Journal of Religion* 88:1 (Jan. 2008): 1–28.

Drey, Johann Sebastian. "Von der Landesreligion und der Weltreligion" (in two parts). *Tübinger Quartalschrift* (1827): 234–74 and 391–435.

———. *Die Apologetik als wissenschaftliche Nachweisung der Göttlichkeit des Christenthums in seiner Erscheinung*, Bd. 1. Mainz, 1838.

———. *Die Apologetik als wissenschaftliche Nachweisung der Göttlichkeit des Christenthums in seiner Erscheinung*. Bd. 2. Mainz, 1843.

———. *Die Apologetik als wissenschaftliche Nachweisung der Göttlichkeit des Christenthums in seiner Erscheinung*, Bd. 3. Mainz, 1847.

———. *Brief Introduction to the Study of Theology*. Translated by Michael Himes. Notre Dame: University of Notre Dame Press, 1994.

Duffy, Stephen J. "A Theology of the Religions and/or a Comparative Theology?" *Horizons* 26 (1999): 105–15.

Dunn, James D. G. *The Parting of the Ways Between Christianity and Judaism and Their Significance for the Character of Christianity*. London: SCM Press and Trinity Press International, 1991.

Dupré, Louis. "Toward a Revaluation of Schleiermacher's 'Philosophy of Religion.'" *Journal of Religion* 44:2 (Apr. 1964): 109–12.

———. *The Common Life*. New York: Crossroad, 1984.

———. *Passage to Modernity*. New Haven: Yale University Press, 1993.

Eck, Diana L. *Encountering God: A Spiritual Journey from Bozeman to Benares*. Boston: Beacon Press, 1993.

Farquhar, J. N. *The Crown of Hinduism*. New York: H. Milford, 1913.

Fehr, Wayne L. *The Birth of the Catholic Tübingen School: The Dogmatics of Johann Sebastian Drey*. Chico, Calif.: Scholars Press, 1981.

Feyerabend, Paul. *Against Method*. New York: Verso, 1993.

Firsching, Horst, and Matthias Schlegel. "Religiöse Innerlichkeit und Geselligkeit: Zum Verhältnis von Erfahrung, Kommunikabilität und Socialität—unter besonderer Berücksichtigung des Religionsverständnisses Friedrich Schleiermachers." In *Religion als Kommunikation*, edited by Hartmann Tyrell, Volkhard Krech, and Hubert Knoblauch, 31–81. Würzburg: Ergon Verlag, 1998.

Fitzgerald, Timothy. *The Ideology of Religious Studies*. New York: Oxford University Press, 2000.

Fort, Andrew O. "Beyond Pleasure: Śaṅkara on Bliss." *Journal of Indian Philosophy* 16 (1988): 177–89.

Fredericks, James L. *Faith among Faiths*. New York: Paulist Press, 1999.

———. *Buddhists and Christians*. Maryknoll, N.Y.: Orbis Books, 2004.

Geertz, Clifford. *The Interpretation of Cultures*. New York: Basic Books, 1973.

Giddens, Anthony. *The Consequences of Modernity*. Stanford, Calif.: Stanford University Press, 1990.

Gilkey, Langdon. "A Theological Voyage with Wilfred Cantwell Smith." *Religious Studies Review* 7:4 (Oct. 1981): 298–306.

Gombrich, Richard. *Theravada Buddhism: A Social History from Ancient Benares to Modern Colombo*. New York: Routledge, 2001.

Gottfried, Paul Edward. *Carl Schmitt: Politics and Theory*. New York: Greenwood Press, 1990.

Gough, Archibald Edward. *The Philosophy of the Upanishads*. Delhi: ESS Publications, 1975.

Green, W. S. "Otherness Within: Towards a Theory of Difference in Rabbinic Judaism." In *"To See Ourselves as Others See Us": Christians, Jews, "Others" in Late Antiquity*, edited by J. Neusner and E. S. Fredrichs, 49–69. Chico, Calif.: Scholars Press, 1985.

Griffiths, Paul. *An Apology for Apologetics*. Maryknoll, N.Y.: Orbis Books, 1991.

———. "On the Future of the Study of Religion in the Academy." *Journal of the American Academy of Religion* 74:1 (2006): 66–74.

Grossman, Cathy Lynn. "Some Call Inaugural Prayers to Jesus Exclusionary." *USA Today*, January 24, 2001.

Grundmann, Herbert. "Die geschichtlichen Grundlagen der deutschen Mystik." In *Altdeutsche und Altniederländische Mystik*, edited by Kurt Ruh, 72–99. Darmstadt: Wissenschaftliche Buchgesellschaft, 1964.

———. *Religious Movements of the Middle Ages*. Translated by Steven Rowan. Notre Dame: University of Notre Dame Press, 1995.

Haas, Alois M. "Seinsspekulation und Geschöpflichkeit in der Mystik Meister Eckharts." In *Sein und Nichts in der Abendländischen Mystik*, edited by Walter Strolz, 33–58. Freiburg: Herder, 1984.

Hacker, Paul. *Upadeśasahasri: Unterweisung in der All-Einheits-Lehre der Indier*. Bonn, 1949.

———. *Vivarta: Studien zur Geschichte der illusionistischen Kosmologie und Erkenntnistheorie der Indier*. Mainz: Akademie der Wissenschaften und der Literatur, 1953.

———. "Westöstliche Mystik." In *Kleine Schriften*, edited by Lambert Schmithausen, 819–22. Wiesbaden: Franz Steiner, 1978.

———. "Distinctive Features of the Doctrine and Terminology of Śaṅkara." In *Philology and Confrontation*, edited by Wilhelm Halbfass, 57–100. Albany: State University of New York Press, 1995.

———. "Śaṅkara the Yogin and Śaṅkara the Advaitin." In *Philology and Confrontation*, edited by Wilhelm Halbfass, 101–34. Albany: State University of New York Press, 1995.

Halbfass, Wilhelm. *India and Europe: An Essay in Understanding*. Albany: State University of New York Press, 1988.

———. *Tradition and Reflection*. Albany: State University of New York Press, 1991.

———. *Karma und Wiedergeburt im indischen Denken*. Munich: Diederichs, 2000.

Hall, Stuart. "The Problem of Ideology—Marxism without Guarantees." In *Marxism: A Hundred Years On*, edited by Betty Matthews, 57–84. London: Lawrence and Wishart, 1983.

Hallisey, Charles. "Roads Taken and Not Taken in the Study of Theravāda Buddhism." In *Curators of the Buddha: The Study of Buddhism under Colonialism*, edited by Donald S. Lopez, 31–61. Chicago: University of Chicago Press, 1995.

Hardt, Michael, and Antonio Negri. *Empire*. Cambridge, Mass.: Harvard University Press, 2000.

Harrison, Peter. *"Religion" and the Religions in the English Enlightenment*. Cambridge: Cambridge University Press, 1990.

Hauer, J. W. *Das Religiöse Artbild der Indogermenen und die Grundtypen der Indo-Arischen Religion*. Stuttgart: W. Kohlhammer, 1937.

Hayes, Zachary. "Response to Bernard McGinn." In *God and Creation: An Ecumenical Symposium*, edited by David Burrell and Bernard McGinn, 220–25. Notre Dame: University of Notre Dame Press, 1990.

Hegel, Georg Wilhelm Friedrich. *Lectures on the Philosophy of Religion*. Vol. 2. Translated by E. B. Speirs and J. Burdon Sanderson. New York: Humanities Press, 1962.

———. *On the Episode of the Mahābhārata known by the name Bhagavad-Gītā by Wilhelm von Humboldt*. Edited and translated by Herbert Herring. New Delhi: Indian Council of Philosophical Research, 1995.

Heiler, Friedrich. *Erscheinungsformen und Wesen der Religion*. Stuttgart: W. Kohlhammer, 1949.

———. "Die Bedeutung Rudolf Ottos fur die vergleichende Religionsgeschichte." In *Religionswissenschaft in neuer Sicht*, 13–26. Marburg: N. G. Elwert Verlag, 1951.

———. "The History of Religions as a Preparation for the Co-Operation of Religions." In *The History of Religions: Essays in Methodology*, edited by Mircea Eliade and Joseph Kitagawa, 132–60. Chicago: University of Chicago Press, 1959.

Heim, S. Mark. *Salvations: Truth and Difference in Religion*. Maryknoll, N.Y.: Orbis Books, 1995.

Henninger, Mark G. *Relations: Medieval Theories 1250–1325*. Oxford: Oxford University Press, 1989.

Hewitt, Marsha A. "How New Is the 'New Comparativism'? Difference, Dialectics, and World-Making." *Method and Theory in the Study of Religion* 8:1 (1996): 15–20.

Hick, John. *God and the Universe of Faiths*. New York: St. Martin's Press, 1973.

———. "The Non-Absoluteness of Christianity." In *The Myth of Christian Uniqueness*, edited by John Hick and Paul F. Knitter, 16–36. Maryknoll, N.Y.: Orbis Books, 1994.

——— and Paul F. Knitter, eds. *The Myth of Christian Uniqueness*. Maryknoll, N.Y.: Orbis Books, 1994.

Himes, Michael J. "Historical Theology as *Wissenschaft*: Johann Sebastian Drey and the Structure of Theology." In *Revisioning the Past: Prospects in Historical Theology*, edited by Mary Potter Engel and Walter E. Wyman, 191–213. Minneapolis: Fortress Press, 1992.

Hiriyanna, Mysore. "What is Ananyatvam?" In *Festschrift Moriz Winternitz*, edited by Otto Stein and Wilhelm Gampert, 221–24. Leipzig: Harrassowitz, 1933.

Hirst, J. G. Suthren. *Śaṃkara's Advaita Vedānta: A Way of Teaching*. New York: Routledge, 2005.

Hjelde, Sigurd. "The Science of Religion and Theology: The Question of Their Interrelationship." In *Religion in the Making*, edited by Arie L. Molendijk and Peter Pels, 99–128. Boston: Brill, 1998.

Hollywood, Amy. *The Soul as Virgin Wife*. Notre Dame: University of Notre Dame Press, 1995.

Honig, Bonnie. *Political Theory and the Displacement of Politics*. Ithaca, N.Y.: Cornell University Press, 1993.

Hume, David. *The Natural History of Religion*. Stanford, Calif.: Stanford University Press, 1956.

Inden, Ronald B. *Imagining India*. Bloomington: Indiana University Press, 1990.

Ingalls, Daniel H. H. "The Study of Śaṅkarācārya." *Annals of the Bhandarkar Oriental Institute* 33 (1952): 1–14.

———. "Śaṅkara's Arguments Against the Buddhists." *Philosophy East and West* 3:4 (Jan. 1954): 291–306.

———. "Bhāskara the Vedāntin." *Philosophy East and West* 17:1/4 (Jan.–Oct. 1967): 61–67.

Irenaeus of Lyons. *Against the Heresies*. Translated by Dominic J. Unger. New York: Paulist Press, 1992.

Jacob, G. A., ed. *Vedāntasāra of Sadānanda*. Varanasi: Chaukhamba, 1893.

Jacobi, Hermann. "Über das Verhältnis des Vedānta zum Sānkhya." In *Kleine Schriften*, Teil 2, edited by Bernhard Kölver, 755–64. Wiesbaden: Franz Steiner Verlag, 1970.

———. "Über den nominalen Stil des wissenschaftlichen Sanskrits." In *Kleine Schriften*, Teil 1, edited by Bernhard Kölver, 236–51. Wiesbaden: Franz Steiner, 1970.

Jakobson, Roman. "The Concept of Mark." In *On Language*, edited by Linda R. Waugh and Monique Monville-Burston, 134–40. Cambridge, Mass.: Harvard University Press, 1990.

Jameson, Fredric. *The Prison House of Language*. Princeton, N.J.: Princeton University Press, 1972.

———. *The Political Unconscious*. Ithaca, N.Y.: Cornell University Press, 1981.

———. *Postmodernism, or, the Cultural Logic of Late Capitalism*. Durham, N.C.: Duke University Press, 1991.

Jantzen, Grace. *Power, Gender and Christian Mysticism*. New York: Cambridge University Press, 1995.

Jonas, Anton. "Der transcendentale Idealismus Arthur Schopenhauers und der Mysticismus des Meister Eckhart." In *Philosophische Monatshefte*, Bd. 2., edited by J. Bergmann, 43–74; 161–196. Berlin: Nicholaische Verlagsbuchhandlung, 1868–69.

Jordan, Henry Louis. *Comparative Religion: Its Genesis and Growth*. New York: Charles Scribner's Sons, 1905.

Juergensmeyer, Mark. *The New Cold War?* Berkeley and Los Angeles: University of California Press, 1993.

Kapstein, Matthew. *Reason's Traces*. Boston: Wisdom Publications, 2001.

Kateb, George. *The Inner Ocean: Individualism and Democratic Culture*. Ithaca, N.Y.: Cornell University Press, 1992.

Kelsey, David. *The Uses of Scripture in Recent Theology*. Philadelphia: Fortress Press, 1975.

Kertzer, David I. *Ritual, Politics, and Power*. New Haven, Conn.: Yale University Press, 1988.

Kiblinger, Kristin Beise. "Relating Theology of Religions and Comparative Theology." In *The New Comparative Theology*, edited by Francis X. Clooney, SJ, 21–42. New York: T & T Clark, 2010.

Kieckhefer, Richard. "Meister Eckhart's Conception of Union with God." *Harvard Theological Review* 71:3/4 (July–Oct. 1978): 203–25.

King, Richard. *Orientalism and Religion*. New York: Routledge, 1999.

Kitagawa, Joseph M. "The History of Religions in America." In *The History of Religions: Essays in Methodology*, edited by Mircea Eliade and Joseph M. Kitagawa, 1–30. Chicago: University of Chicago Press, 1959.

———. "Humanistic and Theological History of Religions with Special Reference to the North American Scene." In *Traditions in Contact and Change: Selected Proceedings of the XIVth Congress of the International Association for the History of Religions*, edited by Peter Slater and Donald N. Wiebe, 553–63. Waterloo, Ont.: Wilfrid Laurier University Press, 1983.

Knitter, Paul F. *No Other Name*. Maryknoll, N.Y.: Orbis Books, 1985.

———. "Toward a Liberation Theology of Religions." In *The Myth of Christian Uniqueness*, edited by John Hick and Paul F. Knitter, 178–200. Maryknoll, N.Y.: Orbis Books, 1994.

———. Review of *Faith among Faiths: Christian Theology and Non-Christian Religions*, by James L. Fredericks. *Theological Studies* 62:4 (2001): 874.

———. *Introducing Theologies of Religions*. Maryknoll, N.Y.: Orbis Books, 2002.

Koch, Josef. "Meister Eckhart und die jüdische Religionsphilosophie des Mittelalters." *Jahresbericht der Schlesischen Gesellschaft für vaterländische Kultur* 1927 100 (1928): 134–48.

———. "Zur Analogielehre Meister Eckharts." In *Mélanges Offerts a Étienne Gilson*, 327–50. Toronto: Pontifical Institute of Medieval Studies, 1959.

Koselleck, Reinhart. *Futures Past*. Translated by Keith Tribe. Cambridge, Mass.: MIT Press, 1995.

Kuenen, Abraham. *National Religions and Universal Religions*. New York: Charles Scribner's Sons, 1882.

Larrain, Jorge. *The Concept of Ideology*. Athens: University of Georgia Press, 1979.

Lash, Nicholas. *Easter in Ordinary*. Charlottesville: University Press of Virginia, 1986.

Lawson, E. Thomas, and McCauley, Robert N. *Rethinking Religion: Connecting Cognition and Culture*. New York: Cambridge University Press, 1990.

———. "Crisis of Conscience, Riddle of Identity: Making Space for a Cognitive Approach to Religious Phenomena." *Journal for the American Academy of Religion* 61:2 (1993): 201–23.

Lévi-Strauss, Claude. *Structural Anthropology*. Translated by Claire Jacobson and Brooke Grundfest Schoepf. New York: Basic Books, 1963.

Lichtmann, Maria. "Marguerite Porete and Meister Eckhart: *The Mirror of Simple Souls* Mirrored." In *Meister Eckhart and the Beguine Mystics*, edited by Bernard McGinn, 65–86. New York: Continuum, 1997.

Lincoln, Bruce. *Discourse and the Construction of Society*. New York: Oxford University Press, 1989.

———. *Death, War, and Sacrifice*. Chicago: University of Chicago Press, 1991.

———. *Theorizing Myth*. Chicago: University of Chicago Press, 1999.

———. *Holy Terrors*. Chicago: University of Chicago Press, 2003.

Lindbeck, George. "Ecumenism and the Future of Belief." *Una Sancta* 25:3 (1968): 3–18.

———. "The Sectarian Future of the Church." In *The God Experience*, edited by Joseph P. Whelan, S.J., 226–43. New York: Newman Press, 1971.

———. *The Nature of Doctrine*. Philadelphia: Westminster Press, 1984.

———. *The Church in a Postliberal Age*. Edited by James J. Buckley. Grand Rapids, Mich.: William B. Eerdmans, 2002.

Livingston, James C. *Modern Christian Thought*. Volume 1, *The Enlightenment and the Nineteenth Century*. Upper Saddle River, N.J.: Prentice Hall, 1988.

Livingston, James C., et al. *Modern Christian Thought*. Volume 2, *The Twentieth Century*. Minneapolis: Fortress Press, 2000.

Locke, John. *An Essay Concerning Human Understanding*. Oxford: Clarendon Press, 1924.

———. *Treatise of Civil Government and A Letter Concerning Toleration*. Edited by Charles L. Sherman. New York: D. Appleton-Century, 1937.

———. *The Reasonableness of Christianity*. Edited by I. T. Ramsey. Stanford, Calif.: Stanford University Press, 1958.

Lossky, Vladimir. *Théologie Négative et Connaissance de Dieu chez Maître Eckhart*. Paris: J. Vrin, 1960.

Malhotra, S. L. *Social and Political Orientations of Neo-Vedantism*. Delhi: S. Chand, 1970.

Mannheim, Karl. *Ideology and Utopia*. Translated by Louis Wirth and Edward Shils. New York: Harvest Books, 1985.

Marcaurelle, Roger. *Freedom through Inner Renunciation*. Albany: State University of New York Press, 2000.

Markell, Patchen. *Bound by Recognition*. Princeton, N.J.: Princeton University Press, 2003.

Martensen, H. *Meister Eckhart: Eine theologische Studie*. Hamburg: Friedrich Perthes, 1842.

Masuzawa, Tomoko. *In Search of Dreamtime*. Chicago: University of Chicago Press, 1993.

———. *The Invention of World Religions*. Chicago: University of Chicago Press, 2005.

Matheson, George. *The Distinctive Messages of the Old Religions*. New York: Anson D. F. Randolph, 1894.

Maurice, F. D. *The Religions of the World and their Relations to Christianity*. London: John W. Parker, 1847.

McCutcheon, Russell T. "A Default of Critical Intelligence? The Scholar of Religion as Public Intellectual." *Journal for the American Academy of Religion* 65:2 (1997): 443–68.

———. "Myth." In *Guide to the Study of Religion*, edited by Willi Braun and Russell T. McCutcheon, 190–208. New York: Cassell, 2000.

McGinn, Bernard. "The God beyond God: Theology and Mysticism in the Thought of Meister Eckhart." *Journal of Religion* 61:1 (Jan. 1981): 1–19.

———. "Meister Eckhart on God as Absolute Unity." In *Neoplatonism and Christian Thought*, edited by Dominic J. O'Meara, 128–39. Norfolk, VA: International Society for Neoplatonic Studies, 1982.

———. "Introduction." In *Meister Eckhart and the Beguine Mystics*, edited by Bernard McGinn. New York: Continuum, 1997.

———. *The Mystical Thought of Meister Eckhart*. New York: Crossroad, 2001.

———. *The Harvest of Mysticism in Medieval Germany*. New York: Crossroad, 2005.

McGrath, Alister E. *The Genesis of Doctrine*. Oxford: Blackwell, 1990.

Mensching, Gustav. *Tolerance and Truth in Religion*. Translated by H. J. Klimkeit. Tuscaloosa: University of Alabama Press, 1955.

———. *Structures and Patterns of Religion*. Translated by Hans F. Klimkeit and V. Srinavasa. Delhi: Motilal Banarsidass, 1976.

Metcalf, Thomas R. *Ideologies of the Raj*. New York: Cambridge University Press, 1995.

Michalson, Gordon. "The Response to Lindbeck." *Modern Theology* 4:2 (Jan. 1988): 107–20.

Mieth, Dietmar. *Die Einheit von Vita Activa und Vita Contemplativa*. Regensberg: Friedrich Pustet, 1969.

Modi, P. M. *A Critique of the Brahmasūtra (III.2.11–IV) with Reference to Śaṅkarācarya's Commentary*. 2 vols. Baroda: Private Publication, 1956.

Müller, F. Max. *The Six Systems of Indian Philosophy*. New York: Longmans, Green, and Co., 1903.

———. *Introduction to the Science of Religion*. London: Longmans, Green, and Co., 1882.

Mommaers, Paul and Jan Van Bragt. *Mysticism: Buddhist and Christian*. New York: Crossroad, 1995.

Monier-Williams, Monier. *A Sanskrit-English Dictionary*. New York: Oxford University Press, 1992.

Mouffe, Chantal. *The Return of the Political*. New York: Verso, 1993.

———. "Carl Schmitt and the Paradox of Liberal Democracy." In *The Challenge of Carl Schmitt*, edited by Chantal Mouffe, 38–53. New York: Verso, 1999.

Molendijk, Arie L. "Transforming Theology: The Institutionalization of the Science of Religion in the Netherlands." In *Religion in the Making*, edited by Arie L. Molendijk and Peter Pels, 67–95. Boston: Brill, 1998.

Murti, T. R. V. "The Two Definitions of Brahman in the Advaita." In *Studies in Indian Thought: Collected Papers of Prof. T. R. V. Murti*, edited by Harold G. Coward, 72–87. Delhi: Motilal Banarsidass, 1983.

Nakamura, Hajime. *A History of Early Vedānta Philosophy*. Part 1. Translated by Trevor Leggett, Segakul Mayeda, Taitetz Unno, et al. Delhi: Motilal Banarsidass, 1983.

Neville, Robert Cummings, and Wildman, Wesley J. "On Comparing Religious Ideas." In *The Human Condition: A Volume in the Comparative Religious Ideas Project*, edited by Robert Cummings Neville, 9–20. Albany: State University of New York Press, 2001.

———. "On Comparing Religious Ideas." In The *Ultimate Realities: A Volume in the Comparative Religious Ideas Project*, edited by Robert Cummings Neville, 187–210. Albany: State University of New York Press, 2001.

Nicholson, Hugh. "Apologetics and Philosophy in Maṇḍana Miśra's *Brahmasiddhi*." *Journal of Indian Philosophy* 30:6 (Dec. 2002): 575–96.

———. "The Political Nature of Doctrine: A Critique of Lindbeck in Light of Recent Scholarship." *Heythrop Journal* 48:6 (Nov. 2007): 858–77.

Oberdorfer, Bernd. *Geselligkeit und Realisierung von Sittlichkeit: Die Theorieentwicklung Friedrich Schleiermachers bis 1799*. Berlin: Walter de Gruyter, 1995.

Olivelle, Patrick. *Renunciation in Hinduism: A Medieval Debate*. Vol. 1. Vienna: Institut für Indologie der Universität Wien, 1986.

———. *The Āśrama System: The History and Hermeneutics of a Religious Tradition*. New York: Oxford University Press, 1993.

Otto, Rudolf. "Parallelisms in the Development of Religion East and West." In *Transactions of the Asiatic Society of Japan* [Yokohama] 40 (1912): 153–58.

———. *Aufsätze das Numinose Betreffend*. Stuttgart: Friedrich Andreas Perthes, 1923.

———. *Siddhānta des Rāmānuja*. Tübingen: J.C.B. Mohr, 1923.

———. *Vischnu-Nārāyaṇa: Texte zur indischen Gottesmystik*. Jena: Eugen Diederichs, 1923.

———. *India's Religion of Grace and Christianity Compared and Contrasted*. Translated by Frank Hugh Foster. New York: Macmillan, 1930.

———. *Gottheit und Gottheiten der Arier*. Giessen: Alfred Töpelmann, 1932.

———. *The Idea of the Holy*. Translated by John L. Harvey. New York: Oxford University Press, 1958.

———. *Mysticism East and West*. Translated by Bertha L. Bracey and Richenda C. Payne. New York: Collier Books, 1962.

Paden, William E. "Elements of a New Comparativism." *Method and Theory in the Study of Religion* 8:1 (1996): 15–20.

———. "Elements of a New Comparativism." In *A Magic Still Dwells*, edited by Kimberley C. Patton and Benjamin C. Ray, 182–92. Berkeley and Los Angeles: University of California Press, 2001.

Paine, Robert. "The Political Uses of Metaphor and Metonym: An Exploratory Statement." In *Politically Speaking: Cross-Cultural Studies of Rhetoric*, edited by Robert Paine, 187–200. Philadelphia: Institute for the Study of Human Issues, 1981.

Pannenberg, Wolfhart. "Religious Pluralism and Conflicting Truth Claims: The Problem of a Theology of the World Religions." In *Christian Uniqueness Reconsidered*, edited by Gavin D'Costa, 96–106. Maryknoll, N.Y.: Orbis Books, 1990.

Paulson, Michael. "Debating the Wisdom of Invoking Jesus at Inauguration; Christian Prayer Detracted from Event, Some Say." *Boston Globe*, January 27, 2001.

Pearson, Birger A. "The Emergence of Christian Religion." In *The Emergence of the Christian Religion: Essays in Early Christianity*, 7–22. Harrisburg, Pa.: Trinity Press International, 1997.

Penner, Hans H., and Edward A. Yonan. "Is a Science of Religion Possible?" *Journal of Religion* 52:2 (1972): 107–33.

Phan, Peter C. *Being Religious Interreligiously*. Maryknoll, N.Y.: Orbis Books, 2004.

Pollock, Sheldon. "Deep Orientalism? Notes on Sanskrit and Power Beyond the Raj." In *Orientalism and the Postcolonial Predicament*, edited by Carol Breckenridge and Peter Van der Veer, 76–133. Philadelphia: University of Pennsylvania Press, 1993.

———. "The Meaning of *Dharma* and the Relationship of the Two Mīmāṃsās: Appayya Dīkṣita's 'Discourse on the Refutation of a Unified Knowledge System of Pūrvamīmāṃsā and Uttaramīmāṃsā.'" *Journal of Indian Philosophy* 32 (2004): 769–811.

———. *The Language of the Gods in the World of Men*. Berkeley and Los Angeles: University of California Press, 2006.

Poole, Fitz John Porter. "Metaphor and Maps: Towards Comparison in the Anthropology of Religion." *Journal of the American Academy of Religion* 54:3 (1986): 411–57.

Potter, Karl H. *Encyclopedia of Indian Philosophies*. Vol. 3, *Advaita Vedānta up to Śaṃkara and His Pupils*. Delhi: Motilal Banarsidass, 1981.

Preger, Wilhelm. *Geschichte der deutschen Mystik im Mittelalter*. Leipzig: Dörffling und Franke, 1874.

Preus, J. Samuel. *Explaining Religion: Criticism and Theory from Bodin to Freud*. New Haven, Conn.: Yale University Press, 1987.

Rabbow, Paul. *Seelenführung: Methodik der Exerzitien in der Antike*. Munich: Kösel, 1954.

Radhakrishnan, S. *Eastern Religions and Western Thought*. Oxford: Oxford University Press, 1940.

———. *The Hindu Way of Life*. London: George Allen and Unwin Ltd., 1961.

Rambachan, Anantanand. "Hierarchies in the Nature of God? Questioning the Saguna-Nirguna Distinction in Advaita Vedanta." *Hindu-Christian Studies Bulletin* 14 (2001): 13–18.

———. *The Advaita Worldview*. Albany: State University of New York Press, 2006.

Rao, Srinivasa. "Two 'Myths' in Advaita." *Journal of Indian Philosophy* 24:3 (1996): 265–79.

Redfield, Robert. *The Primitive World and Its Transformations*. Ithaca, N.Y.: Cornell University Press, 1953.

Reynolds, P. L. "*Bullitio* and the God beyond God: Meister Eckhart's Trinitarian Theology. Part I: The Inner Life of God." *New Blackfriars* 70:826 (Apr. 1989): 169–81.

———. "*Bullitio* and the God beyond God. Part II: Distinctionless Godhead and Trinitarian God." *New Blackfriars* 70:827 (May 1989): 235–44.

Ricoeur, Paul. "The Metaphorical Process." *Semeia*. Vol. 4. Missoula, Mont.: Scholars Press, 1975.

———. *From Text to Action*. Translated by Kathleen Blamey and John B. Thompson. Evanston: Northwestern University Press, 1991.

———. *The Rule of Metaphor*. Translated by Robert Czerny. Toronto: University of Toronto Press, 1977.

Roberts, Tyler. "Exposure and Explanation: On the New Protectionism in the Study of Religion." *Journal of the American Academy of Religion* 72:1 (2004): 143–72.

Rollman, Hans. "Rudolf Otto and India." *Religious Studies Review* 5:3 (July 1979): 199–203.

Römer, Ruth. *Sprachwissenschaft und Rassenideologie in Deutschland*. Munich: Wilhelm Fink, 1985.

Roscoe, Paul B. "The Perils of 'Positivism' in Cultural Anthropology." *American Anthropologist* 97:3 (1995): 492–504.

Ruh, Kurt. "Meister Eckhart und die Spiritualität der Beginen." In *Kleine Schriften*, Bd. 2, edited by Volker Mertens, 327–36. Berlin: Walter de Gruyter, 1984.

Rüping, Klaus. *Philologische Untersuchungen zu den Brahmasūtra-Kommentaren des Śaṅkara und des Bhāskara*. Wiesbaden: Franz Steiner Verlag, 1977.

Said, Edward. *Orientalism*. New York: Vintage Books, 1979.

Schaller, Toni. "Die Meister Eckhart-Forschung von der Jahrhundertwende bis zur Gegenwart." *Freiburger Zeitschrift für Philosophie und Theologie* 15 (1968): 262–316; 403–26.

Schlegel, Friedrich. On the language and wisdom of the Indians. In *The Aesthetic and Miscellaneous Works of Friedrich von Schlegel*, translated by E. J. Millington, 425–526. London: George Bell and Sons, 1889.

Schleiermacher, Friedrich. *Über die Religion: Reden an die Gebildeten unter ihren Verächtern*. Stuttgart: Reclam, 1985.

———. *On Religion: Speeches to its Cultured Despisers*. Translated and edited by Richard Crouter. Cambridge: Cambridge University Press, 1996.

Schlovsky, Victor. "Art as Technique." In *Russian Formalist Criticism: Four Essays*, edited by L. T. Lemon and M. J. Reis, 3–24. Lincoln: University of Nebraska Press, 1965.

Schmidt, Carl. "Meister Eckhart: Ein Beitrag zur Geschichte der Theologie und Philosophie des Mittelalters." *Theologische Studien und Kritiken* 12 (1839): 663–744.

Schmidt, Richard. Review of J. W. Hauer, *Glaubensgeschichte der Indogermanen* (Stuttgart: W. Kohlhammer, 1937). *Orientalistische Literaturzeitung* 8/9 (1939): 546–48.

Schmitt, Carl. "Das Zeitalter der Neutralisierungen und Entpolitisierungen." in *Positionen und Begriffe im Kampf mit Weimar—Genf—Versailes* 1923–1939, 120–32. Berlin: Duncker & Humblot, 1988.

———. *The Concept of the Political*, Translated by George Schwab. Chicago: University of Chicago Press, 1996.

Schmoldt, Benno. *Die deutsche Begriffssprache Meister Eckharts*. Heidelberg: Quelle & Meyer, 1954.

Schürmann, Reiner. *Meister Eckhart: Mystic and Philosopher*. Bloomington: Indiana University Press, 1978.

Schutz, Alfred. *Collected Papers I: The Problem of Social Reality*. The Hague: Martinus Nijhoff, 1971.

Schwab, Raymond. *The Oriental Renaissance*. Translated by Gene Patterson-Black and Victor Reinking. New York: Columbia University Press, 1984.

Schweitzer, Albert. *Indian Thought and Its Development*. Boston: Beacon Press, 1956.

Segal, Robert A. "The Postmodernist Challenge to the Comparative Method." In *Comparing Religions*, edited by Thomas A. Idinopulos, Brian C. Wilson, and James C. Hanges, 249–70. Leiden/Boston: Brill, 2006.

Sells, Michael. *Mystical Languages of Unsaying*. Chicago: University of Chicago Press, 1994.

Sharpe, Eric J. *Comparative Religion: A History*. La Salle, Ill.: Open Court, 1986.

Simmel, Georg. *Conflict and the Web of Group-Affiliations*. Translated by Kurt H. Wolff and Reinhard Bendix. New York: Free Press, 1955.

Smith, Jonathan Z. *Imagining Religion: From Babylon to Johnstown*. Chicago: University of Chicago Press, 1982.

———. *Drudgery Divine*. Chicago: University of Chicago Press, 1990.

———. "The 'End' of Comparison." In *A Magic Still Dwells*, edited by Kimberley C. Patton and Benjamin C. Ray, 237–41. Berkeley and Los Angeles: University of California Press, 2000.

———. *Relating Religion*. Chicago: University of Chicago Press, 2004.

Smith, Wilfred Cantwell. "Comparative Religion: Whither and Why?" In *The History of Religions: Essays in Methodology*, edited by Mircea Eliade and Joseph M. Kitagawa, 31–58. Chicago: University of Chicago Press, 1959.

———. *Faith and Belief*. Princeton, N.J.: Princeton University Press, 1979.

———. *Towards a World Theology*. Philadelphia: Westminster Press, 1981.

———. *The Meaning and End of Religion*. Minneapolis: Fortress Press, 1991.

Stalnaker, Aaron. *Overcoming Our Evil*. Washington, D.C.: Georgetown University Press, 2006.

Stoeber, Michael. *Theo-Monistic Mysticism*. New York: St. Martin's Press, 1994.

Strenski, Ivan. *Thinking about Religion: An Historical Introduction to Theories of Religion*. Malden, Mass.: Blackwell Publishing, 2006.

Sullivan, Winnifred Fallers. "American Religion is Naturally Comparative." In *A Magic Still Dwells*, edited by Kimberley C. Patton and Benjamin C. Ray, 117–30. Berkeley and Los Angeles: University of California Press, 2000.

Surin, Kenneth. "A 'Politics' of Speech: Religious Pluralism in the Age of the McDonald's Hamburger." In *Christian Uniqueness Reconsidered*, edited by Gavin D'Costa, 192–212. Maryknoll, N.Y.: Orbis Books, 1990.

———. "Towards a 'Materialist' Critique of Religious Pluralism: An Examination of the Discourse of John Hick and Wilfred Cantwell Smith." In *Religious Pluralism and Belief*, edited by Ian Hammett, 114–29. New York: Routledge, 1990.

Suzuki, D. T. *Mysticism: Christian and Buddhist*. New York: Collier Books, 1962.

Talghatti, S.R. "Advaita in Marathi." In *Advaita Vedānta*. Vol. 2, Part 2, *History of Science, Philosophy, and Culture in Indian Civilization*, edited by

R. Balasubramanian, 544–68. New Delhi: Centre for Studies in Civilizations, 2000.

Tanner, Kathryn. *The Politics of God.* Minneapolis: Fortress Press, 1992.

———. "Two Kinds of Apologetics." Unpublished manuscript.

———. "Respect for Other Religions: A Christian Antidote to Colonialist Discourse." *Modern Theology* 9:1 (Jan. 1993): 1–18.

———. *Theories of Culture.* Minneapolis: Fortress Press, 1997.

———. *Jesus, Humanity, and the Trinity.* Minneapolis: Fortress Press, 2001.

———. *Economy of Grace.* Minneapolis: Fortress Press, 2005.

Thatamanil, John J. *The Immanent Divine.* Minneapolis: Fortress Press, 2006.

Thiel, John E. *Nonfoundationalism.* Minneapolis: Fortress Press, 1994.

Thompson, John B. *Studies in the Theory of Ideology.* Cambridge: Polity Press, 1984.

Thompson, Marianne Maye. *The God of the Gospel of John.* Grand Rapids, Mich.: William B. Eerdmans, 2001.

Tiele, C. P. "Religions." In *Encyclopaedia Britannica.* 9th ed. 358–71. Edinburgh, 1885.

———. "On the Study of Comparative Theology." In *A Museum of Faiths,* edited by Eric J. Ziolkowski, 75–84. Atlanta: Scholars Press, 1993.

Tindal, Matthew. *Christianity as Old as the Creation.* New York: Garland Publishing, 1978.

Tobin, Frank J. "Eckhart's Mystical Use of Language: The Contexts of *eigenschaft.*" *Seminar* 8:3 (Oct. 1972): 160–68.

———. *Meister Eckhart: Thought and Language.* Philadelphia: University of Pennsylvania Press, 1986.

Toland, John. *Christianity not Mysterious.* New York: Garland Publishing, 1978.

Tracy, David. "Lindbeck's New Program for Theology: A Reflection." *The Thomist* 4:9 (July 1985): 392–416.

———. *The Analogical Imagination.* New York: Crossroad, 1991.

Troeltsch, Ernst. "The Place of Christianity among the World Religions." In *Christian Thought: Its History and Application,* edited by F. von Hügel, 35–63. New York: Meridian Books, 1957.

———. "Christianity and the History of Religion." In *Religion in History,* translated by James Luther Adams and Walter F. Bense, 77–86. Edinburgh: T&T Clark, 1991.

Tull, Herman. F. Max Müller and A. B. Keith: "'Twaddle,' the 'Stupid' Myth, and the Disease of Indology." *Numen* 38:1 (June 1991): 27–58.

Ueda, Shizuteru. *Die Gottesgeburt in der Seele und der Durchbruch zur Gottheit.* Gütersloh: Mohn, 1965.

Ullmann, C. *Reformers before the Reformation.* Vol. 2. Translated by Robert Menzies. Edinburgh: T&T Clark, 1855.

Urban, Greg. "The Role of Comparison in the Light of the Theory of Culture." In *Critical Comparisons in Politics and Culture,* edited by John R. Bowen and Roger Petersen, 90–109. Cambridge: Cambridge University Press, 1999.

Urban, Hugh B. "Making a Place to Stand: Jonathan Z. Smith and the Politics and Poetics of Comparison." *Method and Theory in the Study of Religion* 12 (2000): 339–78.

Viyagappa, S. J., Ignatius. *G. W. F. Hegel's Concept of Indian Philosophy*. Rome: Universita Gregoriana Editrice, 1980.

Voigt, Johannes H. *Max Mueller: The Man and His Ideas*. Calcutta: K. L. Mukhopadhyay, 1967.

Wach, Joachim. "The Meaning and Task of the History of Religions (Religionswissenschaft)." In *Understanding and Believing: Essays by Joachim Wach*, edited by Joseph M. Kitagawa, 125–41. New York: Harper and Row, 1968.

Werblowsky, R. J. Zwi. "The Comparative Study of Religions—A Review Essay." *Judaism* 8:4 (1959): 352–60.

Welch, Claude. *Protestant Thought in the Nineteenth Century*. Vol. 2, 1870–1914. New Haven, Conn.: Yale University Press, 1985.

Whitney, William Dwight. "On the So-Called Science of Religion" *Princeton Review* 57 (May 1881): 429–52.

Wiebe, Donald. *The Politics of Religious Studies*. New York: St. Martin's Press, 1999.

Wildman, Wesley J. "Comparing Religious Ideas: There's a Method in the Mob's Madness." In *Comparing Religions*, edited by Thomas A. Idinopulos, Brian C. Wilson, and James C. Hanges, 77–113. Leiden/Boston: Brill, 2006.

Wiley, Basil. *The Seventeenth-Century Background*. New York: Columbia University Press, 1965.

Winquist, Charles E. *Desiring Theology*. Chicago: University of Chicago Press, 1995.

Witzel, Michael. *On Magical Thought in the Veda*. Leiden: Universitaire Pers Leiden, 1979.

Wolff, Robert Paul. "Beyond Tolerance." In *A Critique of Pure Tolerance*, edited by Robert Paul Wolff, Barrington Moore, and Herbert Marcuse, 3–52. Boston: Beacon Press, 1965.

Wolin, Richard. "Carl Schmitt: The Conservative Revolutionary, Habitus and the Aesthetics of Horror." *Political Theory* 20:3 (Aug. 1992): 424–47.

Wuthnow, Robert. *Rediscovering the Sacred*. Grand Rapids, Mich.: William B. Eerdmans, 1992.

Young, Iris Marion. *Justice and the Politics of Difference*. Princeton, N.J.: Princeton University Press, 1990.

Zaehner, R. C. *Mysticism, Sacred and Profane*. Oxford: Oxford University Press, 1957.

Žižek, Slavoj. "How Did Marx Invent the Symptom?" In *Mapping Ideology*, edited by Slavoj Zizek, 296–331. New York: Verso, 1994.

———. "The Spectre of Ideology." In *Mapping Ideology*, edited by Slavoj Zizek, 1–33. New York: Verso, 1994.

Index